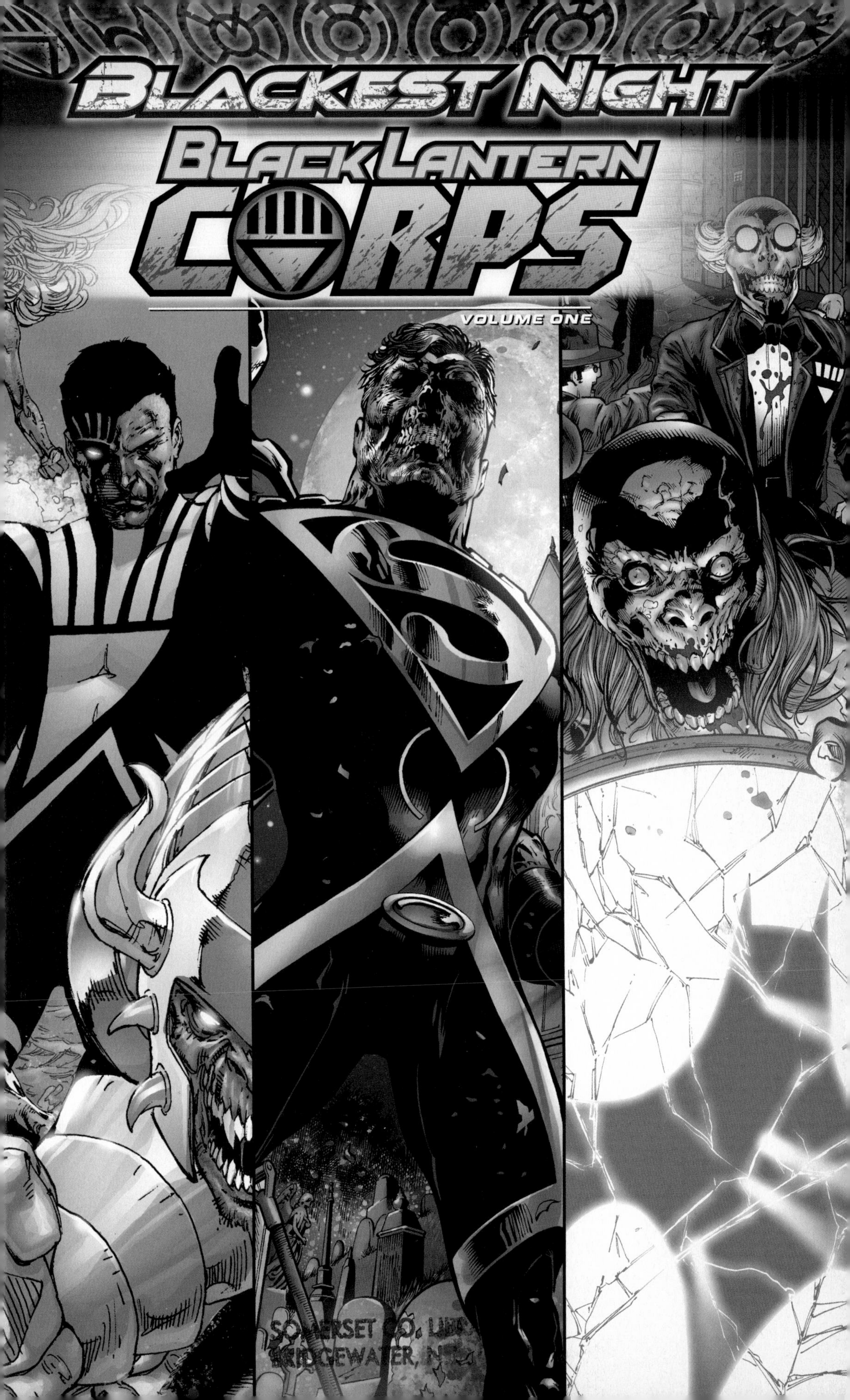
BLACKEST NIGHT
BLACK LANTERN
CORPS
VOLUME ONE

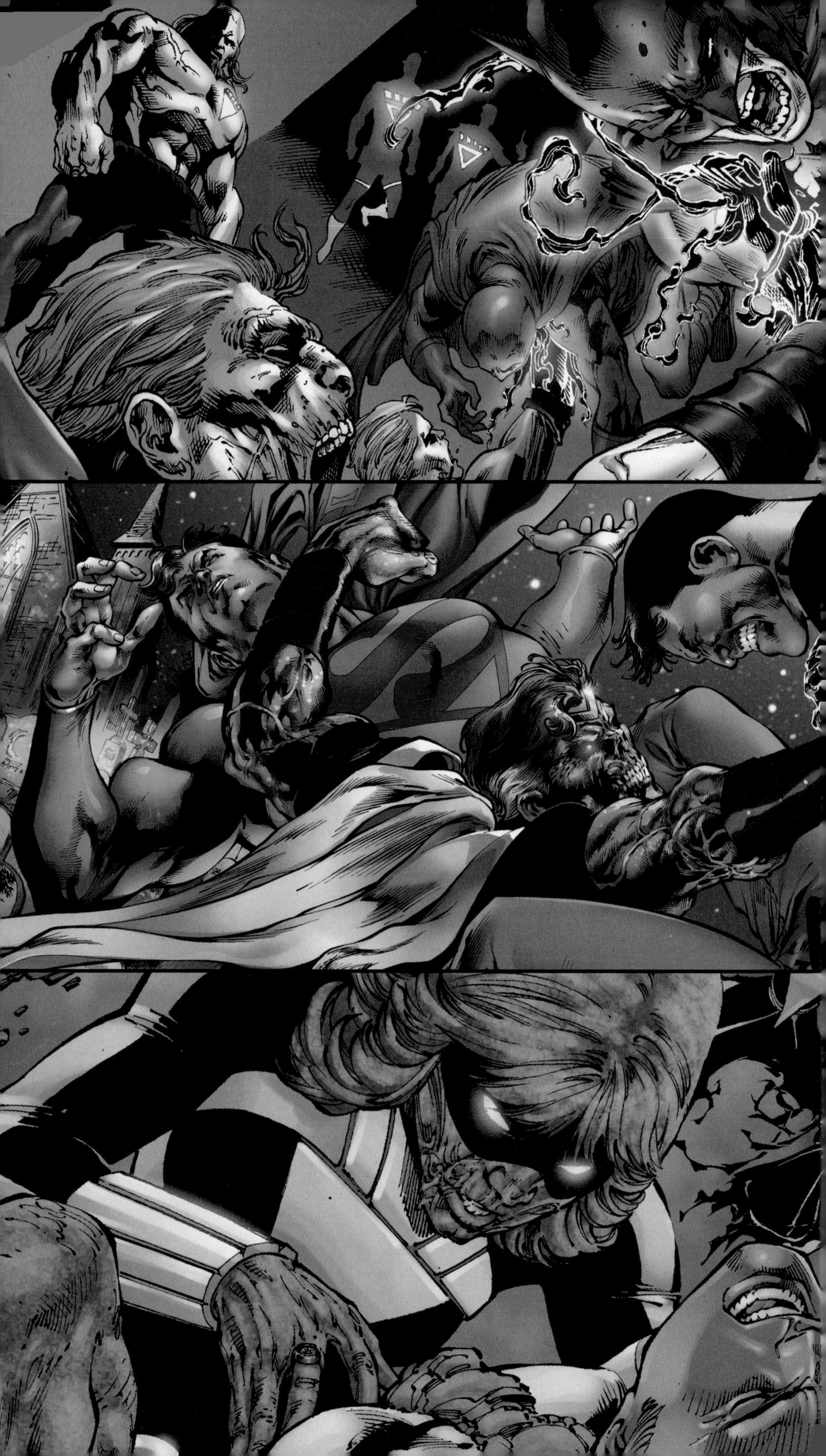

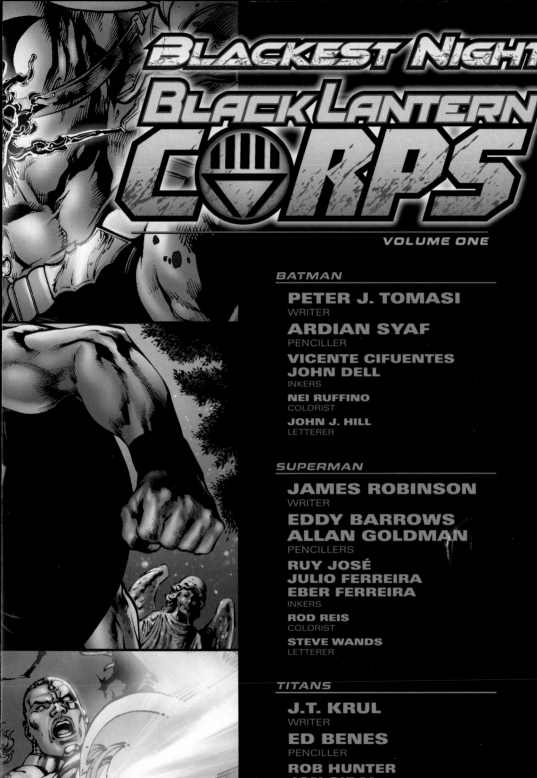

BLACKEST NIGHT
BLACK LANTERN CORPS

VOLUME ONE

BATMAN

PETER J. TOMASI
WRITER

ARDIAN SYAF
PENCILLER

VICENTE CIFUENTES
JOHN DELL
INKERS

NEI RUFFINO
COLORIST

JOHN J. HILL
LETTERER

SUPERMAN

JAMES ROBINSON
WRITER

EDDY BARROWS
ALLAN GOLDMAN
PENCILLERS

RUY JOSÉ
JULIO FERREIRA
EBER FERREIRA
INKERS

ROD REIS
COLORIST

STEVE WANDS
LETTERER

TITANS

J.T. KRUL
WRITER

ED BENES
PENCILLER

ROB HUNTER
JON SIBAL
JP MAYER
SCOTT WILLIAMS
ED BENES
INKERS

HI-FI DESIGN
COLORIST

ROB CLARK JR.
LETTERER

BATMAN CREATED BY **BOB KANE**

SUPERMAN CREATED BY **JERRY SIEGEL & JOE SHUSTER**

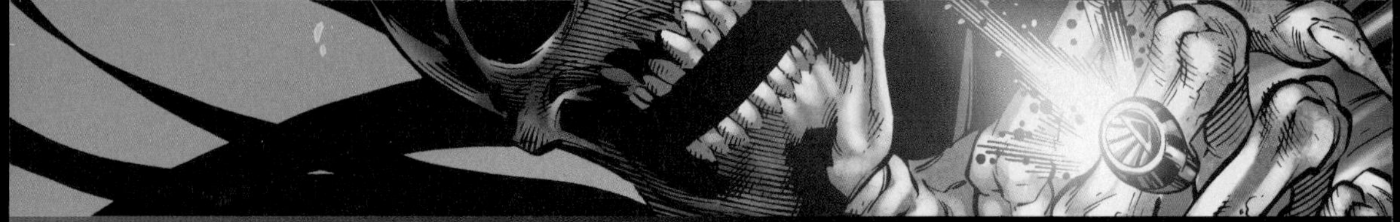

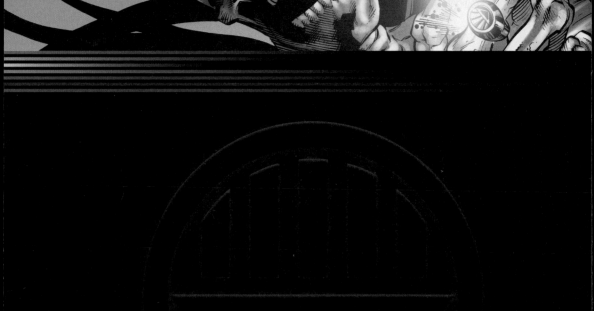

Eddie Berganza Adam Schlagman Brian Cunningham *Editors-original series*
Rex Ogle *Assistant Editor-original series* / Bob Harras *Group Editor-Collected Editions*
Bob Joy *Editor* / Robbin Brosterman *Design Director-Books* / Curtis King Jr. *Senior Art Director*

DC COMICS / Diane Nelson *President* / Dan DiDio and Jim Lee *Co-Publishers*
Geoff Johns *Chief Creative Officer* / Patrick Caldon *EVP–Finance and Administration*
John Rood *EVP–Sales, Marketing and Business Development* / Amy Genkins *SVP–Business and Legal Affairs*
Steve Rotterdam *SVP–Sales and Marketing* / John Cunningham *VP–Marketing*
Terri Cunningham *VP–Managing Editor* / Alison Gill *VP–Manufacturing* / David Hyde *VP–Publicity*
Sue Pohja *VP–Book Trade Sales* / Alysse Soll *VP–Advertising and Custom Publishing*
Bob Wayne *VP–Sales* / Mark Chiarello *Art Director*

Cover by Rodolfo Migliari

BLACKEST NIGHT: BLACK LANTERN CORPS VOLUME 1 Published by DC Comics.

DC COMICS 1700 Broadway, New York, NY 10019 A Warner Bros. Entertainment Company

Printed by RR Donnelley, Salem, VA, USA. 6/16/10. First printing.

HC ISBN: 978-1-4012-2784-5
SC ISBN: 978-1-4012-2804-0

SUSTAINABLE FORESTRY INITIATIVE
Certified Chain of Custody
Promoting Sustainable Forest Management

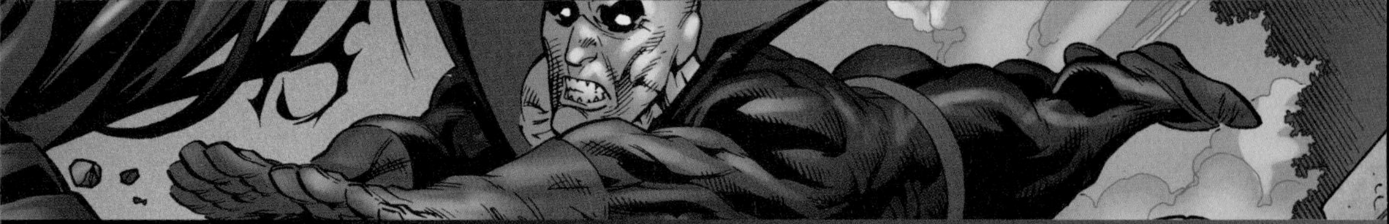

THE STORY SO FAR...

Billions of years ago, the self-appointed Guardians of the Universe recruited thousands of sentient beings from across the cosmos to join their intergalactic police force: the Green Lantern Corps.

Chosen because they are able to overcome great fear, the Green Lanterns patrol their respective space sectors armed with power rings capable of wielding the emerald energy of willpower into whatever constructs they can imagine.

Hal Jordan is the greatest of them all.

When the dying Green Lantern Abin Sur crashed on Earth, he chose Hal Jordan to be his successor, for his indomitable will and ability to overcome great fear. As the protector of Sector 2814, Hal has saved Earth from destruction, even died in its service and been reborn.

Thaal Sinestro of Korugar was once considered the greatest Green Lantern of them all.

As Abin Sur's friend, Sinestro became Jordan's mentor in the Corps. But after being sentenced to the Anti-Matter Universe for abusing his power, Sinestro learned of the yellow light of fear being mined on Qward. Wielding a new golden power ring fueled by terror, Sinestro drafted thousands of the most horrific, psychotic and sadistic beings in the universe, and with their doctrine of fear, burned all who opposed them.

When the Green Lantern Corps battled their former ally during the Sinestro Corps War, the skies burned with green and gold as Earth erupted into an epic battle between good and evil. Though the Green Lanterns won, their brotherhood was broken and the peace they achieved was short-lived. In its aftermath, the Guardians rewrote the Book of Oa, the very laws by which their corps abides, and dissent grew within their members.

Now Hal Jordan will face his greatest challenge yet, as the prophecy foretold by Abin Sur in his dying moments finally comes to pass...

The emotional spectrum has splintered into seven factions. Seven corps were born.

The Green Lanterns. The Sinestro Corps. Atrocitus and the enraged Red Lanterns. Larfleeze, the avaricious keeper of the Orange Light. Former Guardians Ganthet and Sayd's small but hopeful Blue Lantern Corps. The Zamarons and their army of fierce and loving Star Sapphires. And the mysterious Indigo Tribe.

As the War of Light ignited between these Lantern bearers, the skies on every world darkened. In Sector 666, on the planet Ryut, a black lantern grew around the Anti-Monitor's corpse, using his vast energies to empower it.

The first of the Black Lanterns, the Black Hand, has risen from the dead, heralding a greater power that will extinguish all of the light—and life—in the universe.

Now across thousands of worlds, the dead have risen, and Hal Jordan and all of Earth's greatest heroes must bear witness to Blackest Night, which will descend upon them all, without prejudice, mercy or reason.

BLACKEST NIGHT: BATMAN 1
Cover by Andy Kubert with Alex Sinclair

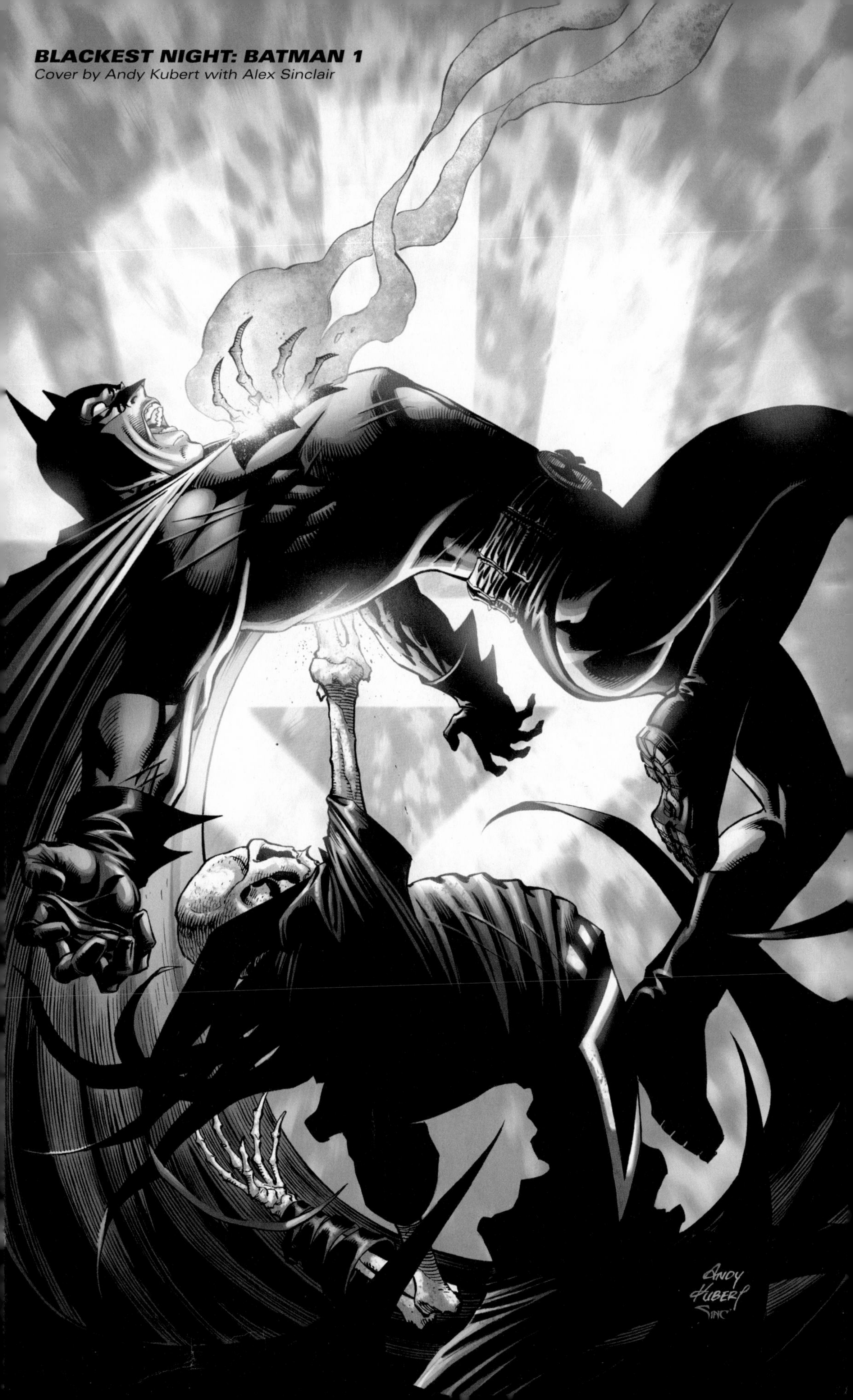
ANDY
KUBERT
SINC

WHO BURNS WHO
PART ONE

PETER J. TOMASI
WRITER

ARDIAN SYAF
PENCILS

JOHN DELL
VICENTE CIFUENTES
INKS

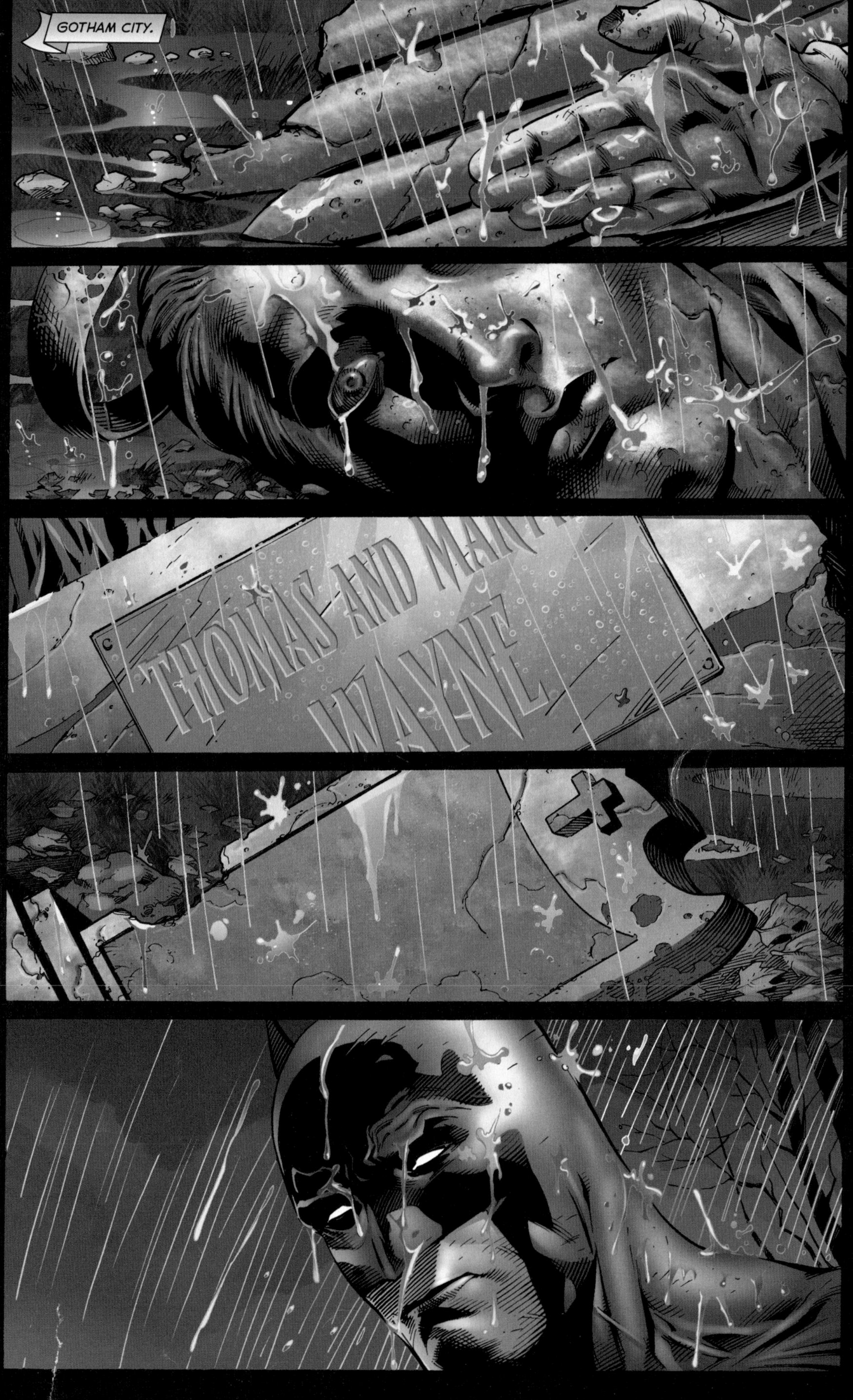
GOTHAM CITY.
THOMAS AND
WAYNE

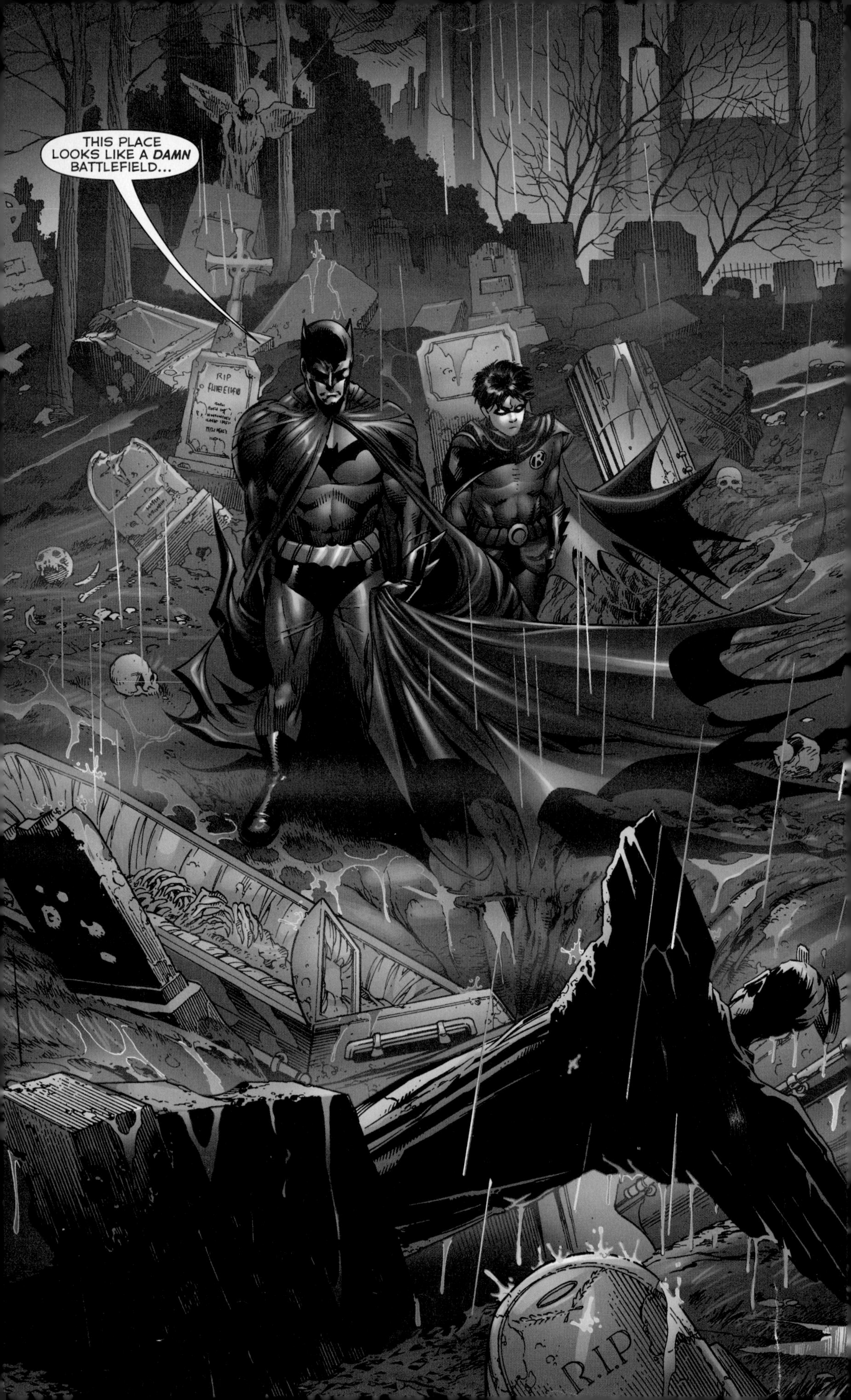
THIS PLACE LOOKS LIKE A *DAMN* BATTLEFIELD...
R.I.P.

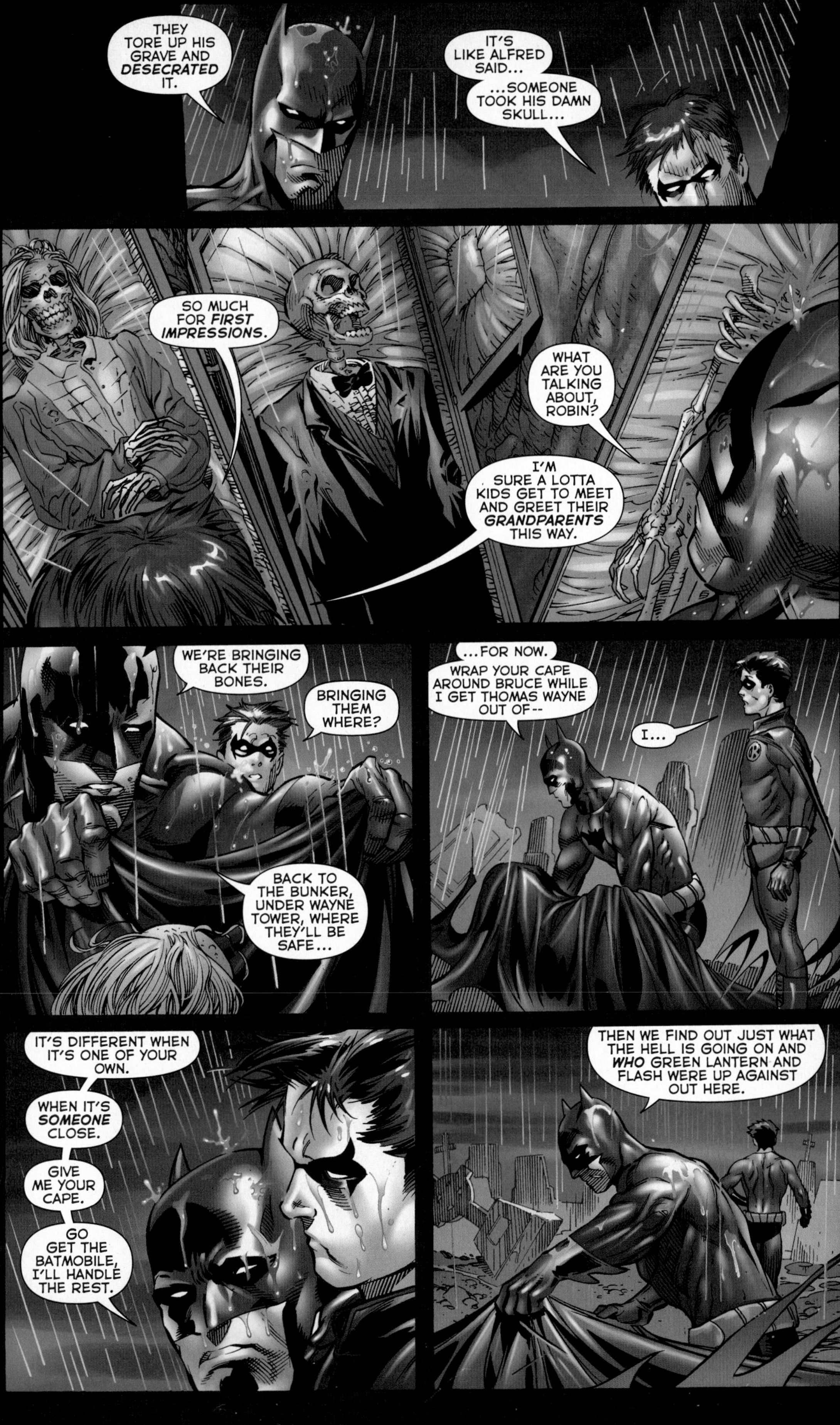

THEY TORE UP HIS GRAVE AND DESECRATED IT.
IT'S LIKE ALFRED SAID...
...SOMEONE TOOK HIS DAMN SKULL...
SO MUCH FOR FIRST IMPRESSIONS.
WHAT ARE YOU TALKING ABOUT, ROBIN?
I'M SURE A LOTTA KIDS GET TO MEET AND GREET THEIR GRANDPARENTS THIS WAY.
WE'RE BRINGING BACK THEIR BONES.
BRINGING THEM WHERE?
BACK TO THE BUNKER, UNDER WAYNE TOWER, WHERE THEY'LL BE SAFE...
...FOR NOW.
WRAP YOUR CAPE AROUND BRUCE WHILE I GET THOMAS WAYNE OUT OF--
I...
IT'S DIFFERENT WHEN IT'S ONE OF YOUR OWN.
WHEN IT'S SOMEONE CLOSE.
GIVE ME YOUR CAPE.
GO GET THE BATMOBILE, I'LL HANDLE THE REST.
THEN WE FIND OUT JUST WHAT THE HELL IS GOING ON AND WHO GREEN LANTERN AND FLASH WERE UP AGAINST OUT HERE.

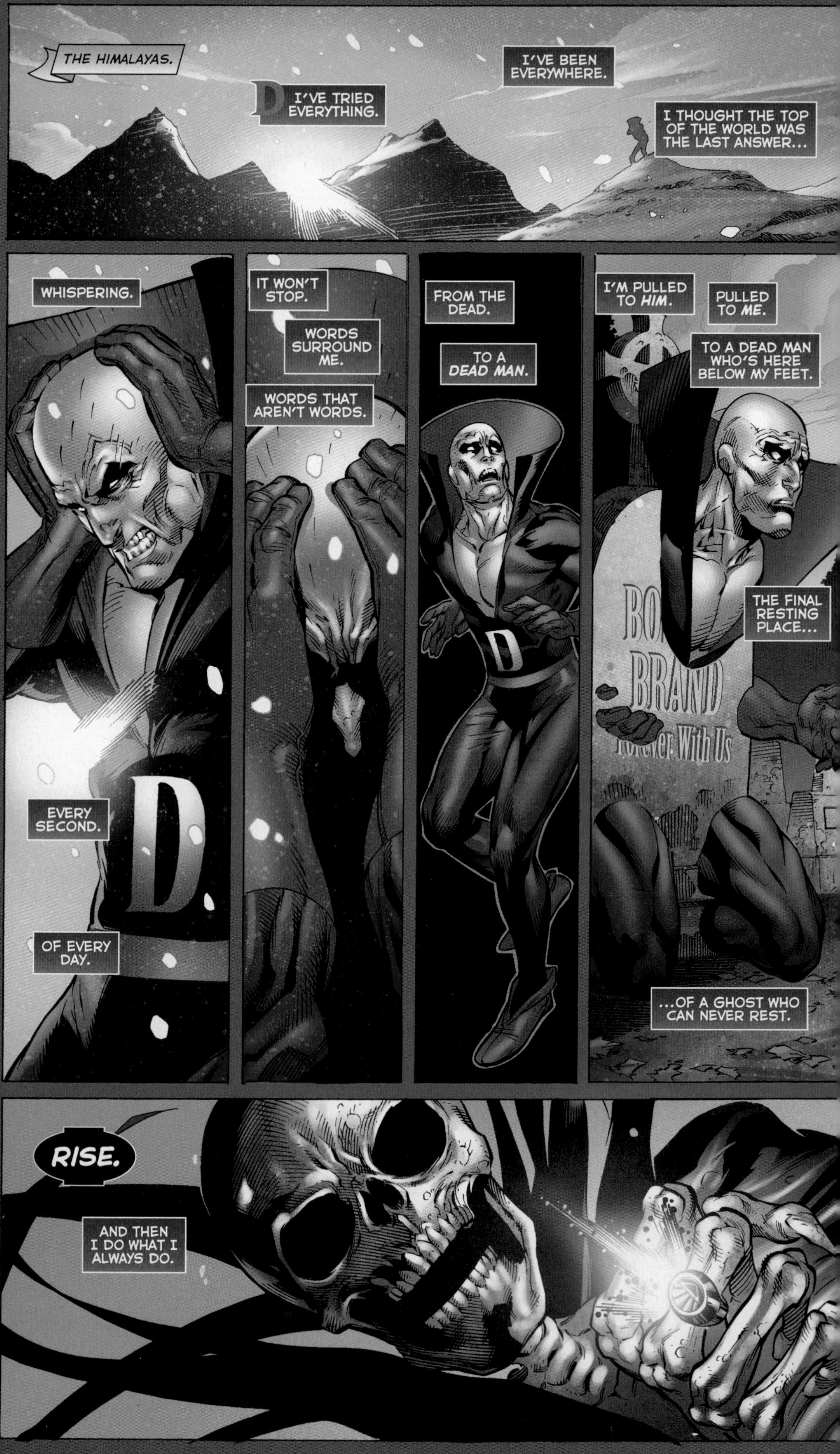
THE HIMALAYAS.
I'VE TRIED EVERYTHING.
I'VE BEEN EVERYWHERE.
I THOUGHT THE TOP OF THE WORLD WAS THE LAST ANSWER...
WHISPERING.
EVERY SECOND.
OF EVERY DAY.
IT WON'T STOP.
WORDS SURROUND ME.
WORDS THAT AREN'T WORDS.
FROM THE DEAD.
TO A DEAD MAN.
I'M PULLED TO HIM.
PULLED TO ME.
TO A DEAD MAN WHO'S HERE BELOW MY FEET.
BRAND
Forever With Us
THE FINAL RESTING PLACE...
...OF A GHOST WHO CAN NEVER REST.
RISE.
AND THEN I DO WHAT I ALWAYS DO.

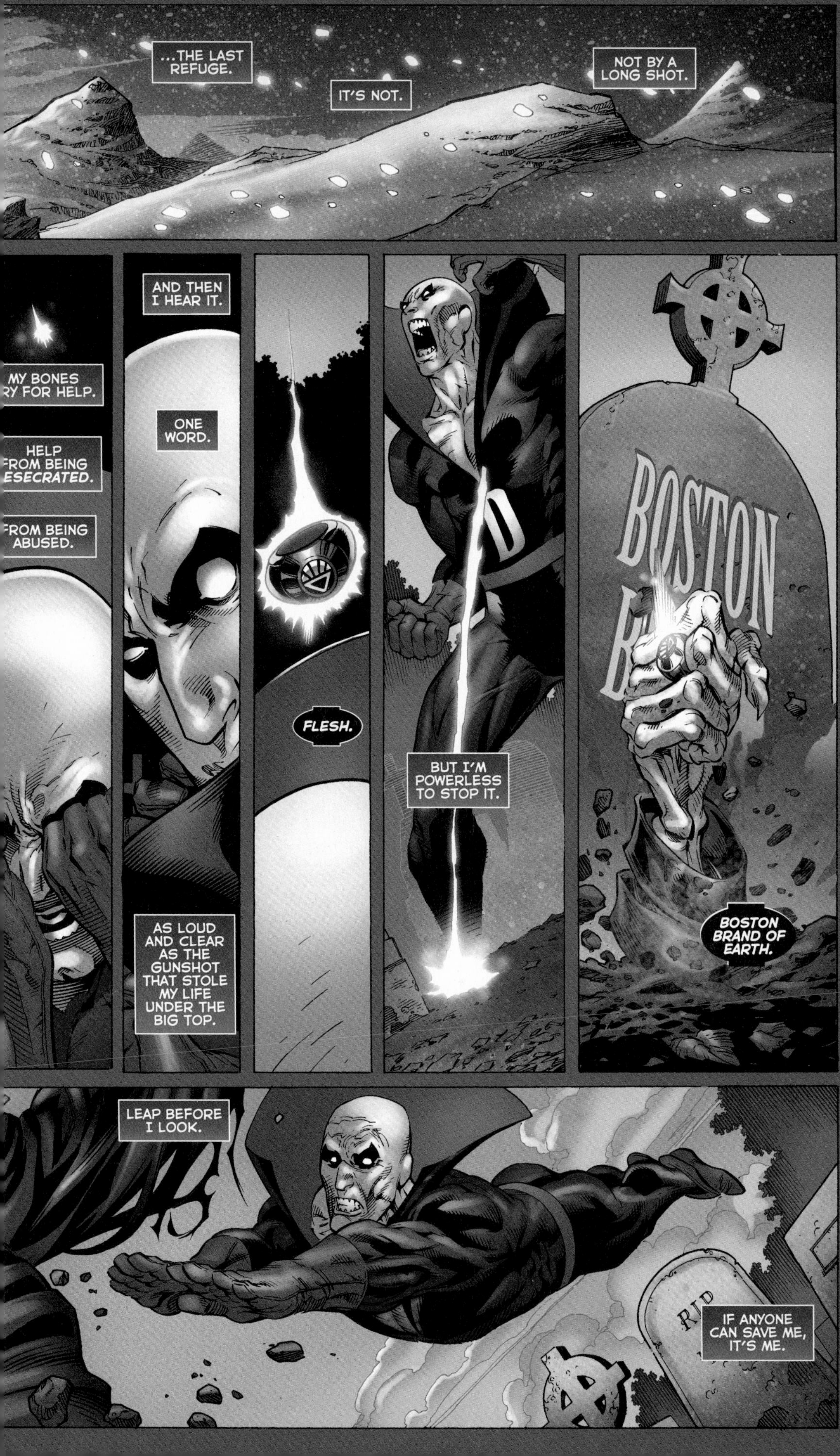

...THE LAST REFUGE.
IT'S NOT.
NOT BY A LONG SHOT.
MY BONES RY FOR HELP.
HELP ROM BEING ESECRATED.
ROM BEING ABUSED.
AND THEN I HEAR IT.
ONE WORD.
AS LOUD AND CLEAR AS THE GUNSHOT THAT STOLE MY LIFE UNDER THE BIG TOP.
FLESH.
BUT I'M POWERLESS TO STOP IT.
BOSTON
BOSTON BRAND OF EARTH.
LEAP BEFORE I LOOK.
RIP
IF ANYONE CAN SAVE ME, IT'S ME.

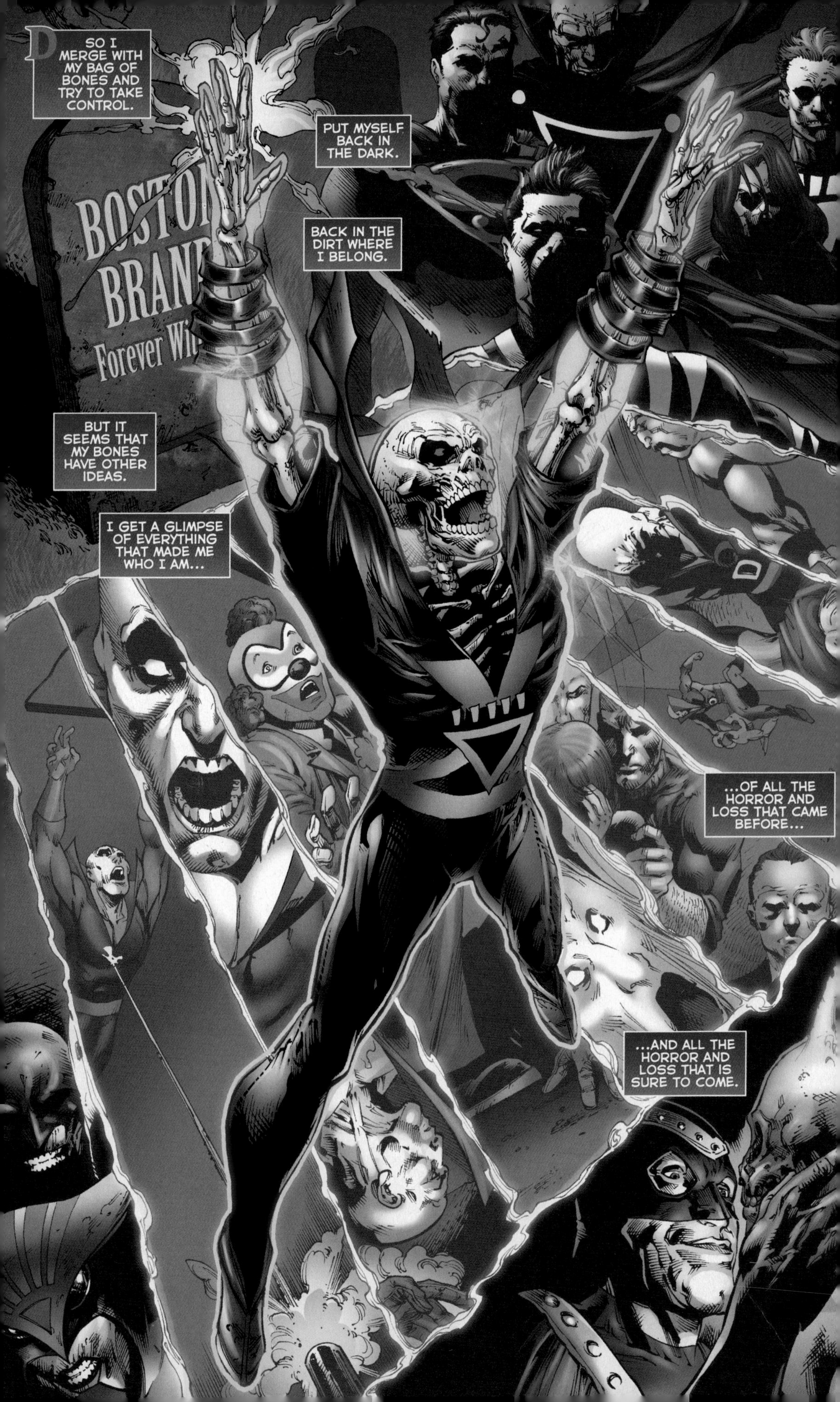
SO I MERGE WITH MY BAG OF BONES AND TRY TO TAKE CONTROL.
PUT MYSELF BACK IN THE DARK.
BACK IN THE DIRT WHERE I BELONG.
BOSTON BRAND Forever Wi
BUT IT SEEMS THAT MY BONES HAVE OTHER IDEAS.
I GET A GLIMPSE OF EVERYTHING THAT MADE ME WHO I AM...
...OF ALL THE HORROR AND LOSS THAT CAME BEFORE...
...AND ALL THE HORROR AND LOSS THAT IS SURE TO COME.

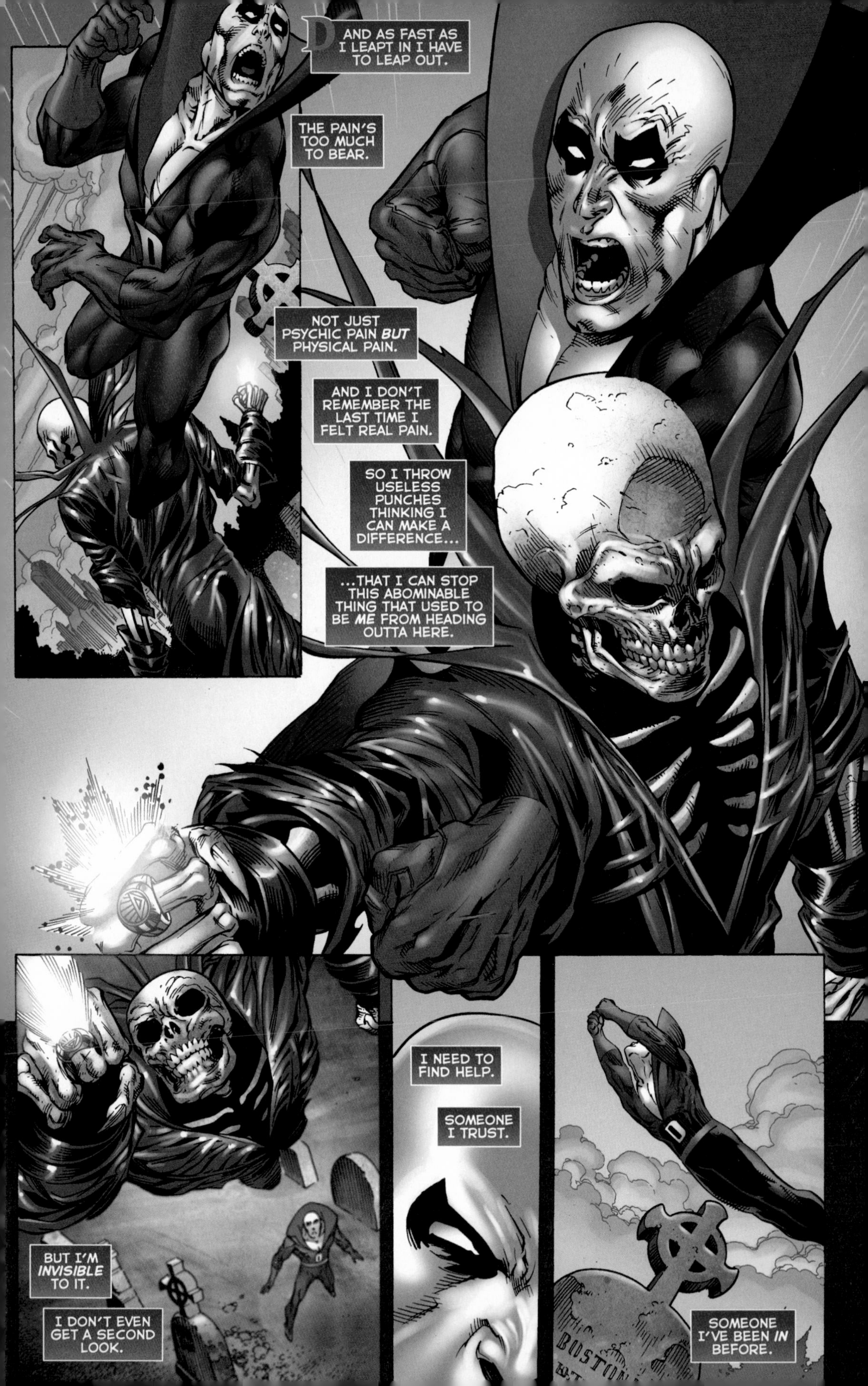
AND AS FAST AS I LEAPT IN I HAVE TO LEAP OUT.
THE PAIN'S TOO MUCH TO BEAR.
NOT JUST PSYCHIC PAIN *BUT* PHYSICAL PAIN.
AND I DON'T REMEMBER THE LAST TIME I FELT REAL PAIN.
SO I THROW USELESS PUNCHES THINKING I CAN MAKE A DIFFERENCE...
...THAT I CAN STOP THIS ABOMINABLE THING THAT USED TO BE *ME* FROM HEADING OUTTA HERE.
BUT I'M *INVISIBLE* TO IT.
I DON'T EVEN GET A SECOND LOOK.
I NEED TO FIND HELP.
SOMEONE I TRUST.
SOMEONE I'VE BEEN *IN* BEFORE.

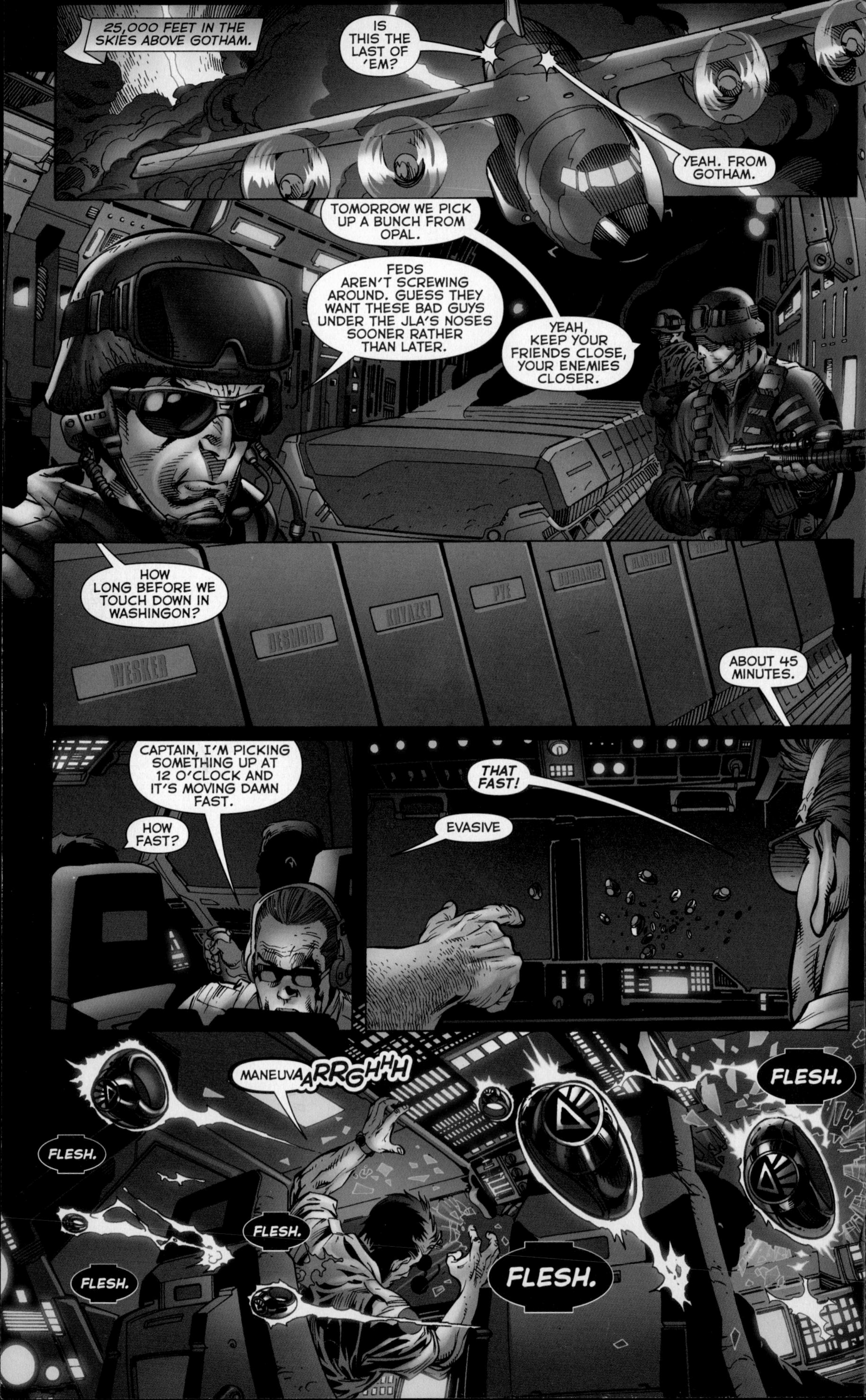

25,000 FEET IN THE SKIES ABOVE GOTHAM.
IS THIS THE LAST OF 'EM?
YEAH. FROM GOTHAM.
TOMORROW WE PICK UP A BUNCH FROM OPAL.
FEDS AREN'T SCREWING AROUND. GUESS THEY WANT THESE BAD GUYS UNDER THE JLA'S NOSES SOONER RATHER THAN LATER.
YEAH, KEEP YOUR FRIENDS CLOSE, YOUR ENEMIES CLOSER.
HOW LONG BEFORE WE TOUCH DOWN IN WASHINGON?
WESKER
DESMOND
KNYAZEV
PYE
ABOUT 45 MINUTES.
CAPTAIN, I'M PICKING SOMETHING UP AT 12 O'CLOCK AND IT'S MOVING DAMN FAST.
HOW FAST?
THAT FAST!
EVASIVE
MANEUVAARRGHHH
FLESH.
FLESH.
FLESH.
FLESH.
FLESH.

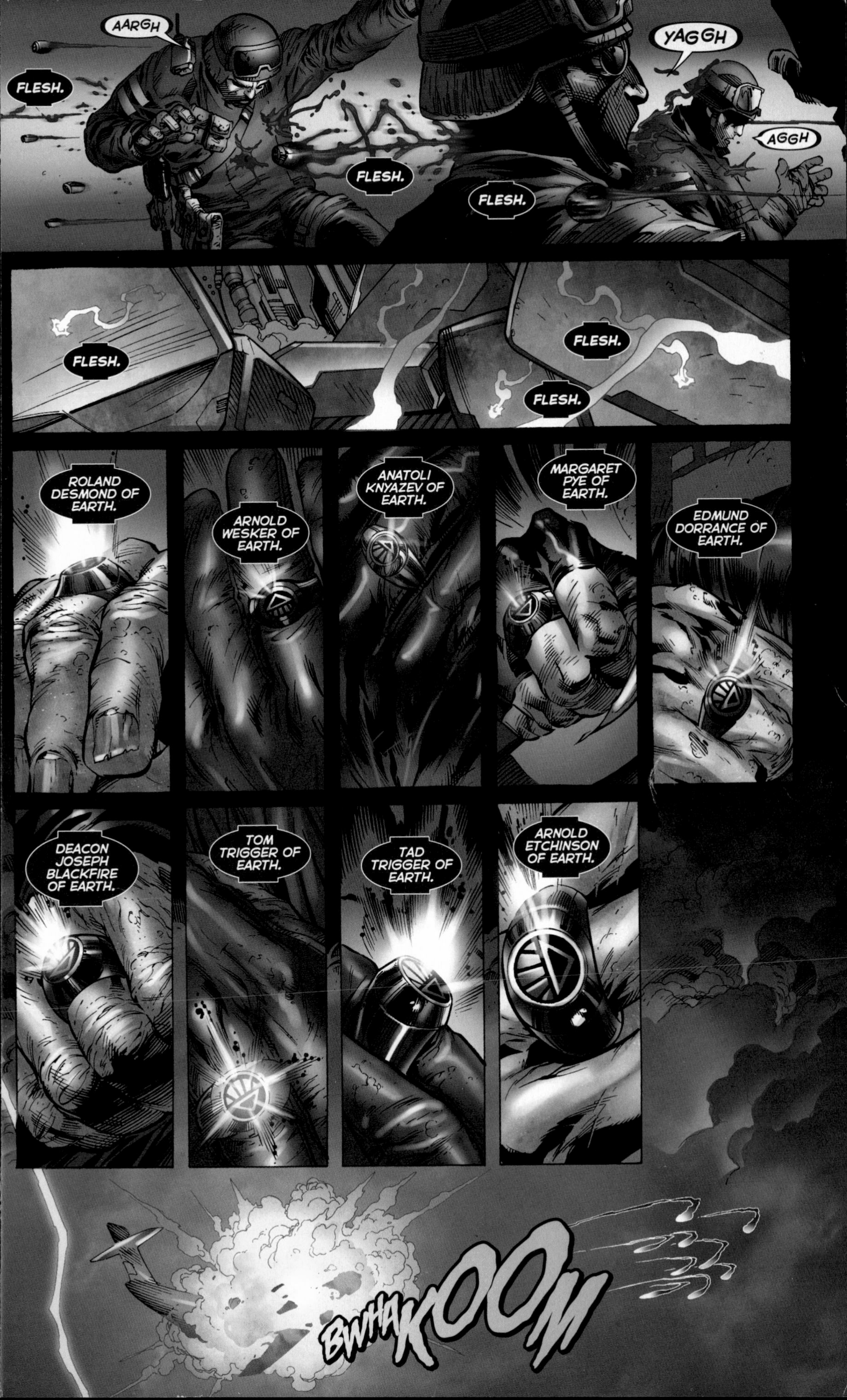

AARGH
FLESH.
YAGGH
AGGH
FLESH.
FLESH.
FLESH.
FLESH.
FLESH.
ROLAND DESMOND OF EARTH.
ARNOLD WESKER OF EARTH.
ANATOLI KNYAZEV OF EARTH.
MARGARET PYE OF EARTH.
EDMUND DORRANCE OF EARTH.
DEACON JOSEPH BLACKFIRE OF EARTH.
TOM TRIGGER OF EARTH.
TAD TRIGGER OF EARTH.
ARNOLD ETCHINSON OF EARTH.
BWHAKOOM

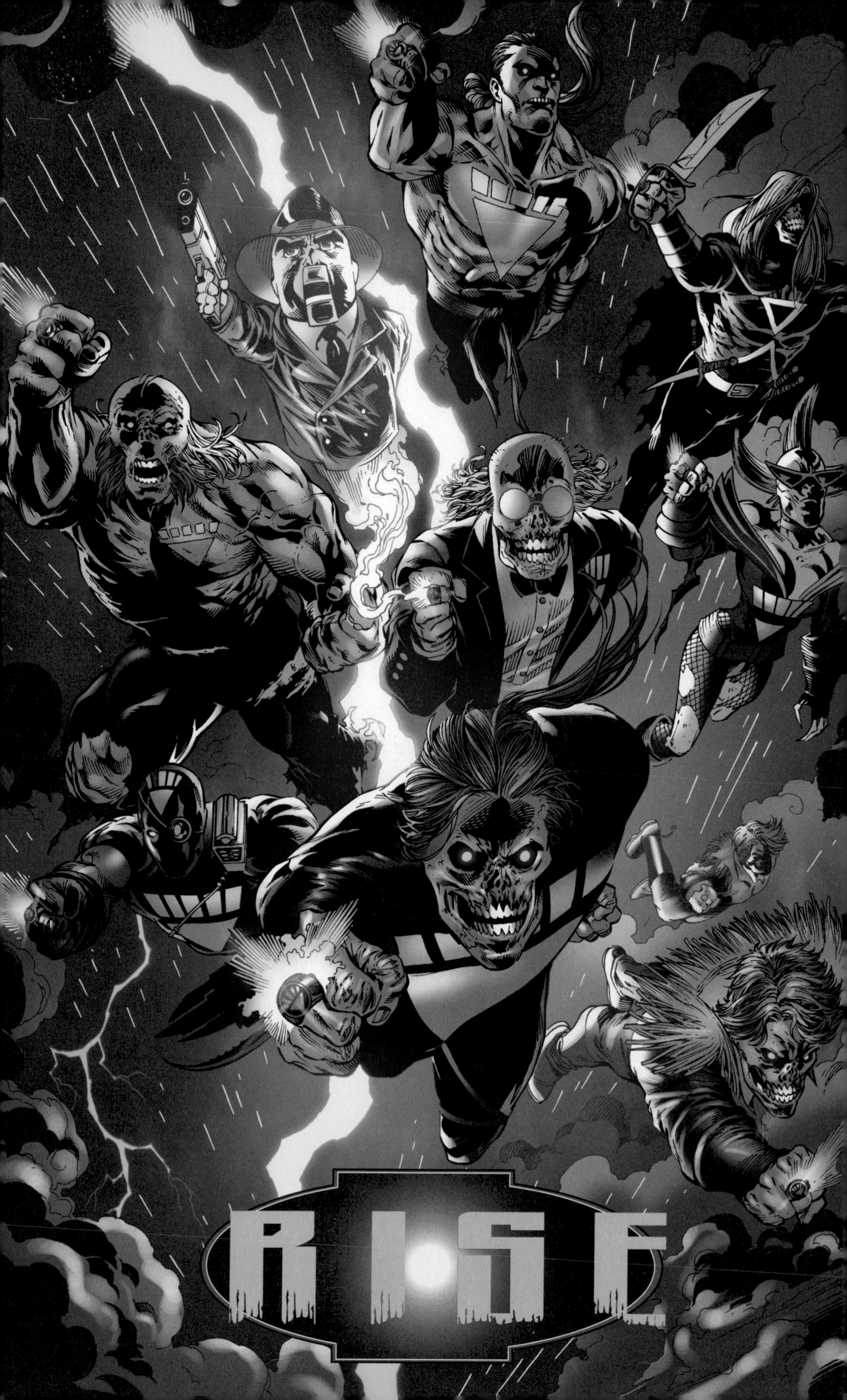
RISE

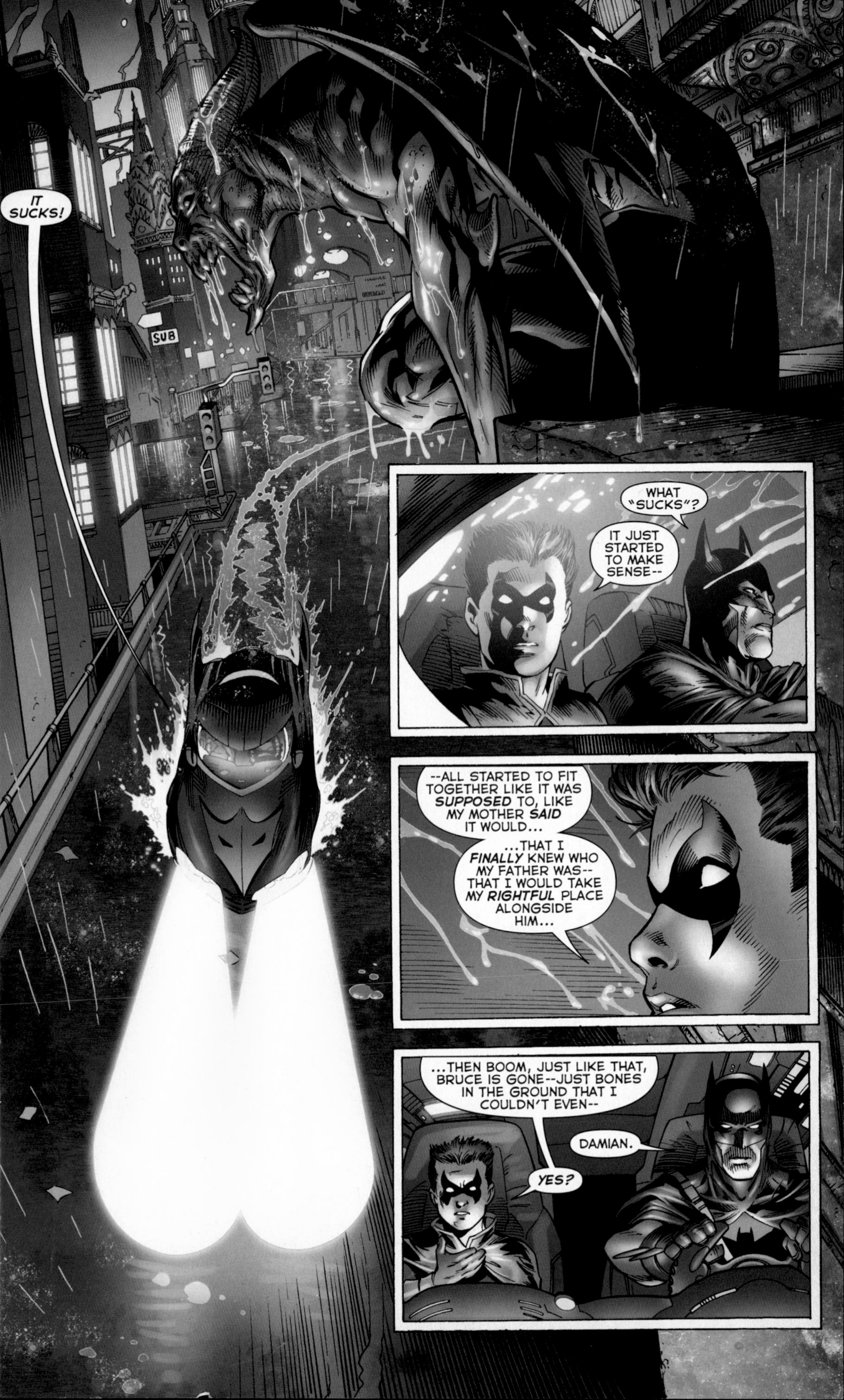
IT SUCKS!
WHAT "SUCKS"?
IT JUST STARTED TO MAKE SENSE--
--ALL STARTED TO FIT TOGETHER LIKE IT WAS SUPPOSED TO, LIKE MY MOTHER SAID IT WOULD...
...THAT I FINALLY KNEW WHO MY FATHER WAS--THAT I WOULD TAKE MY RIGHTFUL PLACE ALONGSIDE HIM...
...THEN BOOM, JUST LIKE THAT, BRUCE IS GONE--JUST BONES IN THE GROUND THAT I COULDN'T EVEN--
DAMIAN.
YES?

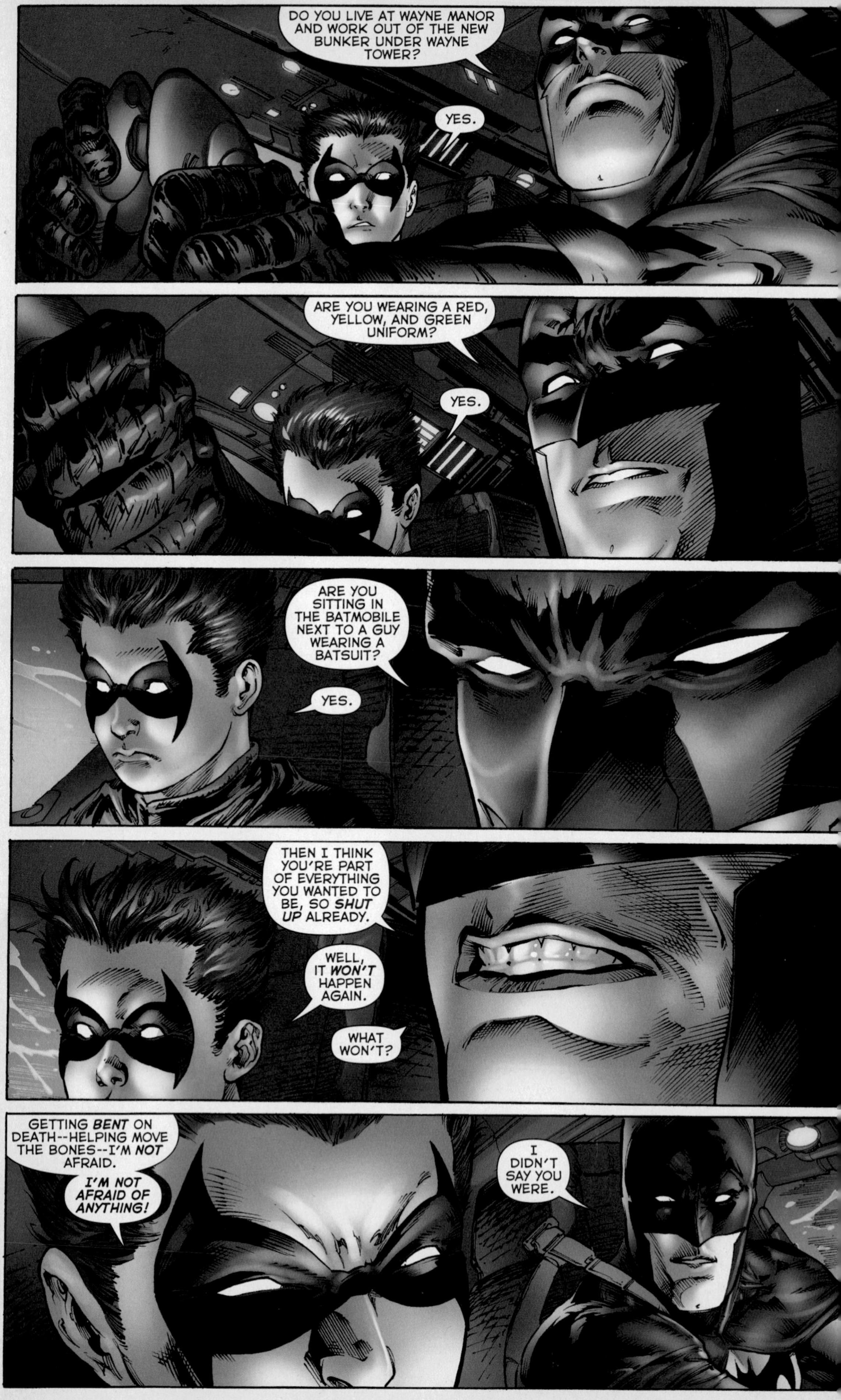

DO YOU LIVE AT WAYNE MANOR AND WORK OUT OF THE NEW BUNKER UNDER WAYNE TOWER?
YES.
ARE YOU WEARING A RED, YELLOW, AND GREEN UNIFORM?
YES.
ARE YOU SITTING IN THE BATMOBILE NEXT TO A GUY WEARING A BATSUIT?
YES.
THEN I THINK YOU'RE PART OF EVERYTHING YOU WANTED TO BE, SO *SHUT UP* ALREADY.
WELL, IT *WON'T* HAPPEN AGAIN.
WHAT WON'T?
GETTING *BENT* ON DEATH--HELPING MOVE THE BONES--I'M *NOT* AFRAID.
I'M NOT AFRAID OF ANYTHING!
I DIDN'T SAY YOU WERE.

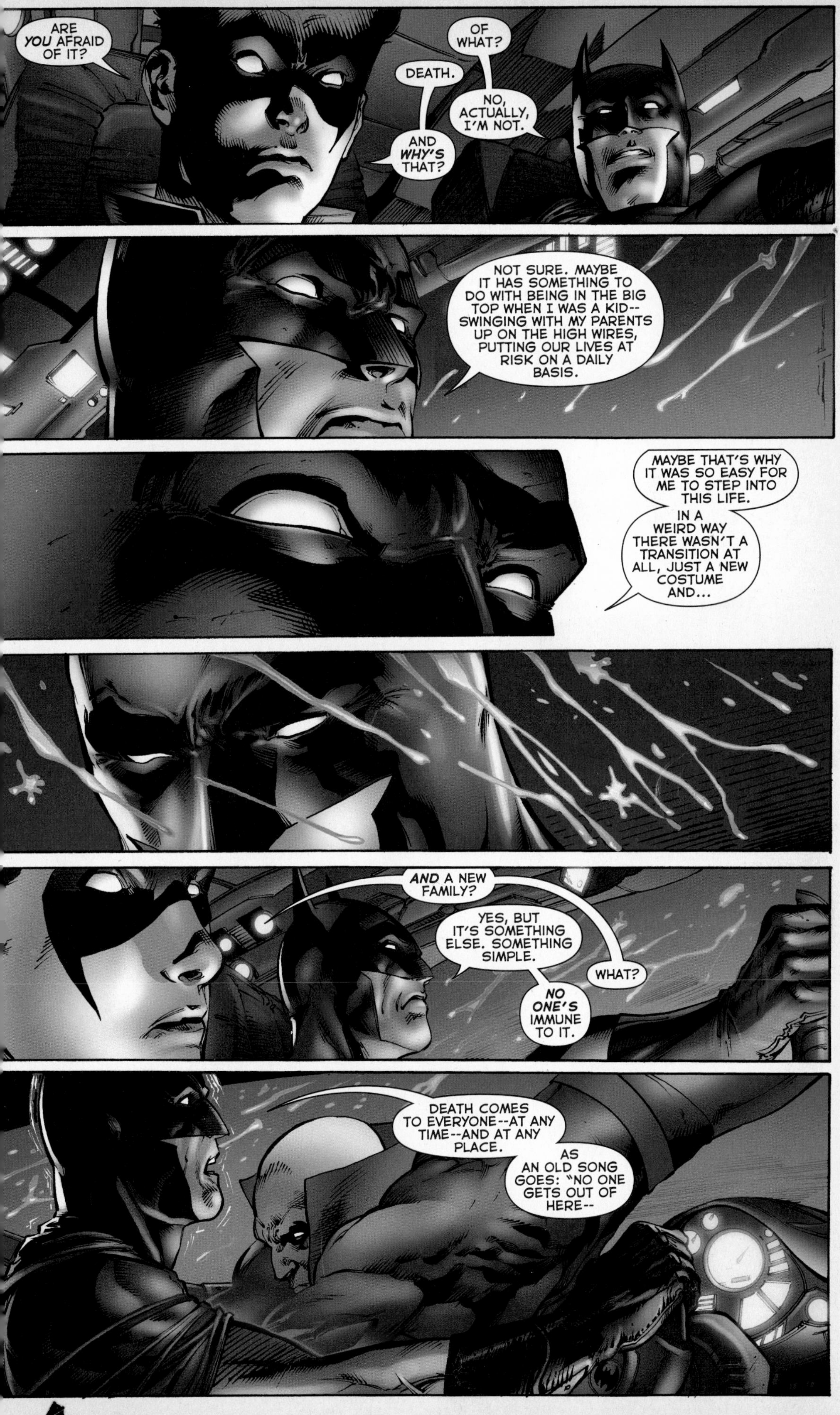

ARE YOU AFRAID OF IT?
OF WHAT?
DEATH.
NO, ACTUALLY, I'M NOT.
AND WHY'S THAT?
NOT SURE. MAYBE IT HAS SOMETHING TO DO WITH BEING IN THE BIG TOP WHEN I WAS A KID-- SWINGING WITH MY PARENTS UP ON THE HIGH WIRES, PUTTING OUR LIVES AT RISK ON A DAILY BASIS.
MAYBE THAT'S WHY IT WAS SO EASY FOR ME TO STEP INTO THIS LIFE.
IN A WEIRD WAY THERE WASN'T A TRANSITION AT ALL, JUST A NEW COSTUME AND...
AND A NEW FAMILY?
YES, BUT IT'S SOMETHING ELSE. SOMETHING SIMPLE.
WHAT?
NO ONE'S IMMUNE TO IT.
DEATH COMES TO EVERYONE--AT ANY TIME--AND AT ANY PLACE.
AS AN OLD SONG GOES: "NO ONE GETS OUT OF HERE--

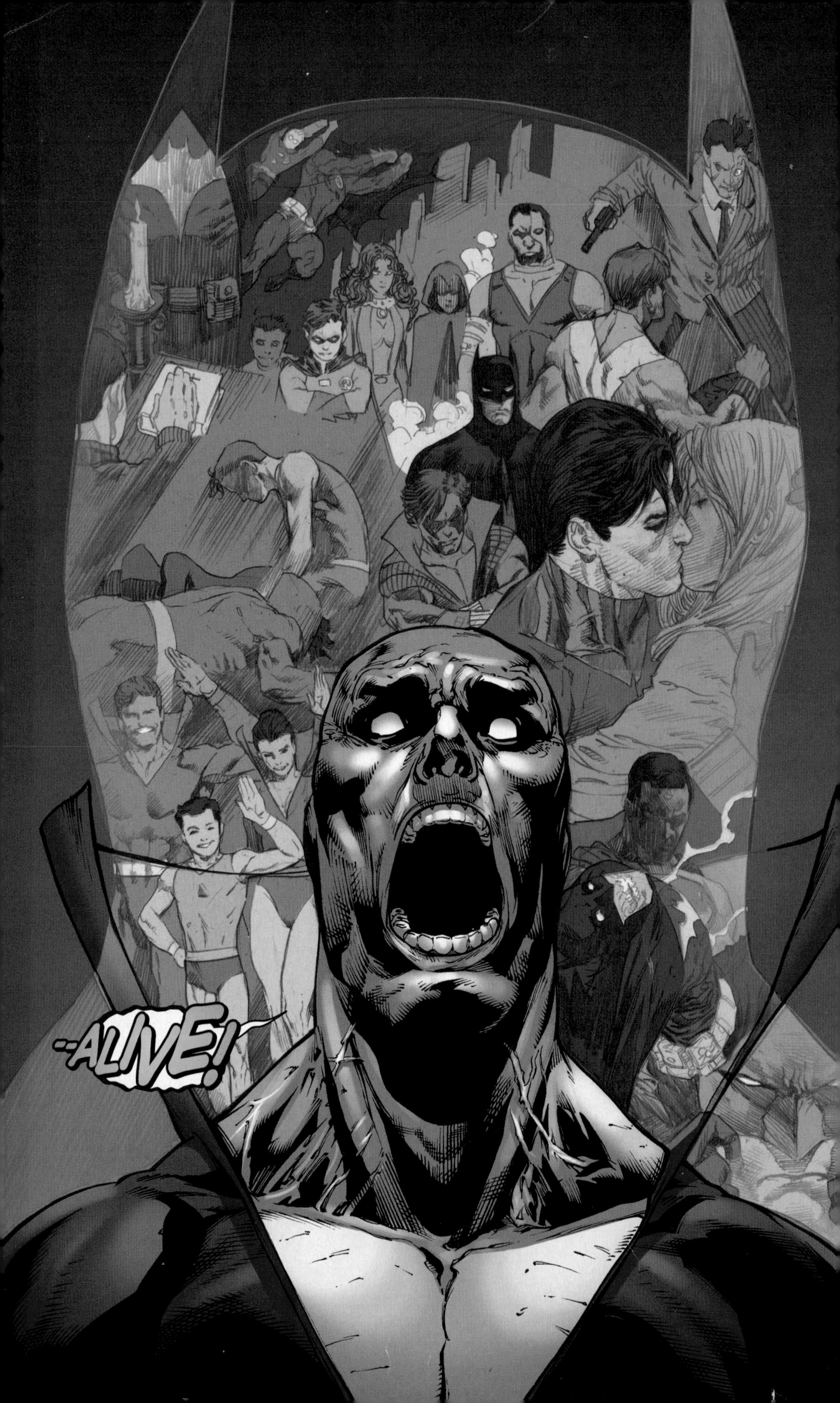
-ALIVE!

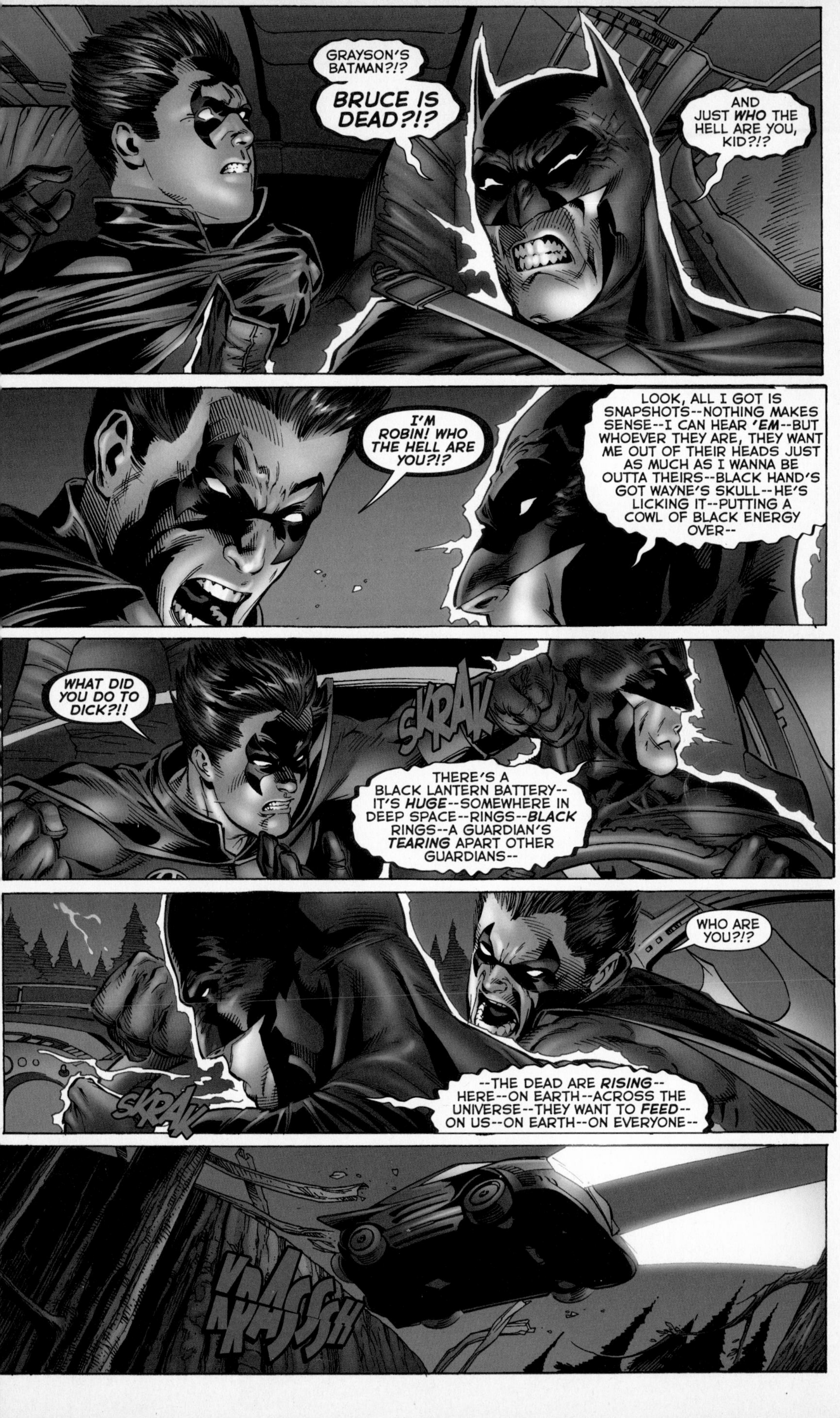
GRAYSON'S BATMAN?!?
BRUCE IS DEAD?!?
AND JUST WHO THE HELL ARE YOU, KID?!?
I'M ROBIN! WHO THE HELL ARE YOU?!?
LOOK, ALL I GOT IS SNAPSHOTS--NOTHING MAKES SENSE--I CAN HEAR 'EM--BUT WHOEVER THEY ARE, THEY WANT ME OUT OF THEIR HEADS JUST AS MUCH AS I WANNA BE OUTTA THEIRS--BLACK HAND'S GOT WAYNE'S SKULL--HE'S LICKING IT--PUTTING A COWL OF BLACK ENERGY OVER--
WHAT DID YOU DO TO DICK?!!
SKRAK
THERE'S A BLACK LANTERN BATTERY--IT'S HUGE--SOMEWHERE IN DEEP SPACE--RINGS--BLACK RINGS--A GUARDIAN'S TEARING APART OTHER GUARDIANS--
WHO ARE YOU?!?
SKRAK
--THE DEAD ARE RISING--HERE--ON EARTH--ACROSS THE UNIVERSE--THEY WANT TO FEED--ON US--ON EARTH--ON EVERYONE--
KRASSH

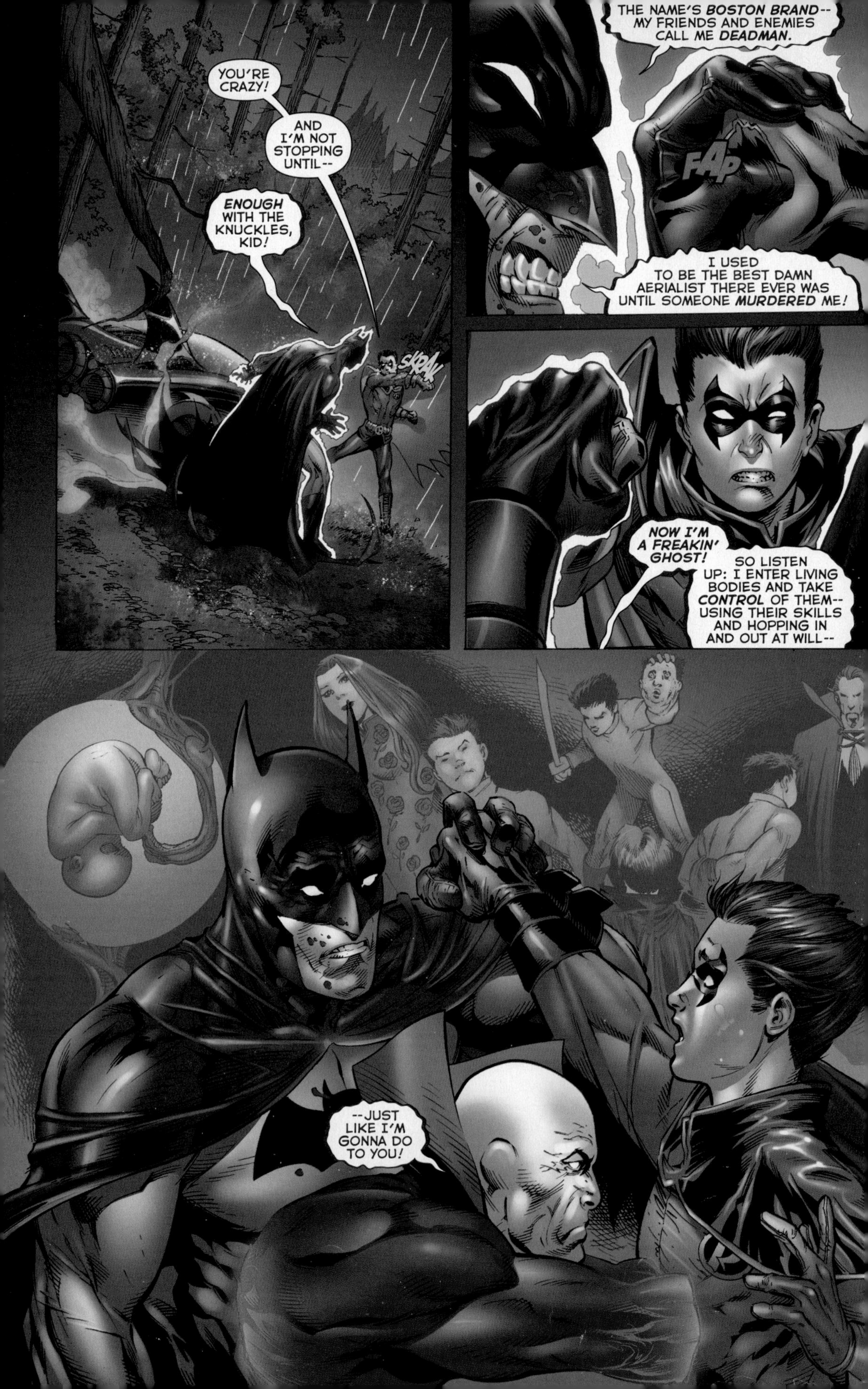
YOU'RE CRAZY!
AND I'M NOT STOPPING UNTIL--
ENOUGH WITH THE KNUCKLES, KID!
SKRAK
THE NAME'S BOSTON BRAND-- MY FRIENDS AND ENEMIES CALL ME DEADMAN.
FAP
I USED TO BE THE BEST DAMN AERIALIST THERE EVER WAS UNTIL SOMEONE MURDERED ME!
NOW I'M A FREAKIN' GHOST!
SO LISTEN UP: I ENTER LIVING BODIES AND TAKE CONTROL OF THEM-- USING THEIR SKILLS AND HOPPING IN AND OUT AT WILL--
--JUST LIKE I'M GONNA DO TO YOU!

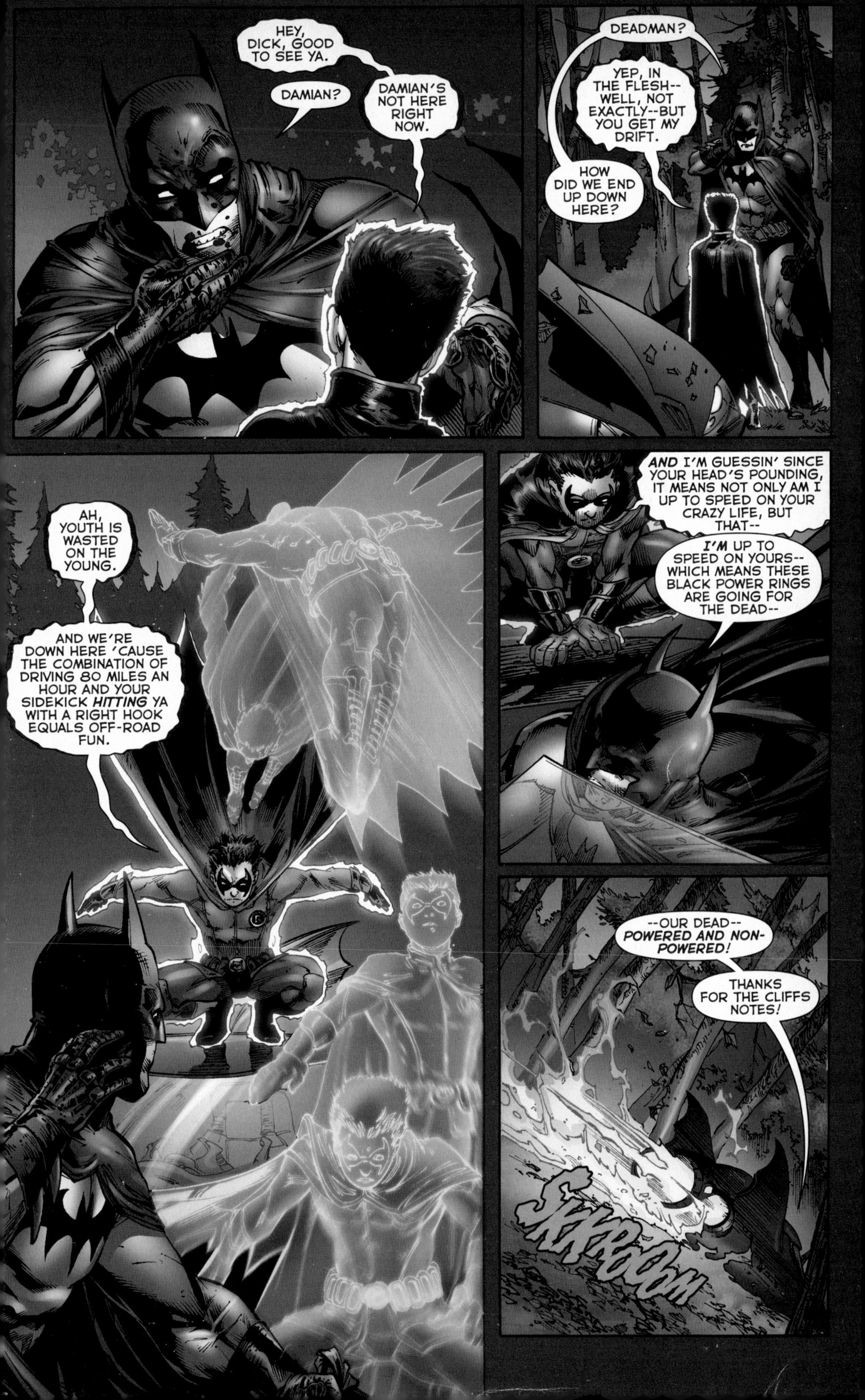
HEY, DICK, GOOD TO SEE YA.
DAMIAN?
DAMIAN'S NOT HERE RIGHT NOW.
DEADMAN?
YEP, IN THE FLESH-- WELL, NOT EXACTLY--BUT YOU GET MY DRIFT.
HOW DID WE END UP DOWN HERE?
AH, YOUTH IS WASTED ON THE YOUNG.
AND WE'RE DOWN HERE 'CAUSE THE COMBINATION OF DRIVING 80 MILES AN HOUR AND YOUR SIDEKICK HITTING YA WITH A RIGHT HOOK EQUALS OFF-ROAD FUN.
AND I'M GUESSIN' SINCE YOUR HEAD'S POUNDING, IT MEANS NOT ONLY AM I UP TO SPEED ON YOUR CRAZY LIFE, BUT THAT--
I'M UP TO SPEED ON YOURS-- WHICH MEANS THESE BLACK POWER RINGS ARE GOING FOR THE DEAD--
--OUR DEAD-- POWERED AND NON-POWERED!
THANKS FOR THE CLIFFS NOTES!
SKKROOOM

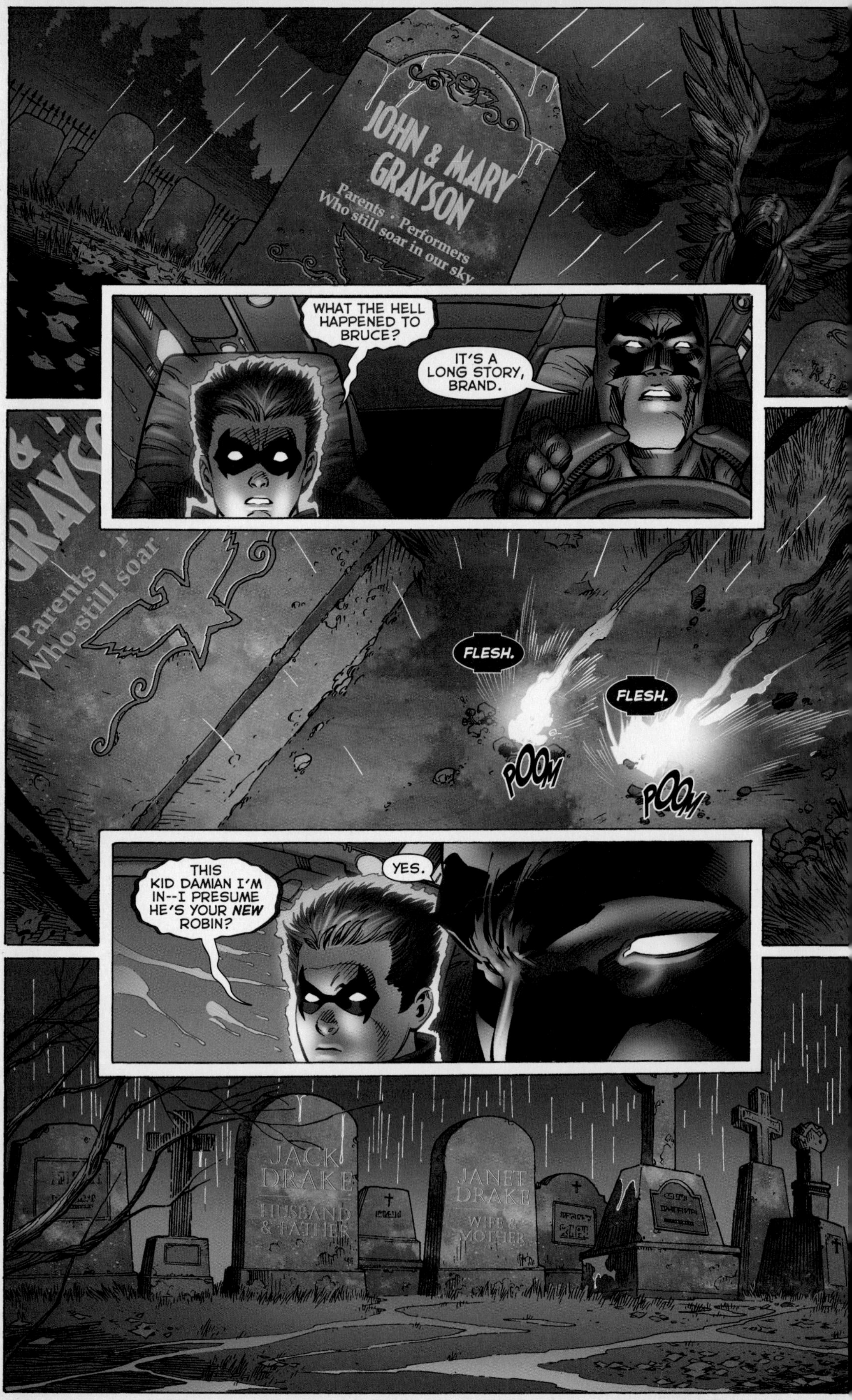
JOHN & MARY GRAYSON
Parents • Performers
Who still soar in our sky
WHAT THE HELL HAPPENED TO BRUCE?
IT'S A LONG STORY, BRAND.
FLESH.
FLESH.
POOM
POOM
THIS KID DAMIAN I'M IN--I PRESUME HE'S YOUR NEW ROBIN?
YES.
JACK DRAKE
HUSBAND & FATHER
JANET DRAKE
WIFE & MOTHER

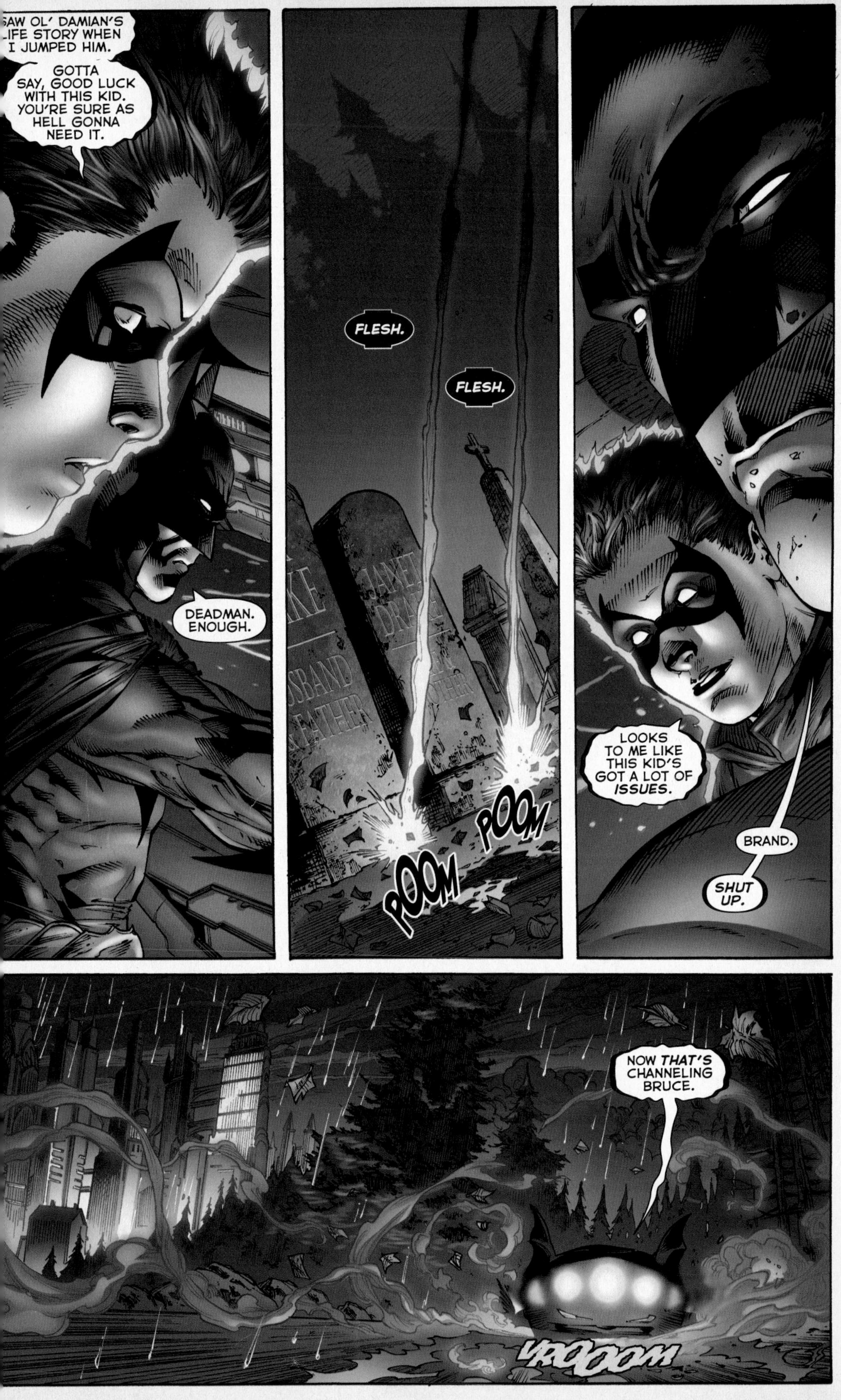
SAW OL' DAMIAN'S LIFE STORY WHEN I JUMPED HIM.
GOTTA SAY, GOOD LUCK WITH THIS KID. YOU'RE SURE AS HELL GONNA NEED IT.
DEADMAN. ENOUGH.
FLESH.
FLESH.
POOM
POOM
LOOKS TO ME LIKE THIS KID'S GOT A LOT OF ISSUES.
BRAND.
SHUT UP.
NOW THAT'S CHANNELING BRUCE.
VROOOOM

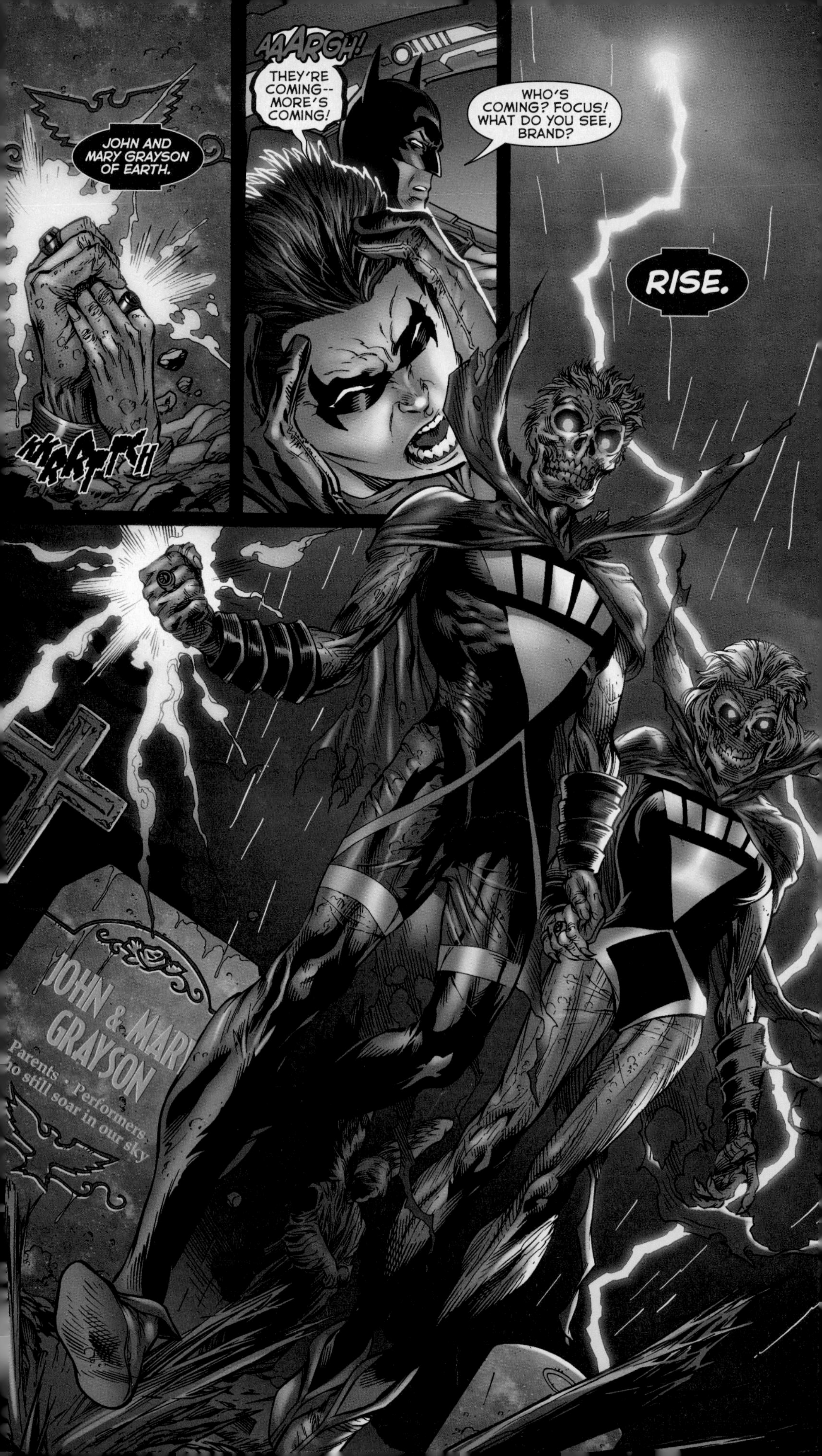
JOHN AND MARY GRAYSON OF EARTH.
KKRRTCH
AAARGH!
THEY'RE COMING-- MORE'S COMING!
WHO'S COMING? FOCUS! WHAT DO YOU SEE, BRAND?
RISE.
JOHN & MARY GRAYSON
Parents • Performers
who still soar in our sky

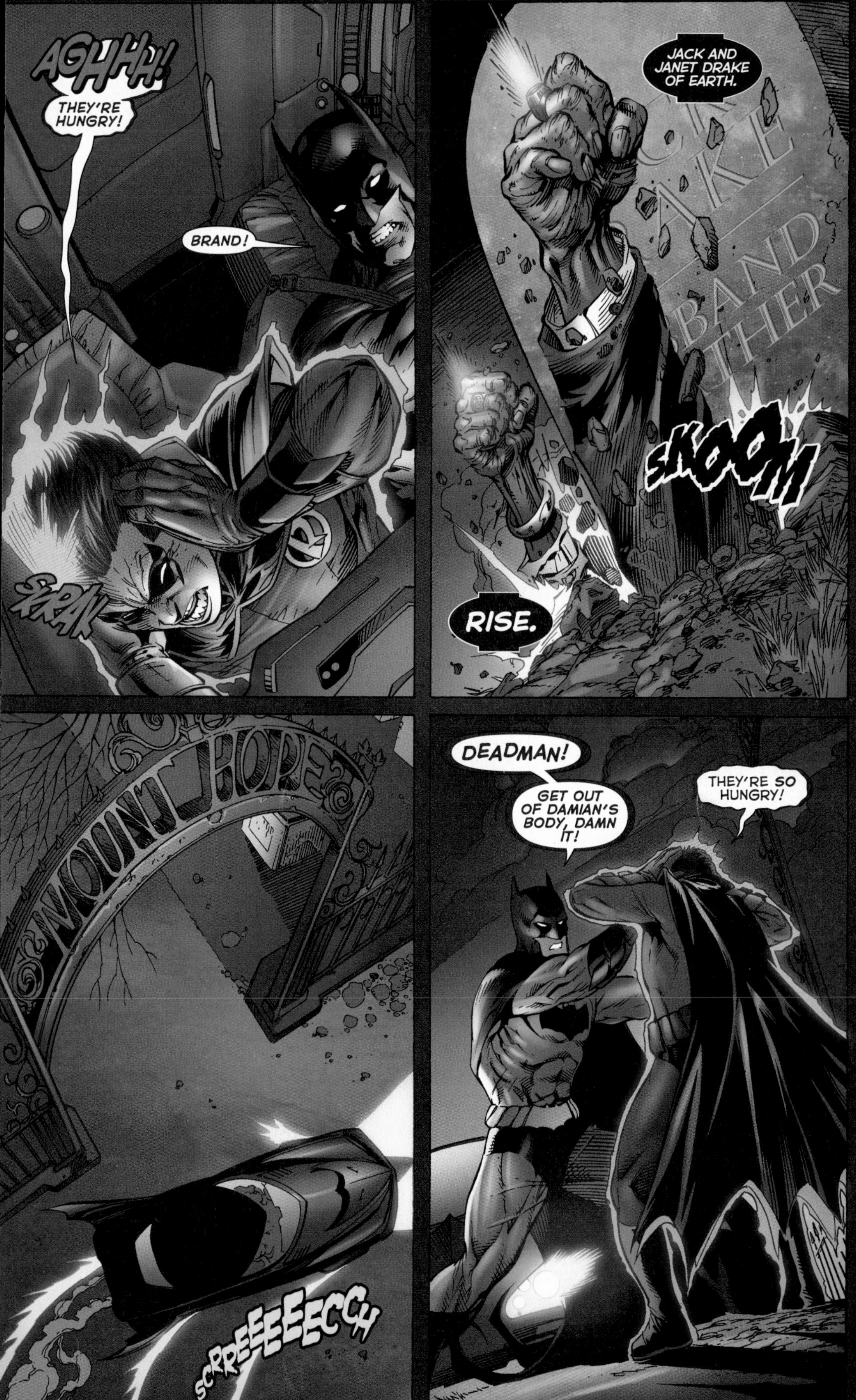
AGHHH!
THEY'RE HUNGRY!
BRAND!
SKRAK
JACK AND JANET DRAKE OF EARTH.
SKOOM
RISE.
MOUNT HOPE
SCREEEEEECCH
DEADMAN!
GET OUT OF DAMIAN'S BODY, DAMN IT!
THEY'RE SO HUNGRY!

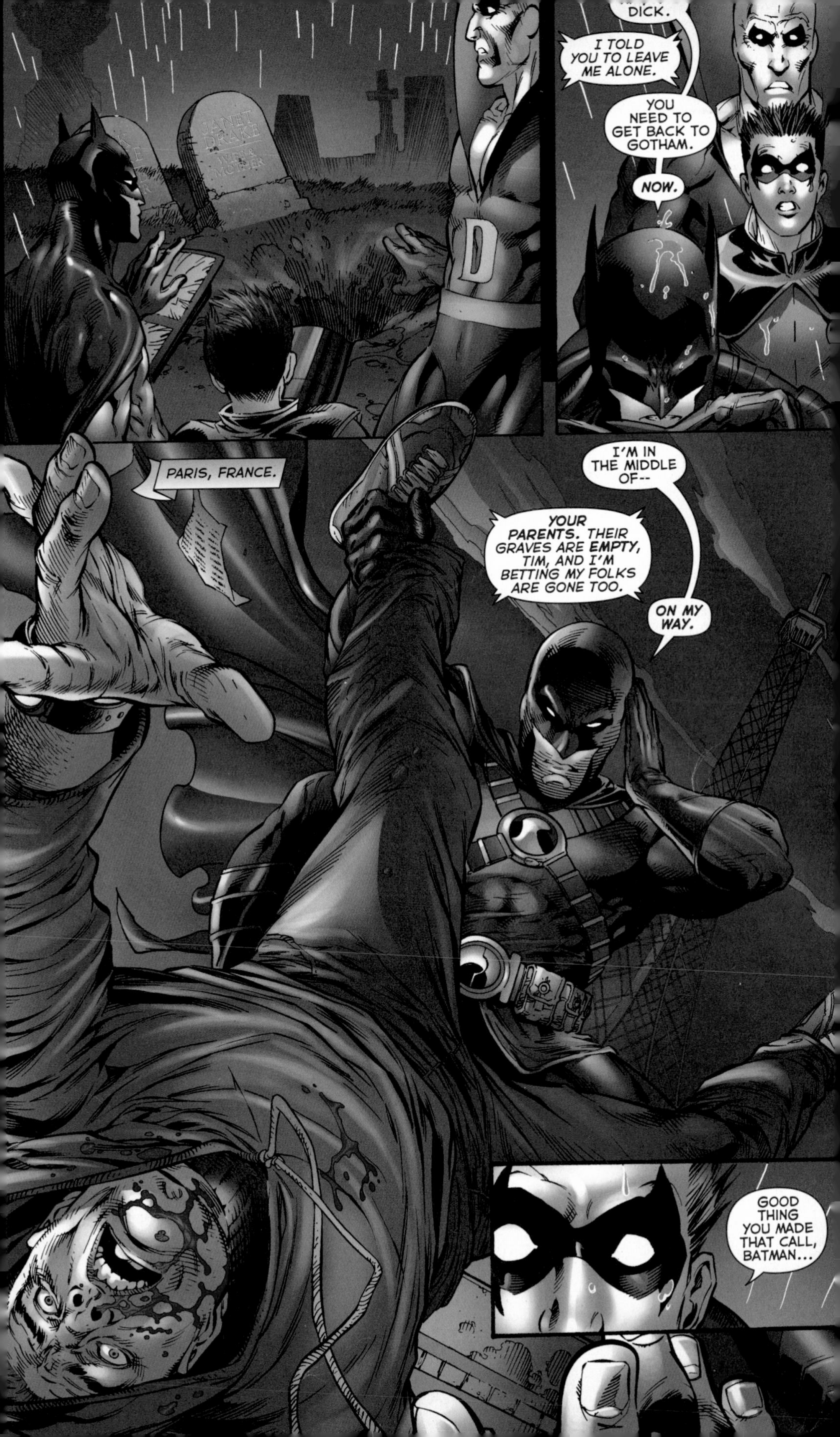
JANET DRAKE
WIFE & MOTHER
DICK.
I TOLD YOU TO LEAVE ME ALONE.
YOU NEED TO GET BACK TO GOTHAM.
NOW.
PARIS, FRANCE.
I'M IN THE MIDDLE OF--
YOUR PARENTS. THEIR GRAVES ARE EMPTY, TIM, AND I'M BETTING MY FOLKS ARE GONE TOO.
ON MY WAY.
GOOD THING YOU MADE THAT CALL, BATMAN...

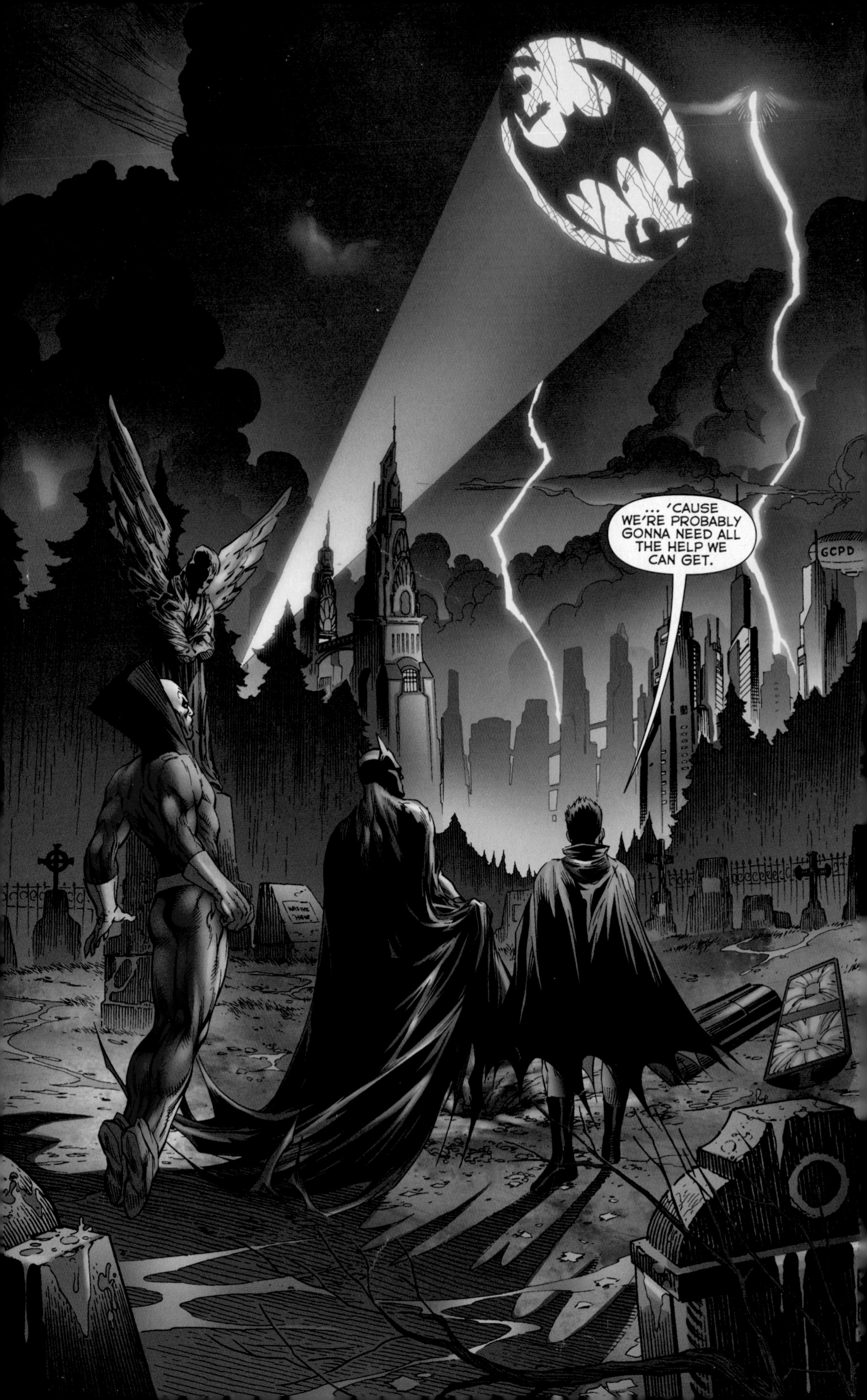
... 'CAUSE WE'RE PROBABLY GONNA NEED ALL THE HELP WE CAN GET.
GCPD

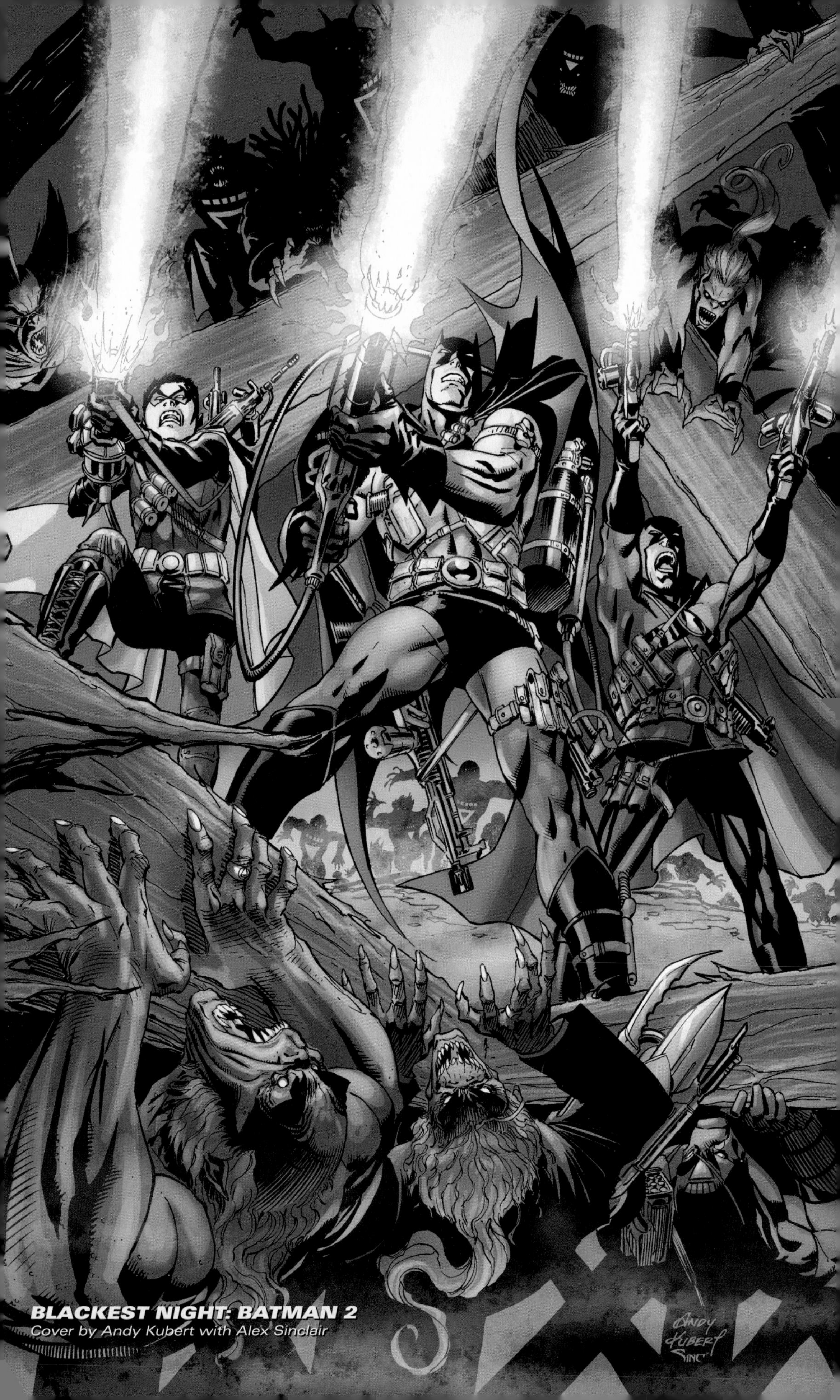

BLACKEST NIGHT: BATMAN 2
Cover by Andy Kubert with Alex Sinclair

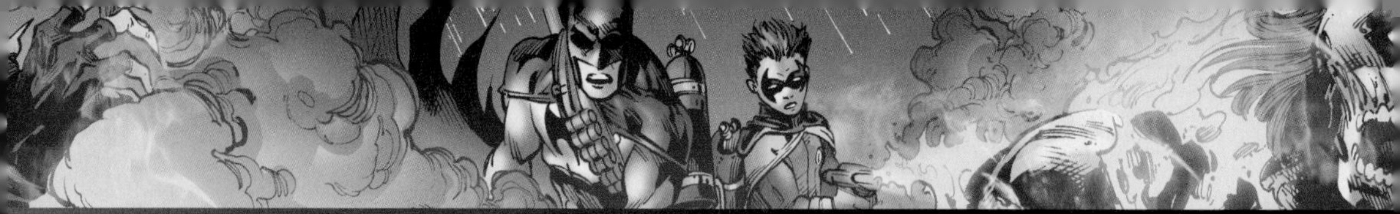

WHO BURNS WHO
PART TWO

PETER J. TOMASI
WRITER

ARDIAN SYAF
PENCILS

VICENTE CIFUENTES
INKS

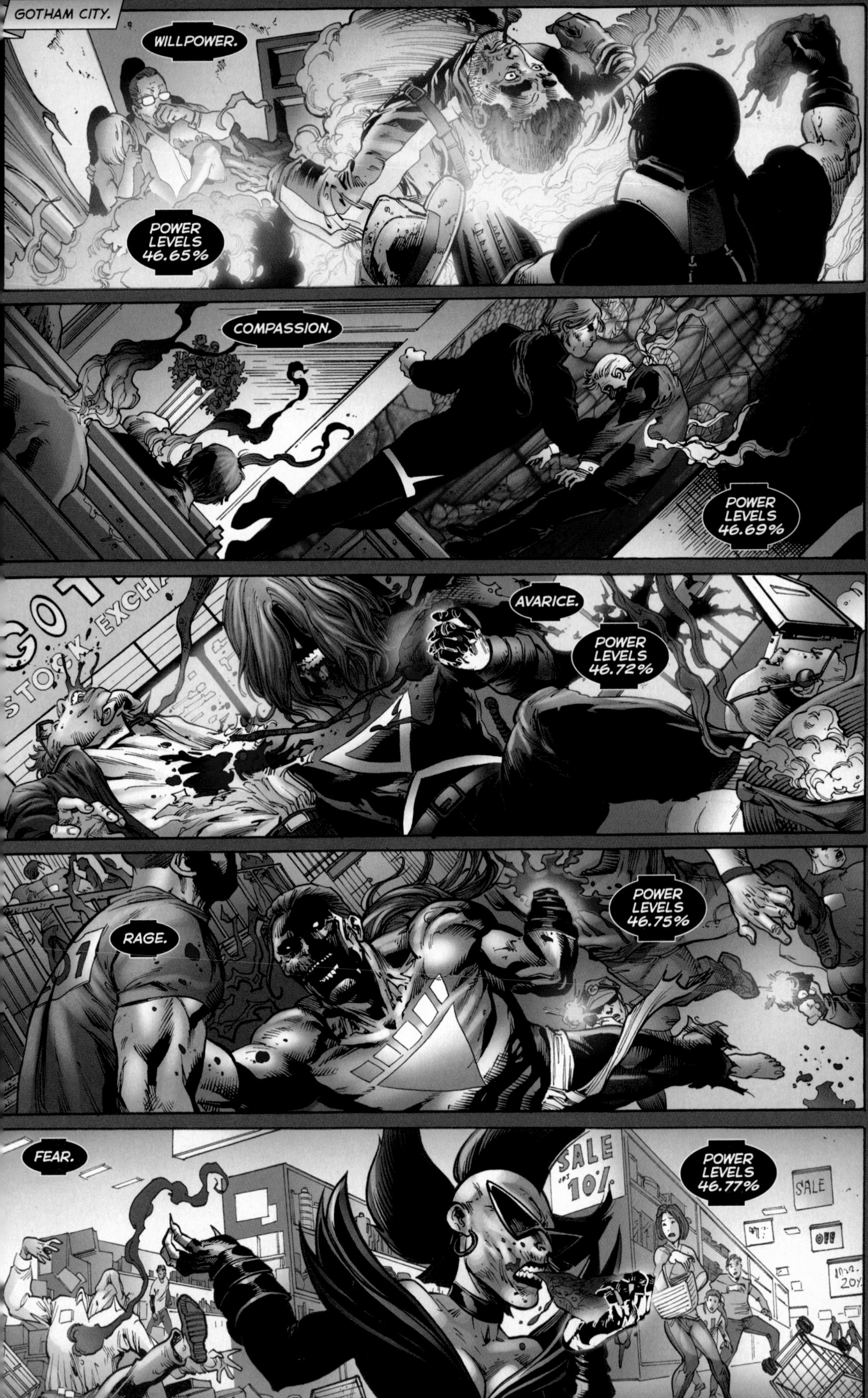
GOTHAM CITY.
WILLPOWER.
POWER LEVELS 46.65%
COMPASSION.
POWER LEVELS 46.69%
AVARICE.
POWER LEVELS 46.72%
RAGE.
POWER LEVELS 46.75%
FEAR.
SALE
POWER LEVELS 46.77%
SALE
OFF

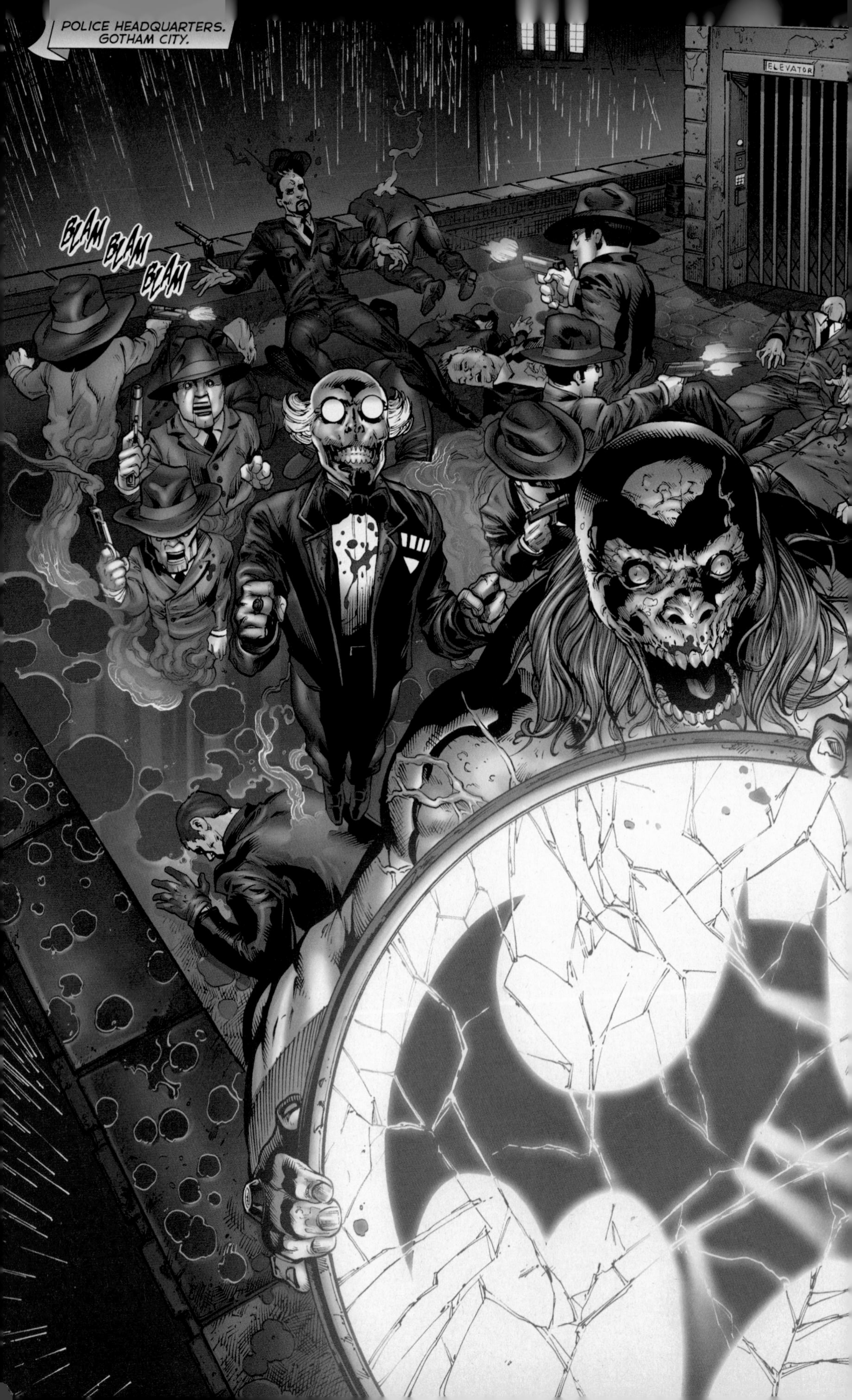
POLICE HEADQUARTERS.
GOTHAM CITY.
ELEVATOR
BLAM BLAM BLAM

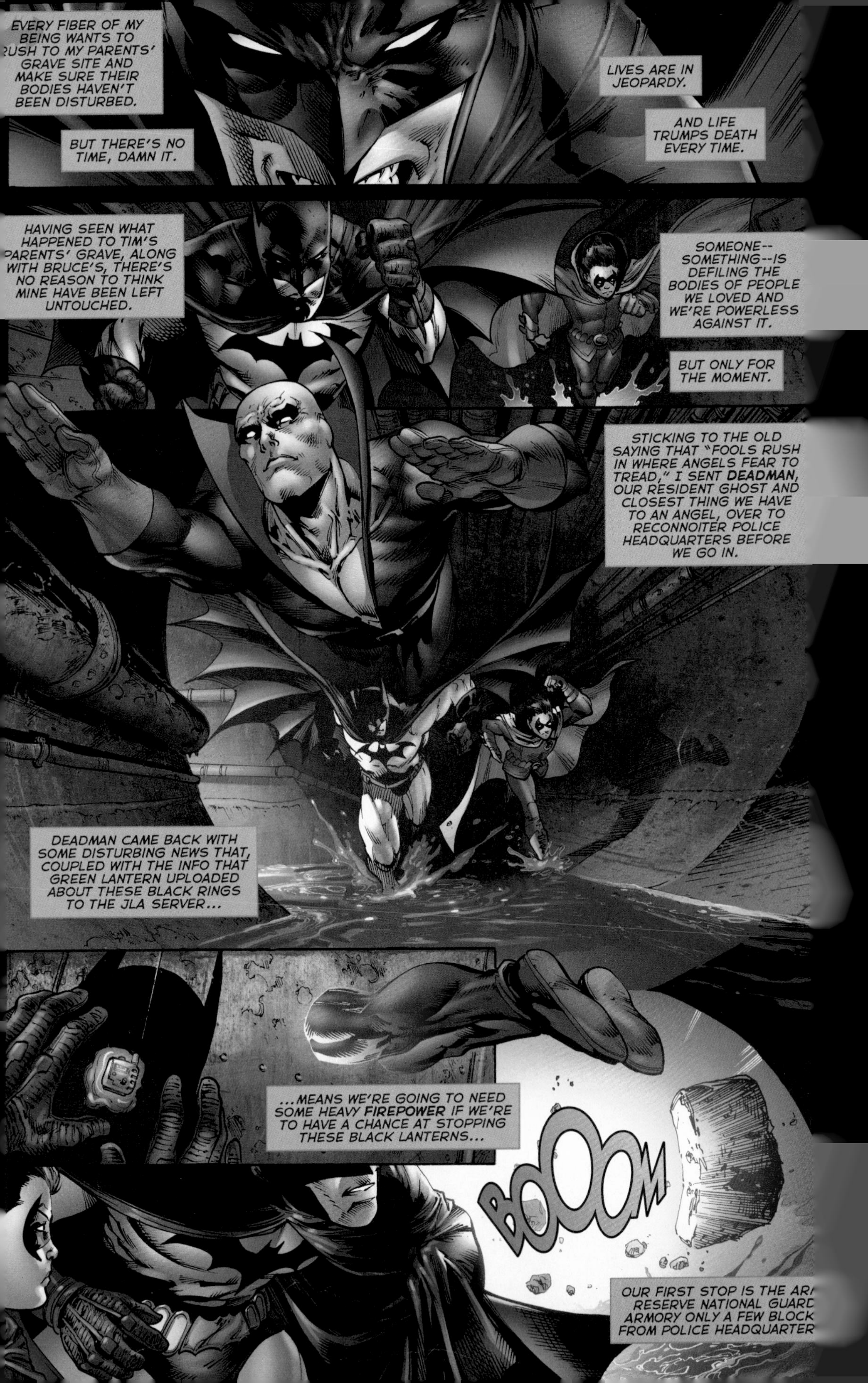
EVERY FIBER OF MY BEING WANTS TO RUSH TO MY PARENTS' GRAVE SITE AND MAKE SURE THEIR BODIES HAVEN'T BEEN DISTURBED.
BUT THERE'S NO TIME, DAMN IT.
LIVES ARE IN JEOPARDY.
AND LIFE TRUMPS DEATH EVERY TIME.
HAVING SEEN WHAT HAPPENED TO TIM'S PARENTS' GRAVE, ALONG WITH BRUCE'S, THERE'S NO REASON TO THINK MINE HAVE BEEN LEFT UNTOUCHED.
SOMEONE-- SOMETHING--IS DEFILING THE BODIES OF PEOPLE WE LOVED AND WE'RE POWERLESS AGAINST IT.
BUT ONLY FOR THE MOMENT.
STICKING TO THE OLD SAYING THAT "FOOLS RUSH IN WHERE ANGELS FEAR TO TREAD," I SENT DEADMAN, OUR RESIDENT GHOST AND CLOSEST THING WE HAVE TO AN ANGEL, OVER TO RECONNOITER POLICE HEADQUARTERS BEFORE WE GO IN.
DEADMAN CAME BACK WITH SOME DISTURBING NEWS THAT, COUPLED WITH THE INFO THAT GREEN LANTERN UPLOADED ABOUT THESE BLACK RINGS TO THE JLA SERVER...
...MEANS WE'RE GOING TO NEED SOME HEAVY FIREPOWER IF WE'RE TO HAVE A CHANCE AT STOPPING THESE BLACK LANTERNS...
BOOOM
OUR FIRST STOP IS THE AR RESERVE NATIONAL GUARD ARMORY ONLY A FEW BLOCK FROM POLICE HEADQUARTER

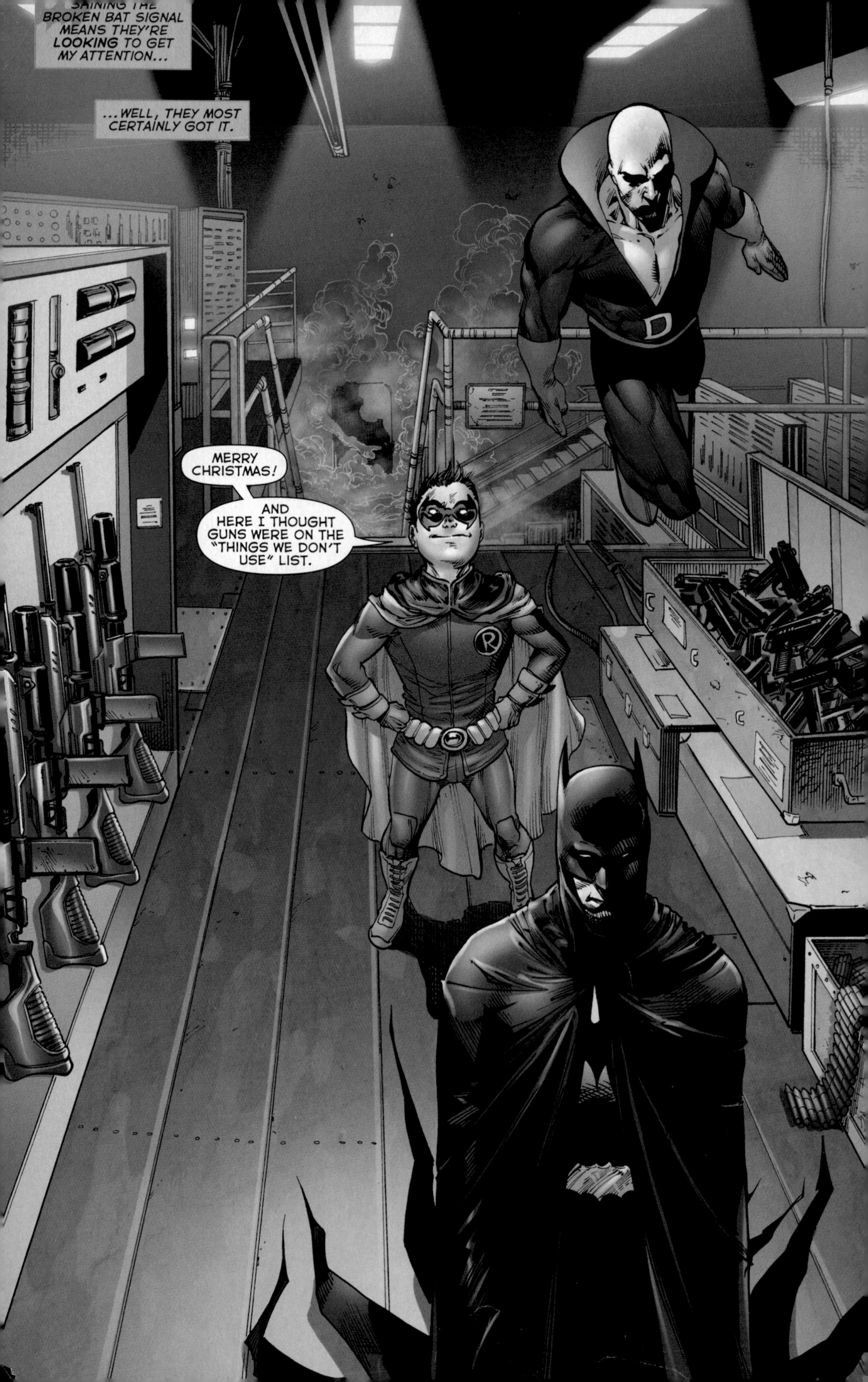
BROKEN BAT SIGNAL MEANS THEY'RE LOOKING TO GET MY ATTENTION...
...WELL, THEY MOST CERTAINLY GOT IT.
MERRY CHRISTMAS!
AND HERE I THOUGHT GUNS WERE ON THE "THINGS WE DON'T USE" LIST.

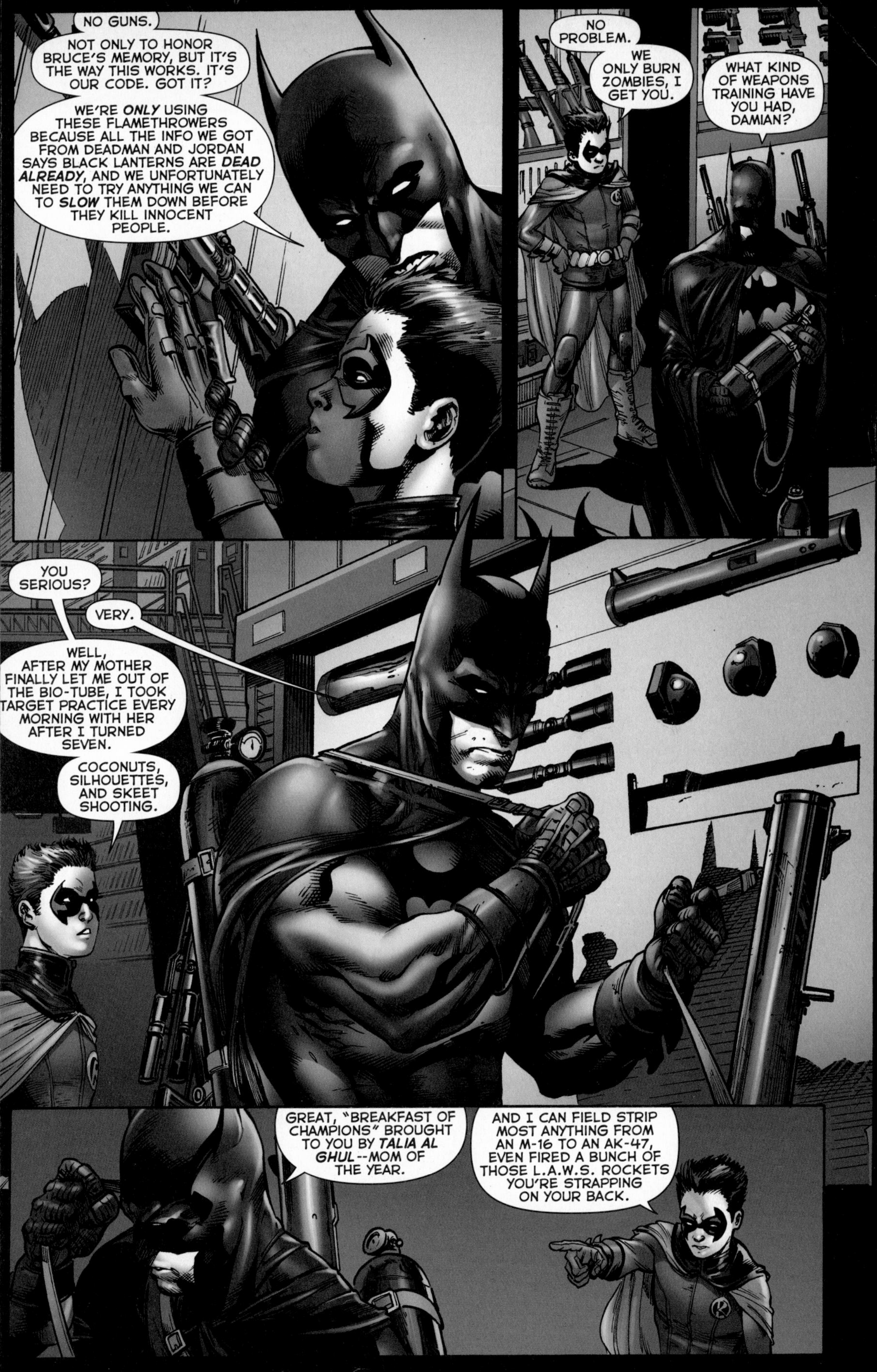
NO GUNS.
NOT ONLY TO HONOR BRUCE'S MEMORY, BUT IT'S THE WAY THIS WORKS. IT'S OUR CODE. GOT IT?
WE'RE *ONLY* USING THESE FLAMETHROWERS BECAUSE ALL THE INFO WE GOT FROM DEADMAN AND JORDAN SAYS BLACK LANTERNS ARE *DEAD ALREADY*, AND WE UNFORTUNATELY NEED TO TRY ANYTHING WE CAN TO *SLOW* THEM DOWN BEFORE THEY KILL INNOCENT PEOPLE.
NO PROBLEM.
WE ONLY BURN ZOMBIES, I GET YOU.
WHAT KIND OF WEAPONS TRAINING HAVE YOU HAD, DAMIAN?
YOU SERIOUS?
VERY.
WELL, AFTER MY MOTHER FINALLY LET ME OUT OF THE BIO-TUBE, I TOOK TARGET PRACTICE EVERY MORNING WITH HER AFTER I TURNED SEVEN.
COCONUTS, SILHOUETTES, AND SKEET SHOOTING.
AND I CAN FIELD STRIP MOST ANYTHING FROM AN M-16 TO AN AK-47, EVEN FIRED A BUNCH OF THOSE L.A.W.S. ROCKETS YOU'RE STRAPPING ON YOUR BACK.
GREAT, "BREAKFAST OF CHAMPIONS" BROUGHT TO YOU BY *TALIA AL GHUL*--MOM OF THE YEAR.

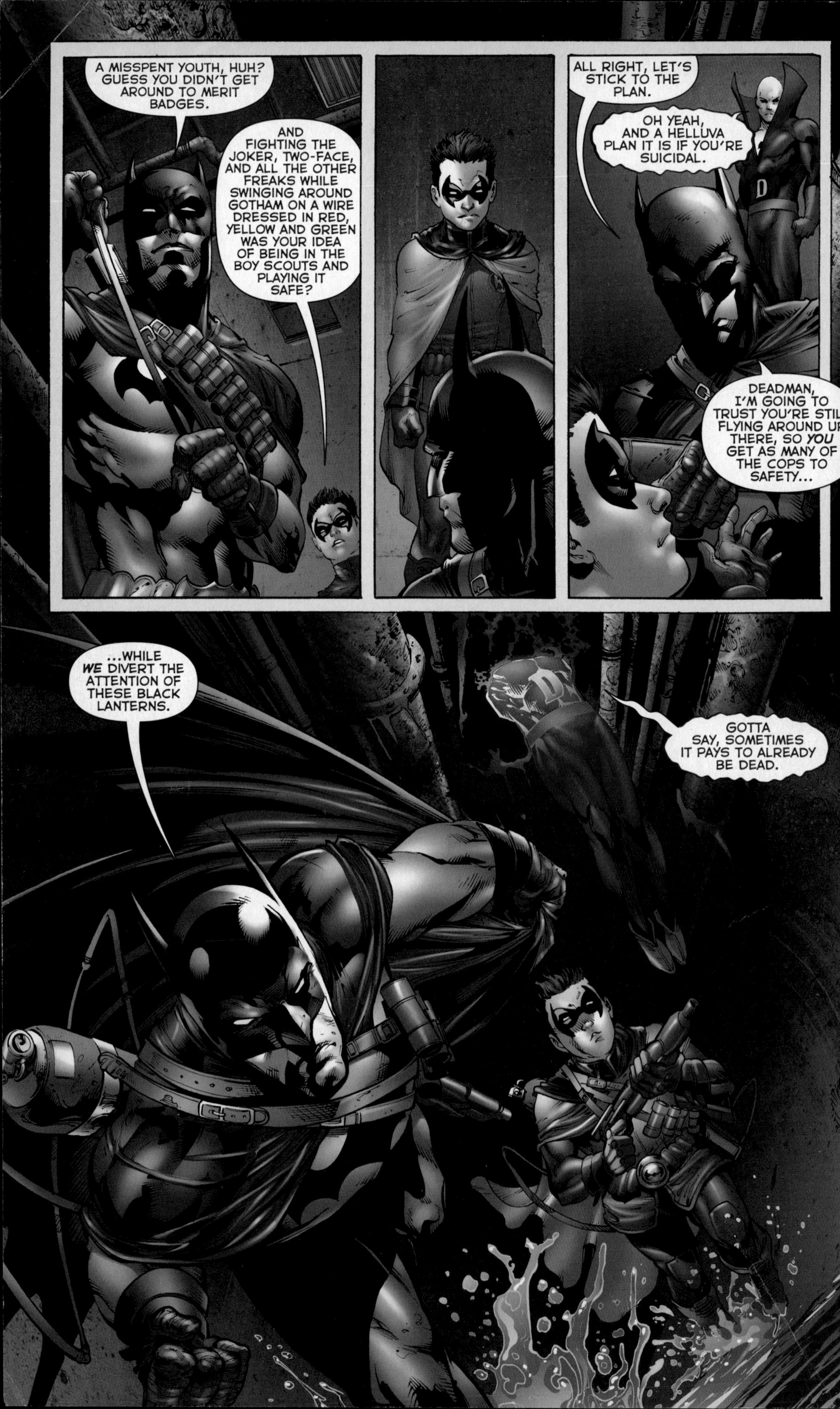
A MISSPENT YOUTH, HUH? GUESS YOU DIDN'T GET AROUND TO MERIT BADGES.
AND FIGHTING THE JOKER, TWO-FACE, AND ALL THE OTHER FREAKS WHILE SWINGING AROUND GOTHAM ON A WIRE DRESSED IN RED, YELLOW AND GREEN WAS YOUR IDEA OF BEING IN THE BOY SCOUTS AND PLAYING IT SAFE?
ALL RIGHT, LET'S STICK TO THE PLAN.
OH YEAH, AND A HELLUVA PLAN IT IS IF YOU'RE SUICIDAL.
DEADMAN, I'M GOING TO TRUST YOU'RE STIL FLYING AROUND UP THERE, SO *YOU* GET AS MANY OF THE COPS TO SAFETY...
...WHILE *WE* DIVERT THE ATTENTION OF THESE BLACK LANTERNS.
GOTTA SAY, SOMETIMES IT PAYS TO ALREADY BE DEAD.

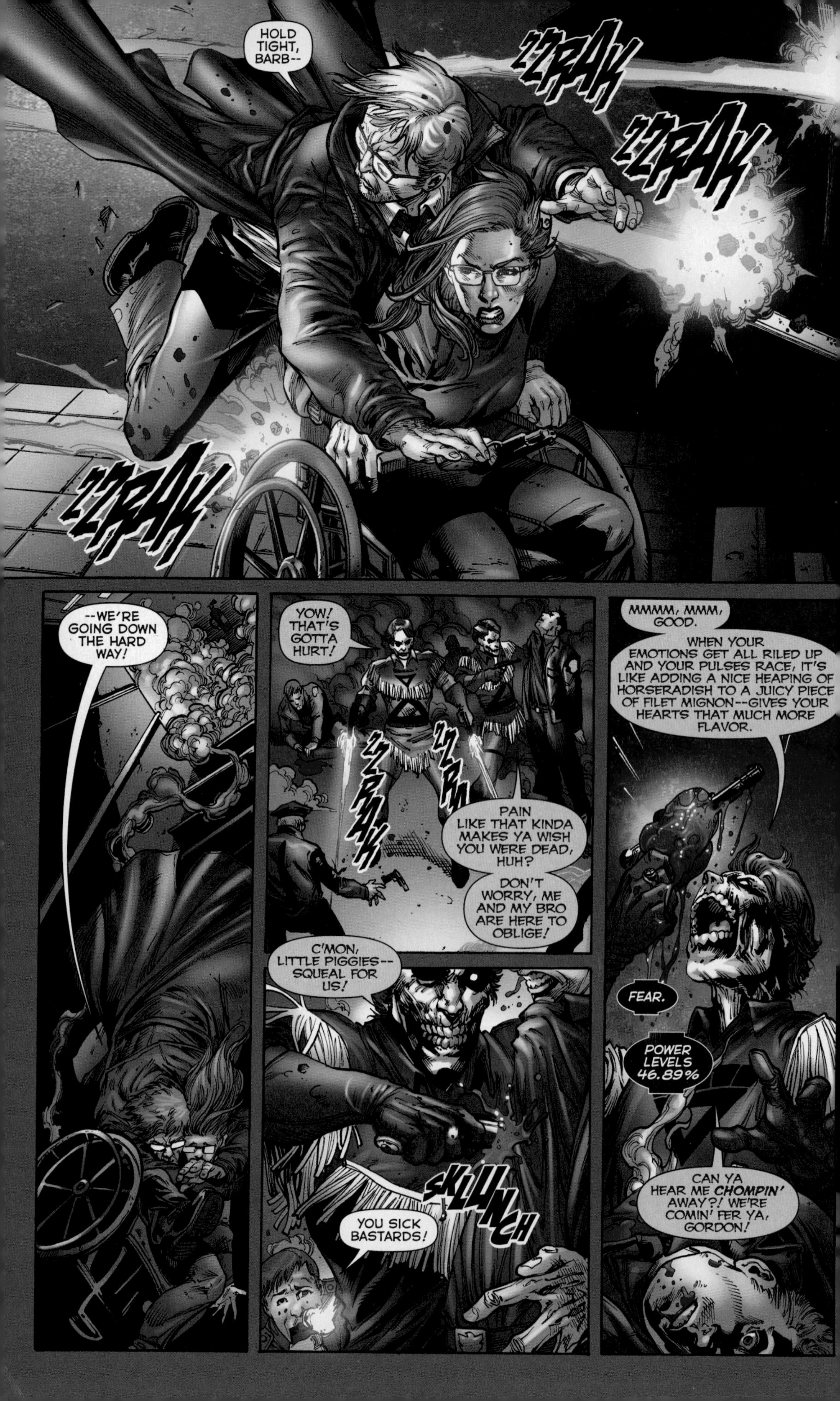
HOLD TIGHT, BARB--
ZZRAK
ZZRAK
ZZRAK
--WE'RE GOING DOWN THE HARD WAY!
YOW! THAT'S GOTTA HURT!
ZZRAK
ZZRAK
PAIN LIKE THAT KINDA MAKES YA WISH YOU WERE DEAD, HUH?
DON'T WORRY, ME AND MY BRO ARE HERE TO OBLIGE!
C'MON, LITTLE PIGGIES-- SQUEAL FOR US!
SKLUNCH
YOU SICK BASTARDS!
MMMM, MMM, GOOD.
WHEN YOUR EMOTIONS GET ALL RILED UP AND YOUR PULSES RACE, IT'S LIKE ADDING A NICE HEAPING OF HORSERADISH TO A JUICY PIECE OF FILET MIGNON--GIVES YOUR HEARTS THAT MUCH MORE FLAVOR.
FEAR.
POWER LEVELS 46.89%
CAN YA HEAR ME CHOMPIN' AWAY?! WE'RE COMIN' FER YA, GORDON!

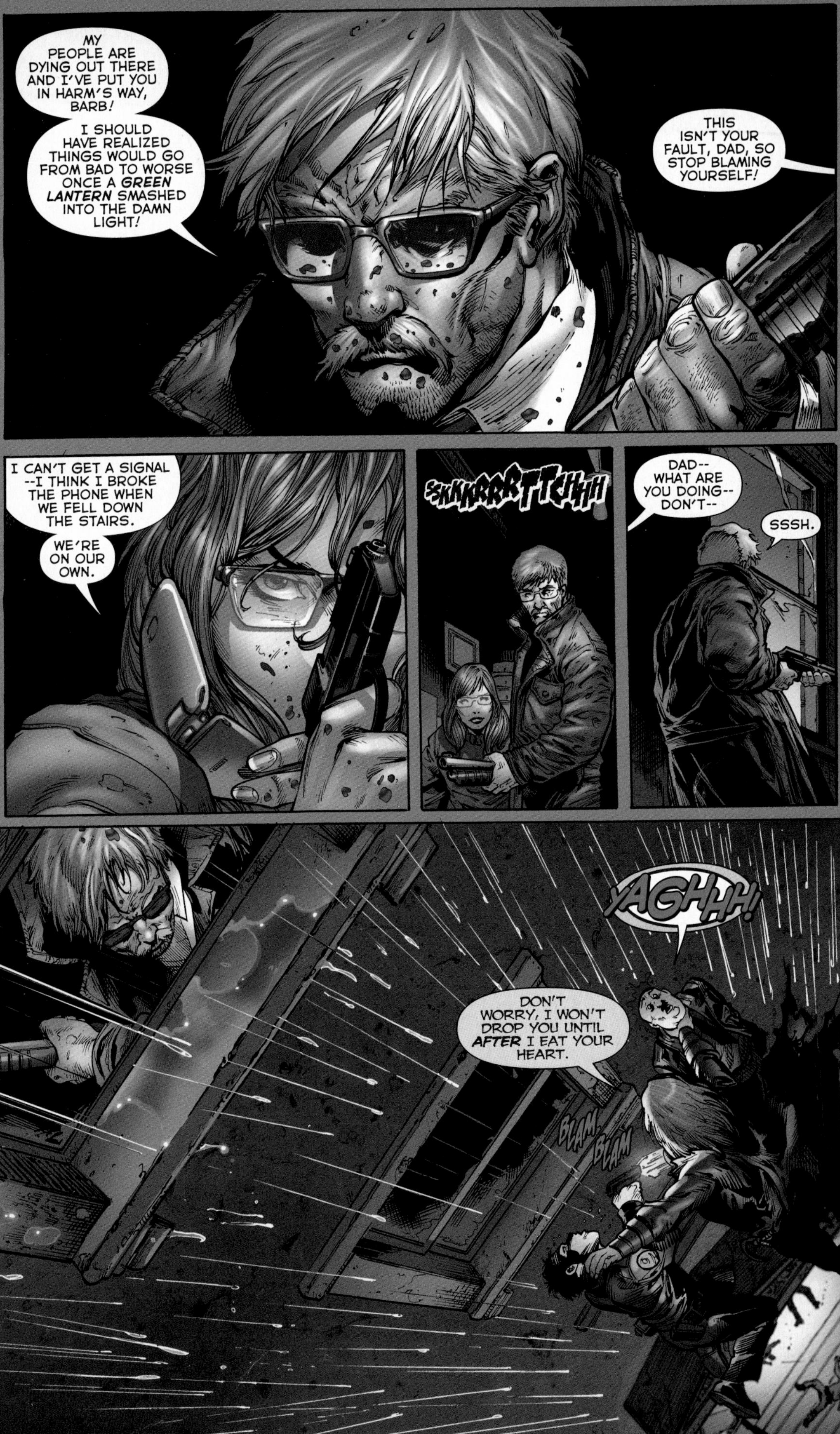

MY PEOPLE ARE DYING OUT THERE AND I'VE PUT YOU IN HARM'S WAY, BARB!
I SHOULD HAVE REALIZED THINGS WOULD GO FROM BAD TO WORSE ONCE A GREEN LANTERN SMASHED INTO THE DAMN LIGHT!
THIS ISN'T YOUR FAULT, DAD, SO STOP BLAMING YOURSELF!
I CAN'T GET A SIGNAL --I THINK I BROKE THE PHONE WHEN WE FELL DOWN THE STAIRS.
WE'RE ON OUR OWN.
SKKKRRRTTCHHH
DAD-- WHAT ARE YOU DOING-- DON'T--
SSSH.
YAGHHH!
DON'T WORRY, I WON'T DROP YOU UNTIL AFTER I EAT YOUR HEART.
BLAM BLAM

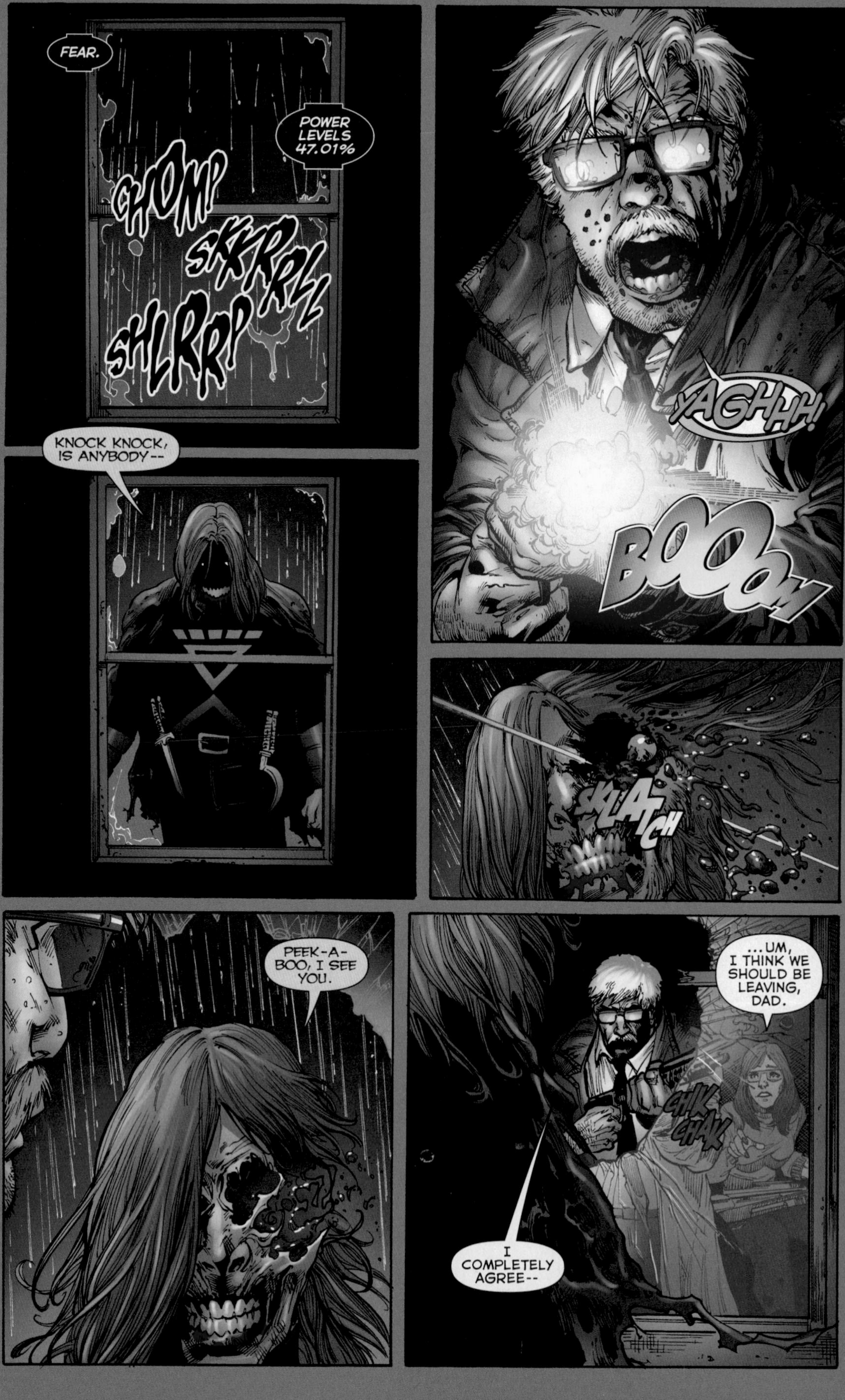
FEAR.
POWER LEVELS 47.01%
CHOMP
SKKRRLL
SHLRRP
YAGHHH!
BOOOOM
KNOCK KNOCK, IS ANYBODY--
SKLAATCH
PEEK-A-BOO, I SEE YOU.
...UM, I THINK WE SHOULD BE LEAVING, DAD.
CHIK CHAK
I COMPLETELY AGREE--

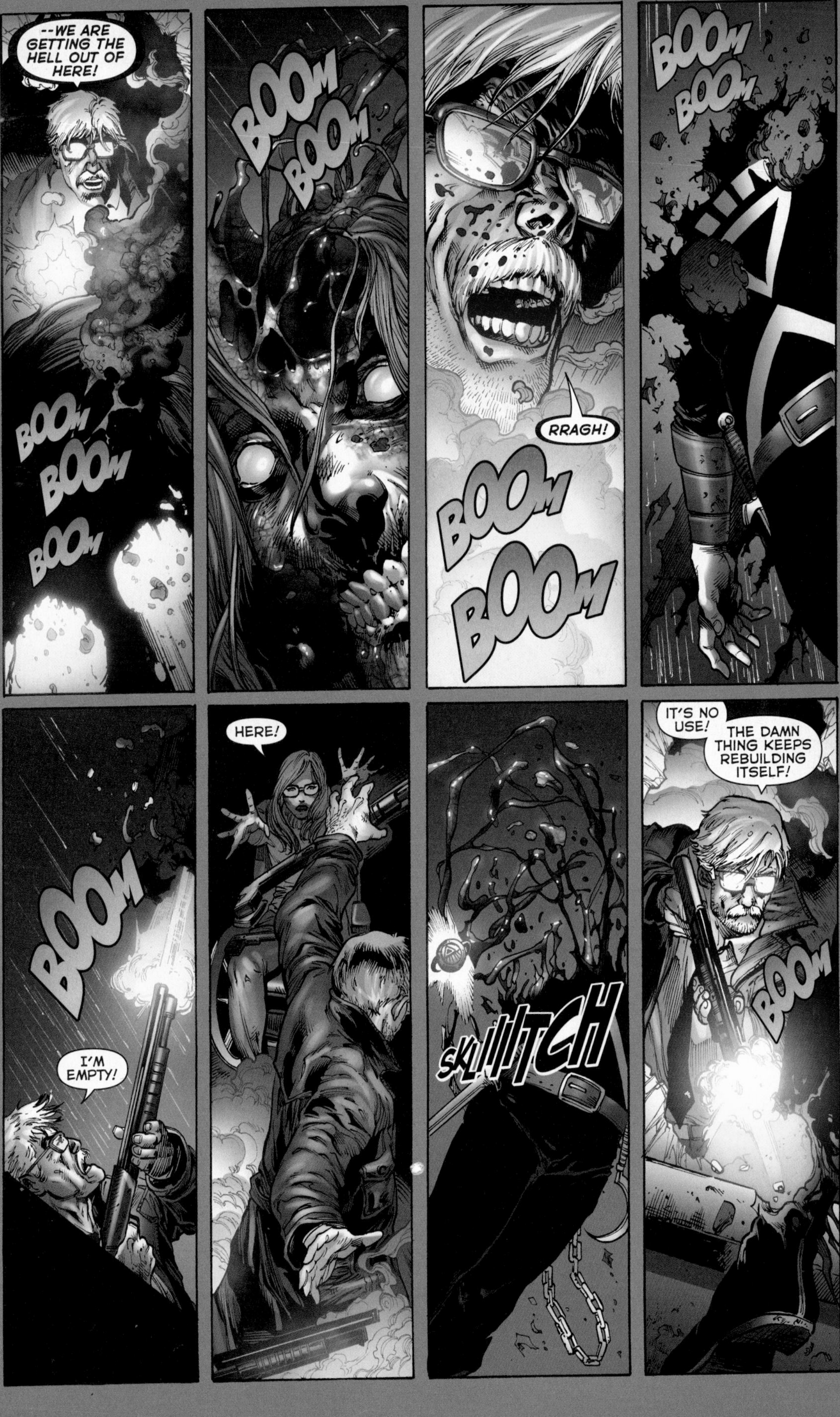
--WE ARE GETTING THE HELL OUT OF HERE!
BOOM BOOM BOOM
BOOM BOOM
RRAGH!
BOOM BOOM
BOOM BOOM
BOOM
I'M EMPTY!
HERE!
SKLIIIITCH
IT'S NO USE!
THE DAMN THING KEEPS REBUILDING ITSELF!
BOOM

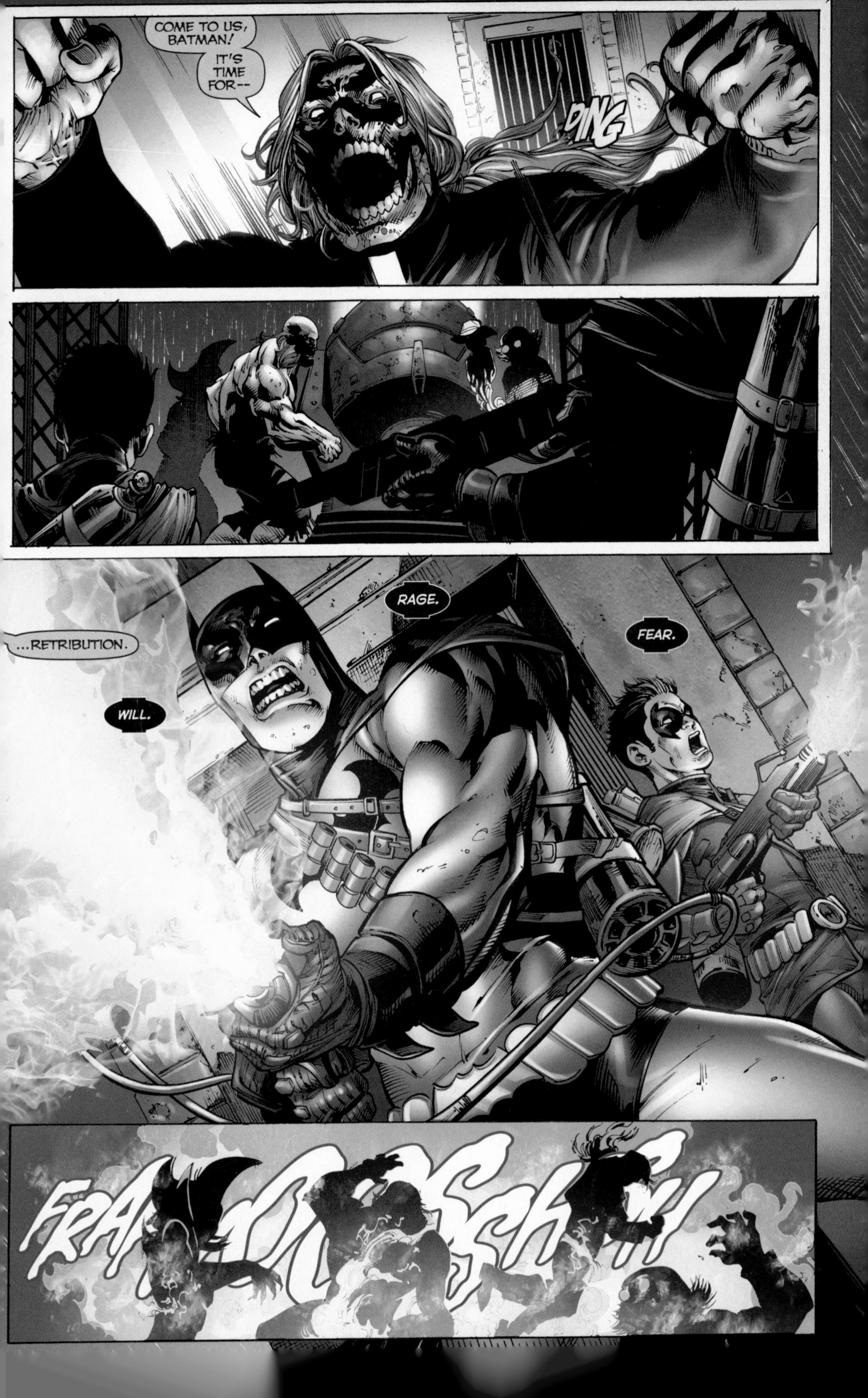

COME TO US, BATMAN!
IT'S TIME FOR--
DING
...RETRIBUTION.
RAGE.
FEAR.
WILL.

SKRA-KROOM

DAD! LOOK--

AH, WE SEEM TO HAVE MISSED A FEW SNAILS.

...BARBARA... NO...

JAMES GORDON. YES. I REMEMBER YOU, WE HAD A FEW ROWS BACK WHEN I TOOK CONTROL OF CHINATOWN FROM THE TRIAD GANGS YOU LET RUN RAMPANT ALL THOSE YEARS AGO.

HEAVY BAGS UNDER YOUR EYES, DEEP WRINKLES, I'D SAY TIME HAS NOT BEEN KIND TO YOU, SIR.

:KAKK: ...LOOK WHO'S CALLING... THE KETTLE BLACK...

LET'S SHOOT 'EM UP AND EAT.

NOT JUST YET, MY TRIGGER-HAPPY FRIEND.

FIRST HE WILL WATCH HIS DAUGHTER DIE.

YOU LOOK SO PROUD OF HER.

BUT NOW YOU'LL NEVER HEAR HER VOICE AGAIN SAY THAT SIMPLE, YET MAGICAL WORD: "DADDY"--WELL, EXCEPT MAYBE YOU'LL HEAR HER SCREAM IT AS WE TEAR OUT HER HEART.

...SON OF A BITCH...

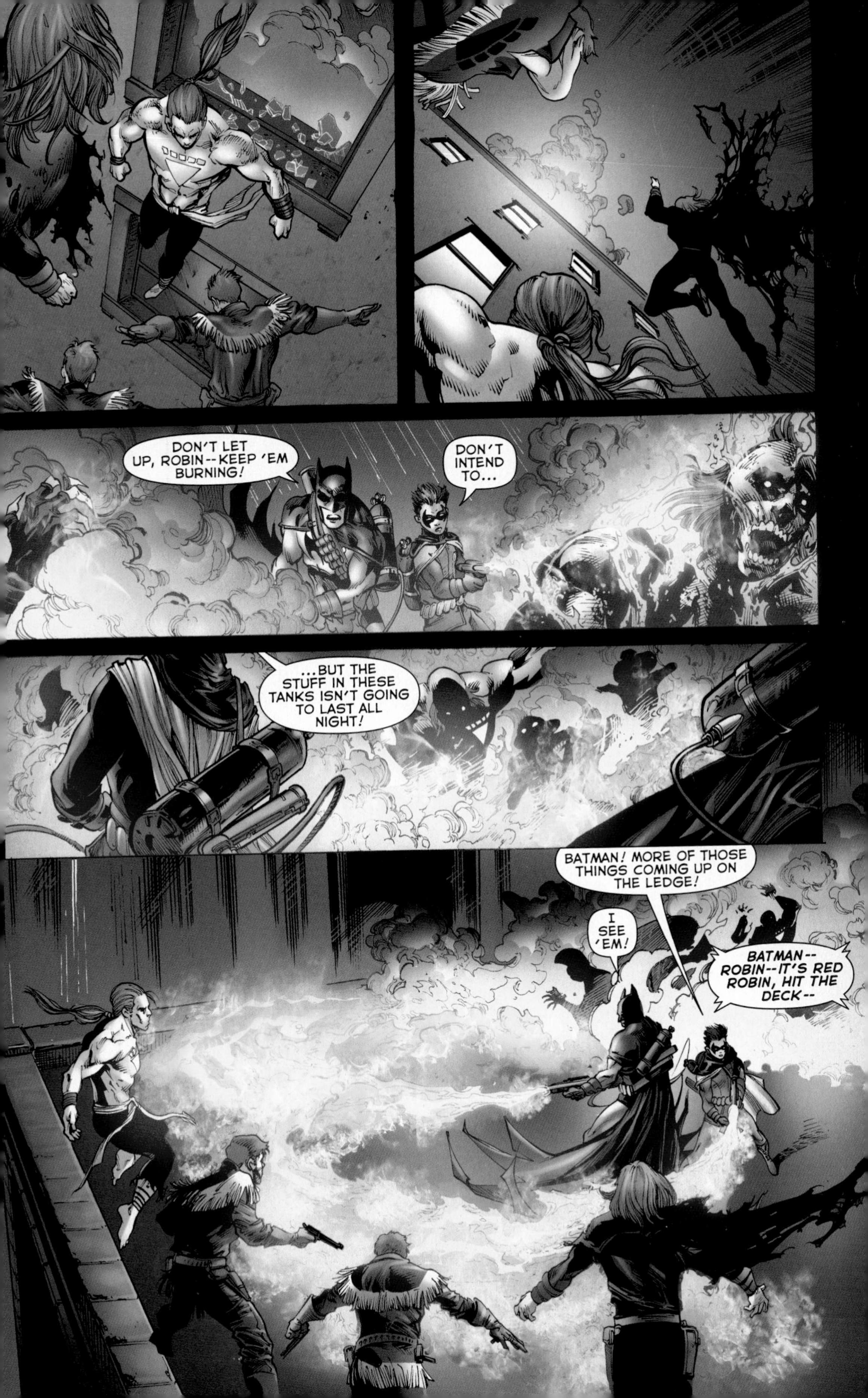
DON'T LET UP, ROBIN--KEEP 'EM BURNING!
DON'T INTEND TO...
...BUT THE STUFF IN THESE TANKS ISN'T GOING TO LAST ALL NIGHT!
BATMAN! MORE OF THOSE THINGS COMING UP ON THE LEDGE!
I SEE 'EM!
BATMAN--ROBIN--IT'S RED ROBIN, HIT THE DECK--

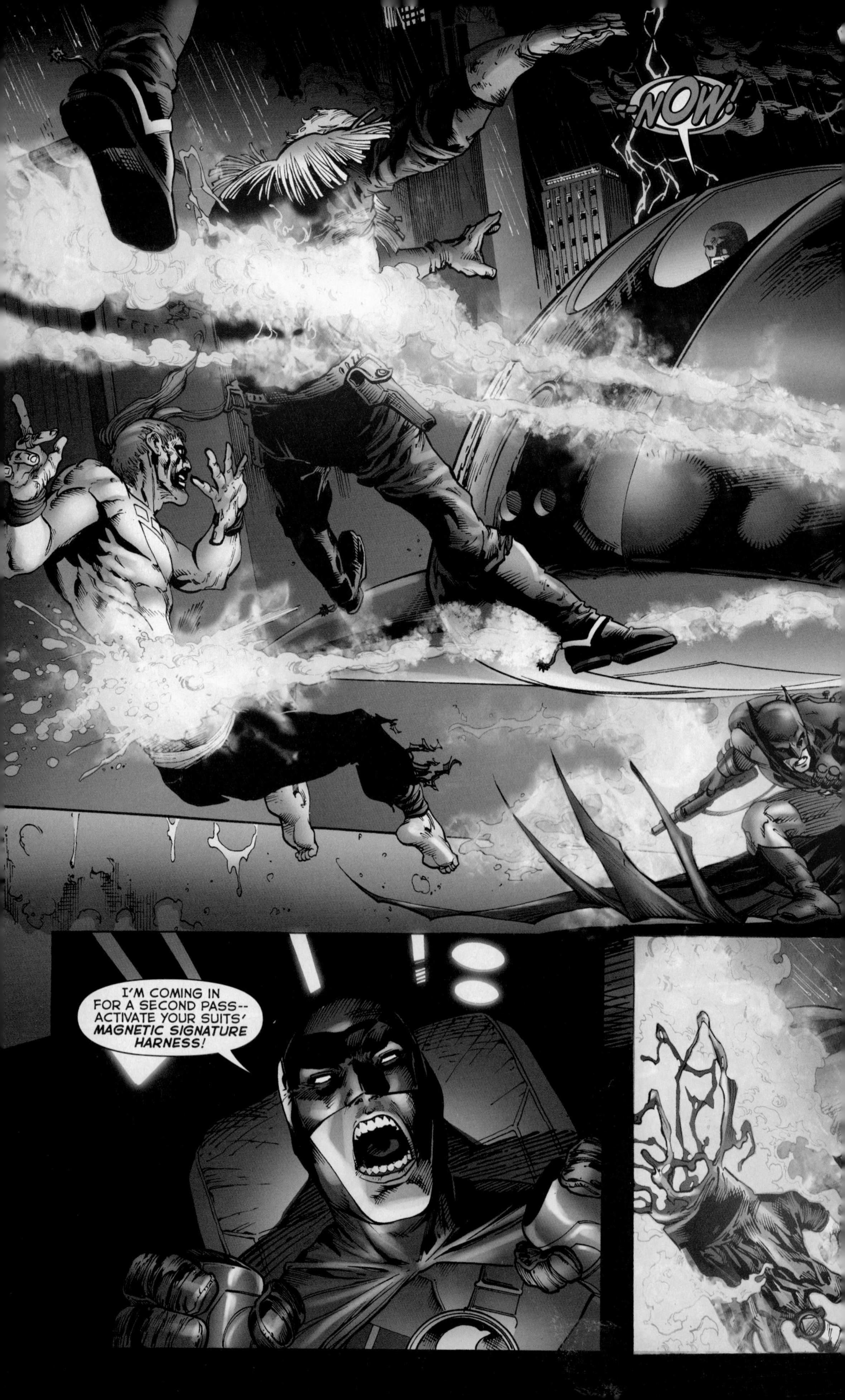
--NOW!
I'M COMING IN FOR A SECOND PASS-- ACTIVATE YOUR SUITS' MAGNETIC SIGNATURE HARNESS!

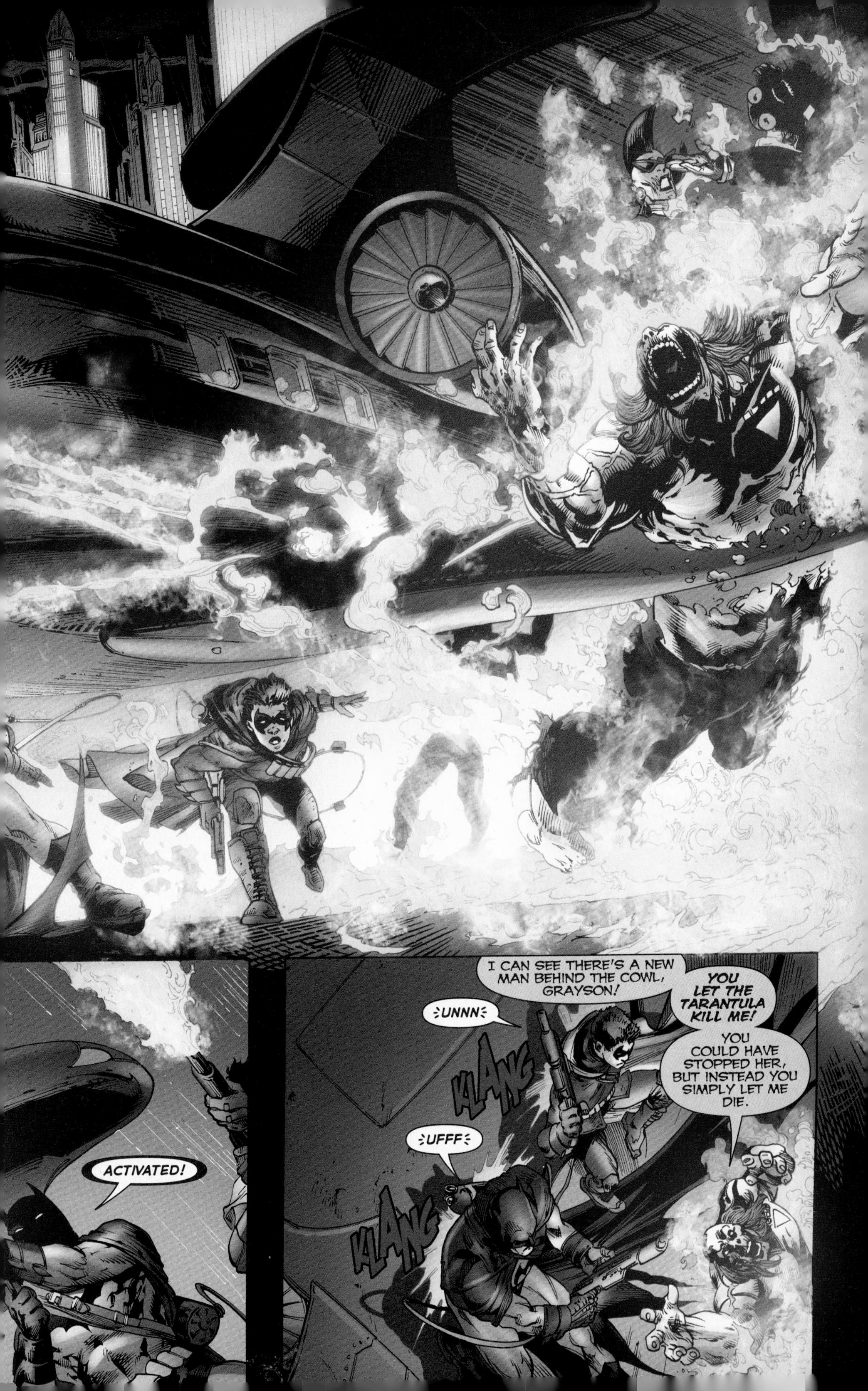
ACTIVATED!
I CAN SEE THERE'S A NEW MAN BEHIND THE COWL, GRAYSON!
UNNN
KLANG
YOU LET THE TARANTULA KILL ME!
YOU COULD HAVE STOPPED HER, BUT INSTEAD YOU SIMPLY LET ME DIE.
UFFF
KLANG

DO YOU THINK THESE PUTRID FLAMES CAN STOP US FOR LONG?!?

HERE'S HOPING!

YAARGGH!!!

I'M SURE YOUR MENTOR WOULD HAVE BEEN DISGUSTED WITH YOUR ACTIONS THAT NIGHT IN BLÜDHAVEN.

I CAN FEEL YOUR AGITATION GROW AS MY WORDS BITE DEEP.

I'M PICKING UP TWO CIVILIANS RIGHT BELOW US!

WHERE? I DON'T SEE...

...THEM.

...BARBARA...

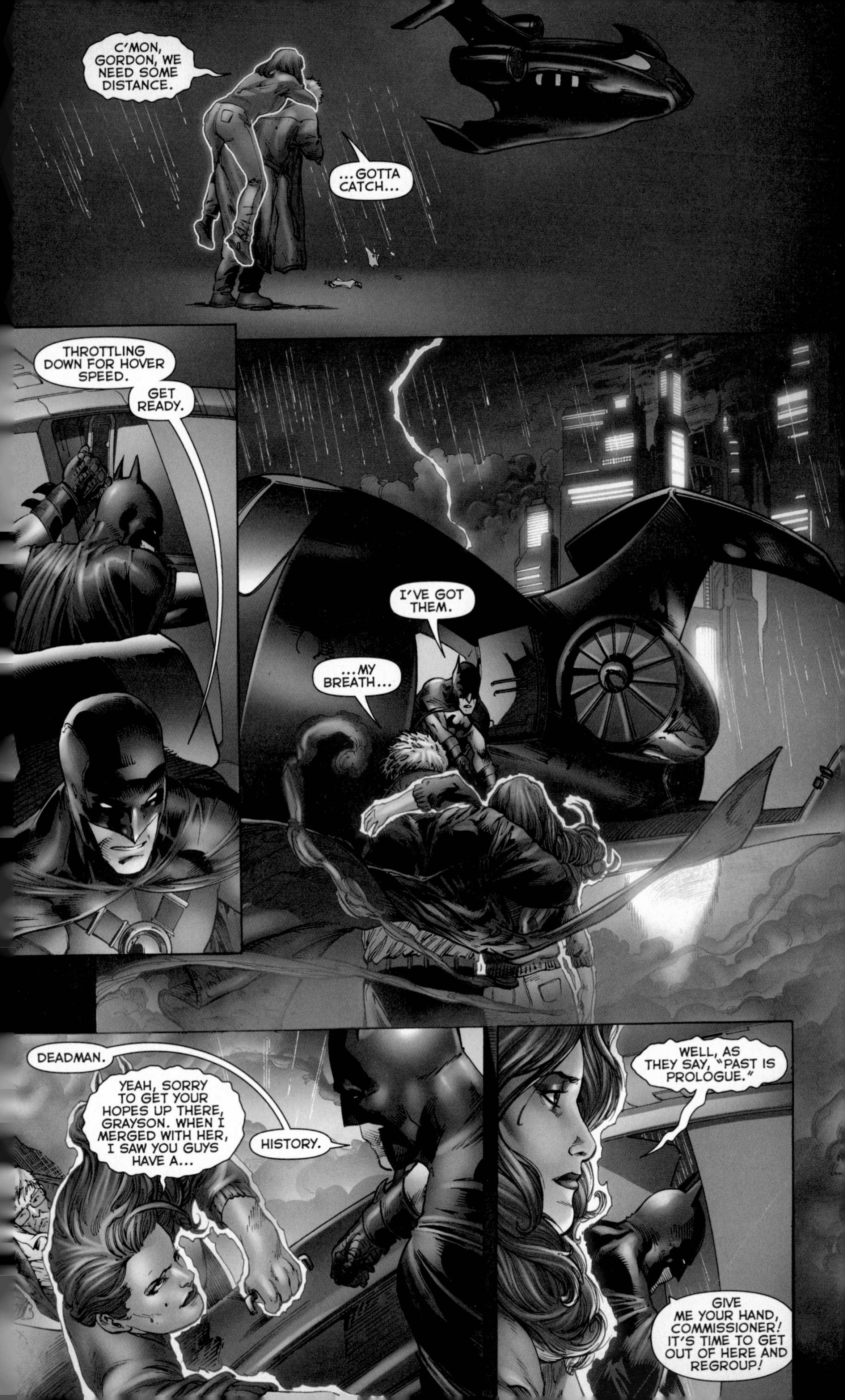
C'MON, GORDON, WE NEED SOME DISTANCE.
...GOTTA CATCH...
THROTTLING DOWN FOR HOVER SPEED.
GET READY.
I'VE GOT THEM.
...MY BREATH...
DEADMAN.
YEAH, SORRY TO GET YOUR HOPES UP THERE, GRAYSON. WHEN I MERGED WITH HER, I SAW YOU GUYS HAVE A...
HISTORY.
WELL, AS THEY SAY, "PAST IS PROLOGUE."
GIVE ME YOUR HAND, COMMISSIONER! IT'S TIME TO GET OUT OF HERE AND REGROUP!

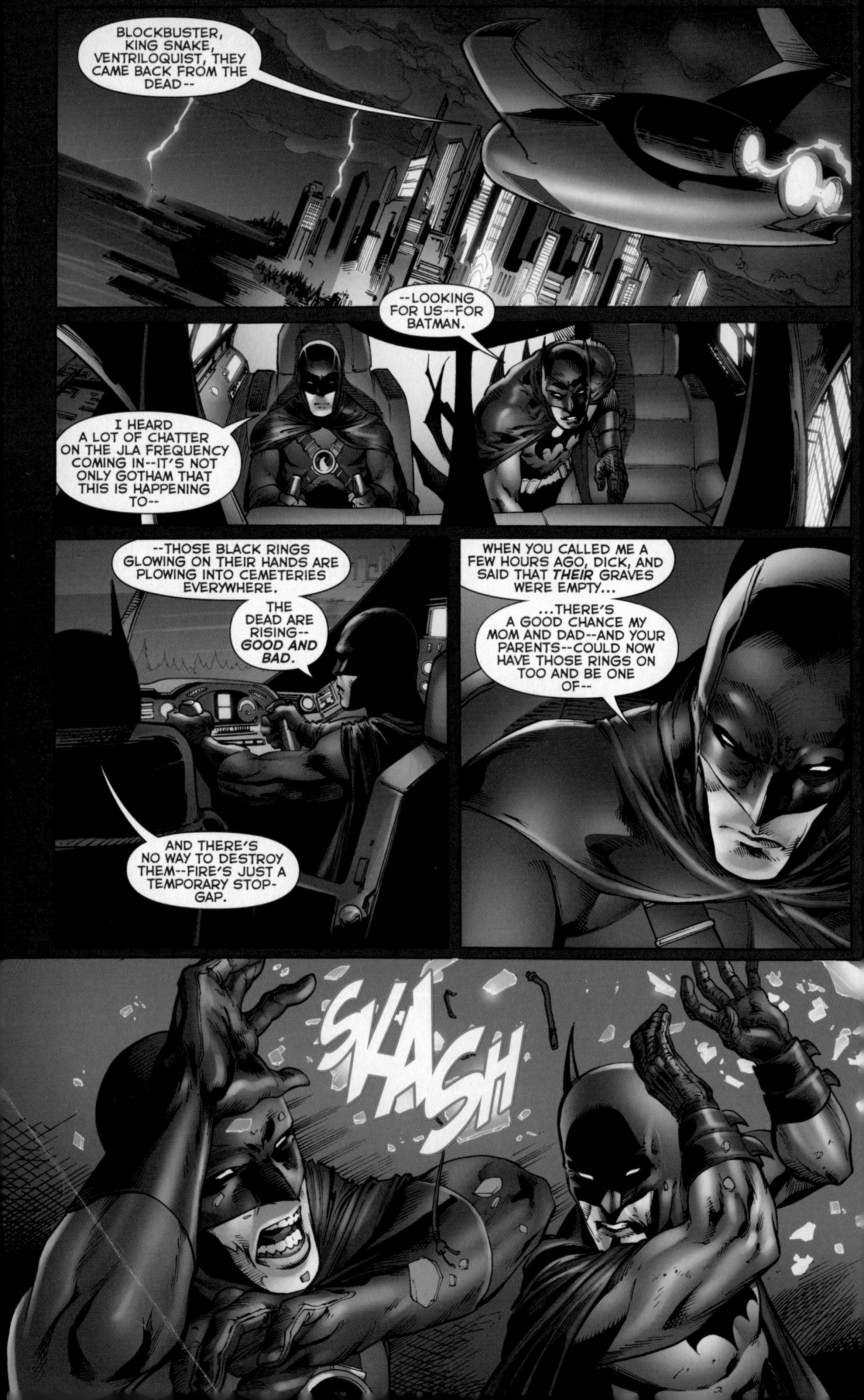

BLOCKBUSTER, KING SNAKE, VENTRILOQUIST, THEY CAME BACK FROM THE DEAD--
--LOOKING FOR US--FOR BATMAN.
I HEARD A LOT OF CHATTER ON THE JLA FREQUENCY COMING IN--IT'S NOT ONLY GOTHAM THAT THIS IS HAPPENING TO--
--THOSE BLACK RINGS GLOWING ON THEIR HANDS ARE PLOWING INTO CEMETERIES EVERYWHERE.
THE DEAD ARE RISING--*GOOD AND BAD*.
AND THERE'S NO WAY TO DESTROY THEM--FIRE'S JUST A TEMPORARY STOP-GAP.
WHEN YOU CALLED ME A FEW HOURS AGO, DICK, AND SAID THAT *THEIR* GRAVES WERE EMPTY...
...THERE'S A GOOD CHANCE MY MOM AND DAD--AND YOUR PARENTS--COULD NOW HAVE THOSE RINGS ON TOO AND BE ONE OF--
SKASH

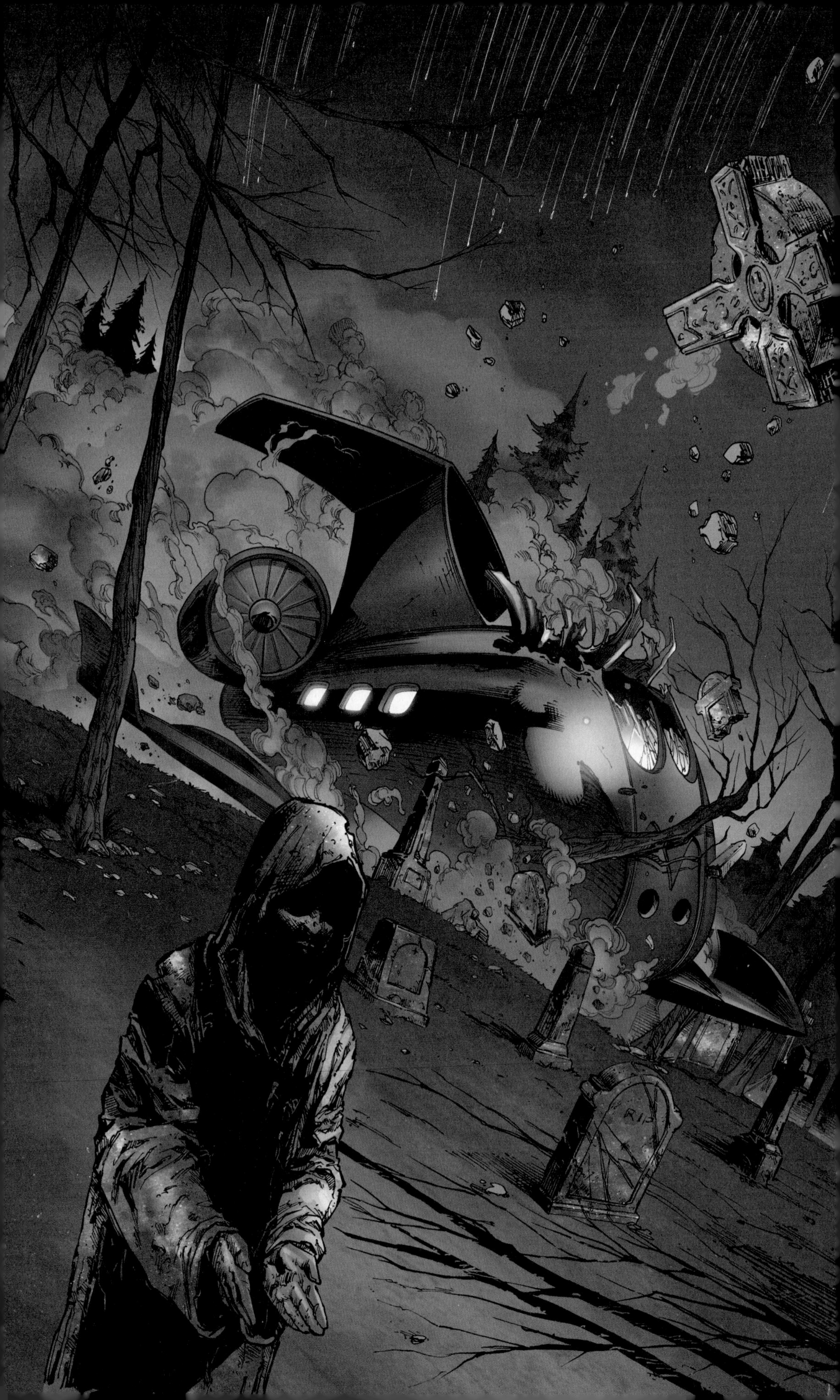
RIP

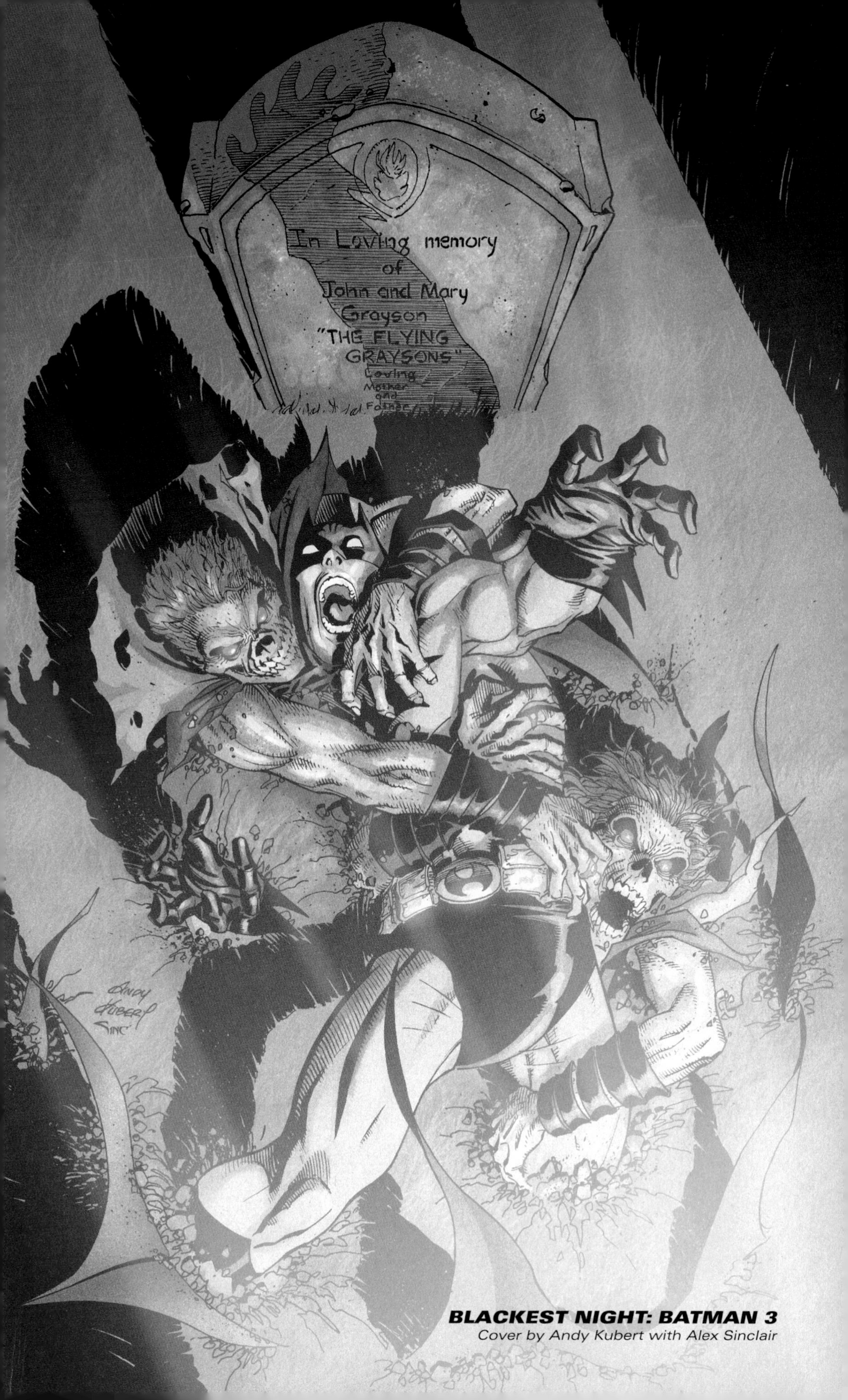
In Loving memory
of
John and Mary
Grayson
"THE FLYING
GRAYSONS"
Loving
Mother
and
Father
ANDY
KUBERT
SINC

BLACKEST NIGHT: BATMAN 3
Cover by Andy Kubert with Alex Sinclair

WHO BURNS WHO
CONCLUSION

PETER J. TOMASI
WRITER

ARDIAN SYAF
PENCILS

VICENTE CIFUENTES
INKS

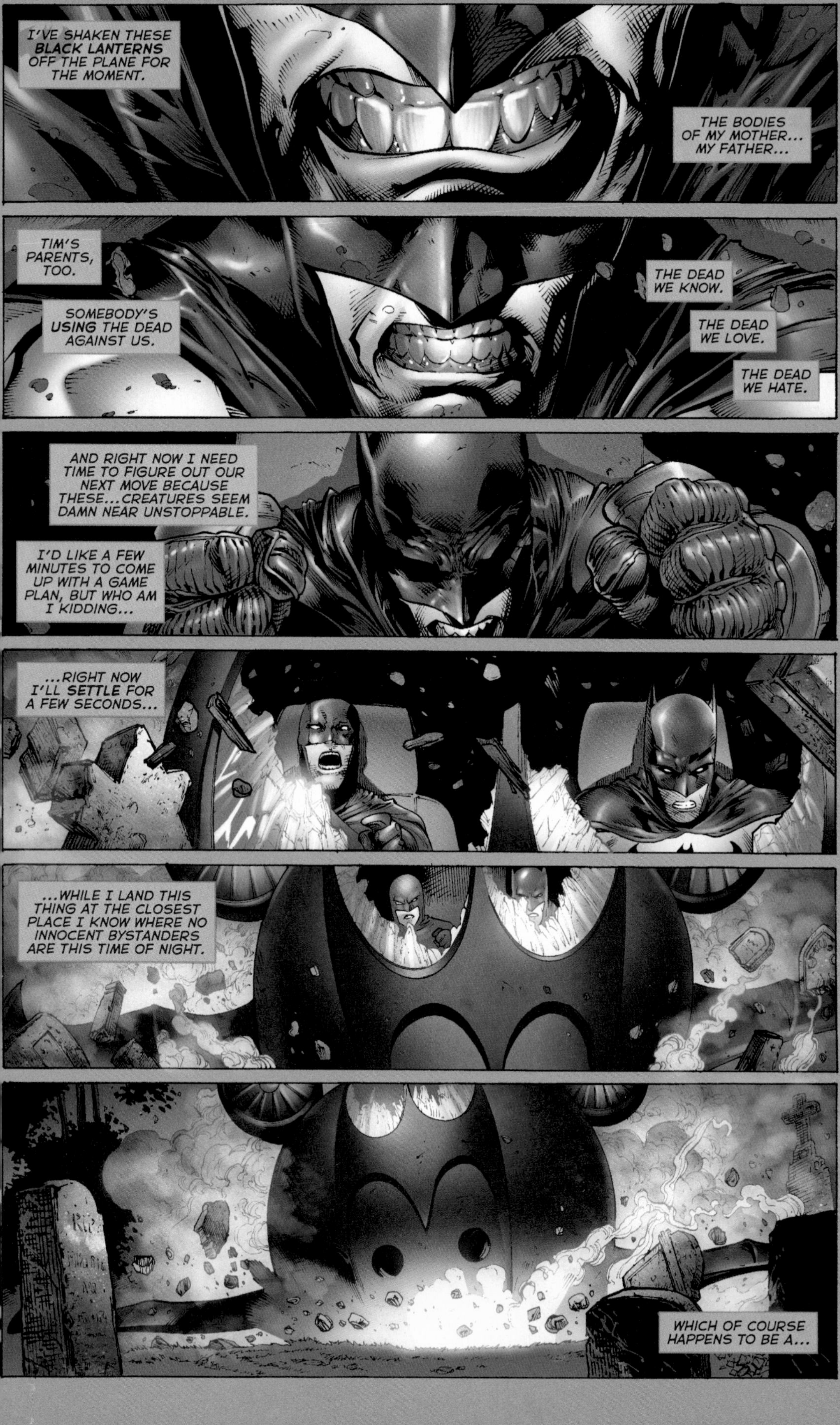
I'VE SHAKEN THESE BLACK LANTERNS OFF THE PLANE FOR THE MOMENT.
THE BODIES OF MY MOTHER... MY FATHER...
TIM'S PARENTS, TOO.
SOMEBODY'S USING THE DEAD AGAINST US.
THE DEAD WE KNOW.
THE DEAD WE LOVE.
THE DEAD WE HATE.
AND RIGHT NOW I NEED TIME TO FIGURE OUT OUR NEXT MOVE BECAUSE THESE...CREATURES SEEM DAMN NEAR UNSTOPPABLE.
I'D LIKE A FEW MINUTES TO COME UP WITH A GAME PLAN, BUT WHO AM I KIDDING...
...RIGHT NOW I'LL SETTLE FOR A FEW SECONDS...
...WHILE I LAND THIS THING AT THE CLOSEST PLACE I KNOW WHERE NO INNOCENT BYSTANDERS ARE THIS TIME OF NIGHT.
WHICH OF COURSE HAPPENS TO BE A...

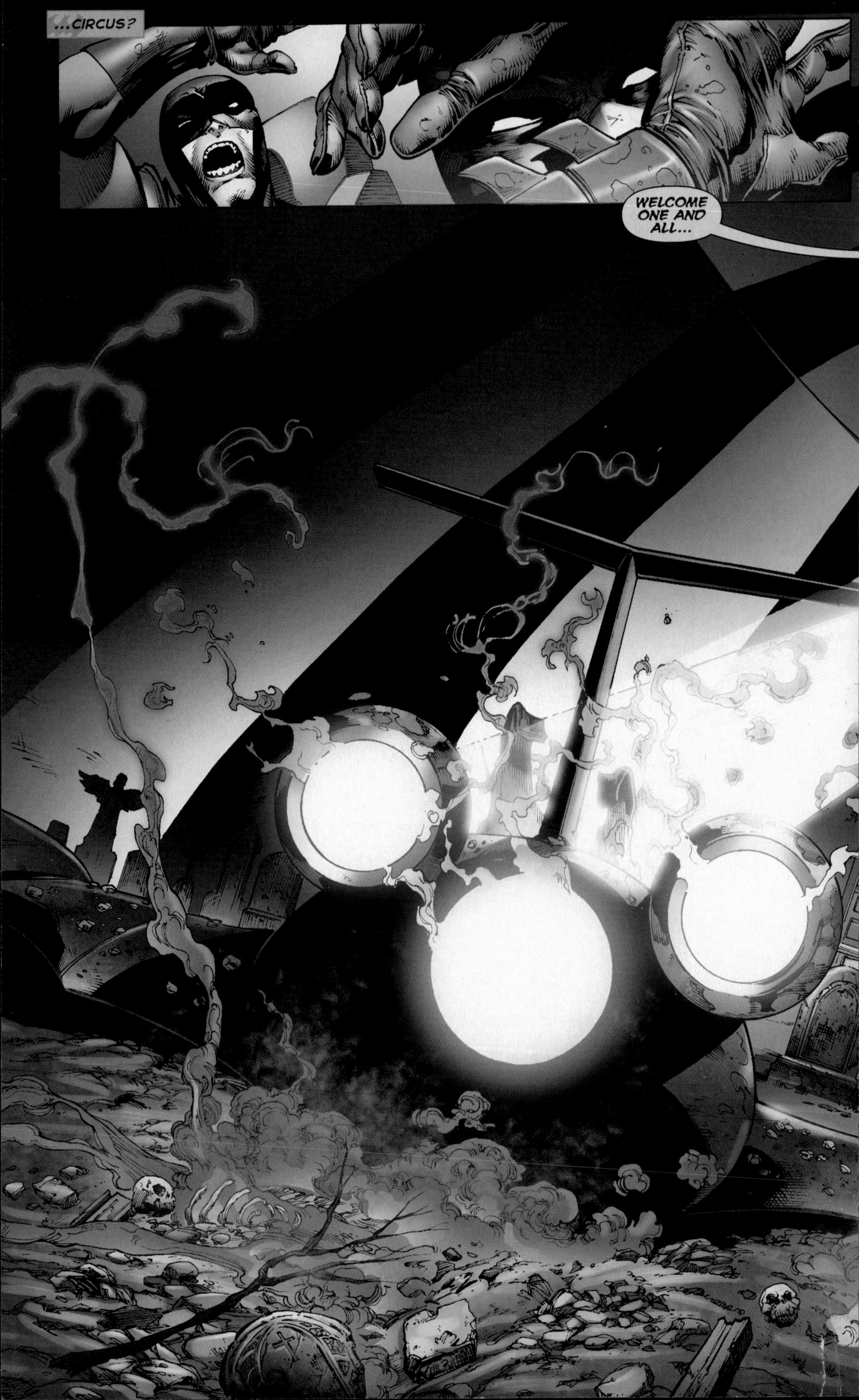
...CIRCUS?
WELCOME ONE AND ALL...

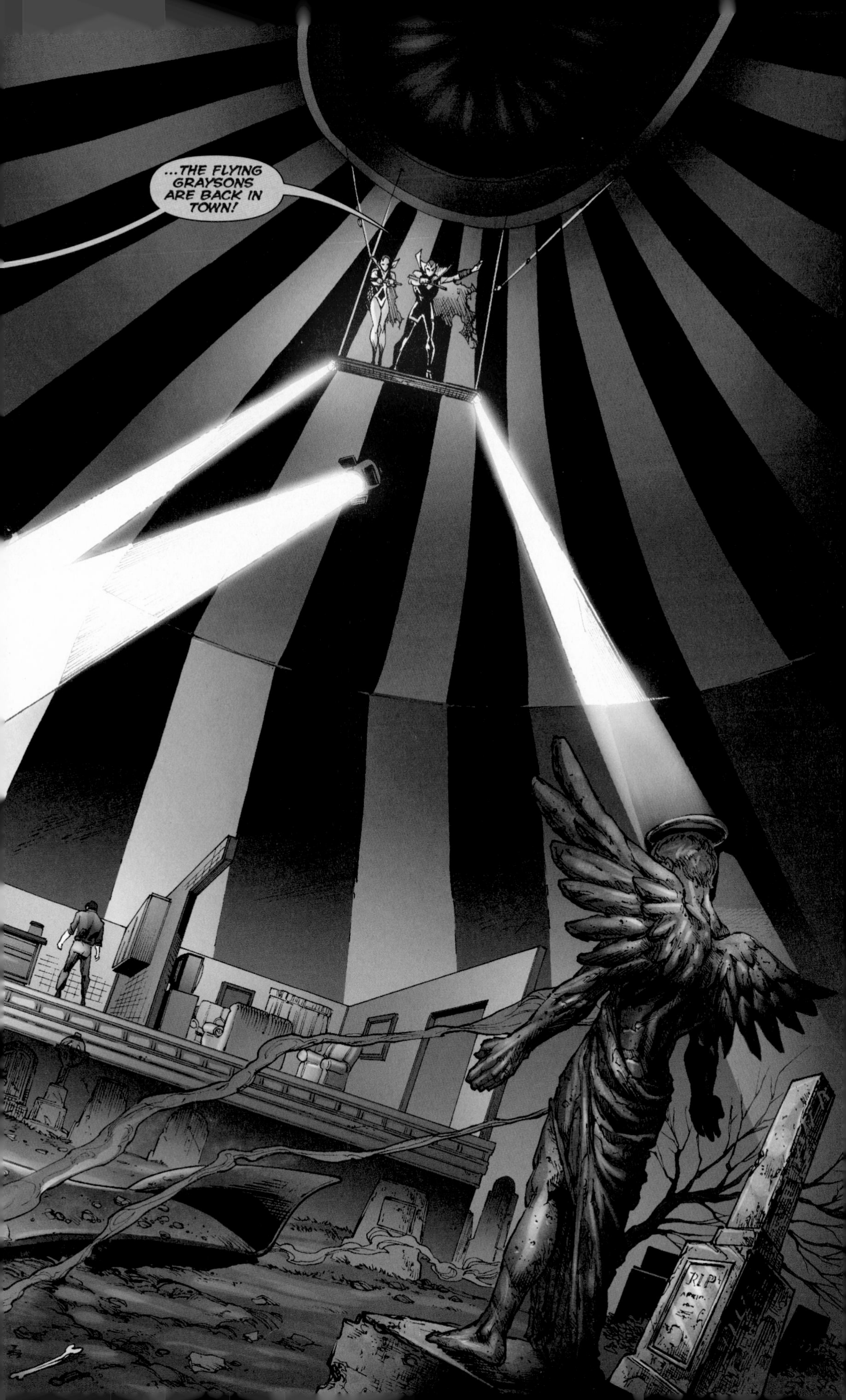
...THE FLYING GRAYSONS ARE BACK IN TOWN!

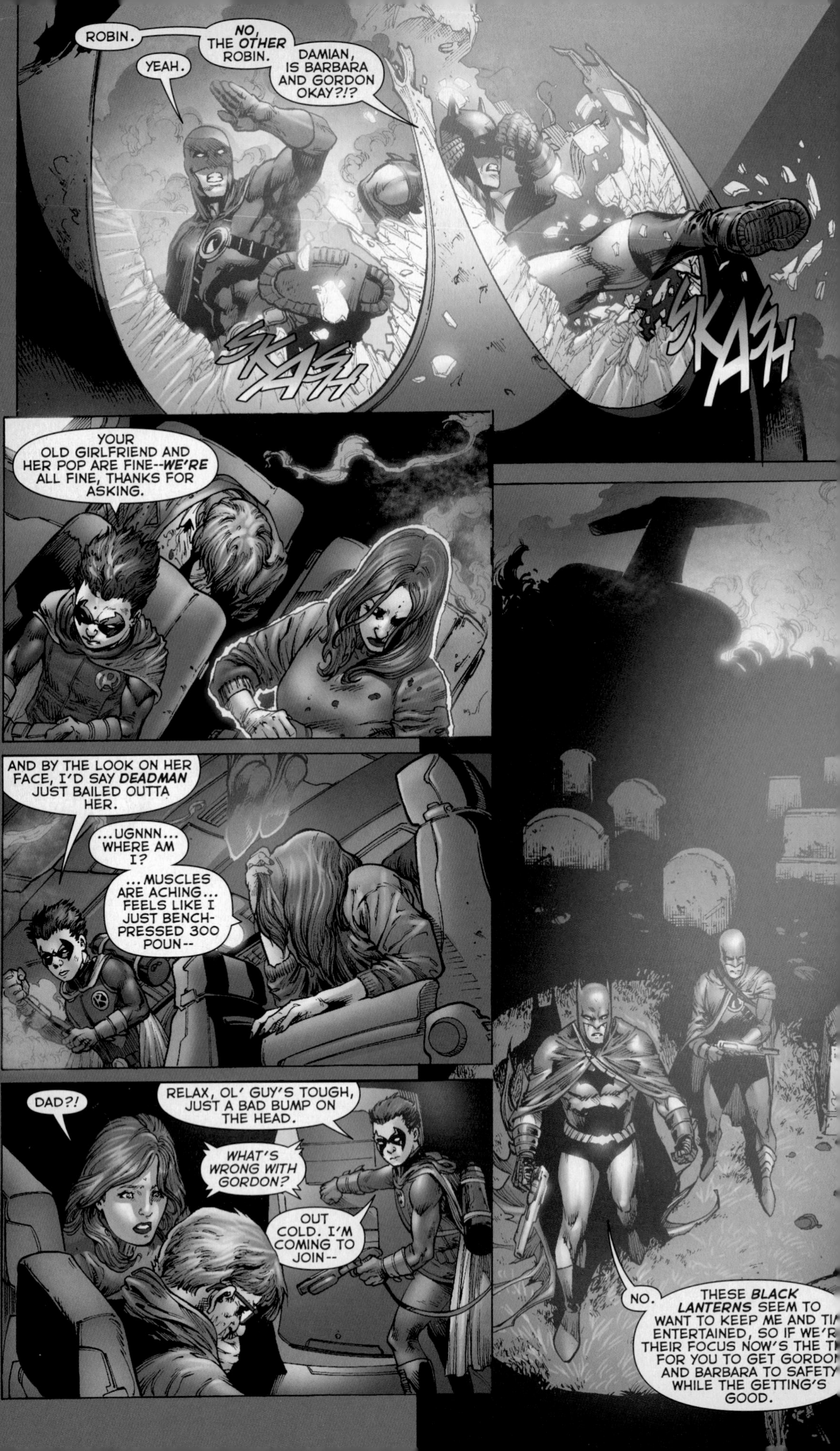
ROBIN.
NO, THE OTHER ROBIN.
YEAH.
DAMIAN, IS BARBARA AND GORDON OKAY?!?
SKASH
SKASH
YOUR OLD GIRLFRIEND AND HER POP ARE FINE--WE'RE ALL FINE, THANKS FOR ASKING.
AND BY THE LOOK ON HER FACE, I'D SAY DEADMAN JUST BAILED OUTTA HER.
...UGNNN... WHERE AM I?
...MUSCLES ARE ACHING... FEELS LIKE I JUST BENCH-PRESSED 300 POUN--
DAD?!
RELAX, OL' GUY'S TOUGH, JUST A BAD BUMP ON THE HEAD.
WHAT'S WRONG WITH GORDON?
OUT COLD. I'M COMING TO JOIN--
NO.
THESE BLACK LANTERNS SEEM TO WANT TO KEEP ME AND TI
ENTERTAINED, SO IF WE'R
THEIR FOCUS NOW'S THE T
FOR YOU TO GET GORDO
AND BARBARA TO SAFETY
WHILE THE GETTING'S GOOD.

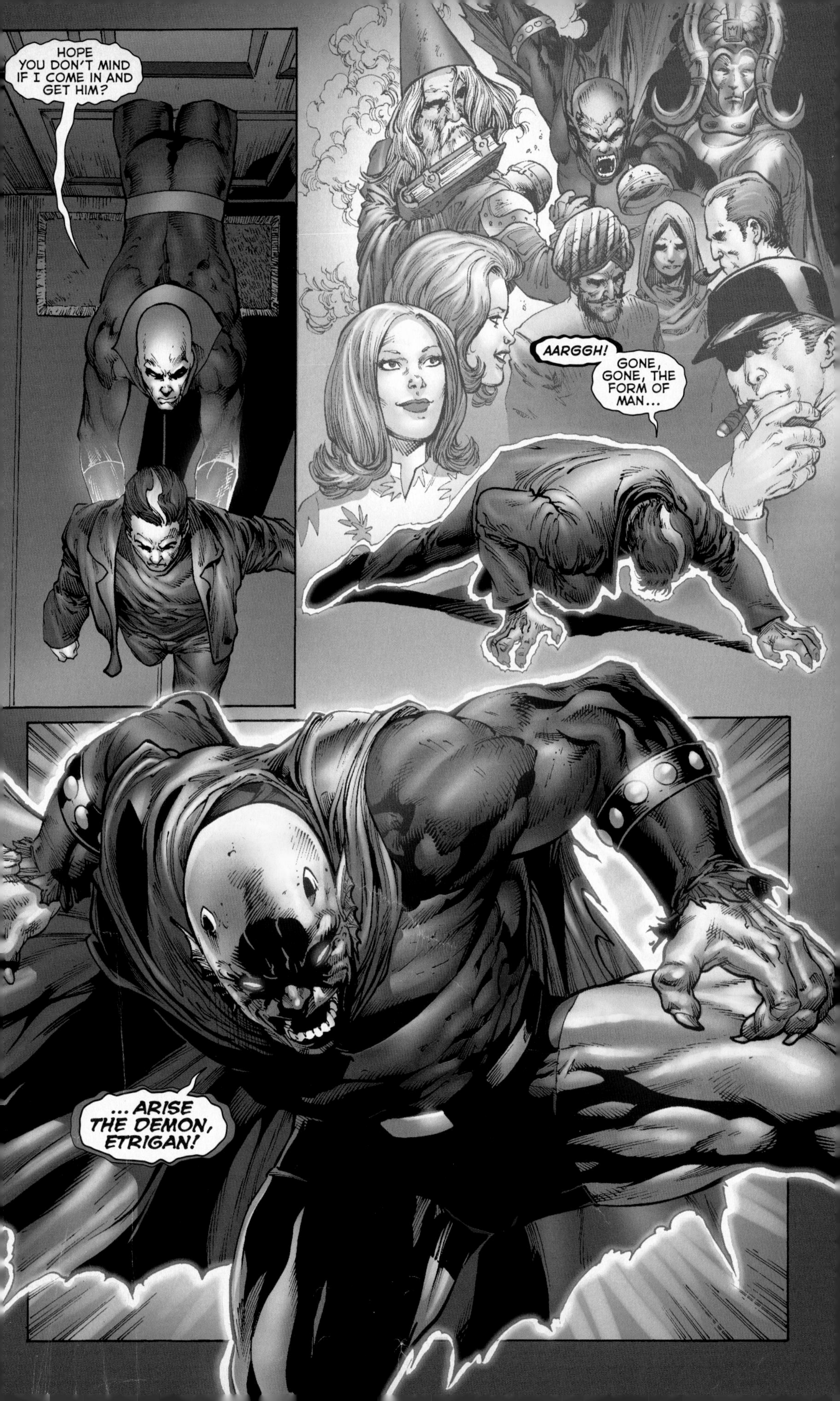
HOPE YOU DON'T MIND IF I COME IN AND GET HIM?
AARGGH!
GONE, GONE, THE FORM OF MAN...
...ARISE THE DEMON, ETRIGAN!

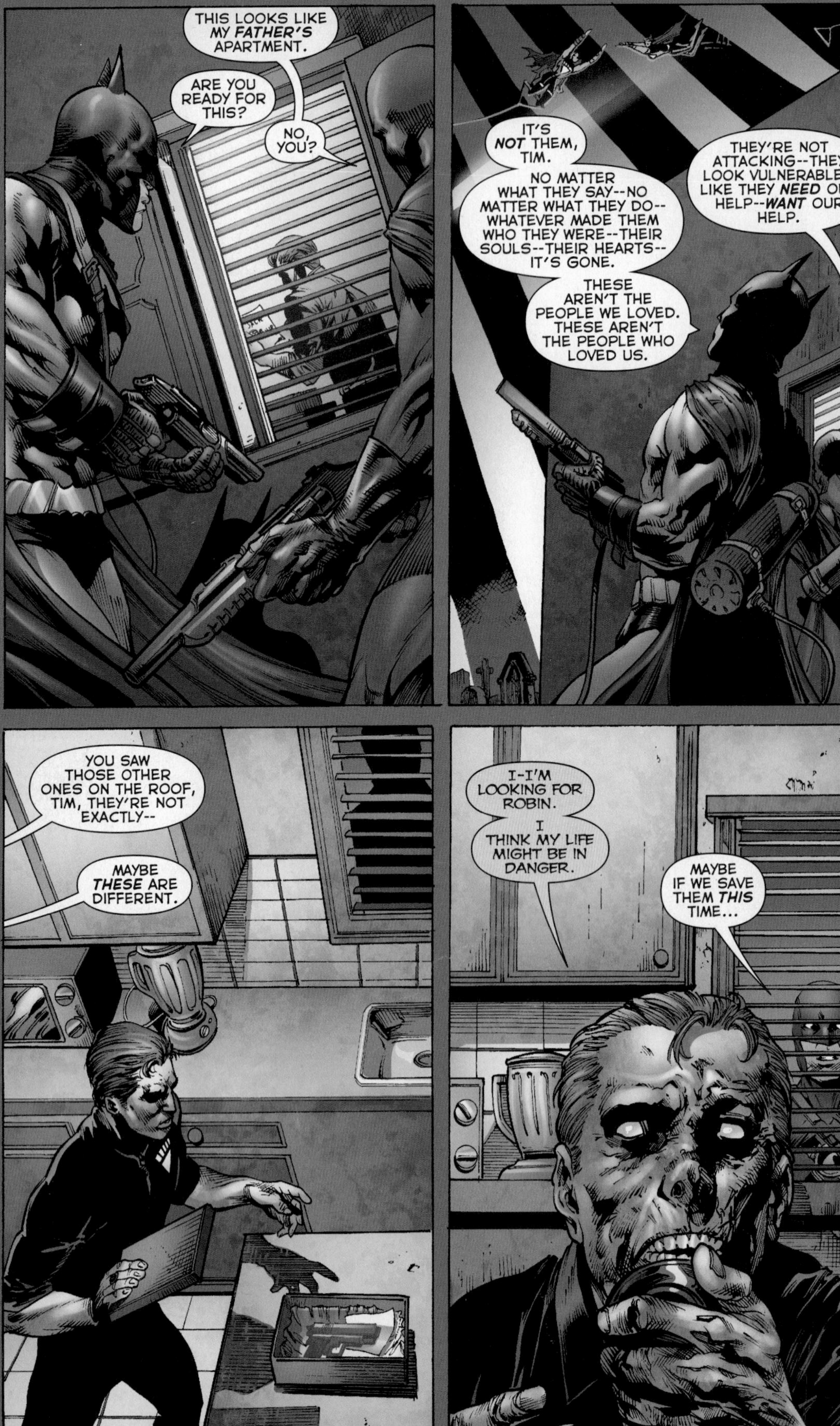
THIS LOOKS LIKE MY *FATHER'S* APARTMENT.
ARE YOU READY FOR THIS?
NO, YOU?
IT'S *NOT* THEM, TIM.
NO MATTER WHAT THEY SAY--NO MATTER WHAT THEY DO--WHATEVER MADE THEM WHO THEY WERE--THEIR SOULS--THEIR HEARTS--IT'S GONE.
THESE AREN'T THE PEOPLE WE LOVED. THESE AREN'T THE PEOPLE WHO LOVED US.
THEY'RE NOT ATTACKING--THEY LOOK VULNERABLE--LIKE THEY *NEED* OUR HELP--*WANT* OUR HELP.
YOU SAW THOSE OTHER ONES ON THE ROOF, TIM, THEY'RE NOT EXACTLY--
MAYBE *THESE* ARE DIFFERENT.
I-I'M LOOKING FOR ROBIN.
I THINK MY LIFE MIGHT BE IN DANGER.
MAYBE IF WE SAVE THEM *THIS* TIME...

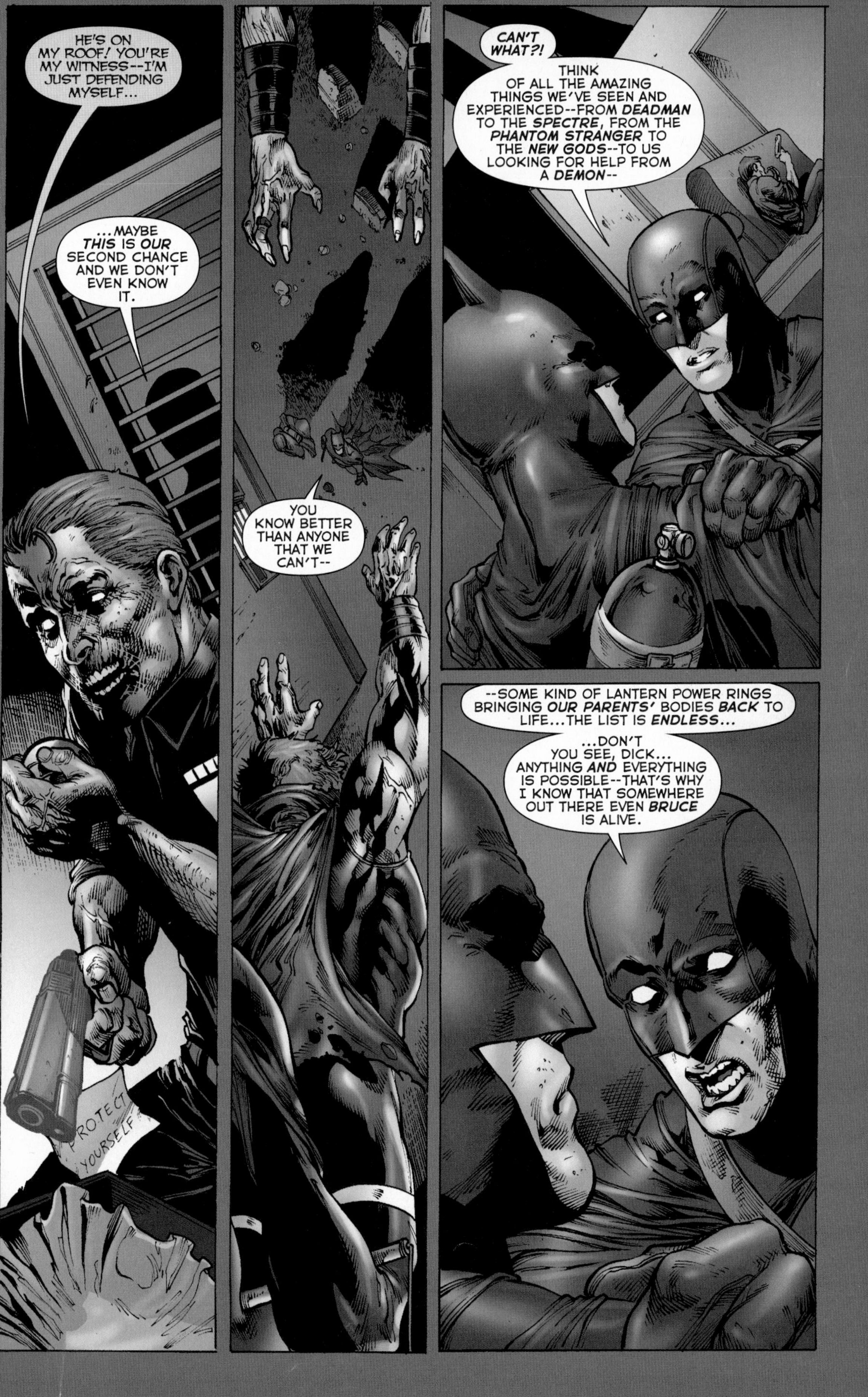
HE'S ON MY ROOF! YOU'RE MY WITNESS--I'M JUST DEFENDING MYSELF...
...MAYBE THIS IS OUR SECOND CHANCE AND WE DON'T EVEN KNOW IT.
PROTECT YOURSELF
YOU KNOW BETTER THAN ANYONE THAT WE CAN'T--
CAN'T WHAT?!
THINK OF ALL THE AMAZING THINGS WE'VE SEEN AND EXPERIENCED--FROM DEADMAN TO THE SPECTRE, FROM THE PHANTOM STRANGER TO THE NEW GODS--TO US LOOKING FOR HELP FROM A DEMON--
--SOME KIND OF LANTERN POWER RINGS BRINGING OUR PARENTS' BODIES BACK TO LIFE...THE LIST IS ENDLESS...
...DON'T YOU SEE, DICK... ANYTHING AND EVERYTHING IS POSSIBLE--THAT'S WHY I KNOW THAT SOMEWHERE OUT THERE EVEN BRUCE IS ALIVE.

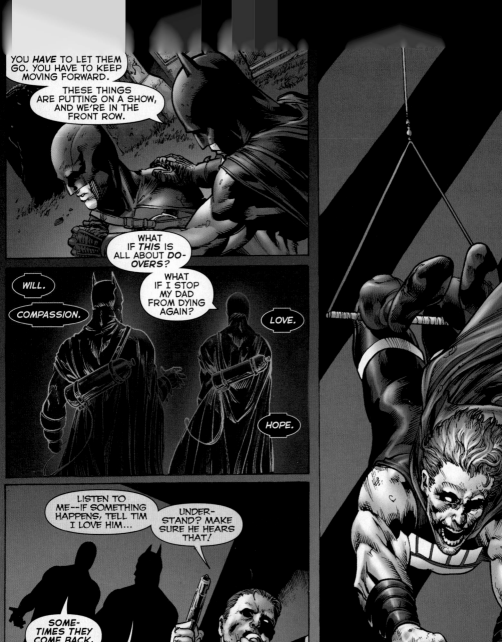

YOU *HAVE* TO LET THEM GO. YOU HAVE TO KEEP MOVING FORWARD.

THESE THINGS ARE PUTTING ON A SHOW, AND WE'RE IN THE FRONT ROW.

WHAT IF *THIS* IS ALL ABOUT *DO-OVERS?*

WHAT IF I STOP MY DAD FROM DYING AGAIN?

WILL.

COMPASSION.

LOVE.

HOPE.

LISTEN TO ME--IF SOMETHING HAPPENS, TELL TIM I LOVE HIM...

UNDER-STAND? MAKE SURE HE HEARS THAT!

SOME-TIMES THEY COME BACK, DICK.

AND *MOST* OF THE TIME THEY DON'T, TIM.

HEADS UP, RICHARD!

IT'S TIME TO FLY!

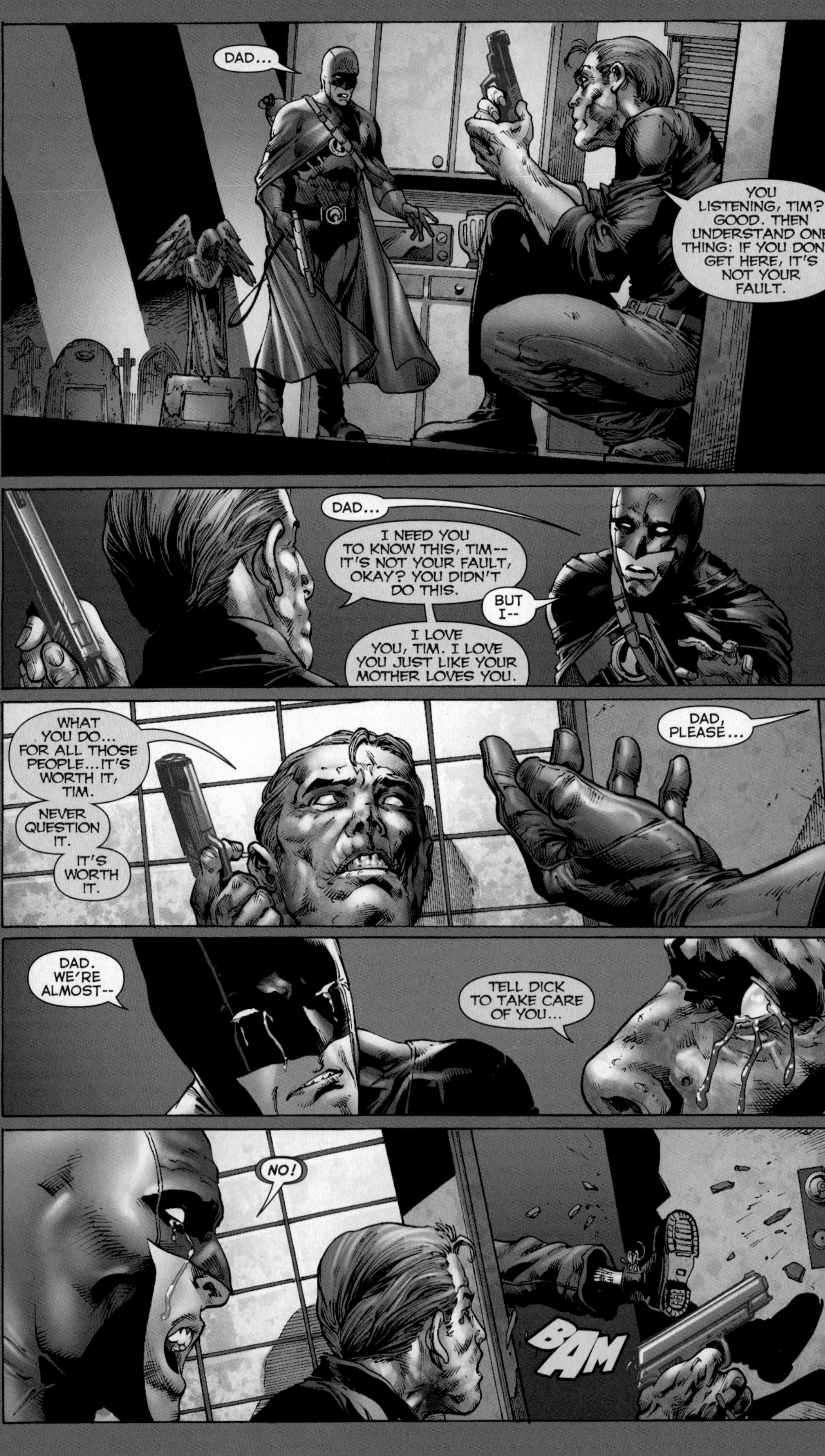
DAD...
YOU LISTENING, TIM? GOOD. THEN UNDERSTAND ONE THING: IF YOU DON'T GET HERE, IT'S NOT YOUR FAULT.
DAD...
I NEED YOU TO KNOW THIS, TIM-- IT'S NOT YOUR FAULT, OKAY? YOU DIDN'T DO THIS.
BUT I--
I LOVE YOU, TIM. I LOVE YOU JUST LIKE YOUR MOTHER LOVES YOU.
WHAT YOU DO... FOR ALL THOSE PEOPLE...IT'S WORTH IT, TIM.
NEVER QUESTION IT.
IT'S WORTH IT.
DAD, PLEASE...
DAD. WE'RE ALMOST--
TELL DICK TO TAKE CARE OF YOU...
NO!
BAM

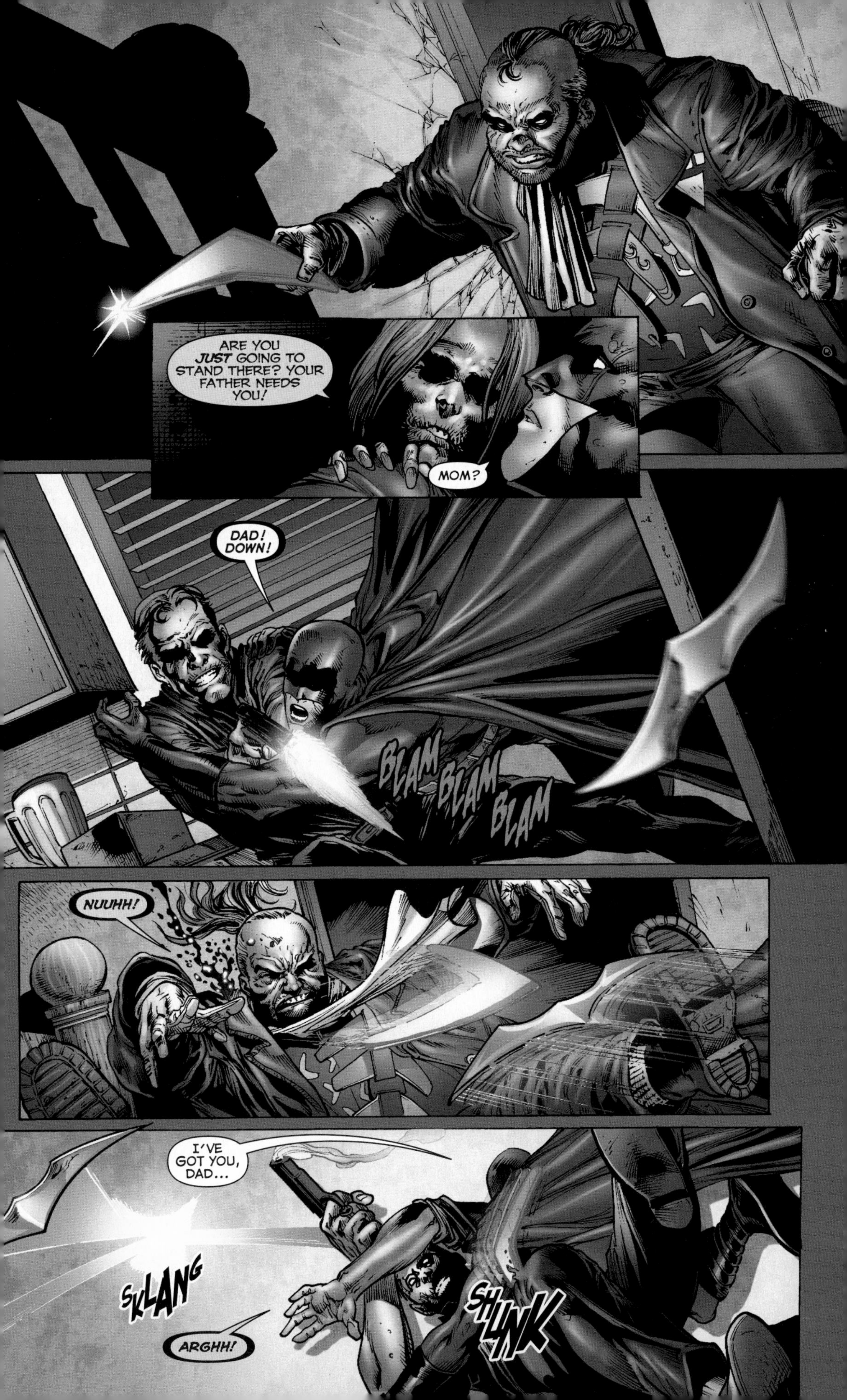
ARE YOU JUST GOING TO STAND THERE? YOUR FATHER NEEDS YOU!
MOM?
DAD! DOWN!
BLAM BLAM BLAM
NUUHH!
I'VE GOT YOU, DAD...
SKLANG
ARGHH!
SHUNK

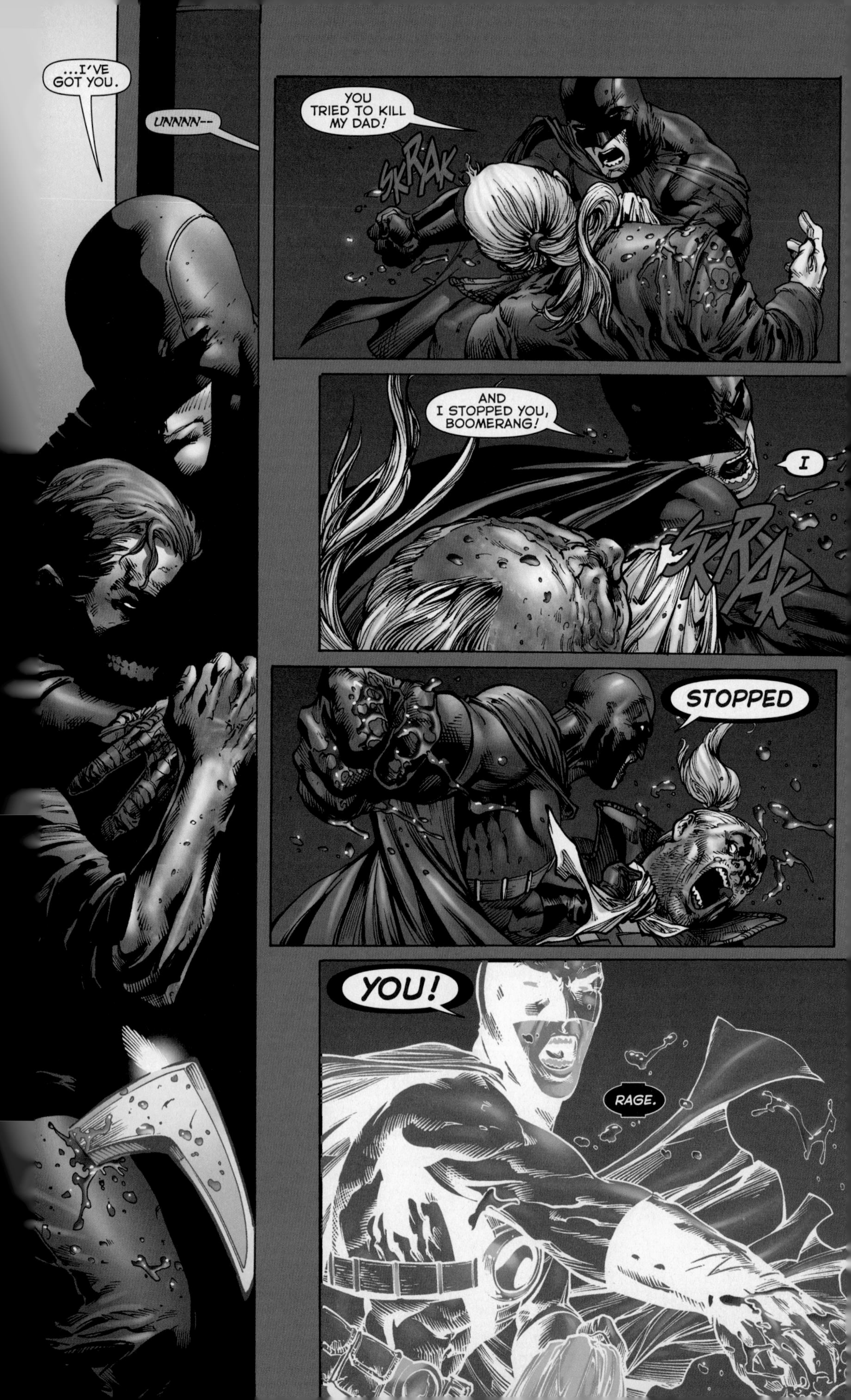
...I'VE GOT YOU.
UNNNN--
YOU TRIED TO KILL MY DAD!
SKRAK
AND I STOPPED YOU, BOOMERANG!
I
SKRAK
STOPPED
YOU!
RAGE.

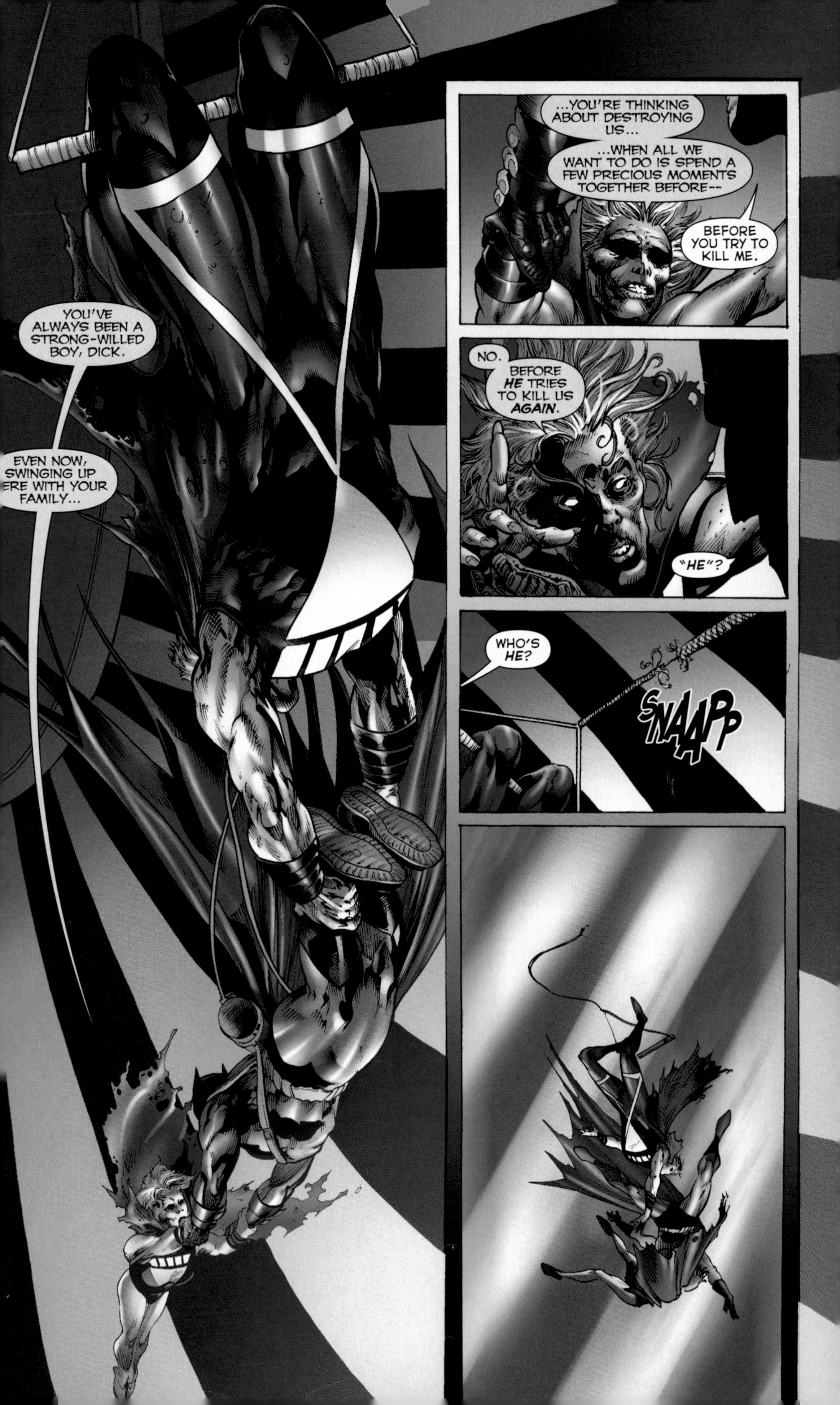
YOU'VE ALWAYS BEEN A STRONG-WILLED BOY, DICK.
EVEN NOW, SWINGING UP ERE WITH YOUR FAMILY...
...YOU'RE THINKING ABOUT DESTROYING US...
...WHEN ALL WE WANT TO DO IS SPEND A FEW PRECIOUS MOMENTS TOGETHER BEFORE--
BEFORE YOU TRY TO KILL ME.
NO.
BEFORE HE TRIES TO KILL US AGAIN.
"HE"?
WHO'S HE?
SNAAPP

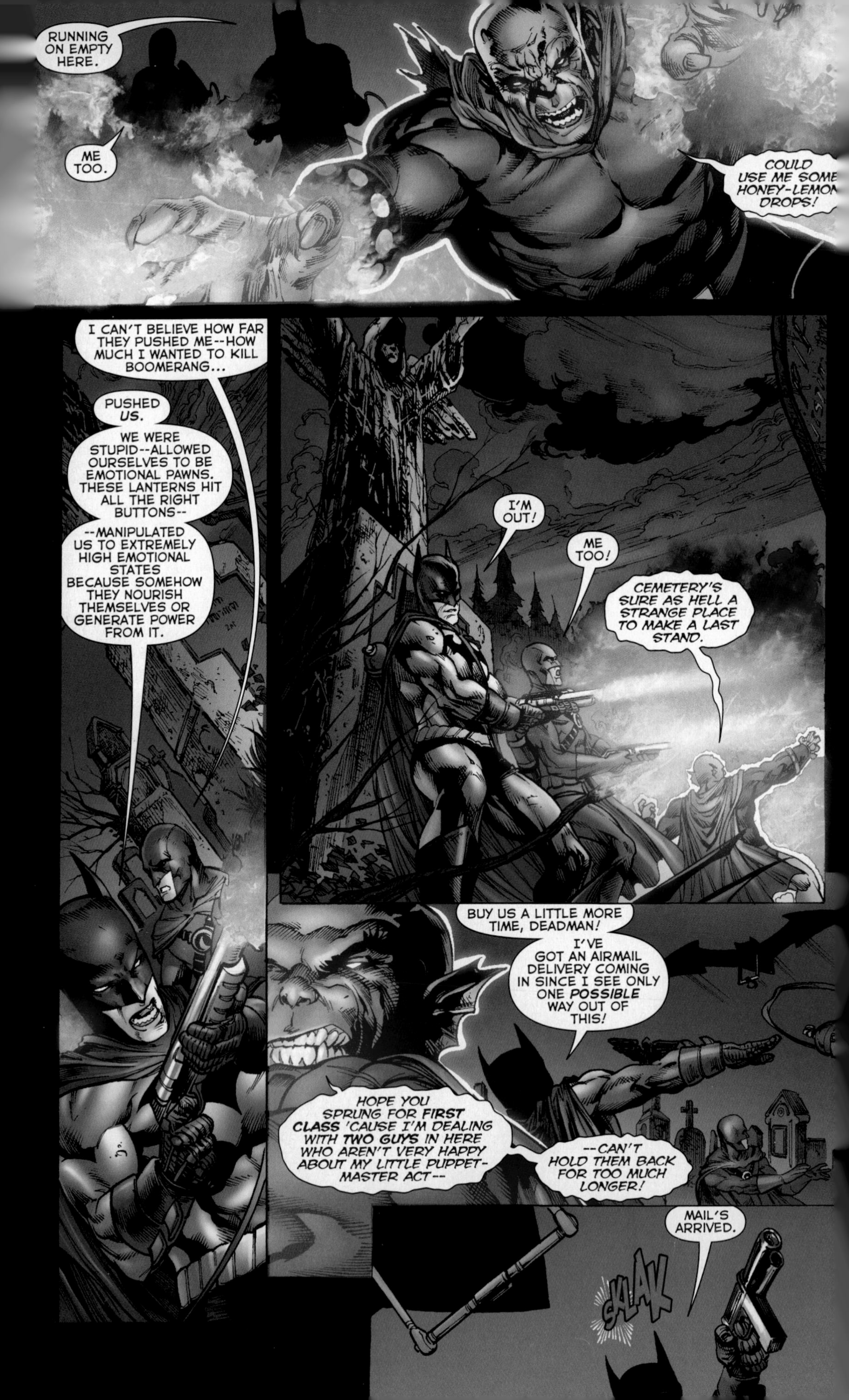
RUNNING ON EMPTY HERE.
ME TOO.
COULD USE ME SOME HONEY-LEMON DROPS!
I CAN'T BELIEVE HOW FAR THEY PUSHED ME--HOW MUCH I WANTED TO KILL BOOMERANG...
PUSHED US.
WE WERE STUPID--ALLOWED OURSELVES TO BE EMOTIONAL PAWNS. THESE LANTERNS HIT ALL THE RIGHT BUTTONS--
--MANIPULATED US TO EXTREMELY HIGH EMOTIONAL STATES BECAUSE SOMEHOW THEY NOURISH THEMSELVES OR GENERATE POWER FROM IT.
I'M OUT!
ME TOO!
CEMETERY'S SURE AS HELL A STRANGE PLACE TO MAKE A LAST STAND.
BUY US A LITTLE MORE TIME, DEADMAN!
I'VE GOT AN AIRMAIL DELIVERY COMING IN SINCE I SEE ONLY ONE POSSIBLE WAY OUT OF THIS!
HOPE YOU SPRUNG FOR FIRST CLASS 'CAUSE I'M DEALING WITH TWO GUYS IN HERE WHO AREN'T VERY HAPPY ABOUT MY LITTLE PUPPET-MASTER ACT--
--CAN'T HOLD THEM BACK FOR TOO MUCH LONGER!
MAIL'S ARRIVED.
SKLAK

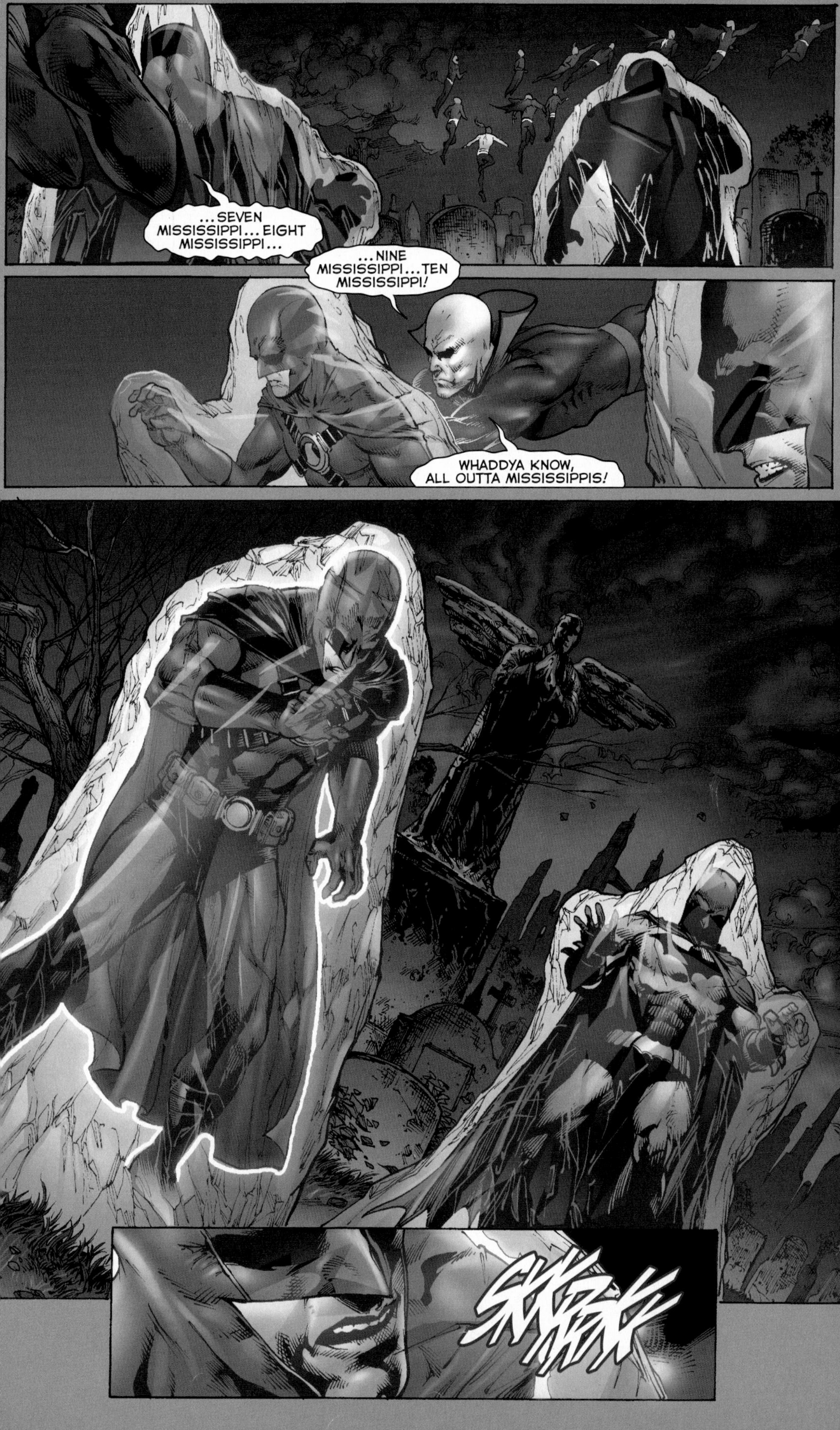

...SEVEN MISSISSIPPI... EIGHT MISSISSIPPI...
...NINE MISSISSIPPI...TEN MISSISSIPPI!
WHADDYA KNOW, ALL OUTTA MISSISSIPPIS!

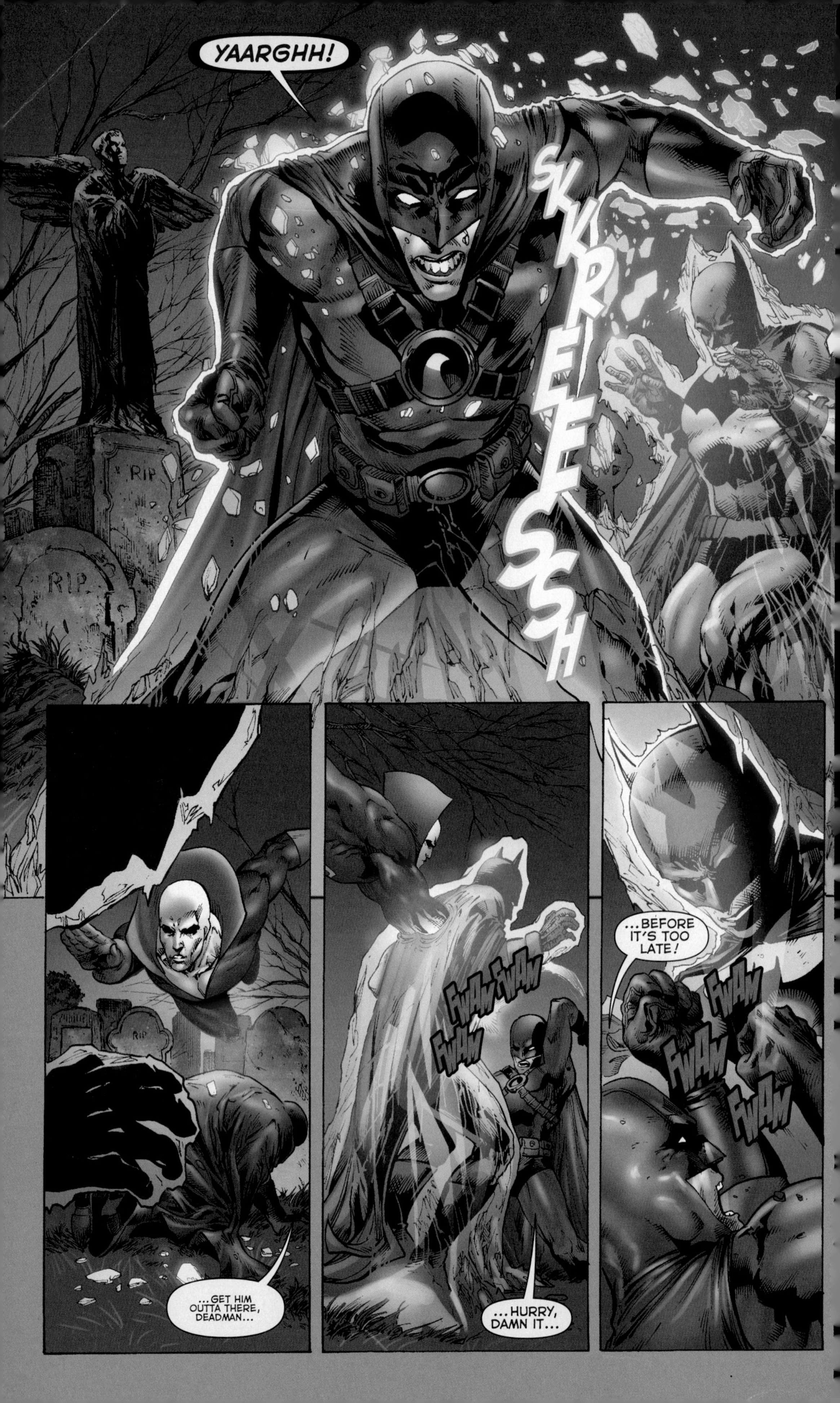
YAARGHH!
SKKREEEESSSH
RIP
RIP
RIP
...GET HIM OUTTA THERE, DEADMAN...
FWAM FWAM FWAM FWAM
...HURRY, DAMN IT...
...BEFORE IT'S TOO LATE!
FWAM FWAM FWAM

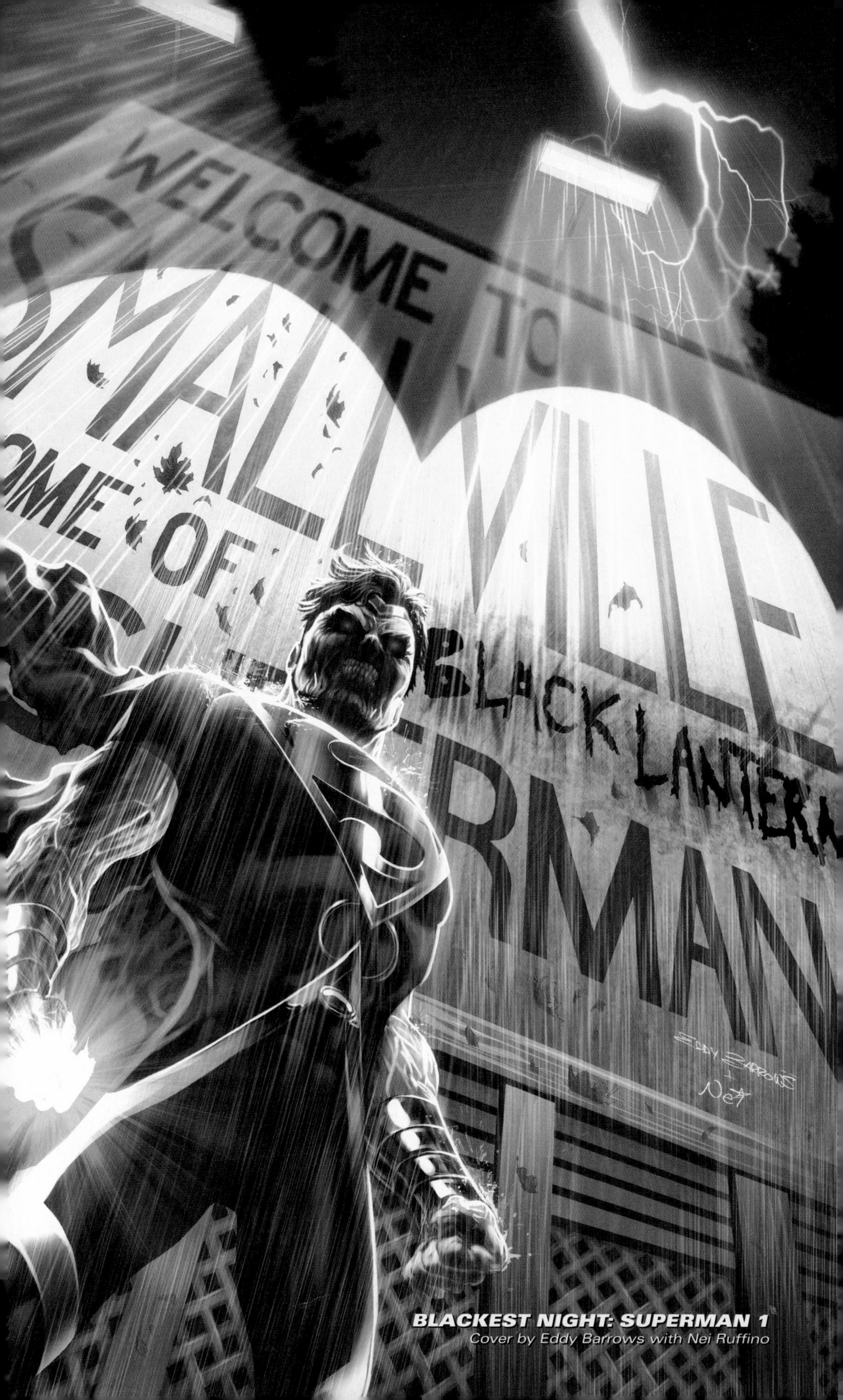
WELCOME TO
BLACK LANTER

BLACKEST NIGHT: SUPERMAN 1
Cover by Eddy Barrows with Nei Ruffino

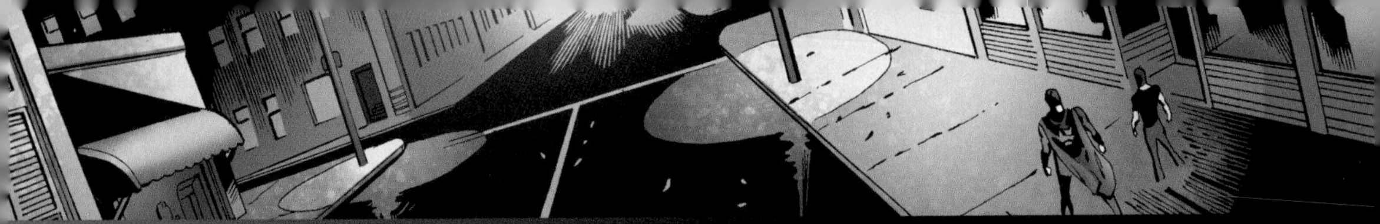

A SLEEPY LITTLE TOWN

JAMES ROBINSON
WRITER

EDDY BARROWS
PENCILS

RUY JOSÉ
JULIO FERREIRA
INKS

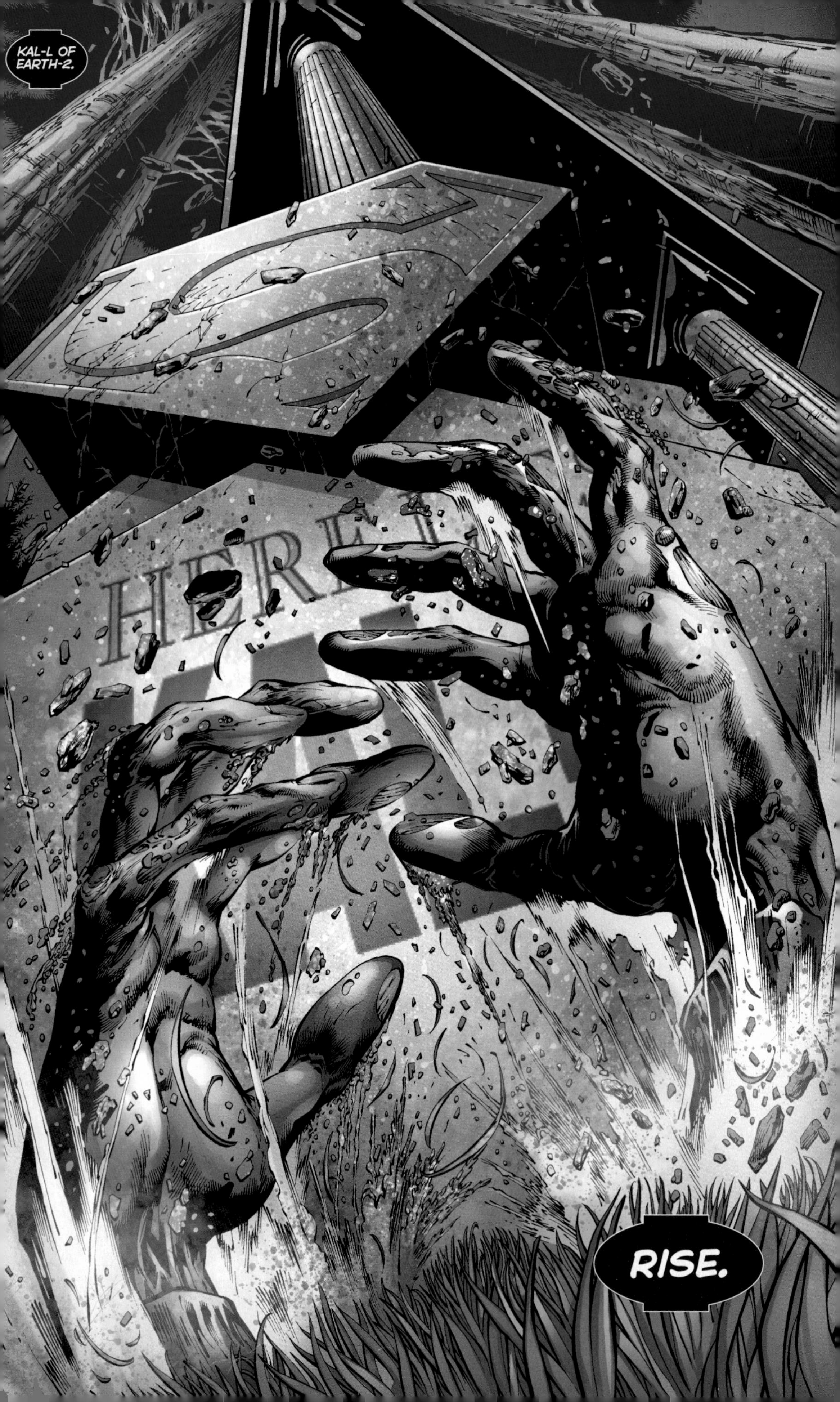
KAL-L OF EARTH-2.
RISE.

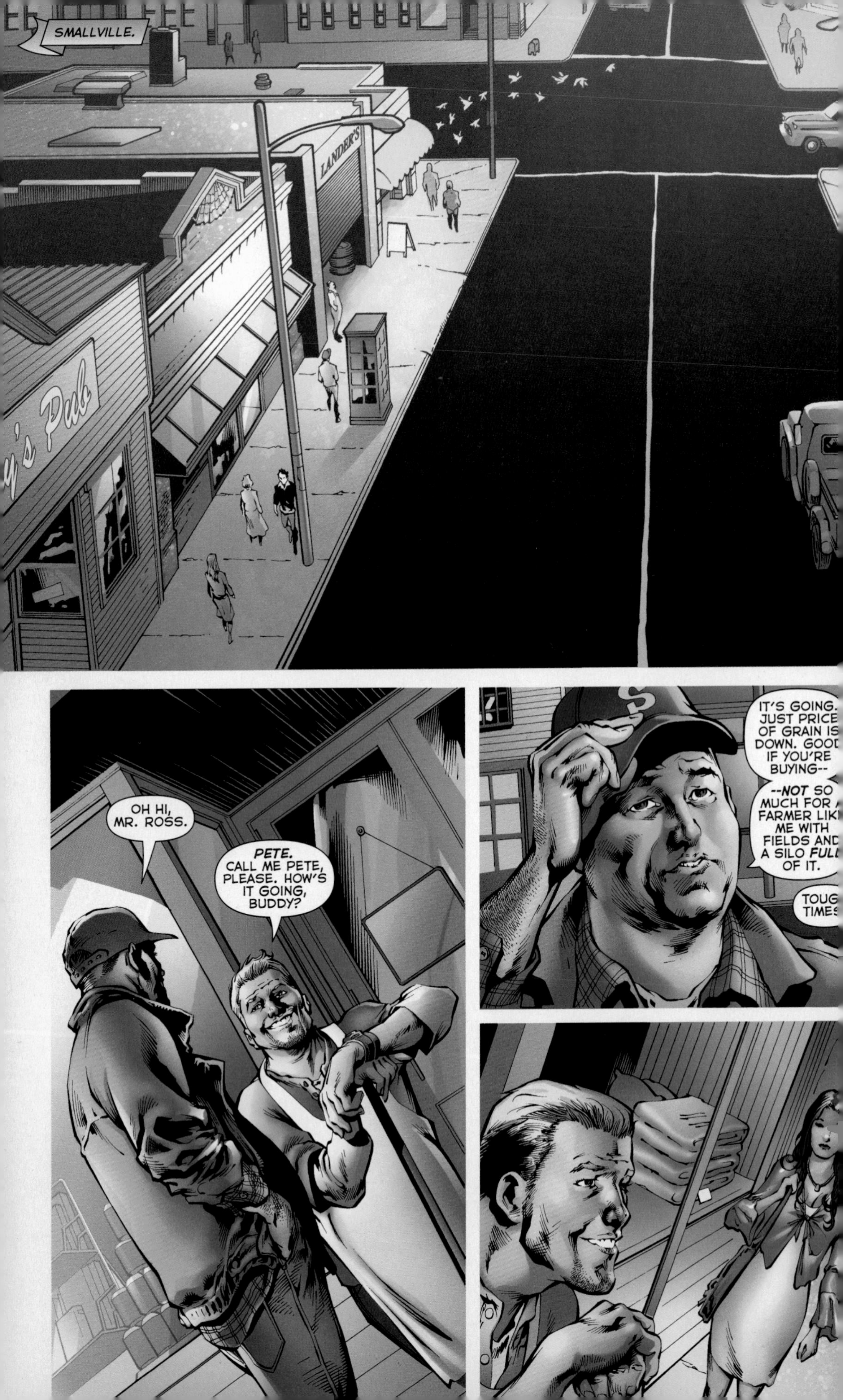
SMALLVILLE.
LANDER'S
OH HI, MR. ROSS.
PETE. CALL ME PETE, PLEASE. HOW'S IT GOING, BUDDY?
IT'S GOING. JUST PRICE OF GRAIN IS DOWN. GOOD IF YOU'RE BUYING--
--NOT SO MUCH FOR A FARMER LIKE ME WITH FIELDS AND A SILO FULL OF IT.
TOUGH TIMES.

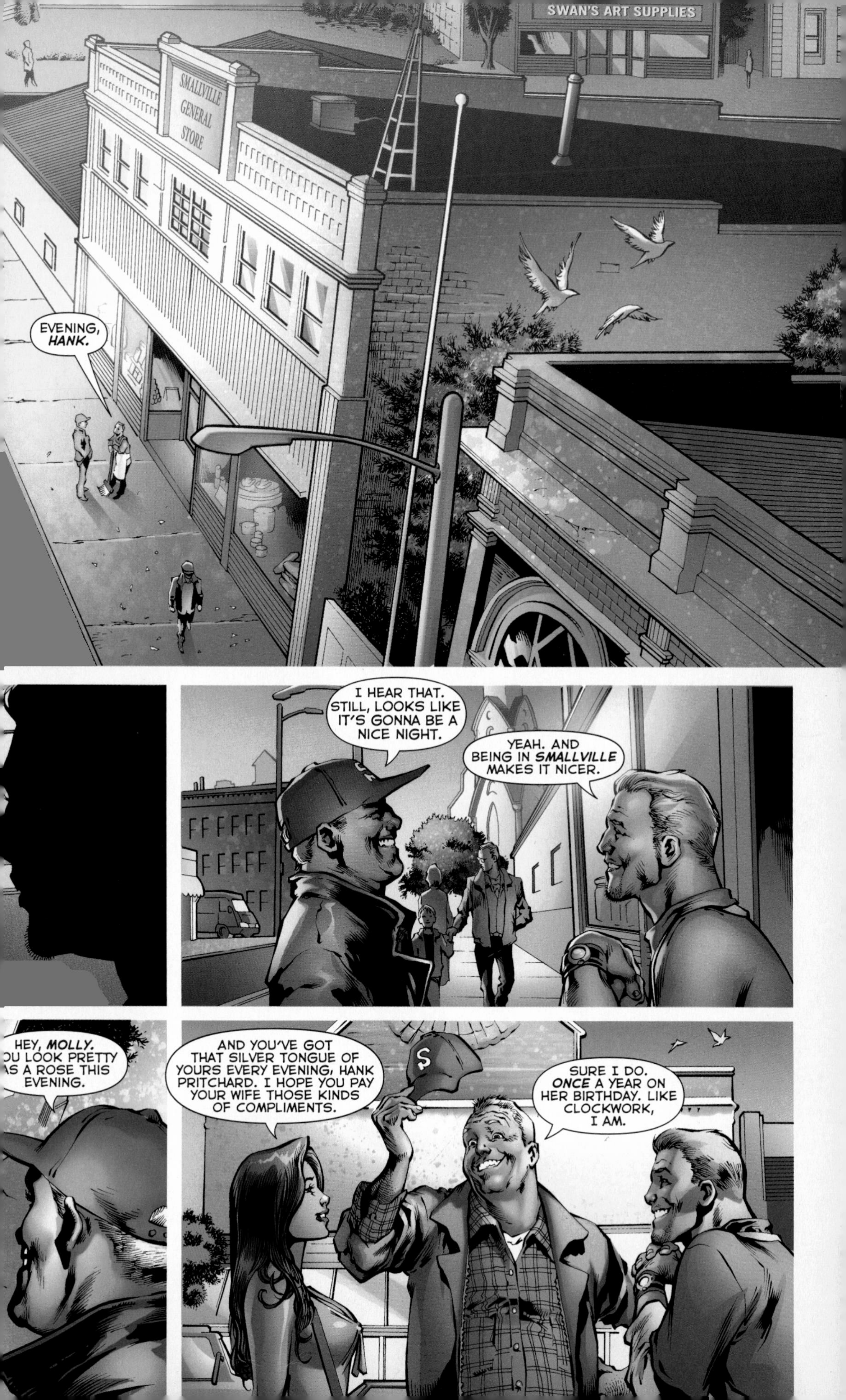
SWAN'S ART SUPPLIES
SMALLVILLE GENERAL STORE
EVENING, HANK.
I HEAR THAT. STILL, LOOKS LIKE IT'S GONNA BE A NICE NIGHT.
YEAH. AND BEING IN SMALLVILLE MAKES IT NICER.
HEY, MOLLY. OU LOOK PRETTY AS A ROSE THIS EVENING.
AND YOU'VE GOT THAT SILVER TONGUE OF YOURS EVERY EVENING, HANK PRITCHARD. I HOPE YOU PAY YOUR WIFE THOSE KINDS OF COMPLIMENTS.
SURE I DO. ONCE A YEAR ON HER BIRTHDAY. LIKE CLOCKWORK, I AM.

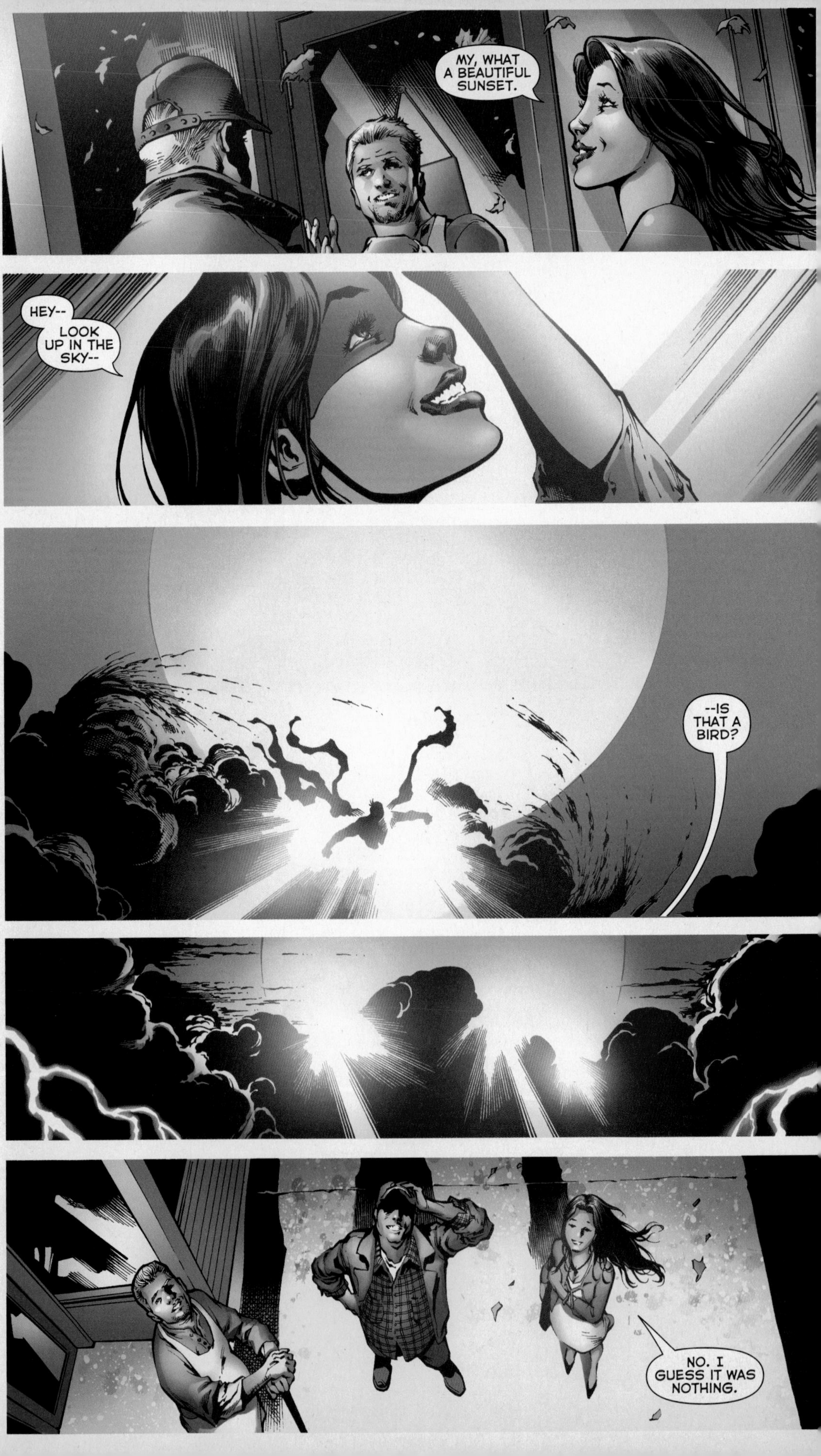
MY, WHAT A BEAUTIFUL SUNSET.
HEY--
LOOK UP IN THE SKY--
--IS THAT A BIRD?
NO. I GUESS IT WAS NOTHING.

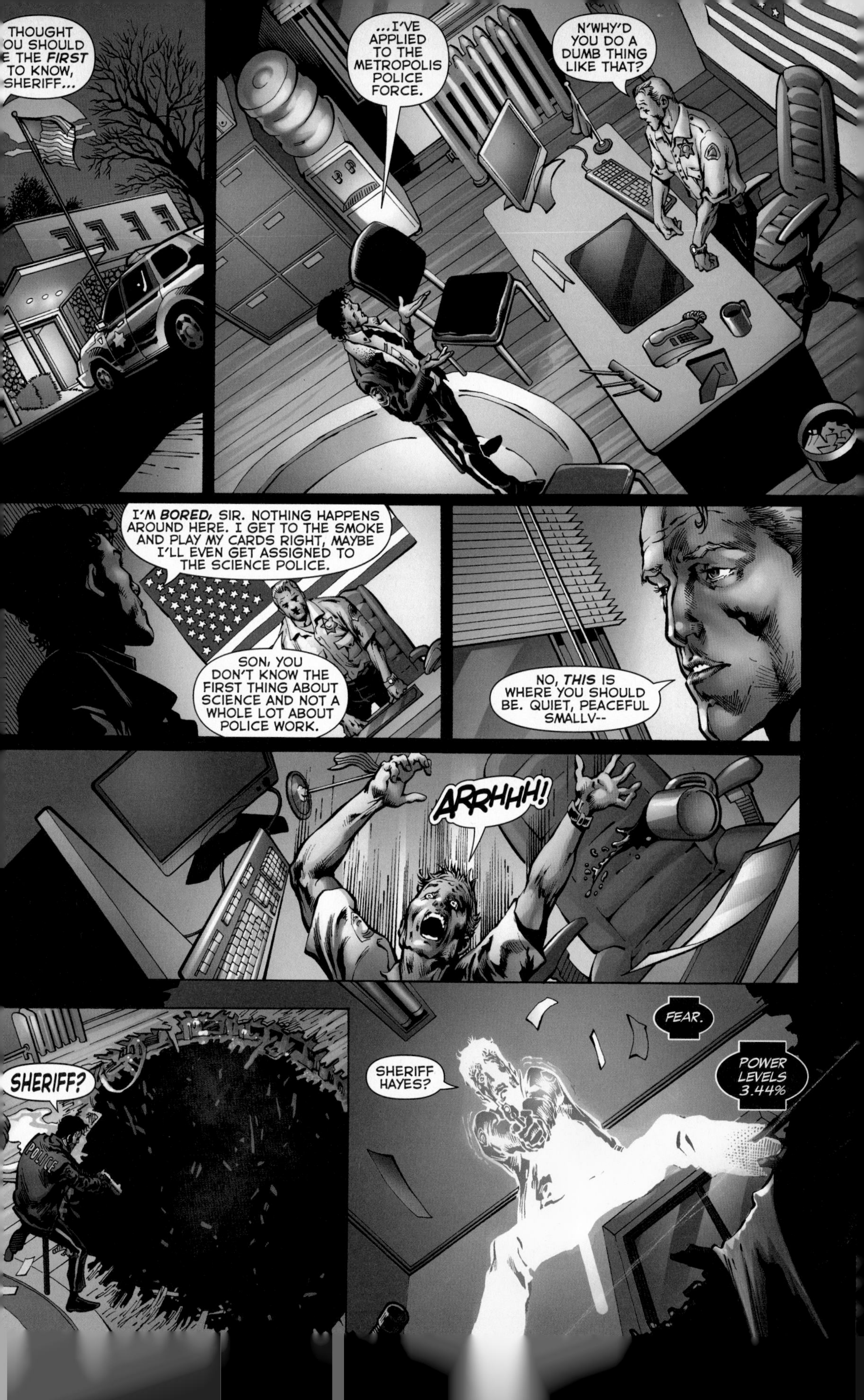

THOUGHT
OU SHOULD
E THE FIRST
TO KNOW,
SHERIFF...
...I'VE APPLIED TO THE METROPOLIS POLICE FORCE.
N'WHY'D YOU DO A DUMB THING LIKE THAT?
I'M BORED, SIR. NOTHING HAPPENS AROUND HERE. I GET TO THE SMOKE AND PLAY MY CARDS RIGHT, MAYBE I'LL EVEN GET ASSIGNED TO THE SCIENCE POLICE.
SON, YOU DON'T KNOW THE FIRST THING ABOUT SCIENCE AND NOT A WHOLE LOT ABOUT POLICE WORK.
NO, THIS IS WHERE YOU SHOULD BE. QUIET, PEACEFUL SMALLV--
ARRHHH!
SHERIFF?
POLICE
SHERIFF HAYES?
FEAR.
POWER LEVELS 3.44%

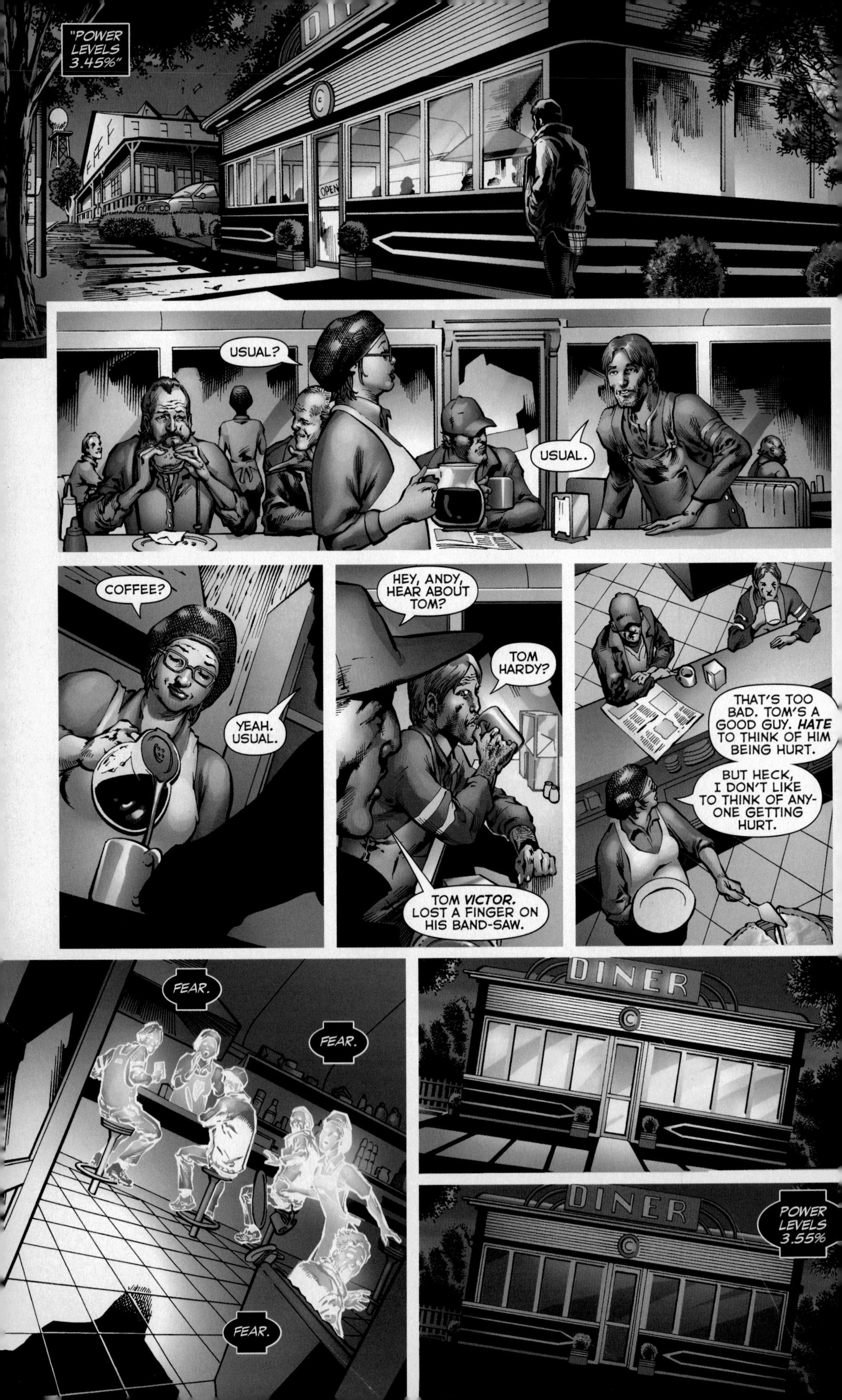

"POWER LEVELS 3.45%"
USUAL?
USUAL.
COFFEE?
YEAH. USUAL.
HEY, ANDY, HEAR ABOUT TOM?
TOM HARDY?
TOM VICTOR. LOST A FINGER ON HIS BAND-SAW.
THAT'S TOO BAD. TOM'S A GOOD GUY. HATE TO THINK OF HIM BEING HURT.
BUT HECK, I DON'T LIKE TO THINK OF ANY-ONE GETTING HURT.
FEAR.
FEAR.
FEAR.
DINER
DINER
POWER LEVELS 3.55%

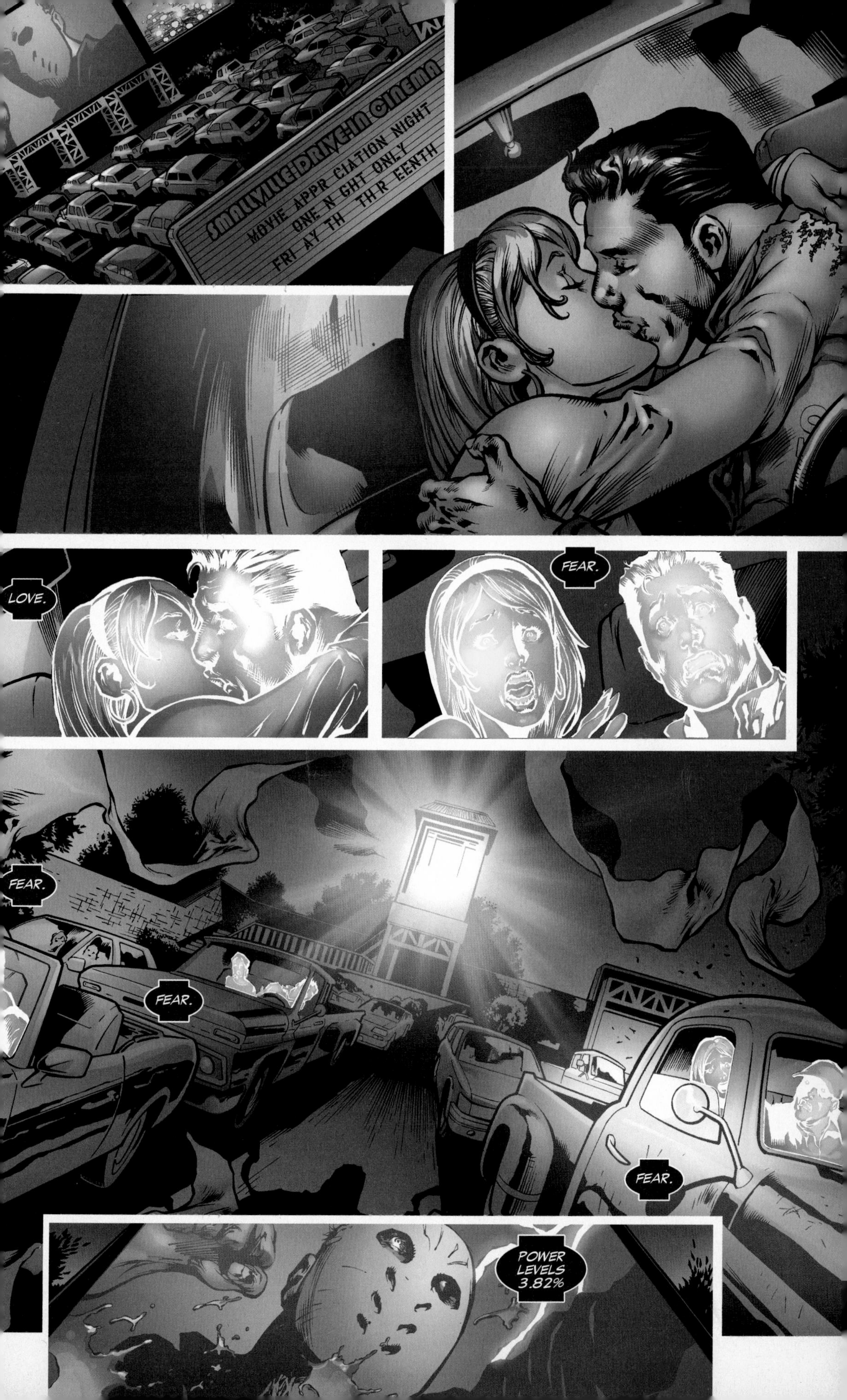
SMALLVILLE DRIVE-IN CINEMA
MOVIE APPR CIATION NIGHT
ONE N GHT ONLY
FRI AY TH THR EENTH
LOVE.
FEAR.
FEAR.
FEAR.
FEAR.
POWER LEVELS 3.82%

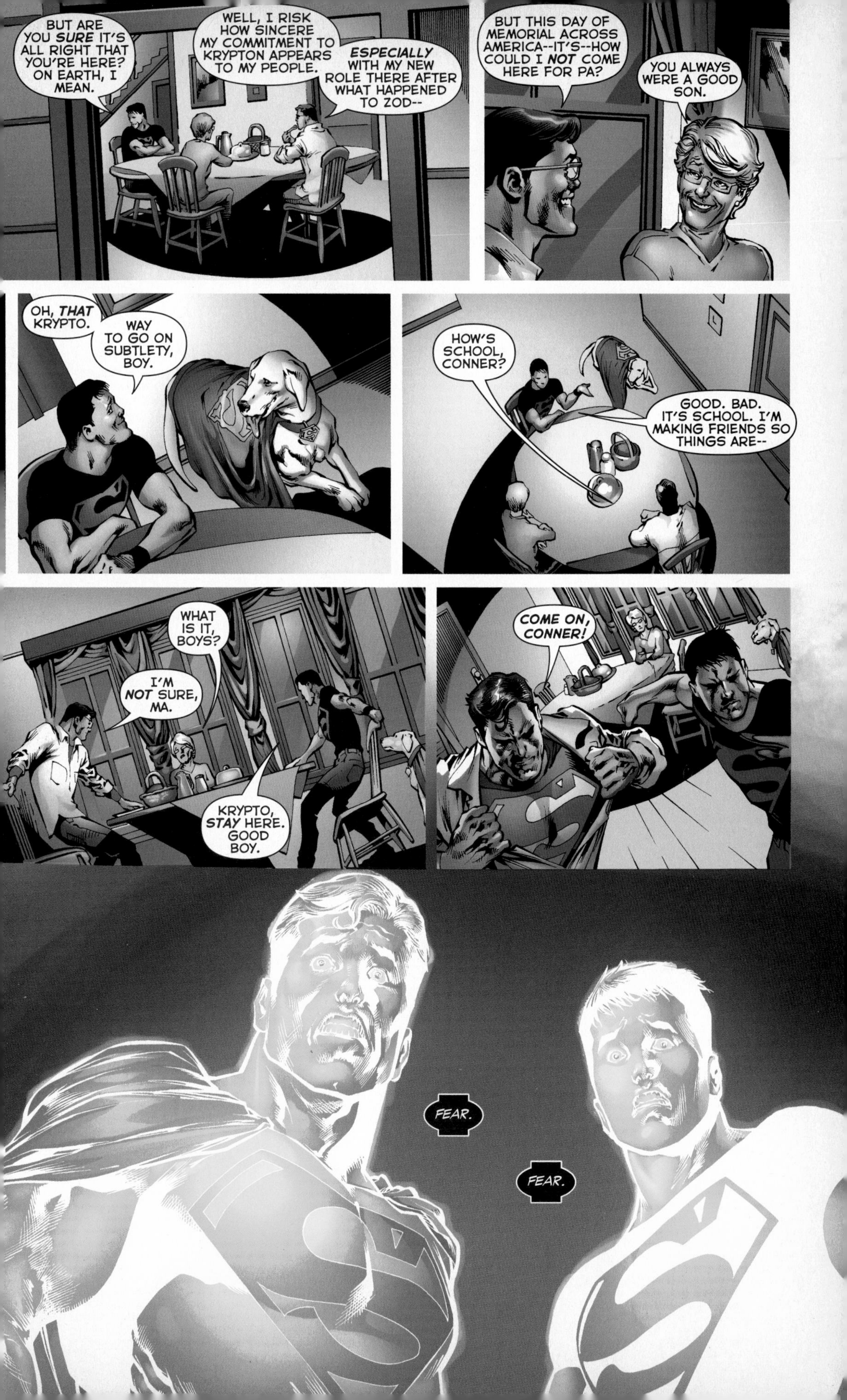
BUT ARE YOU SURE IT'S ALL RIGHT THAT YOU'RE HERE? ON EARTH, I MEAN.
WELL, I RISK HOW SINCERE MY COMMITMENT TO KRYPTON APPEARS TO MY PEOPLE.
ESPECIALLY WITH MY NEW ROLE THERE AFTER WHAT HAPPENED TO ZOD--
BUT THIS DAY OF MEMORIAL ACROSS AMERICA--IT'S--HOW COULD I NOT COME HERE FOR PA?
YOU ALWAYS WERE A GOOD SON.
OH, THAT KRYPTO.
WAY TO GO ON SUBTLETY, BOY.
HOW'S SCHOOL, CONNER?
GOOD. BAD. IT'S SCHOOL. I'M MAKING FRIENDS SO THINGS ARE--
WHAT IS IT, BOYS?
I'M NOT SURE, MA.
KRYPTO, STAY HERE. GOOD BOY.
COME ON, CONNER!
FEAR.
FEAR.

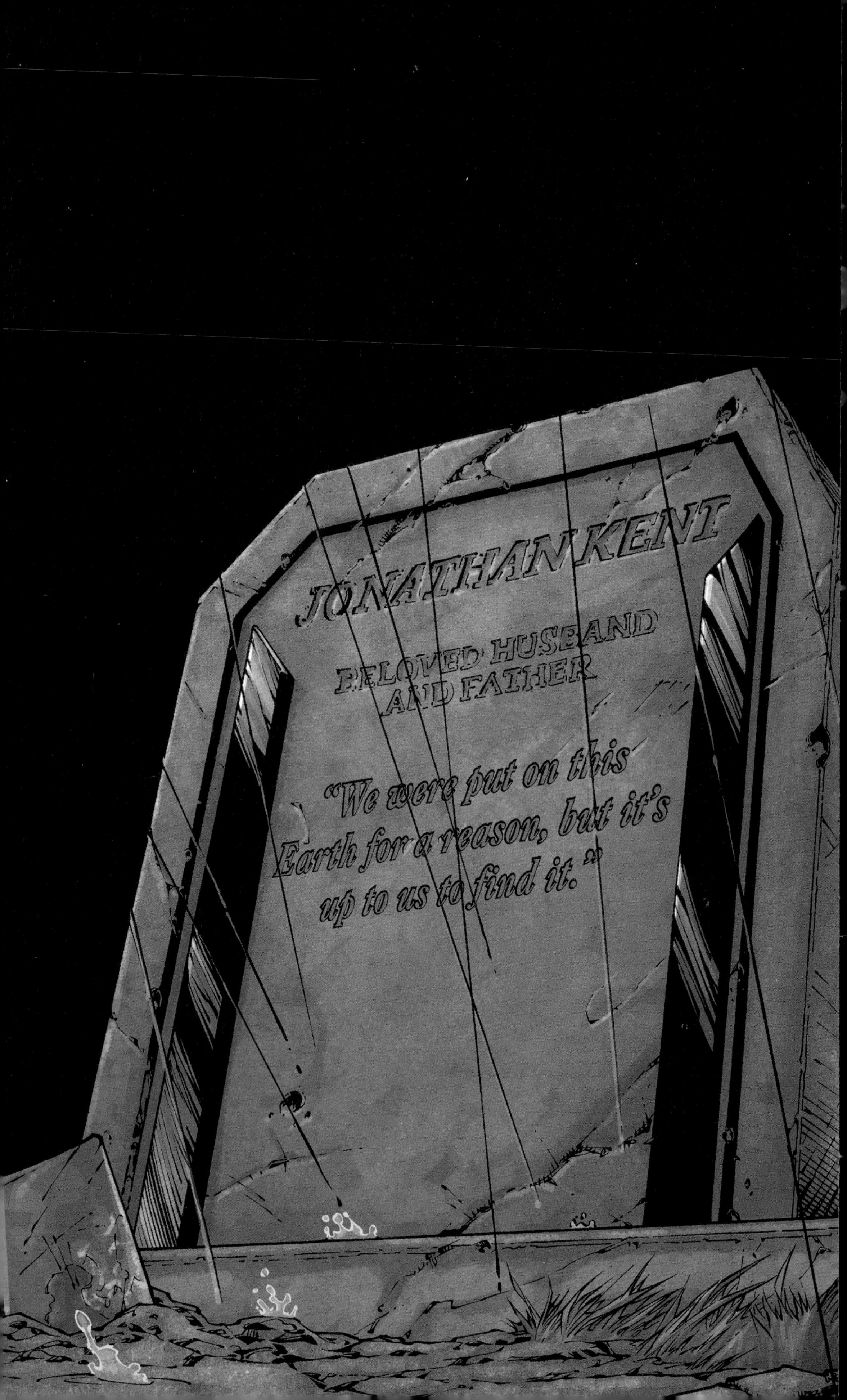
JONATHAN KENT
BELOVED HUSBAND AND FATHER
"We were put on this Earth for a reason, but it's up to us to find it."

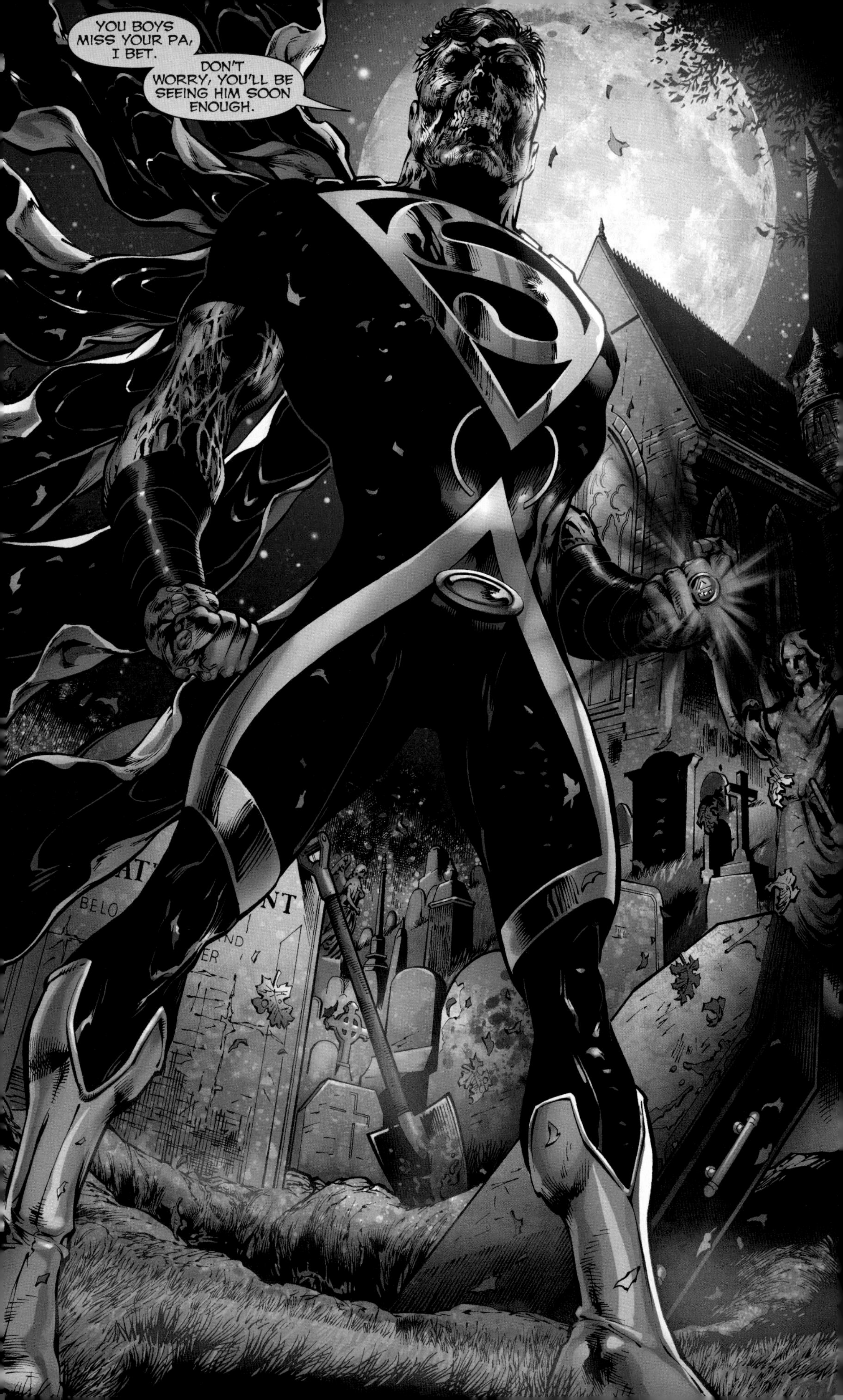
YOU BOYS MISS YOUR PA, I BET.
DON'T WORRY, YOU'LL BE SEEING HIM SOON ENOUGH.

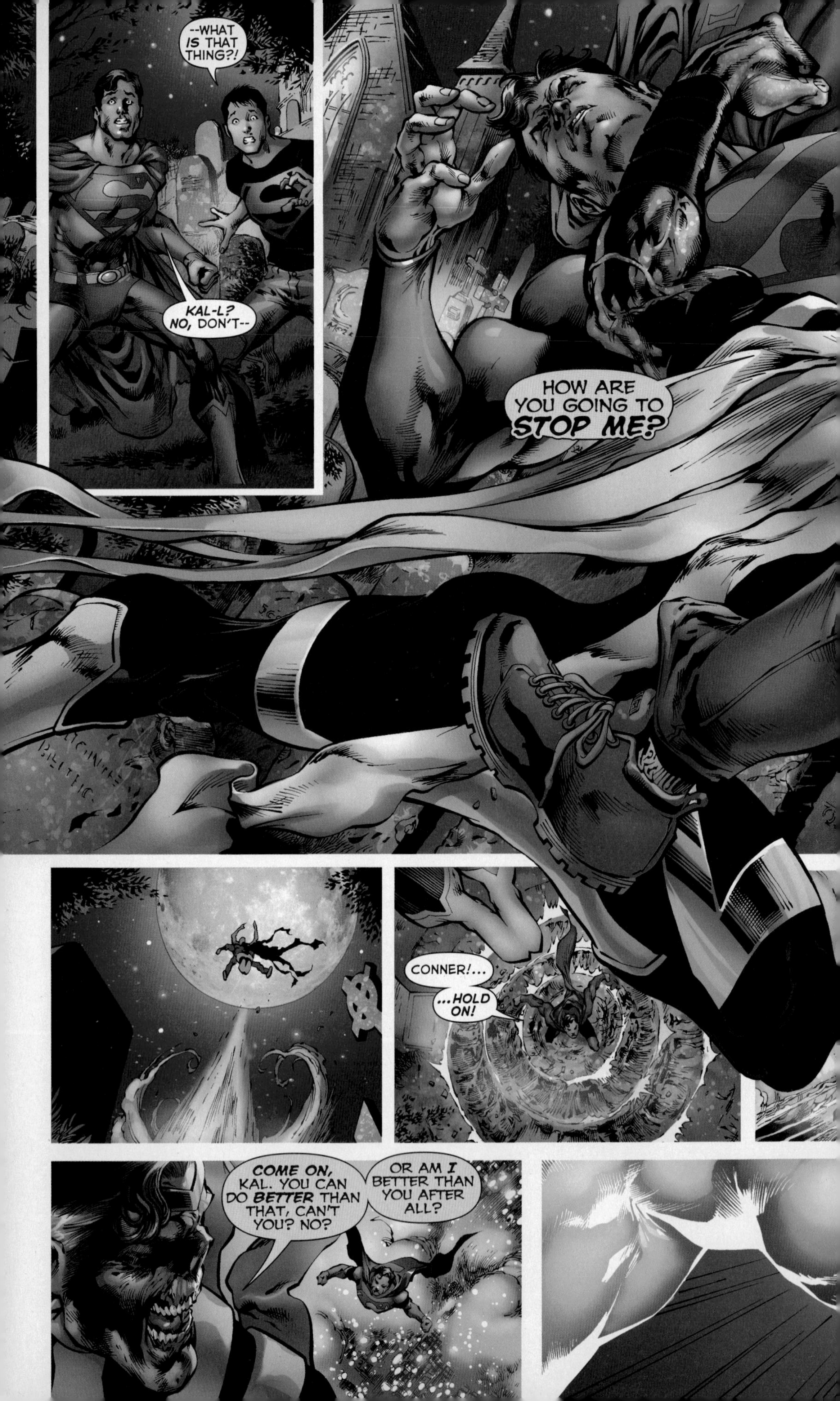
--WHAT *IS* THAT THING?!
KAL-L? NO, DON'T--
HOW ARE YOU GOING TO ***STOP ME?***
CONNER*!*...
...HOLD ON!
COME ON, KAL. YOU CAN DO ***BETTER*** THAN THAT, CAN'T YOU? NO?
OR AM ***I*** BETTER THAN YOU AFTER ALL?

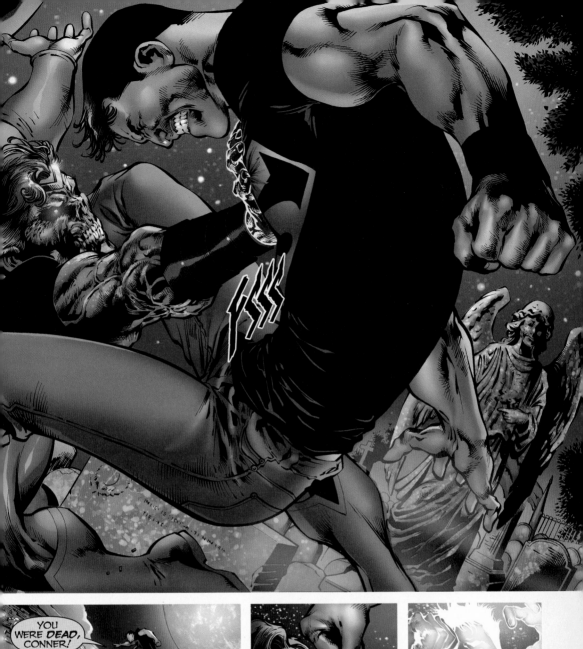

YOU WERE **DEAD**, CONNER!

YOU WERE **ONE** OF US!

BE ONE OF US **AGAIN!**

FEAR.

WILL.

FEAR.

WILL.

RAGE.

HOPE.

LOVE.

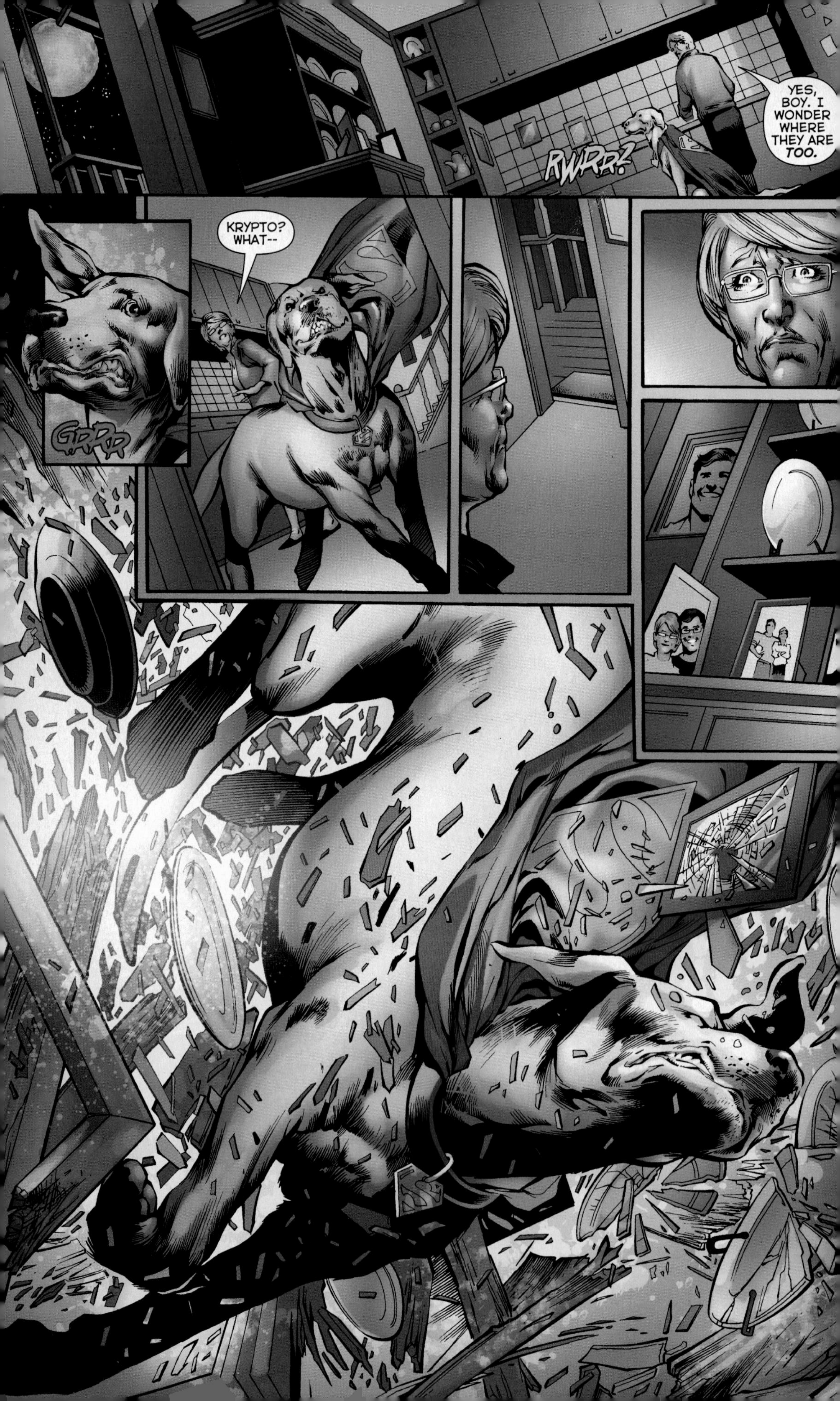
RWRR?
YES, BOY. I WONDER WHERE THEY ARE TOO.
GRRR
KRYPTO? WHAT--

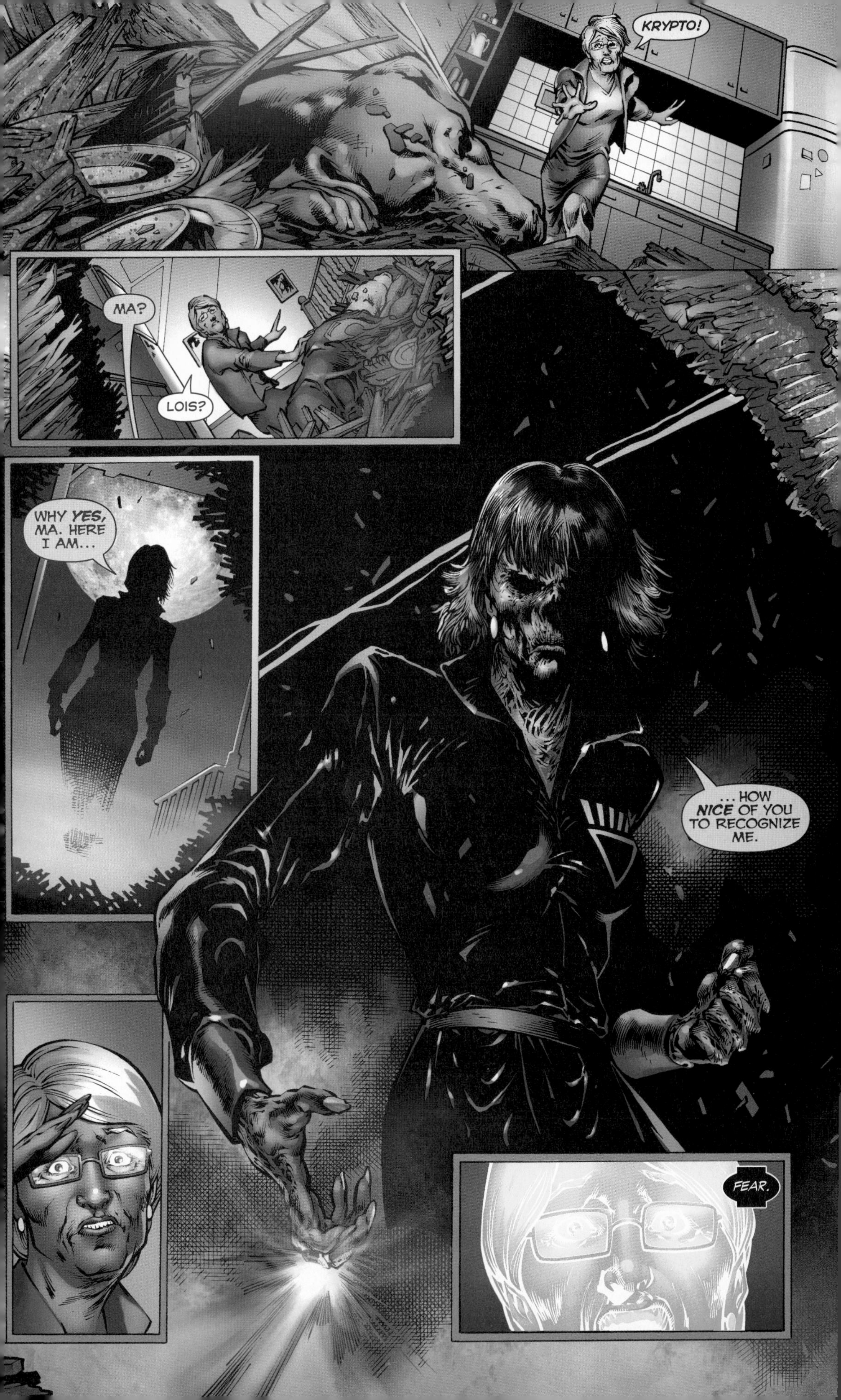
KRYPTO!
MA?
LOIS?
WHY YES, MA. HERE I AM...
...HOW NICE OF YOU TO RECOGNIZE ME.
FEAR.

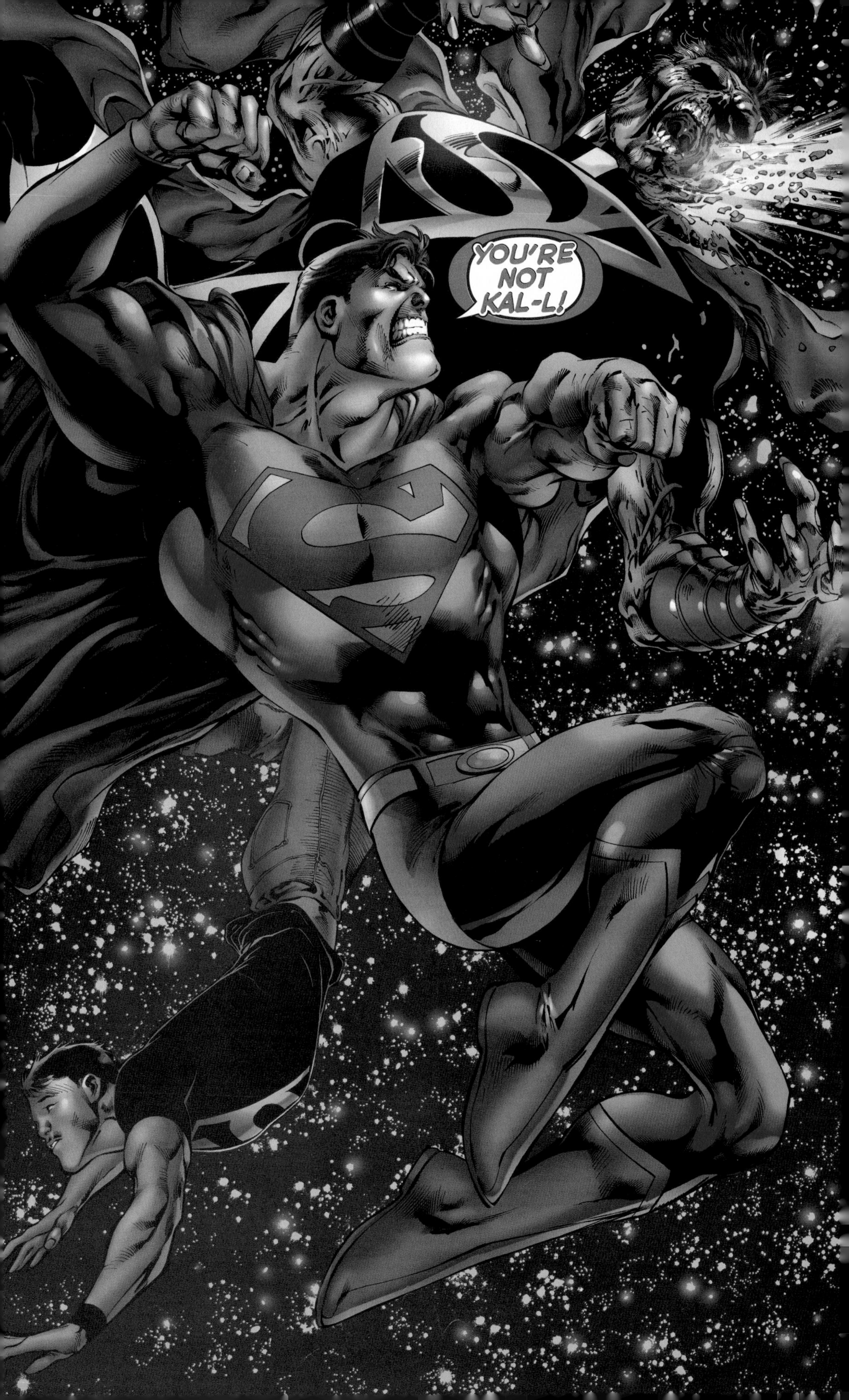
YOU'RE NOT KAL-L!

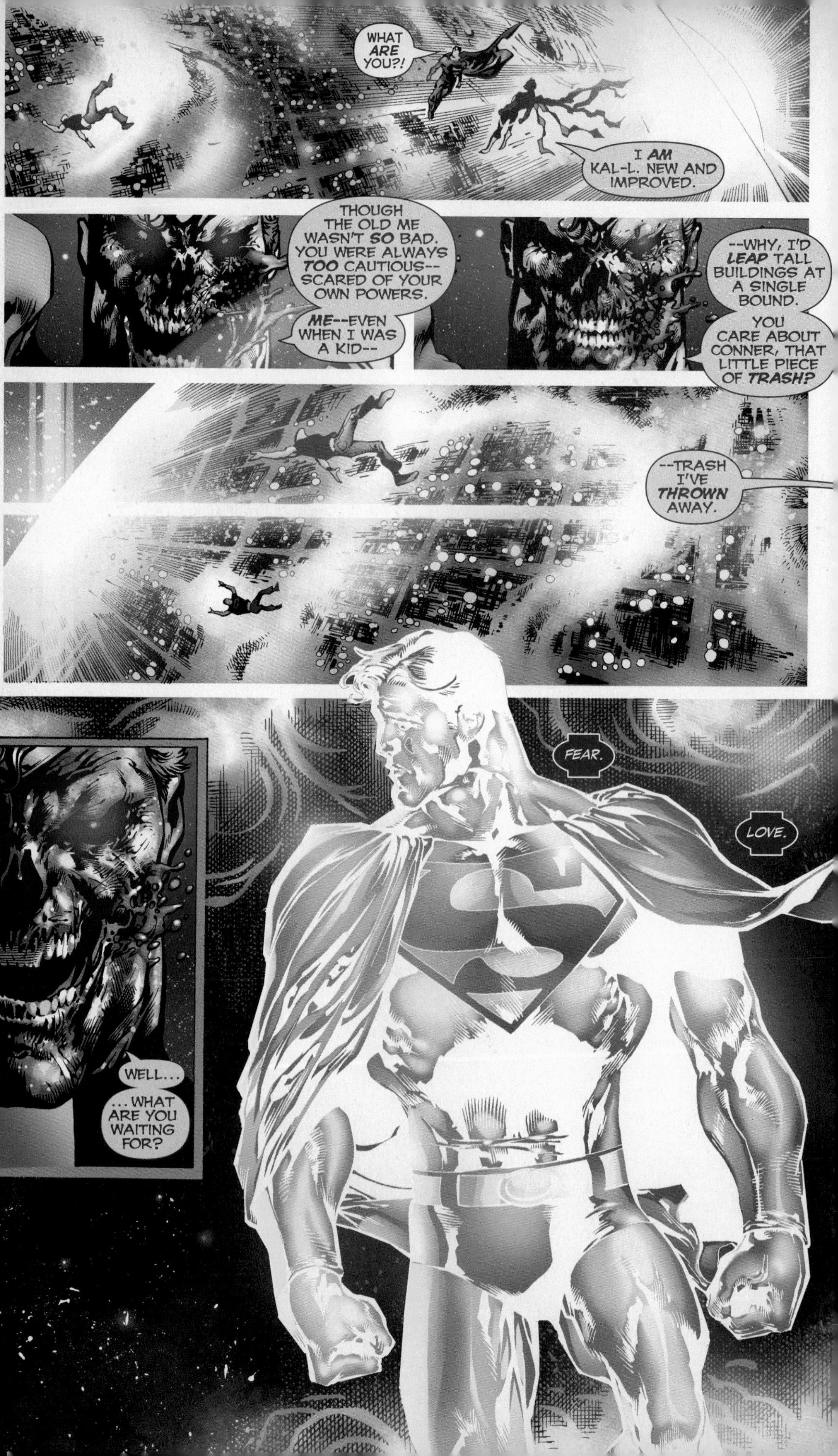
WHAT ARE YOU?!
I AM KAL-L. NEW AND IMPROVED.
THOUGH THE OLD ME WASN'T SO BAD. YOU WERE ALWAYS TOO CAUTIOUS-- SCARED OF YOUR OWN POWERS.
ME--EVEN WHEN I WAS A KID--
--WHY, I'D LEAP TALL BUILDINGS AT A SINGLE BOUND.
YOU CARE ABOUT CONNER, THAT LITTLE PIECE OF TRASH?
--TRASH I'VE THROWN AWAY.
FEAR.
LOVE.
WELL...
...WHAT ARE YOU WAITING FOR?

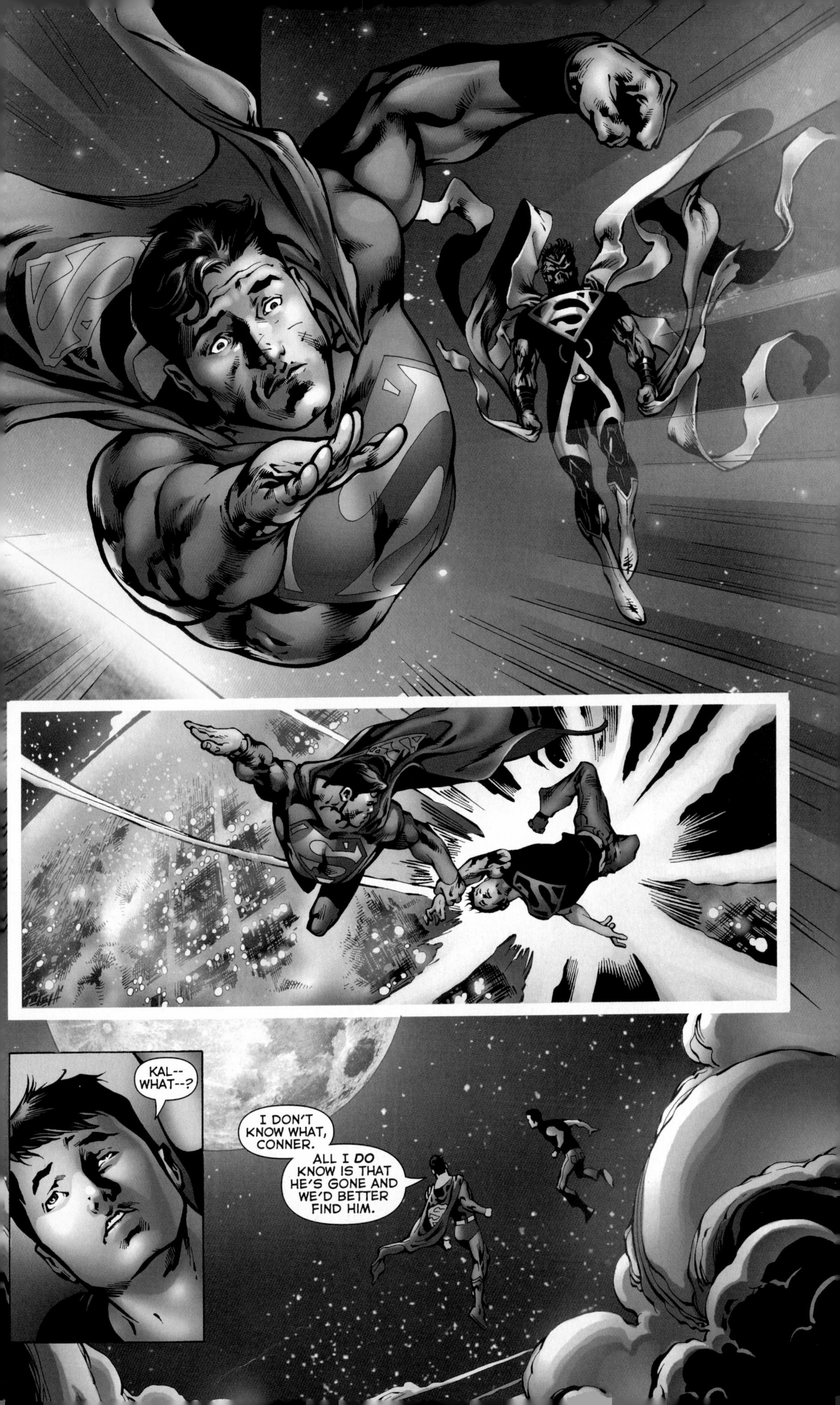
KAL--
WHAT--?
I DON'T KNOW WHAT, CONNER.
ALL I *DO* KNOW IS THAT HE'S GONE AND WE'D BETTER FIND HIM.

NEW KRYPTON.

FLSH

KANDOR.

MOTHER, I'VE BEEN LOOKING FOR YOU.

WELL, YOU FOUND ME, KARA.

I WANTED TO DISCUSS SOME THINGS.

THINGS?

THINGS GOING ON.

HERE?

NO. ON EARTH.

EARTH? HEAVENS, WHAT IS IT ABOUT THAT PLACE THAT DRAWS YOU SO?

I CAN UNDERSTAND YOUR COUSIN, HE GREW UP THERE, BUT YOUR TIME IN THAT PLACE IS BARELY ANYTHING AT ALL.

I'M AFRAID THAT STUFF GOING ON THERE NOW WILL AFFECT KRYPTON IN THE FUTURE.

IN THE FUTURE? THEN IT CAN WAIT WHILE WE PAY OUR RESPECTS TO YOUR FATHER.

COME. REMEMBER HIM WITH ME.

I DO MISS HIM SO. I WISH I COULD SEE HIS FACE JUST ONE MORE T--

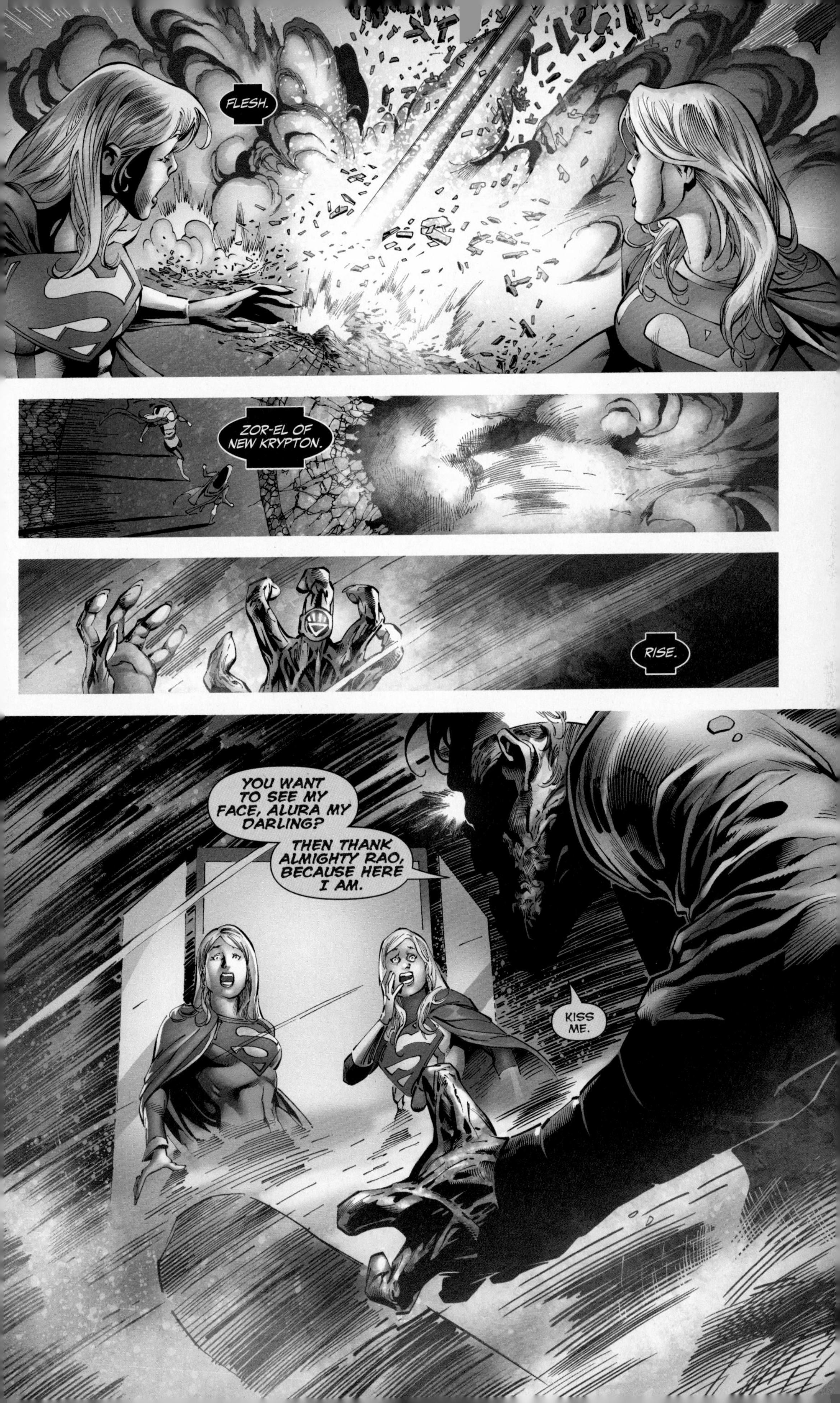
FLESH.
ZOR-EL OF NEW KRYPTON.
RISE.
YOU WANT TO SEE MY FACE, ALURA MY DARLING?
THEN THANK ALMIGHTY RAO, BECAUSE HERE I AM.
KISS ME.

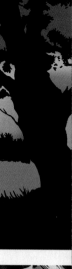

MA!

KRYPTO!

NO.
NO!

OH...

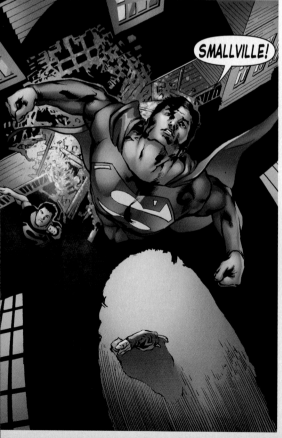
SMALLVILLE!

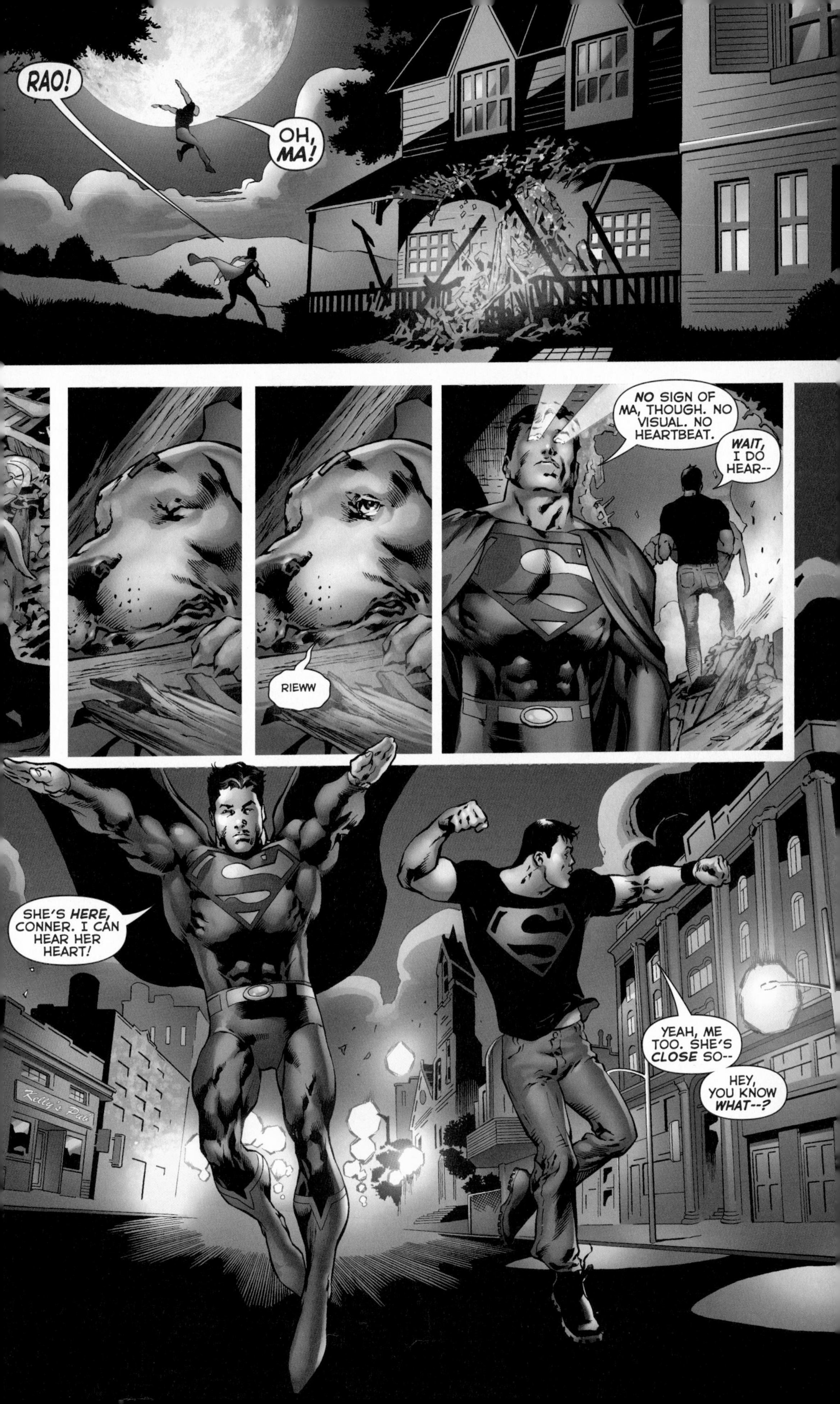
RAO!
OH, MA!
RIEWW
NO SIGN OF MA, THOUGH. NO VISUAL. NO HEARTBEAT.
WAIT, I DO HEAR--
SHE'S HERE, CONNER. I CAN HEAR HER HEART!
YEAH, ME TOO. SHE'S CLOSE SO--
HEY, YOU KNOW WHAT--?
Kelly's Pub

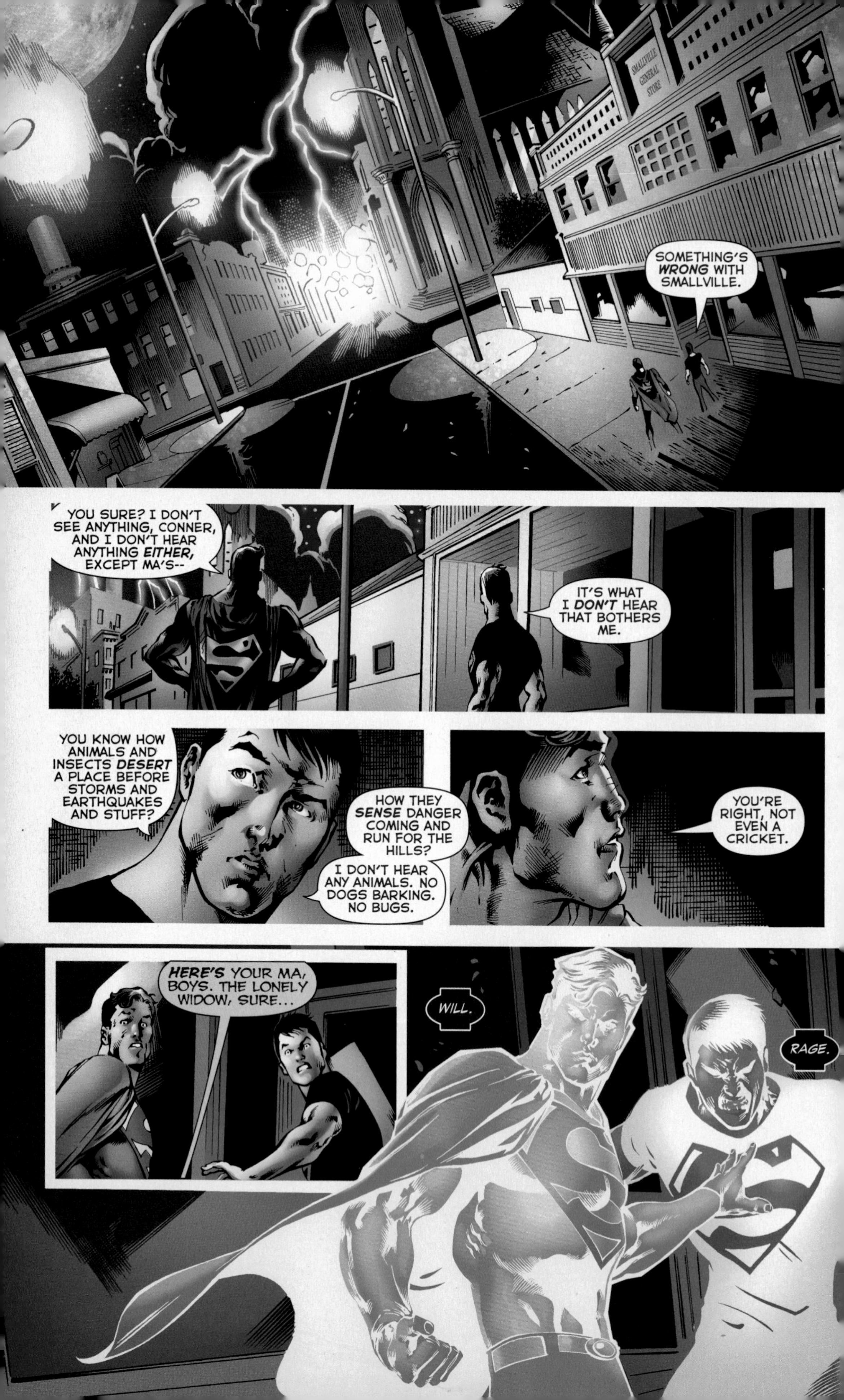
SMALLVILLE GENERAL STORE
SOMETHING'S WRONG WITH SMALLVILLE.
YOU SURE? I DON'T SEE ANYTHING, CONNER, AND I DON'T HEAR ANYTHING EITHER, EXCEPT MA'S--
IT'S WHAT I DON'T HEAR THAT BOTHERS ME.
YOU KNOW HOW ANIMALS AND INSECTS DESERT A PLACE BEFORE STORMS AND EARTHQUAKES AND STUFF?
HOW THEY SENSE DANGER COMING AND RUN FOR THE HILLS?
I DON'T HEAR ANY ANIMALS. NO DOGS BARKING. NO BUGS.
YOU'RE RIGHT, NOT EVEN A CRICKET.
HERE'S YOUR MA, BOYS. THE LONELY WIDOW, SURE...
WILL.
RAGE.

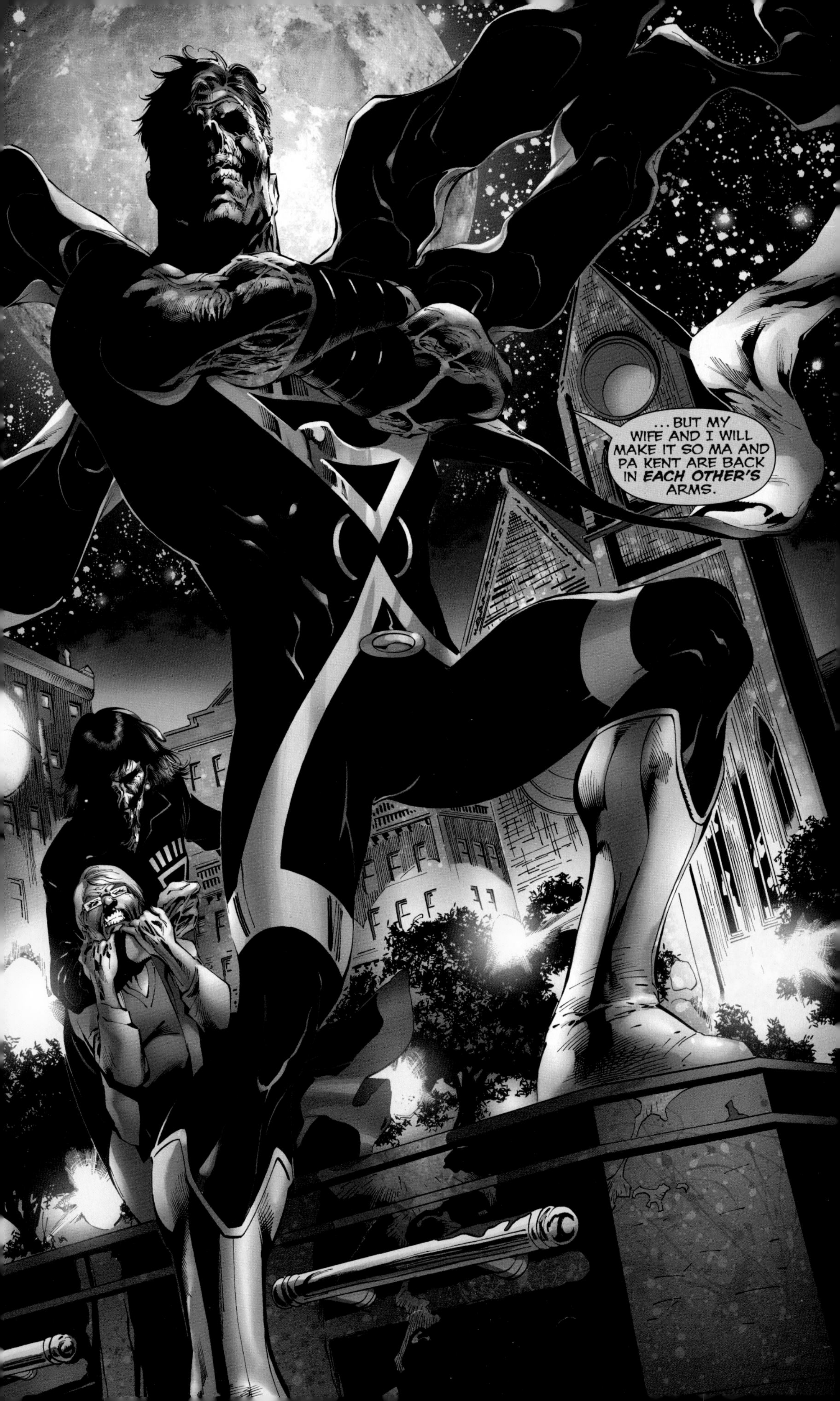
...BUT MY WIFE AND I WILL MAKE IT SO MA AND PA KENT ARE BACK IN EACH OTHER'S ARMS.

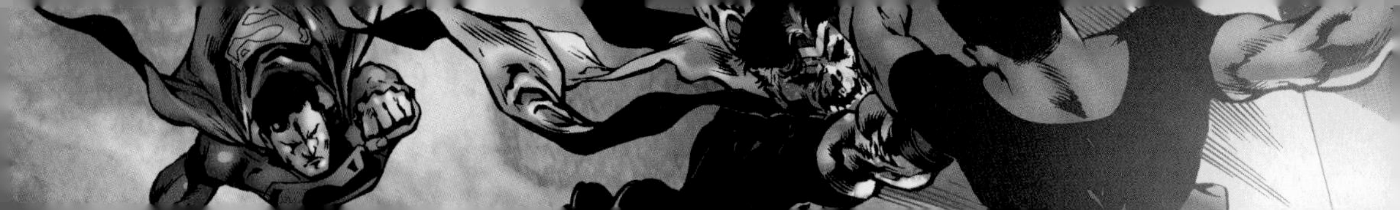

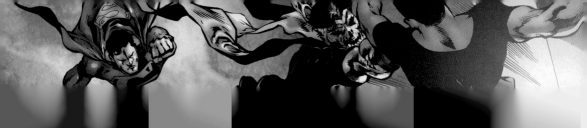

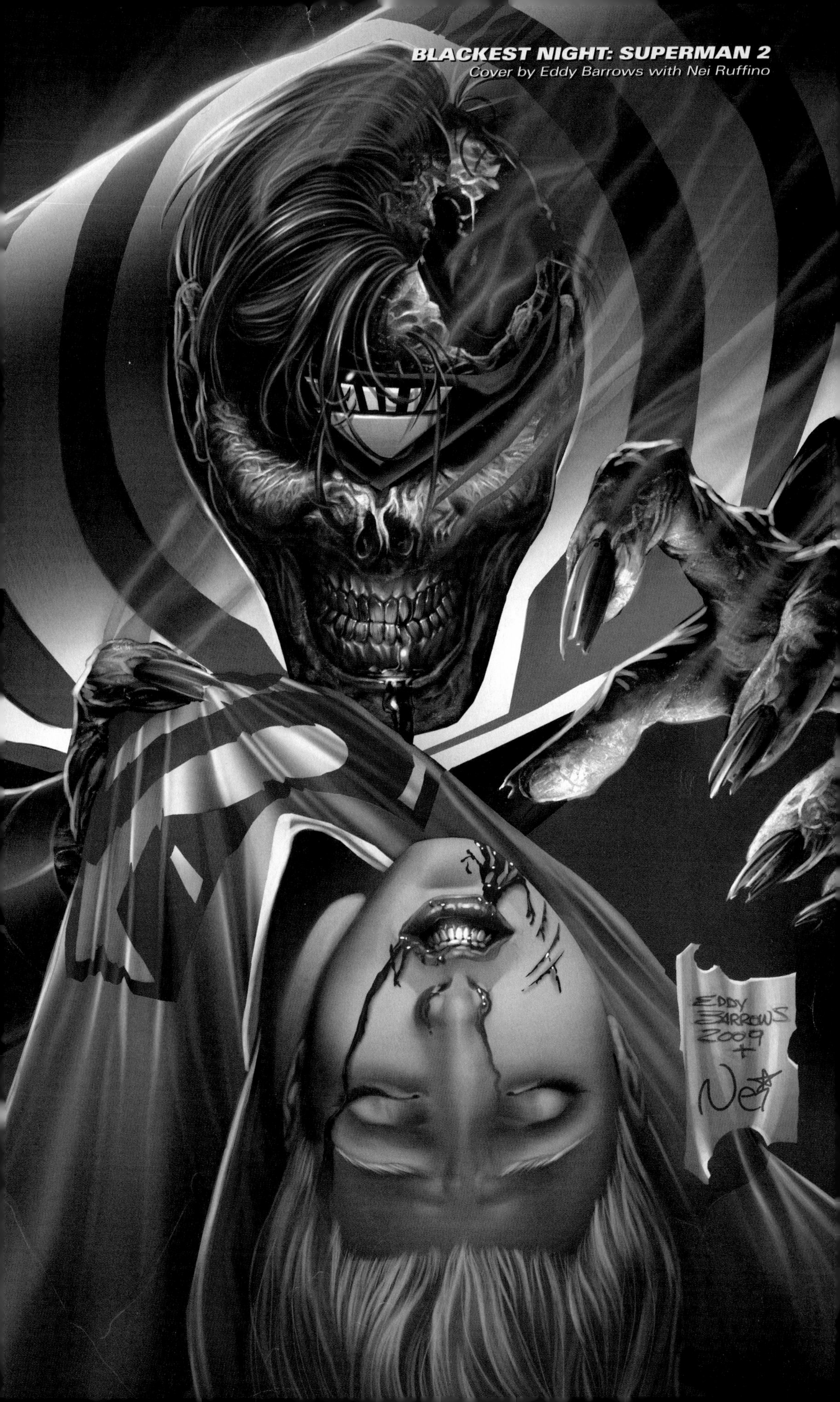
EDDY BARROWS 2009 + Nei

BLACKEST NIGHT: SUPERMAN 2
Cover by Eddy Barrows with Nei Ruffino

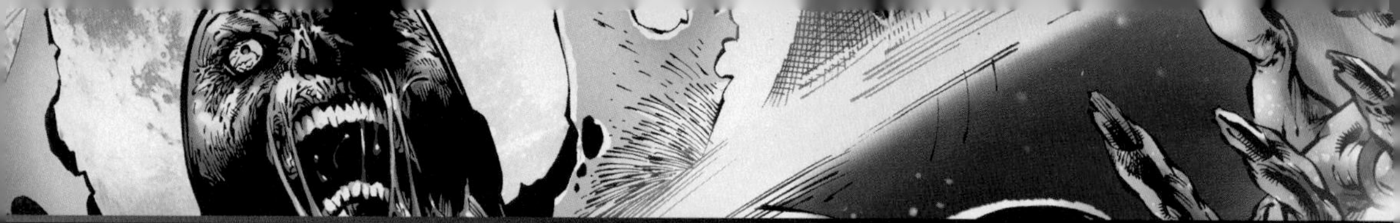

PSYCHO PIRACY!

JAMES ROBINSON
WRITER

EDDY BARROWS
PENCILS

RUY JOSÉ
JULIO FERREIRA

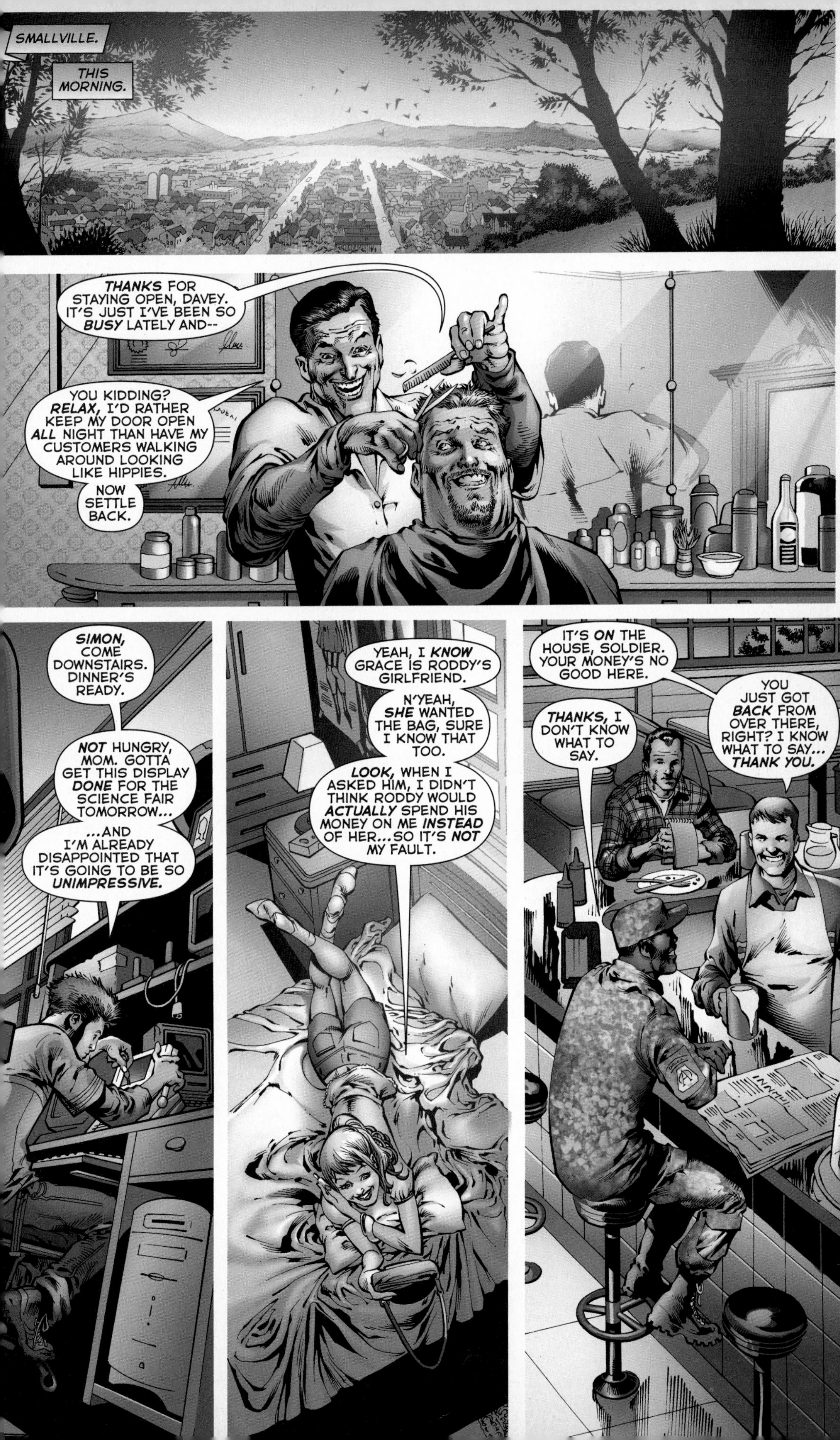
SMALLVILLE.
THIS MORNING.
THANKS FOR STAYING OPEN, DAVEY. IT'S JUST I'VE BEEN SO BUSY LATELY AND--
YOU KIDDING? RELAX, I'D RATHER KEEP MY DOOR OPEN ALL NIGHT THAN HAVE MY CUSTOMERS WALKING AROUND LOOKING LIKE HIPPIES.
NOW SETTLE BACK.
SIMON, COME DOWNSTAIRS. DINNER'S READY.
NOT HUNGRY, MOM. GOTTA GET THIS DISPLAY DONE FOR THE SCIENCE FAIR TOMORROW...
...AND I'M ALREADY DISAPPOINTED THAT IT'S GOING TO BE SO UNIMPRESSIVE.
YEAH, I KNOW GRACE IS RODDY'S GIRLFRIEND.
N'YEAH, SHE WANTED THE BAG, SURE I KNOW THAT TOO.
LOOK, WHEN I ASKED HIM, I DIDN'T THINK RODDY WOULD ACTUALLY SPEND HIS MONEY ON ME INSTEAD OF HER...SO IT'S NOT MY FAULT.
IT'S ON THE HOUSE, SOLDIER. YOUR MONEY'S NO GOOD HERE.
THANKS, I DON'T KNOW WHAT TO SAY.
YOU JUST GOT BACK FROM OVER THERE, RIGHT? I KNOW WHAT TO SAY... THANK YOU.

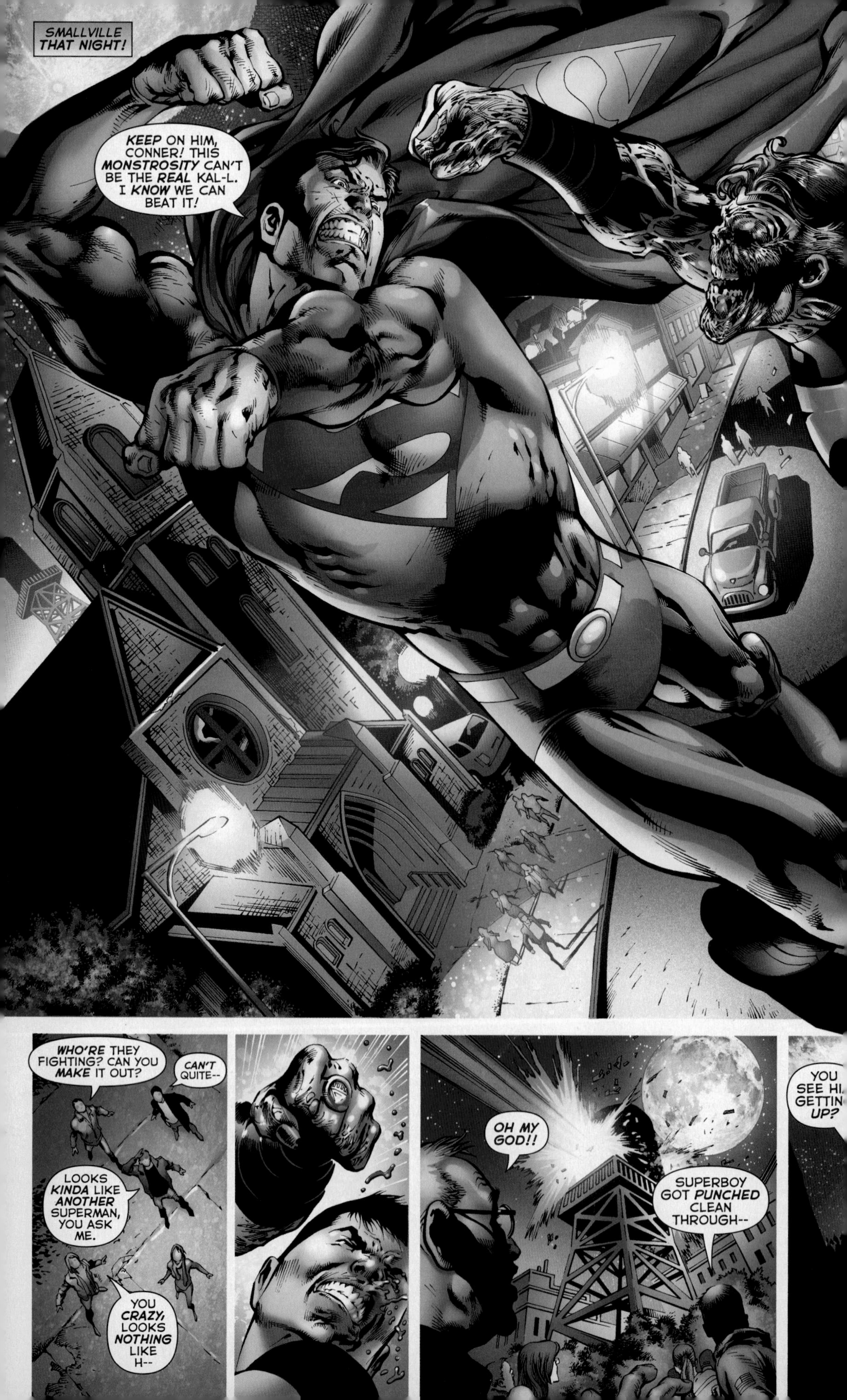
SMALLVILLE THAT NIGHT!
KEEP ON HIM, CONNER! THIS MONSTROSITY CAN'T BE THE REAL KAL-L. I KNOW WE CAN BEAT IT!
WHO'RE THEY FIGHTING? CAN YOU MAKE IT OUT?
CAN'T QUITE--
LOOKS KINDA LIKE ANOTHER SUPERMAN, YOU ASK ME.
YOU CRAZY, LOOKS NOTHING LIKE H--
OH MY GOD!!
SUPERBOY GOT PUNCHED CLEAN THROUGH--
YOU SEE HI GETTIN UP?

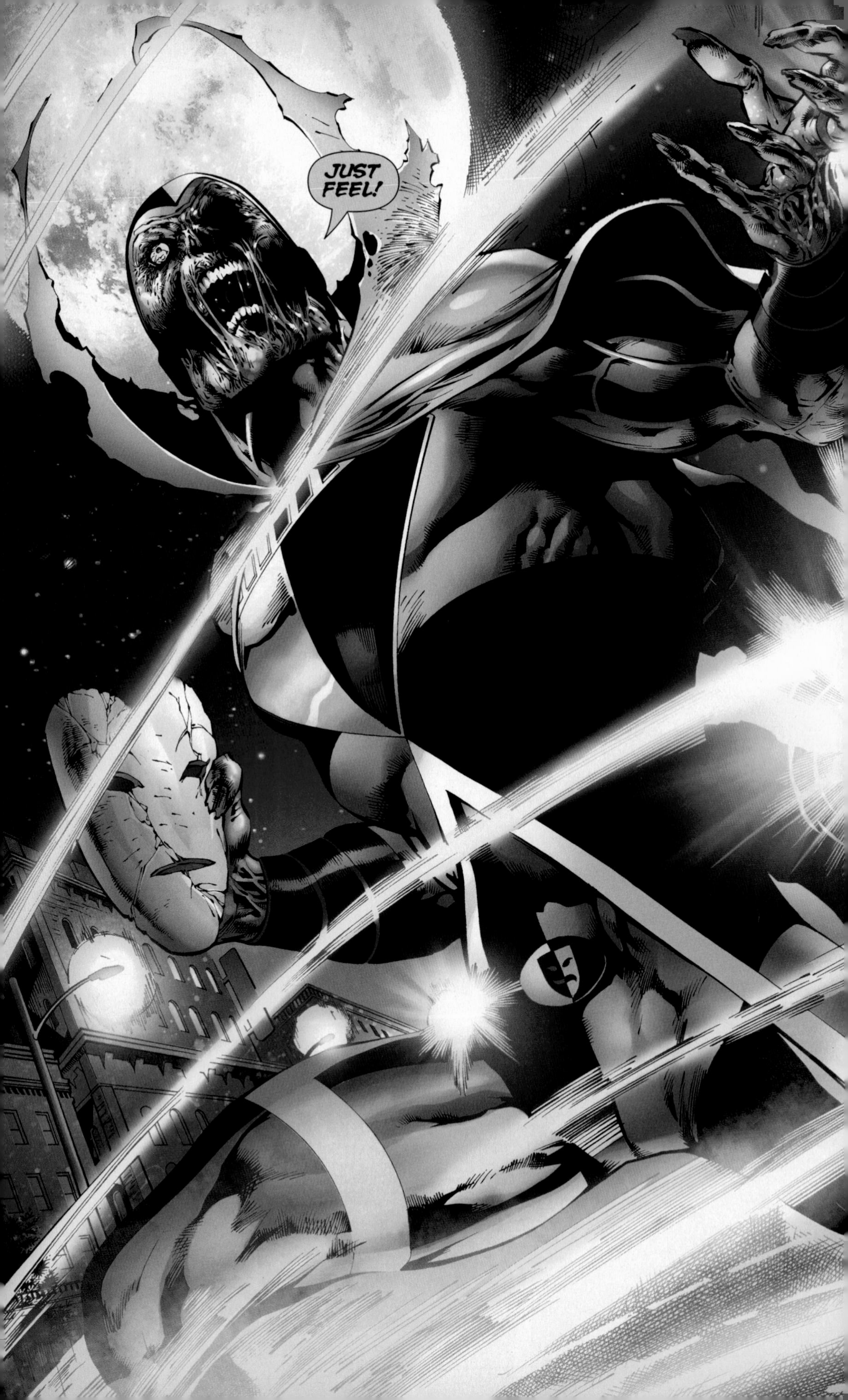
JUST FEEL!

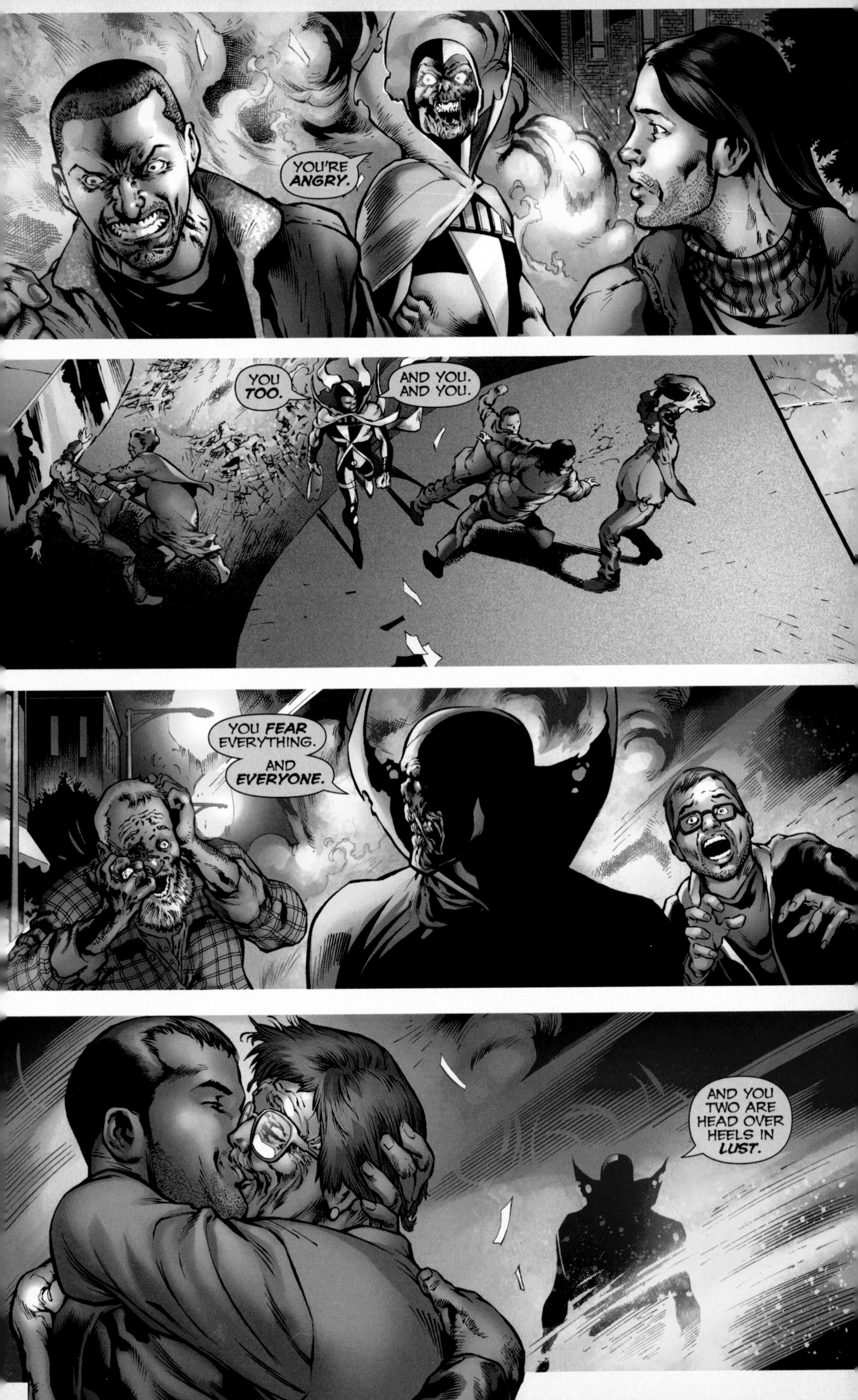
YOU'RE ANGRY.
YOU TOO.
AND YOU. AND YOU.
YOU FEAR EVERYTHING.
AND EVERYONE.
AND YOU TWO ARE HEAD OVER HEELS IN LUST.

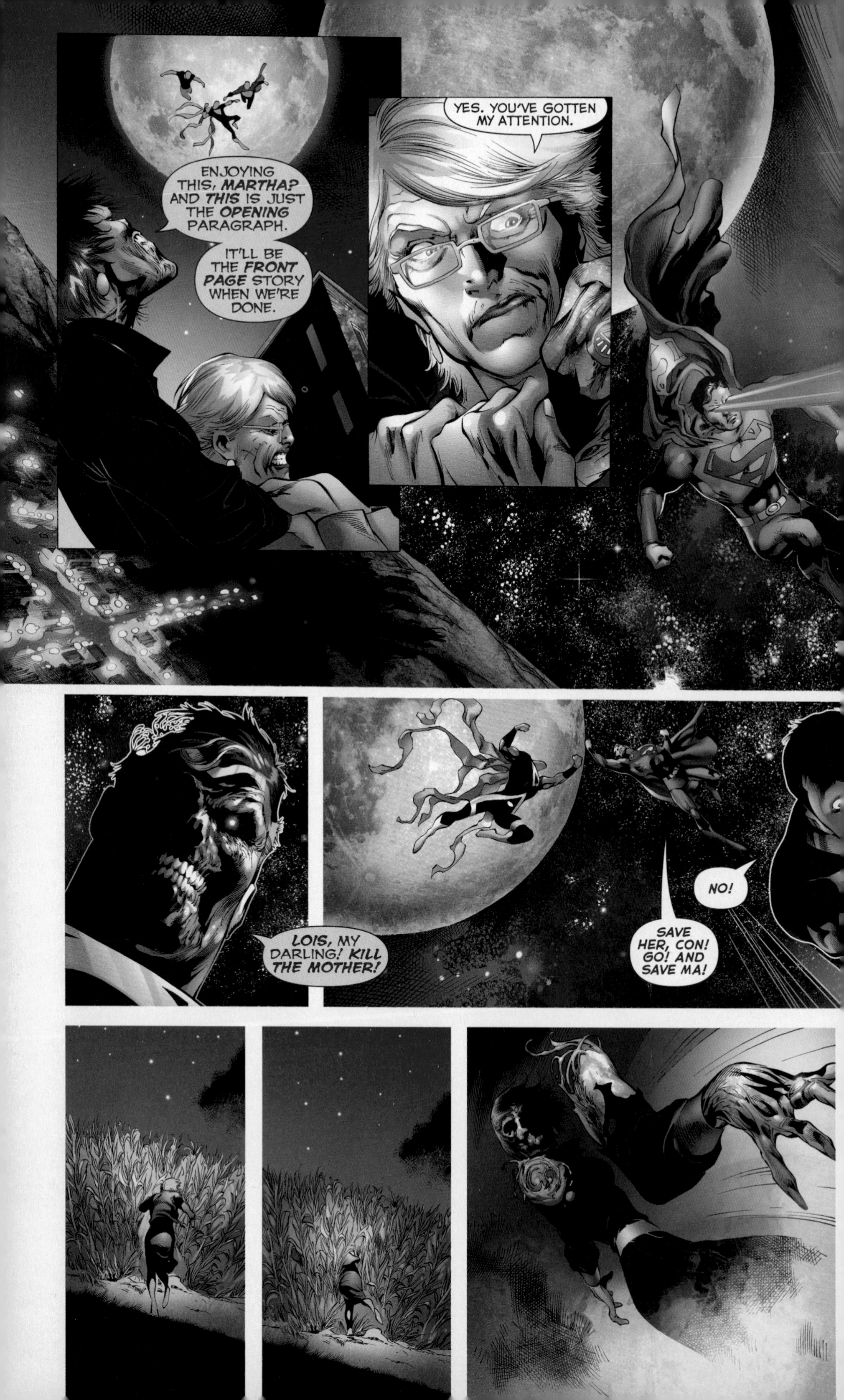
ENJOYING THIS, MARTHA? AND THIS IS JUST THE OPENING PARAGRAPH.
IT'LL BE THE FRONT PAGE STORY WHEN WE'RE DONE.
YES. YOU'VE GOTTEN MY ATTENTION.
LOIS, MY DARLING! KILL THE MOTHER!
NO!
SAVE HER, CON! GO! AND SAVE MA!

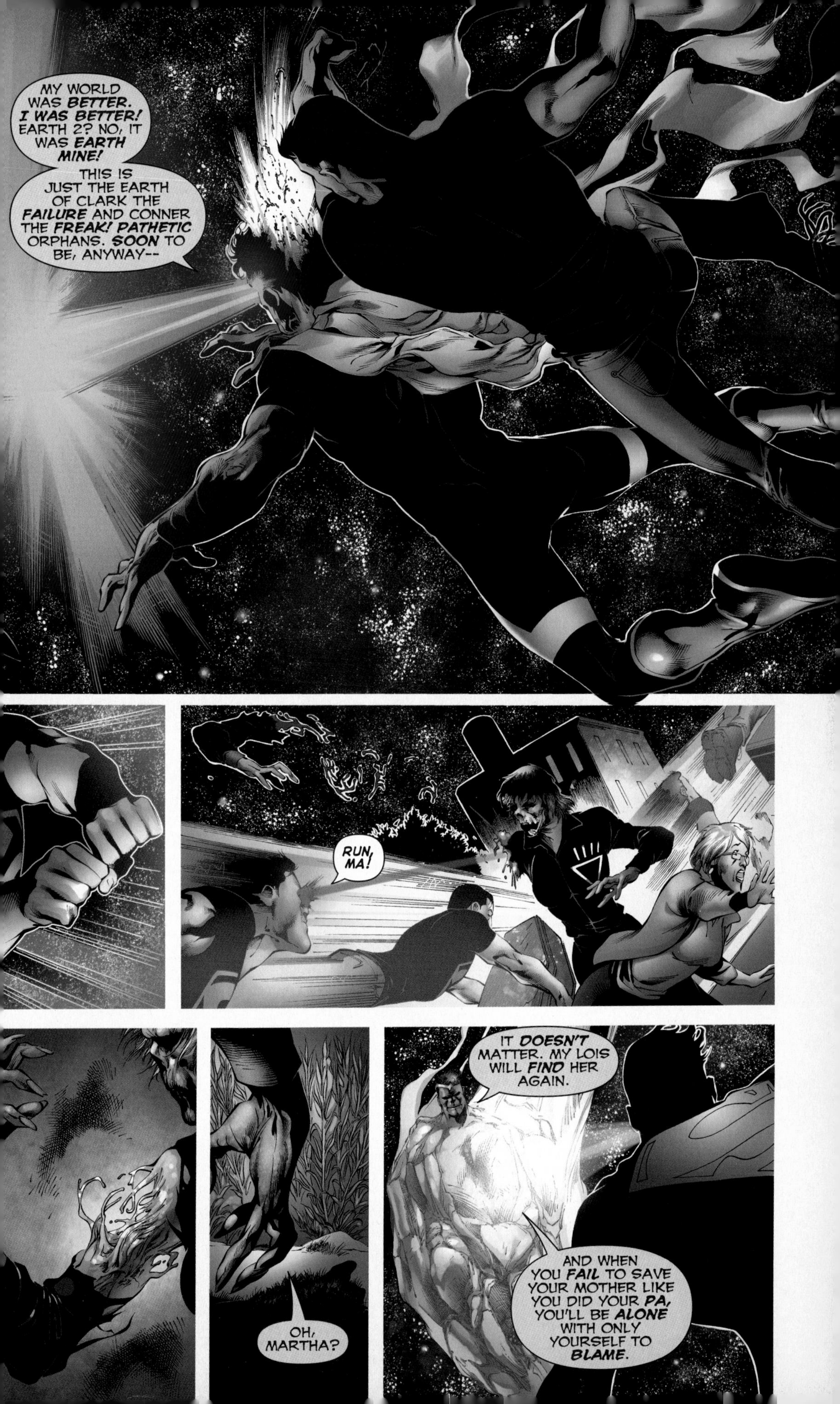
MY WORLD WAS BETTER. I WAS BETTER! EARTH 2? NO, IT WAS EARTH MINE!
THIS IS JUST THE EARTH OF CLARK THE FAILURE AND CONNER THE FREAK! PATHETIC ORPHANS. SOON TO BE, ANYWAY--
RUN, MA!
OH, MARTHA?
IT DOESN'T MATTER. MY LOIS WILL FIND HER AGAIN.
AND WHEN YOU FAIL TO SAVE YOUR MOTHER LIKE YOU DID YOUR PA, YOU'LL BE ALONE WITH ONLY YOURSELF TO BLAME.

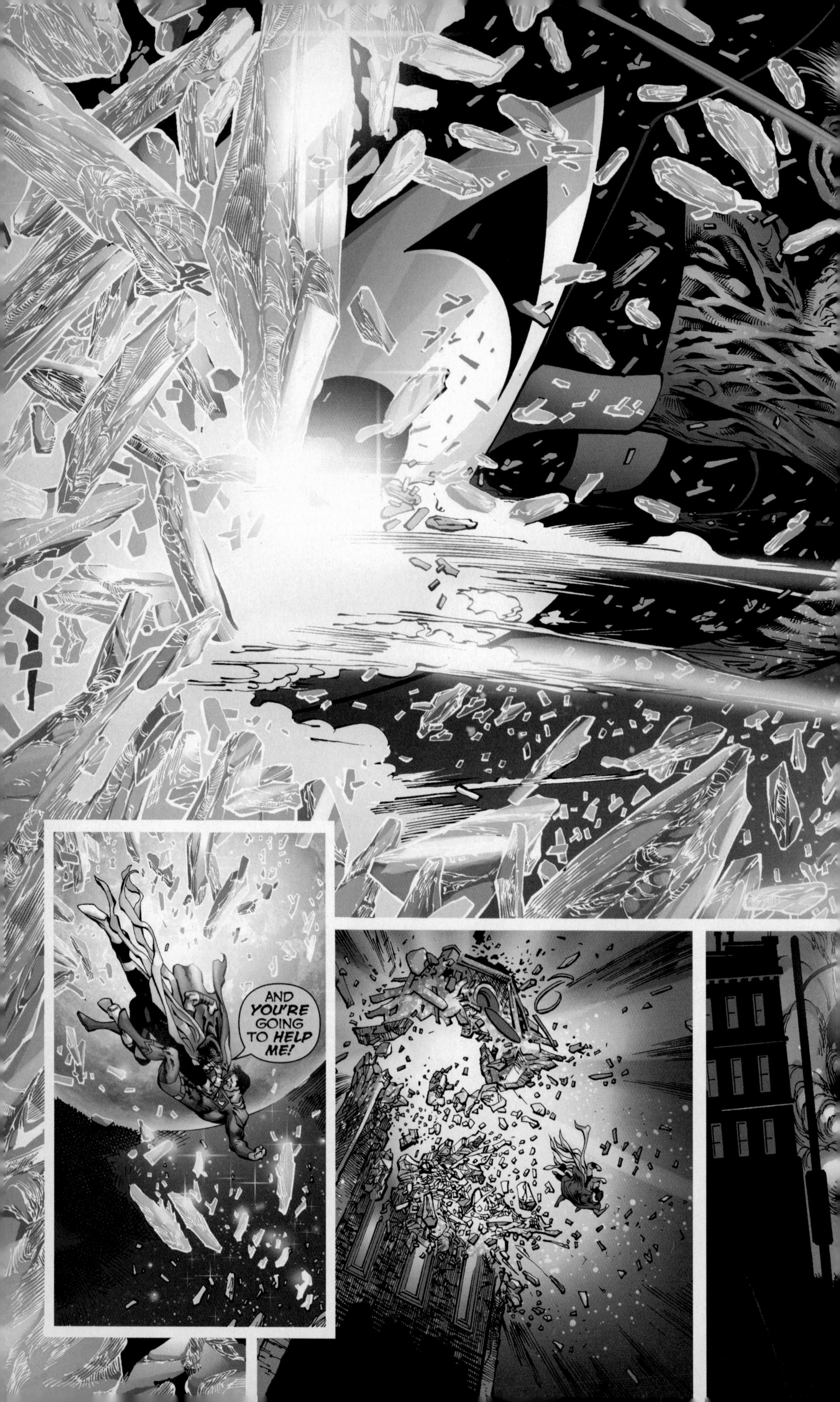
AND YOU'RE GOING TO HELP ME!

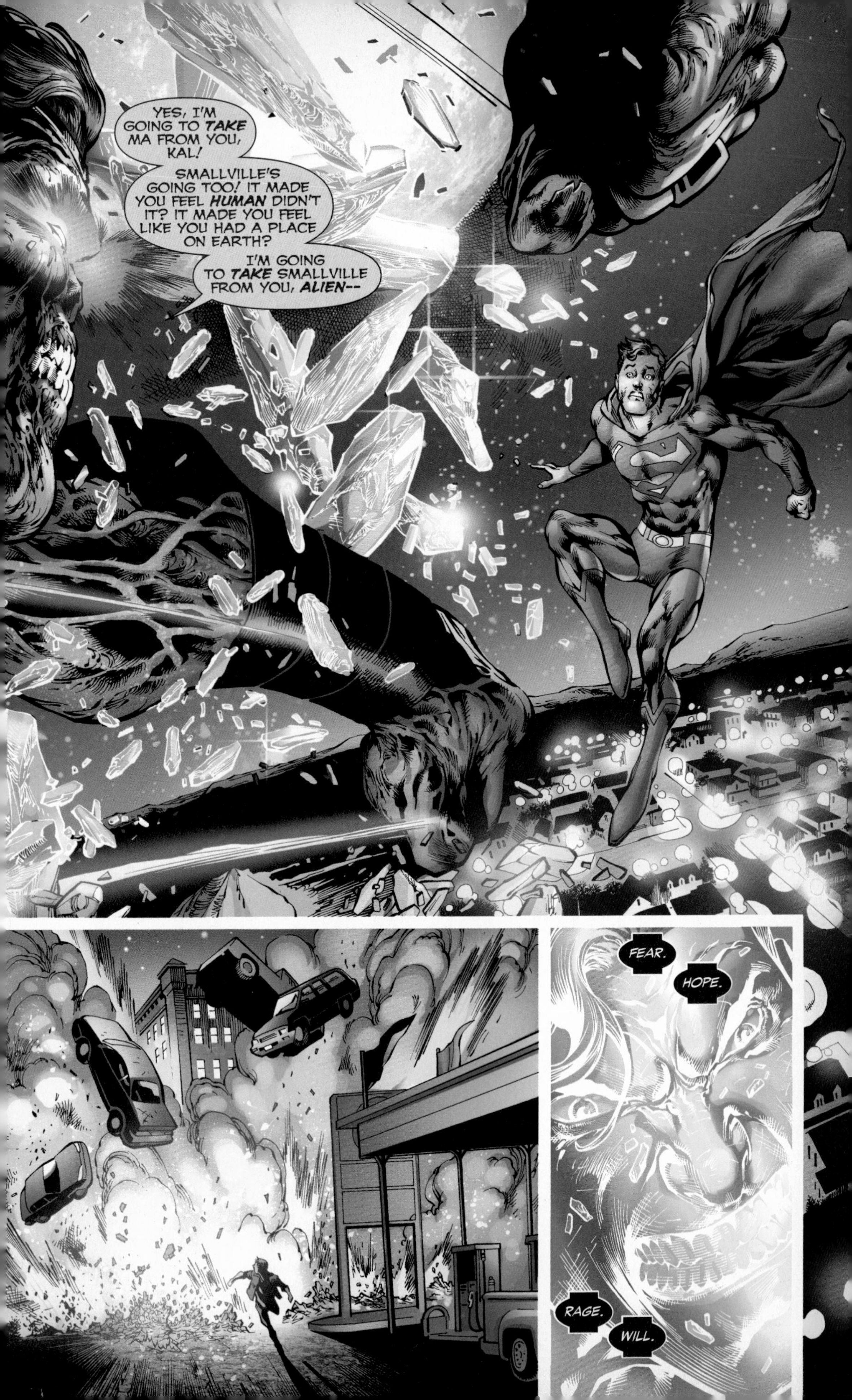
YES, I'M GOING TO *TAKE* MA FROM YOU, KAL!
SMALLVILLE'S GOING TOO! IT MADE YOU FEEL *HUMAN* DIDN'T IT? IT MADE YOU FEEL LIKE YOU HAD A PLACE ON EARTH?
I'M GOING TO *TAKE* SMALLVILLE FROM YOU, *ALIEN*--
FEAR.
HOPE.
RAGE.
WILL.

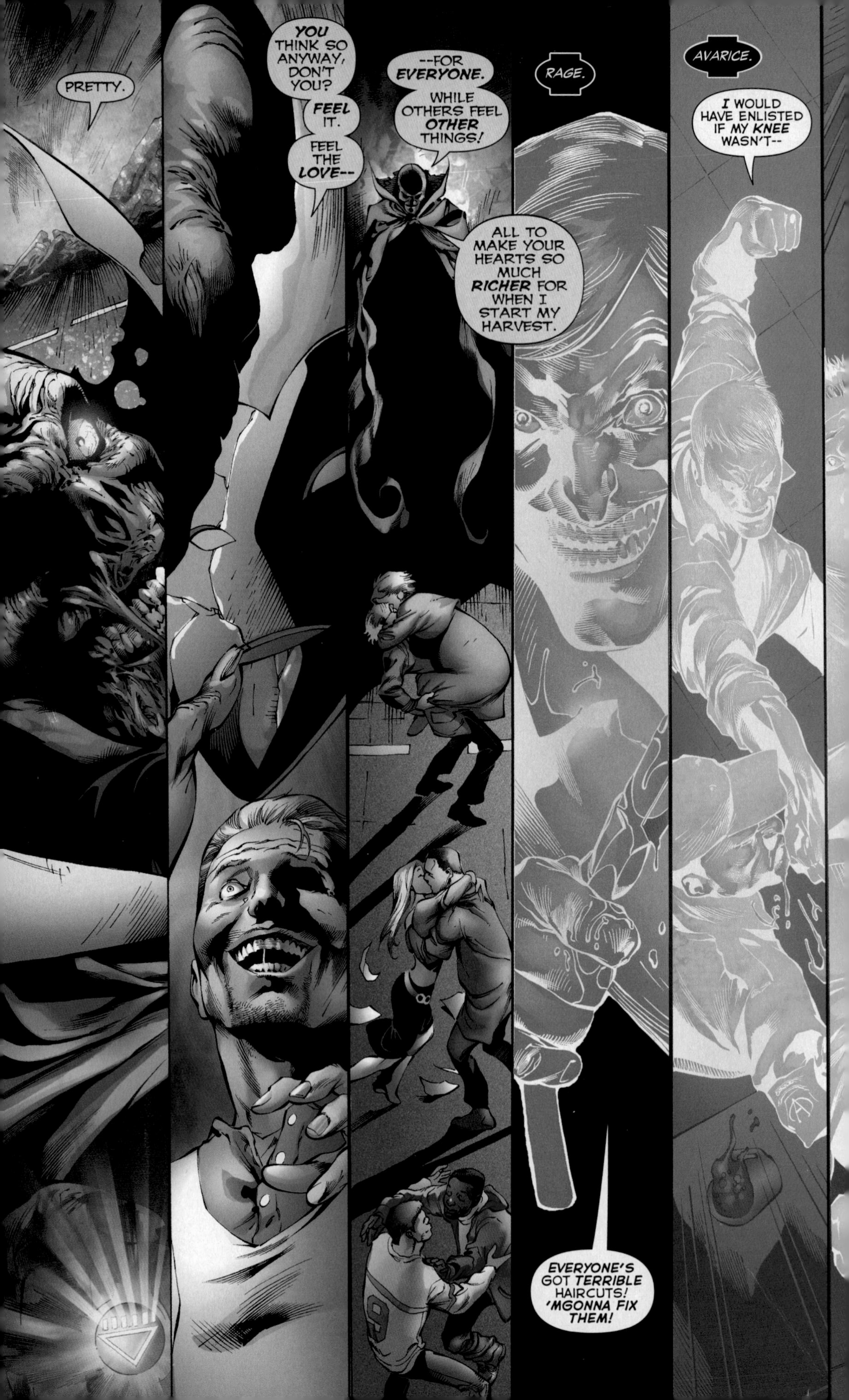
PRETTY.
YOU THINK SO ANYWAY, DON'T YOU?
FEEL IT.
FEEL THE LOVE--
--FOR EVERYONE.
WHILE OTHERS FEEL OTHER THINGS!
ALL TO MAKE YOUR HEARTS SO MUCH RICHER FOR WHEN I START MY HARVEST.
RAGE.
EVERYONE'S GOT TERRIBLE HAIRCUTS! 'MGONNA FIX THEM!
AVARICE.
I WOULD HAVE ENLISTED IF MY KNEE WASN'T--

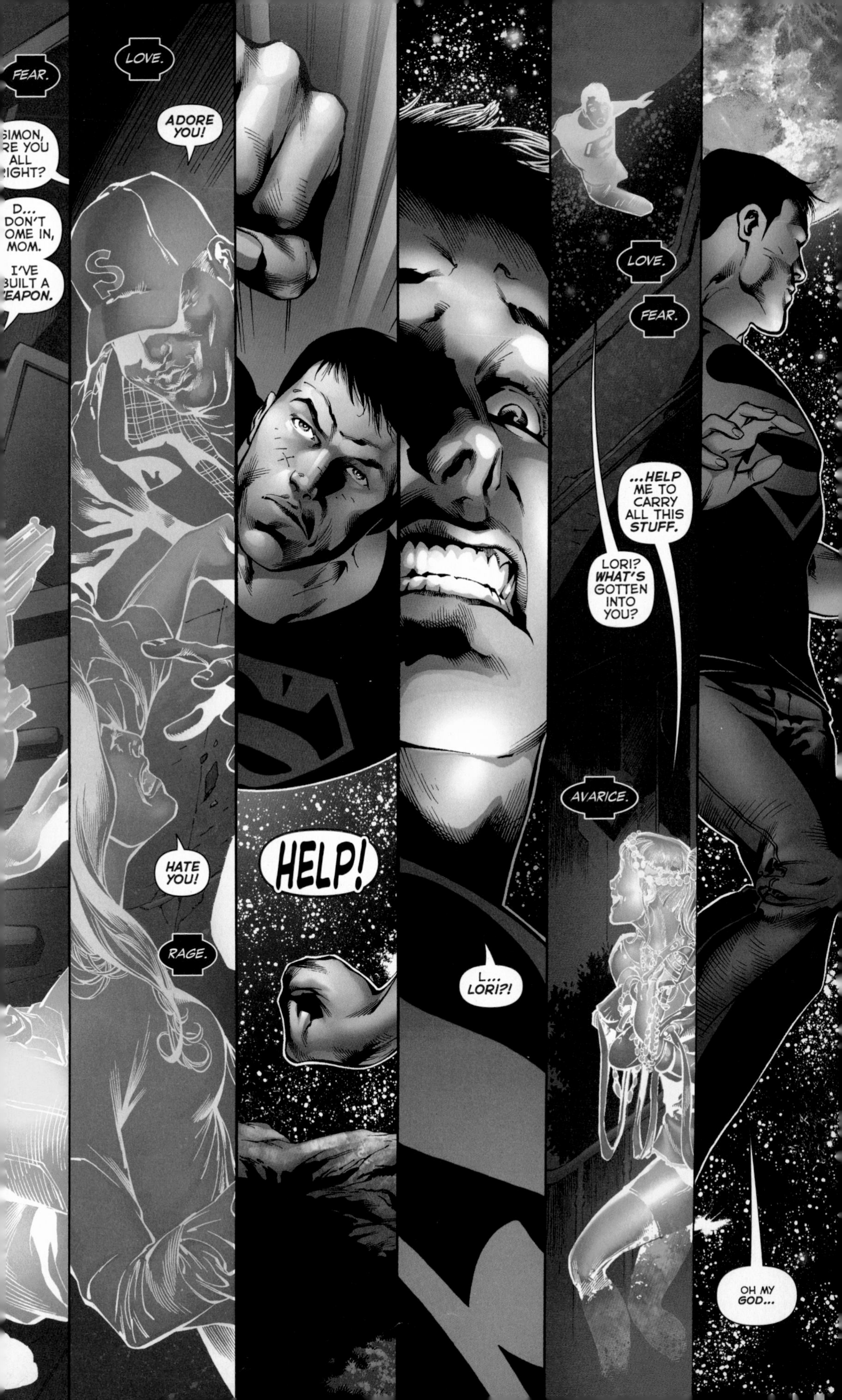

FEAR.
SIMON, ...RE YOU ALL ...RIGHT?
D... DON'T ...OME IN, MOM.
I'VE ...UILT A ...EAPON.
LOVE.
ADORE YOU!
HATE YOU!
RAGE.
HELP!
L... LORI?!
LOVE.
FEAR.
...HELP ME TO CARRY ALL THIS STUFF.
LORI? WHAT'S GOTTEN INTO YOU?
AVARICE.
OH MY GOD...

...WHAT'S GOTTEN INTO EVERYONE?

THAT WOULD BE ME. ROGER HAYDEN, THE PSYCHO-PIRATE!

I STEAL PEOPLE'S EMOTIONS.

AND GIVE THEM MINE.

WILL.

NO WAY, YOU SICK WEIRDO! GIVE ME BACK MY TOWN!

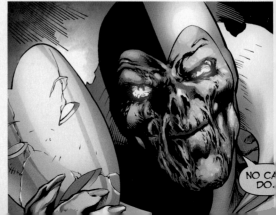

NO CA... DO.

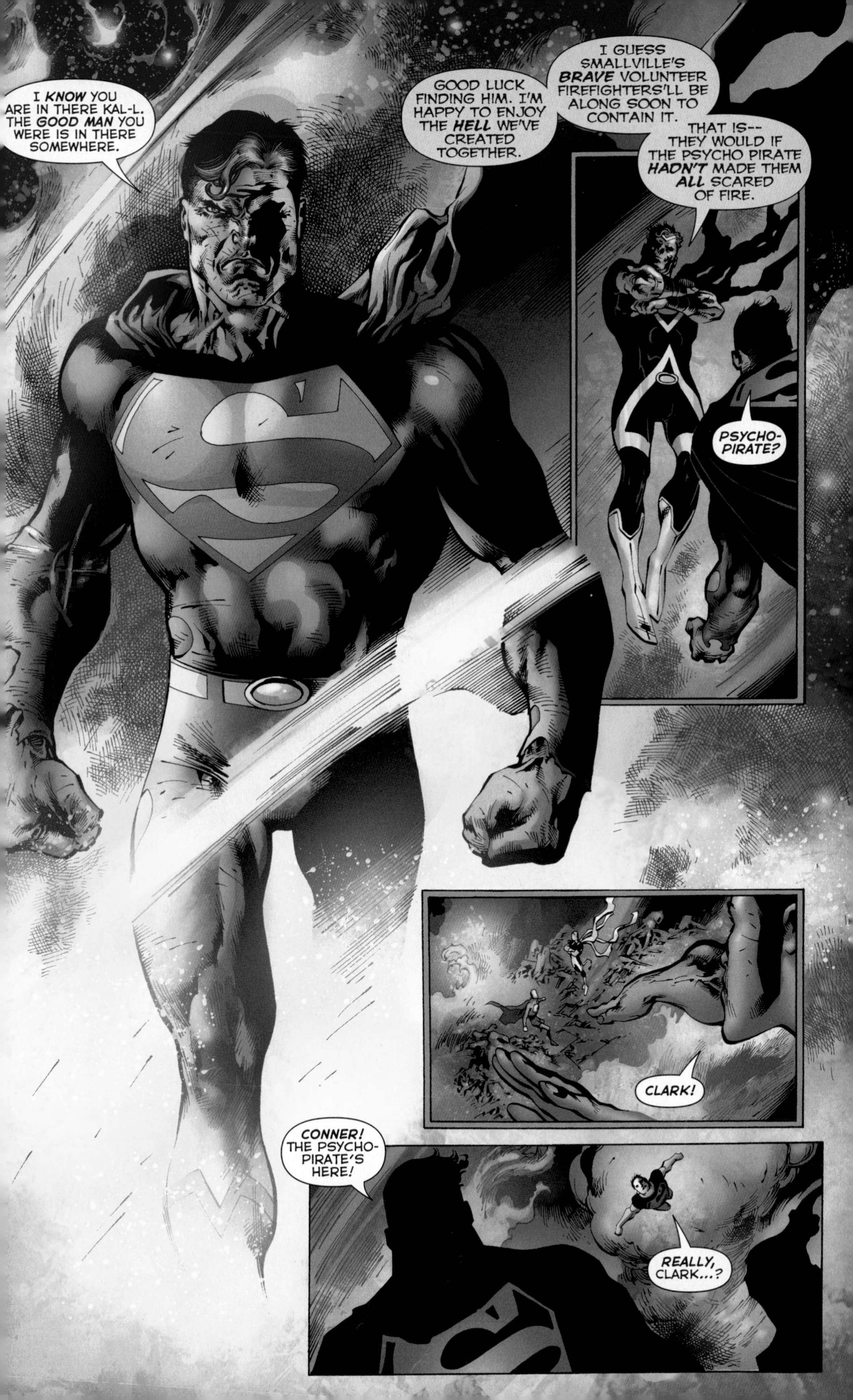
I KNOW YOU ARE IN THERE KAL-L. THE GOOD MAN YOU WERE IS IN THERE SOMEWHERE.
GOOD LUCK FINDING HIM. I'M HAPPY TO ENJOY THE HELL WE'VE CREATED TOGETHER.
I GUESS SMALLVILLE'S BRAVE VOLUNTEER FIREFIGHTERS'LL BE ALONG SOON TO CONTAIN IT.
THAT IS-- THEY WOULD IF THE PSYCHO PIRATE HADN'T MADE THEM ALL SCARED OF FIRE.
PSYCHO-PIRATE?
CLARK!
CONNER! THE PSYCHO-PIRATE'S HERE!
REALLY, CLARK...?

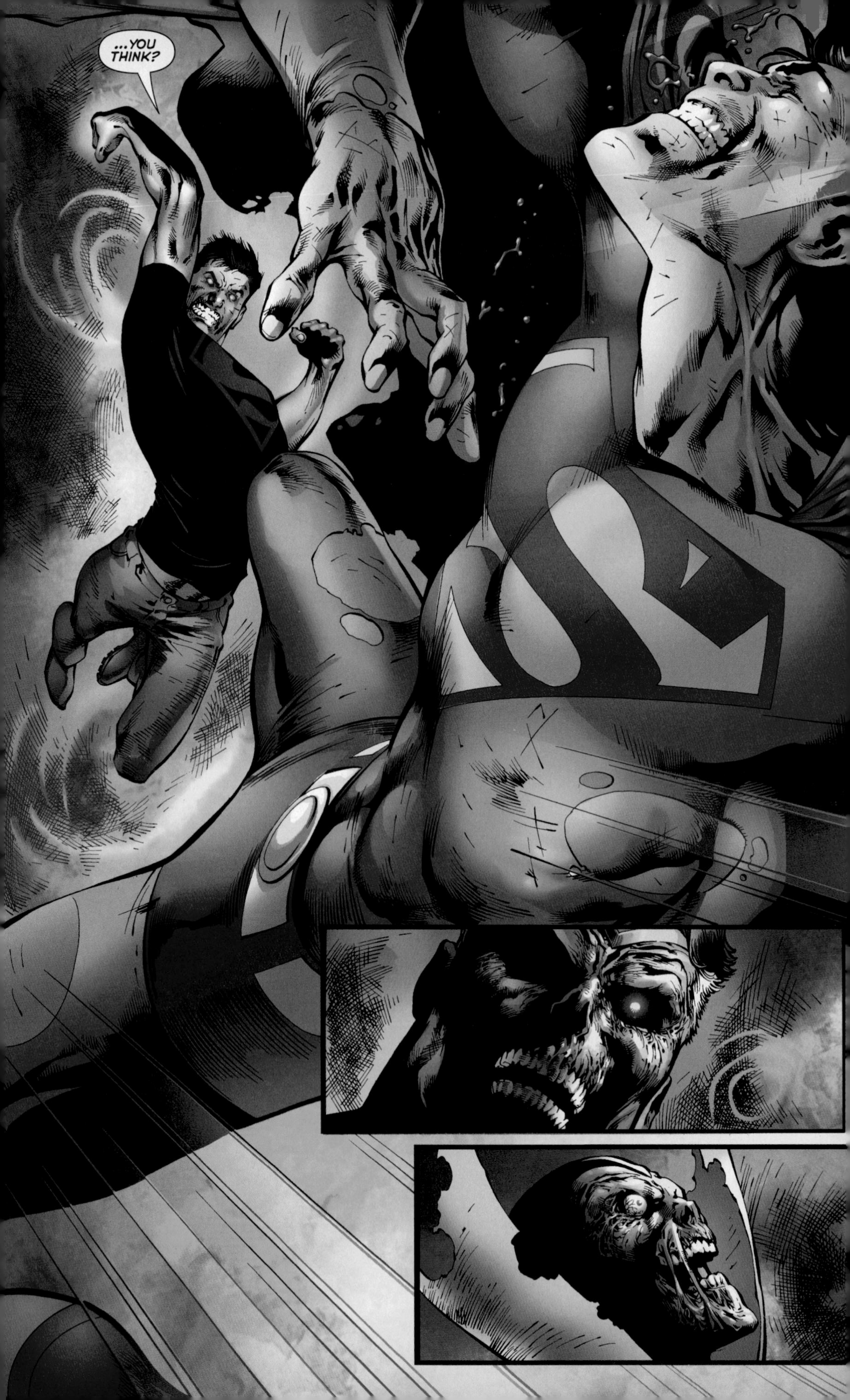
...YOU THINK?

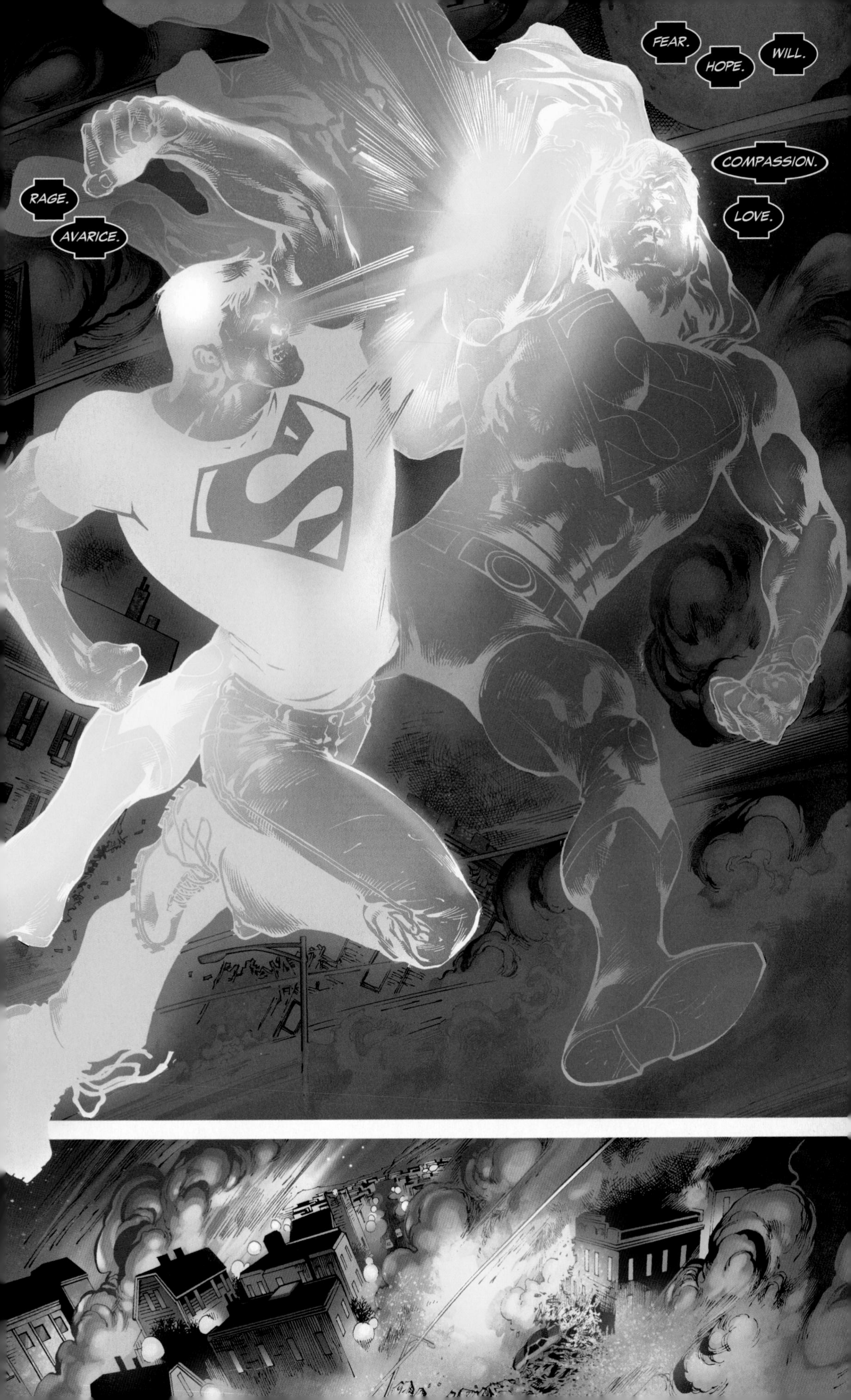
RAGE.
AVARICE.
FEAR.
HOPE.
WILL.
COMPASSION.
LOVE.

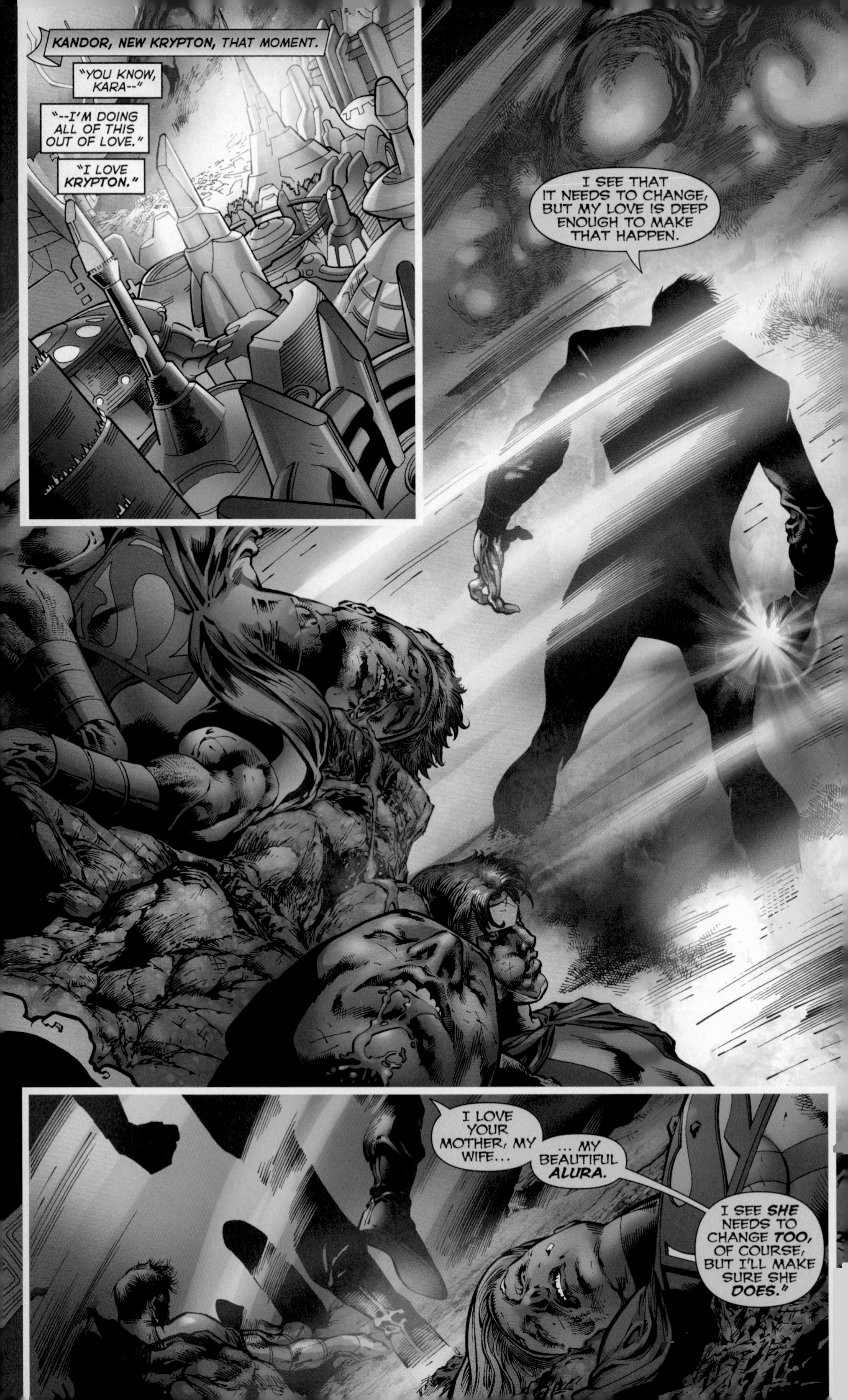
KANDOR, NEW KRYPTON, THAT MOMENT.
"YOU KNOW, KARA--"
"--I'M DOING ALL OF THIS OUT OF LOVE."
"I LOVE KRYPTON."
I SEE THAT IT NEEDS TO CHANGE, BUT MY LOVE IS DEEP ENOUGH TO MAKE THAT HAPPEN.
I LOVE YOUR MOTHER, MY WIFE...
... MY BEAUTIFUL ALURA.
I SEE SHE NEEDS TO CHANGE TOO, OF COURSE, BUT I'LL MAKE SURE SHE DOES."

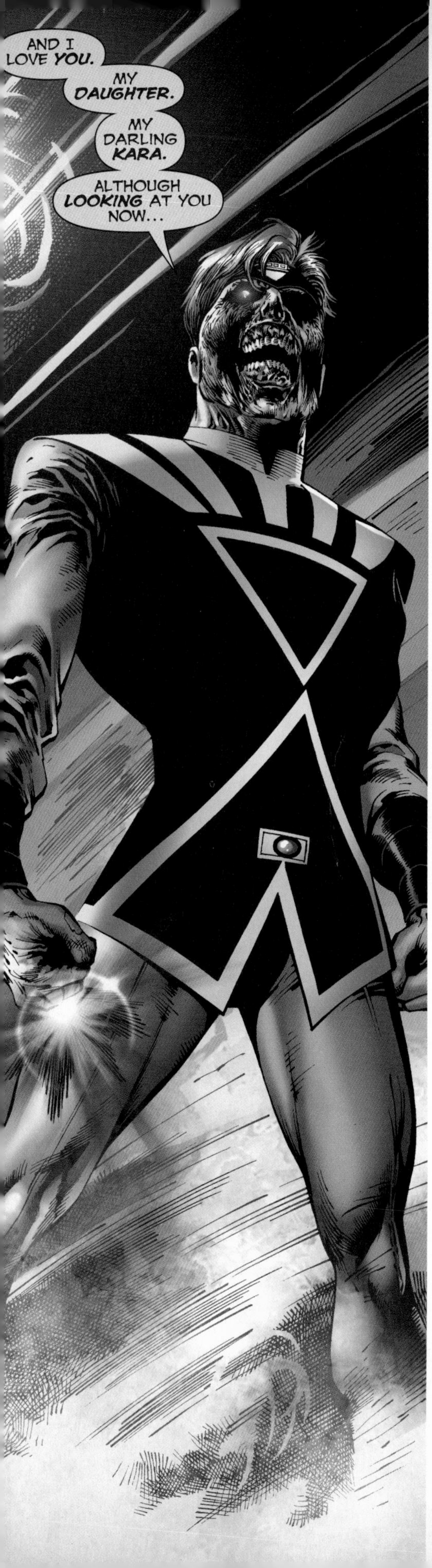
AND I LOVE YOU.
MY DAUGHTER.
MY DARLING KARA.
ALTHOUGH LOOKING AT YOU NOW...
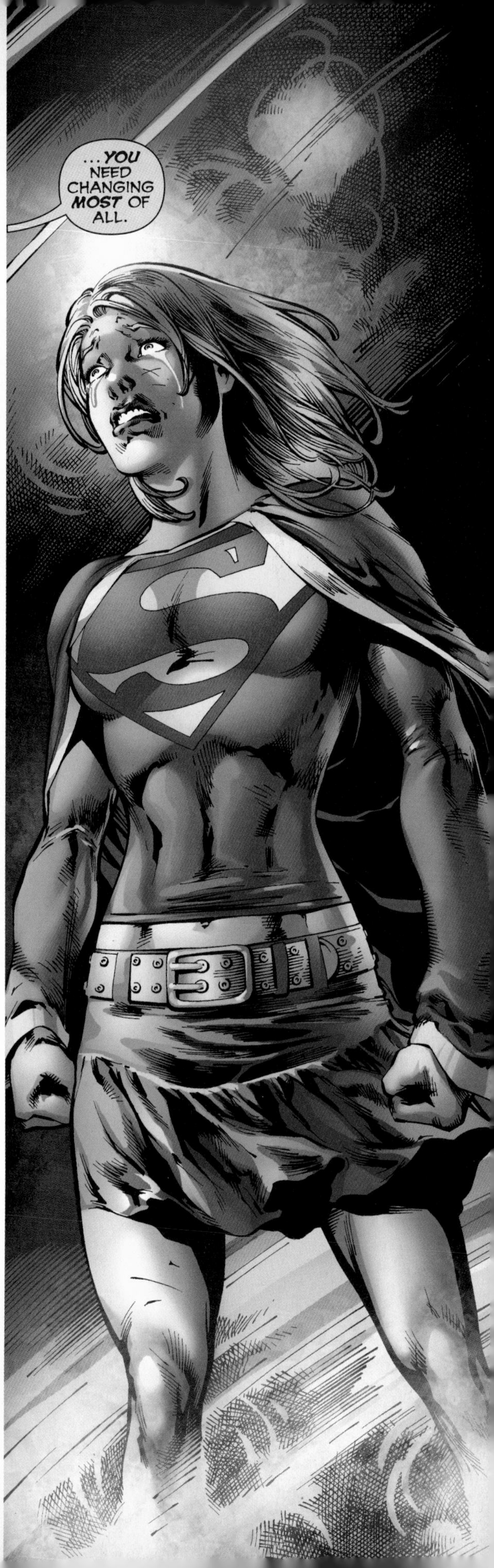
...YOU NEED CHANGING MOST OF ALL.

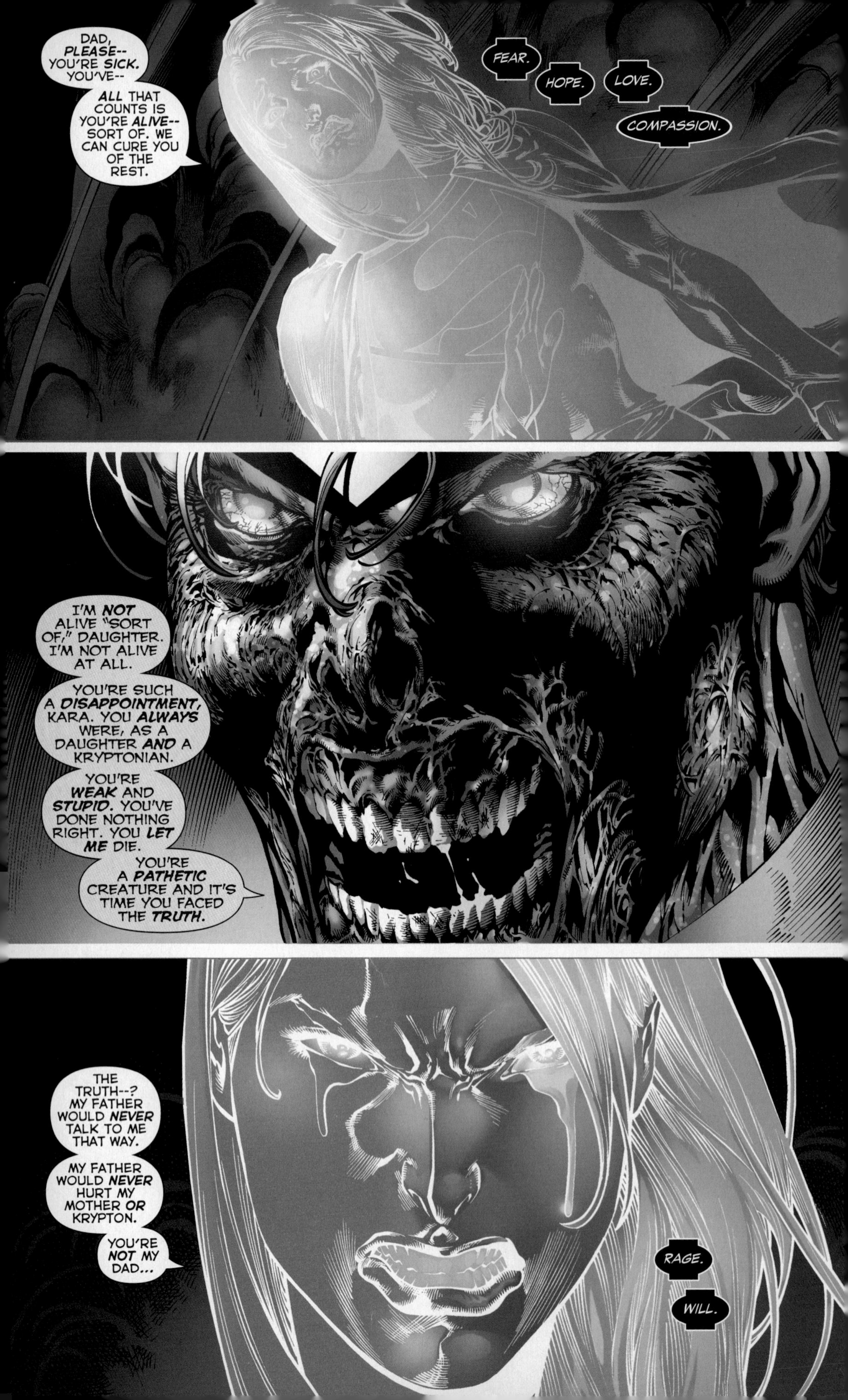
DAD, PLEASE-- YOU'RE SICK. YOU'VE--
ALL THAT COUNTS IS YOU'RE ALIVE-- SORT OF. WE CAN CURE YOU OF THE REST.
FEAR.
HOPE.
LOVE.
COMPASSION.
I'M NOT ALIVE "SORT OF," DAUGHTER. I'M NOT ALIVE AT ALL.
YOU'RE SUCH A DISAPPOINTMENT, KARA. YOU ALWAYS WERE, AS A DAUGHTER AND A KRYPTONIAN.
YOU'RE WEAK AND STUPID. YOU'VE DONE NOTHING RIGHT. YOU LET ME DIE.
YOU'RE A PATHETIC CREATURE AND IT'S TIME YOU FACED THE TRUTH.
THE TRUTH--? MY FATHER WOULD NEVER TALK TO ME THAT WAY.
MY FATHER WOULD NEVER HURT MY MOTHER OR KRYPTON.
YOU'RE NOT MY DAD...
RAGE.
WILL.

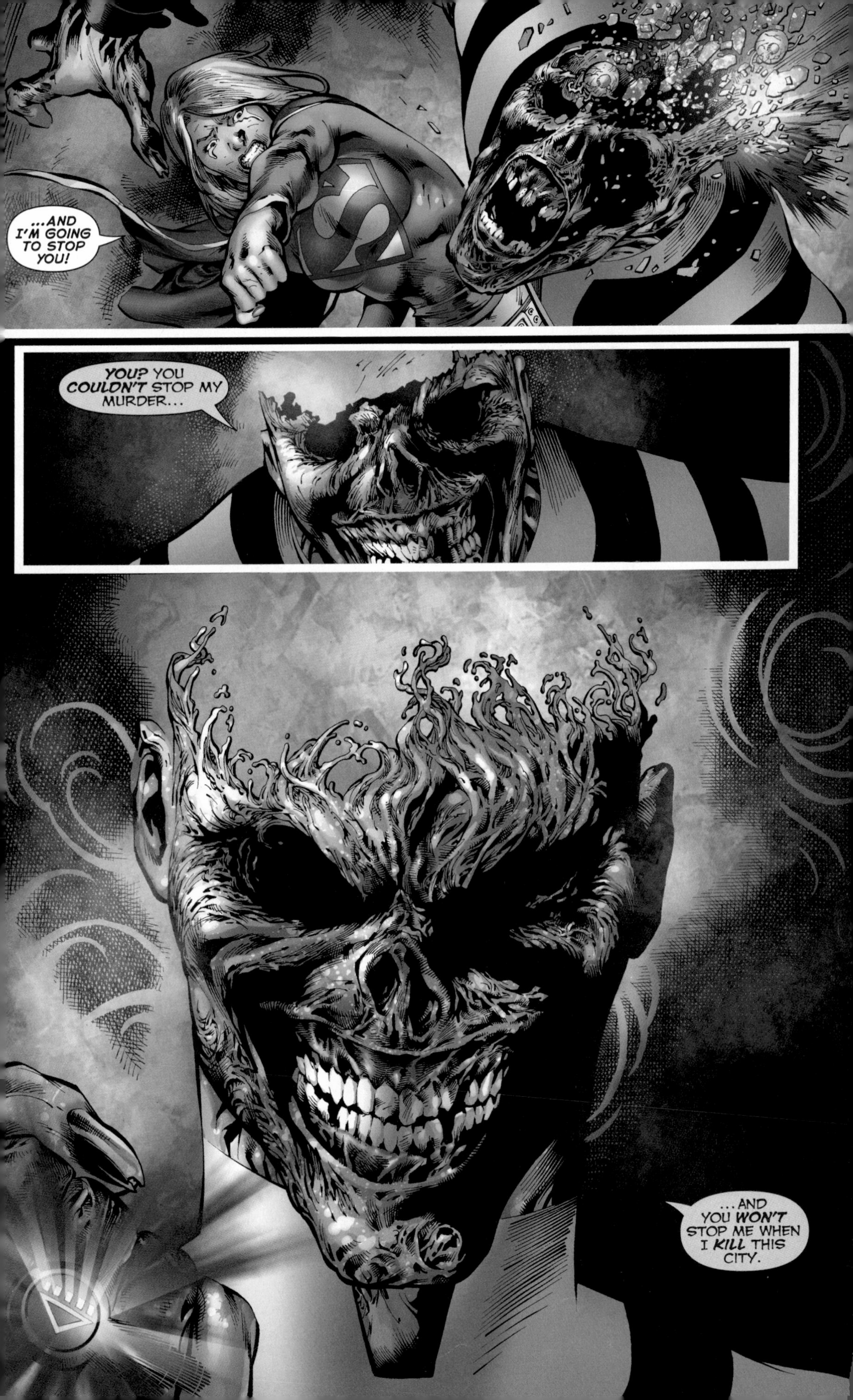
...AND I'M GOING TO STOP YOU!
YOU? YOU COULDN'T STOP MY MURDER...
...AND YOU WON'T STOP ME WHEN I KILL THIS CITY.

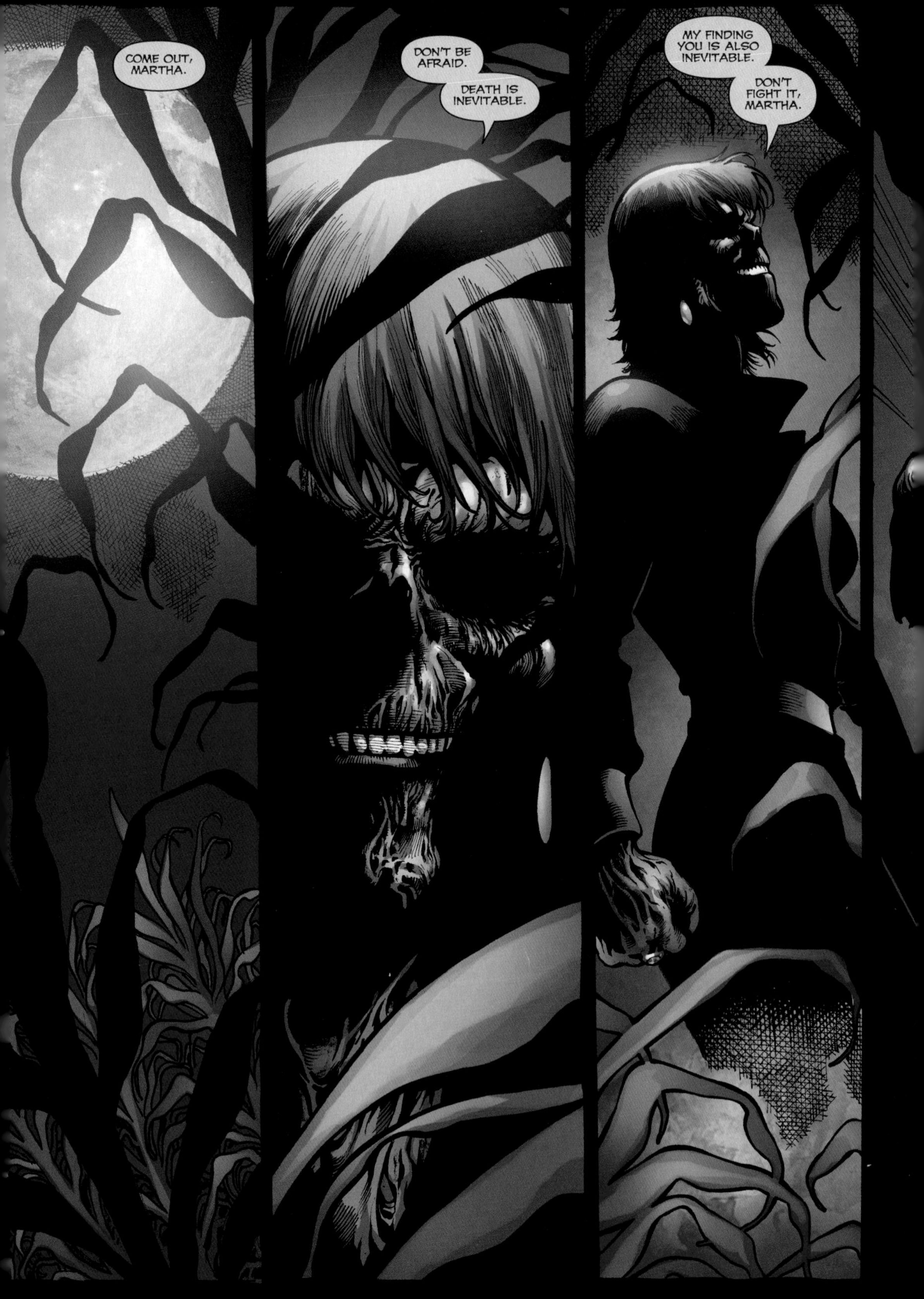
COME OUT, MARTHA.
DON'T BE AFRAID.
DEATH IS INEVITABLE.
MY FINDING YOU IS ALSO INEVITABLE.
DON'T FIGHT IT, MARTHA.

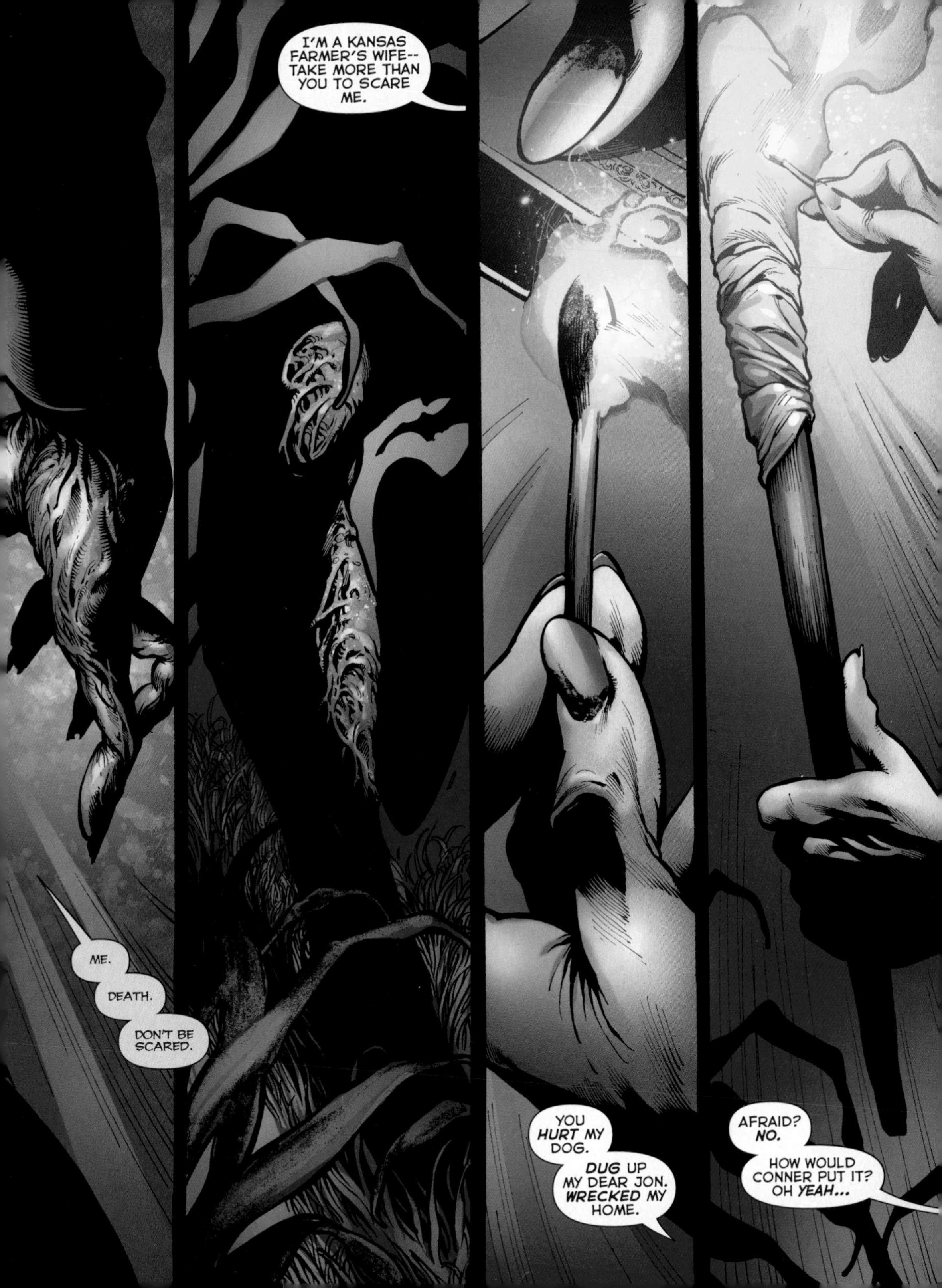
ME.
DEATH.
DON'T BE SCARED.
I'M A KANSAS FARMER'S WIFE-- TAKE MORE THAN YOU TO SCARE ME.
YOU *HURT* MY DOG.
DUG UP MY DEAR JON. *WRECKED* MY HOME.
AFRAID? *NO.*
HOW WOULD CONNER PUT IT? OH *YEAH...*

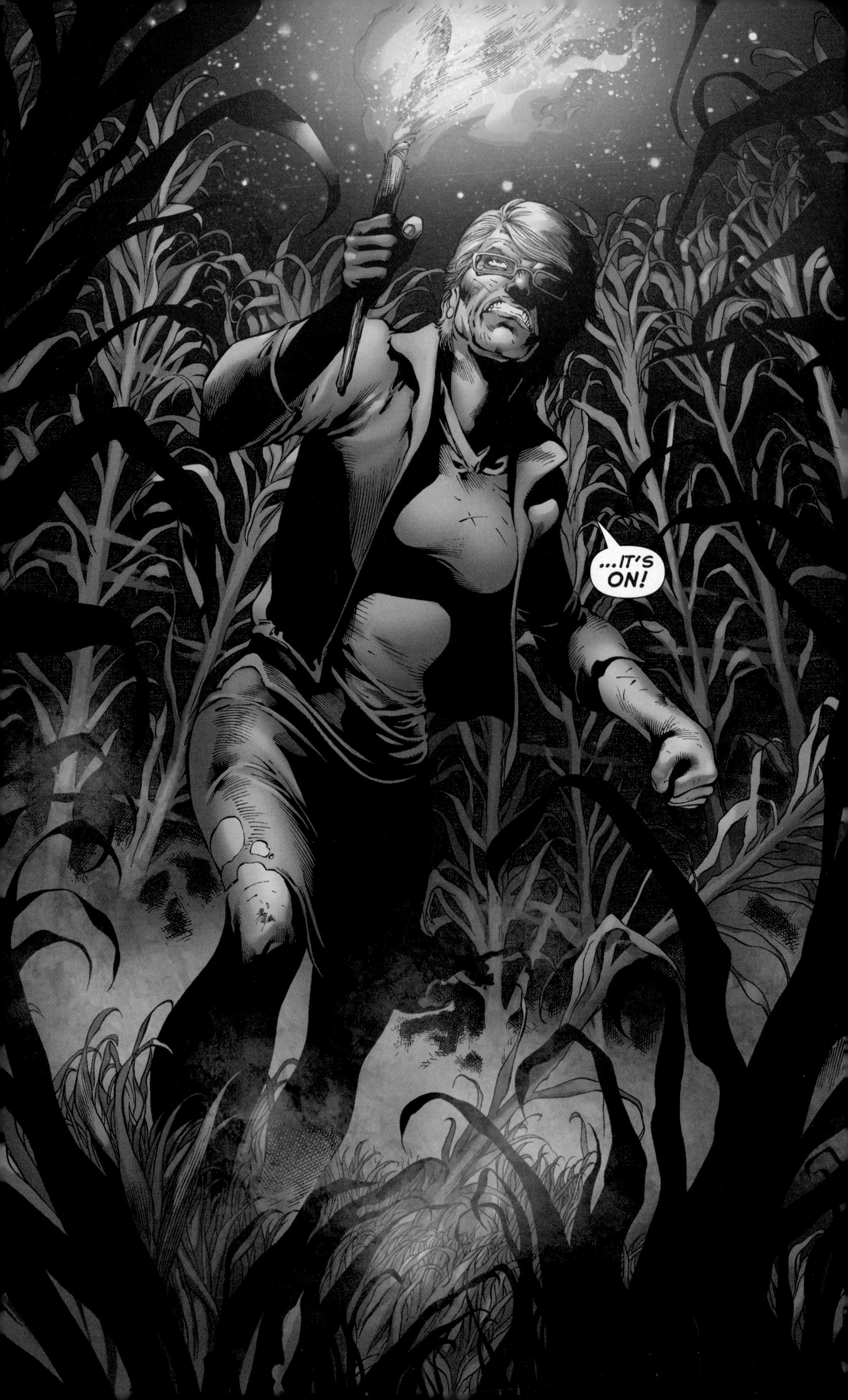
...IT'S ON!

BLACKEST NIGHT: SUPERMAN 3

Cover by Eddy Barrows with Nei Ruffino

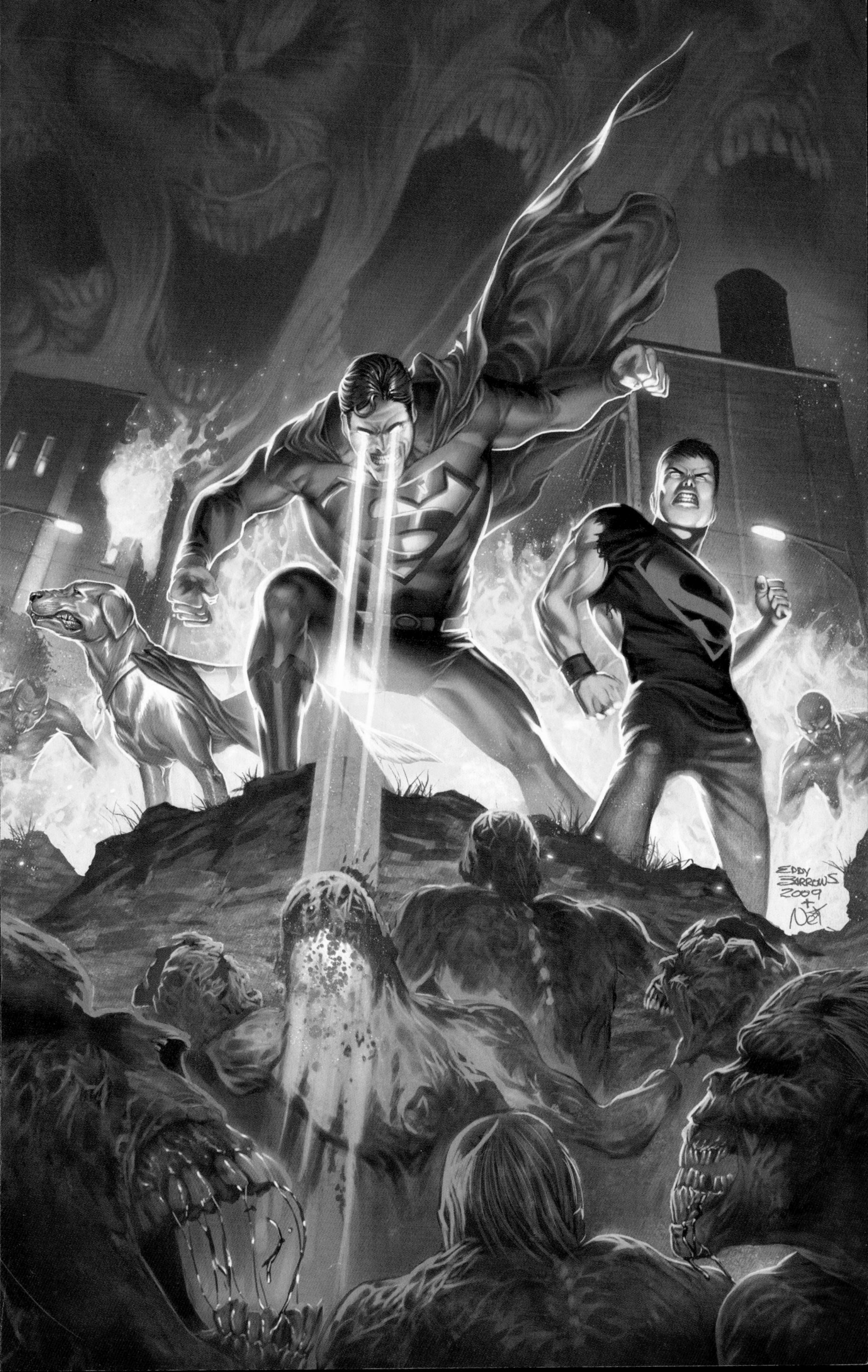
EDDY BARROWS 2009 + NEI

THE LONG DARK NIGHT

JAMES ROBINSON
WRITER

EDDY BARROWS
ALLAN GOLDMAN
PENCILS

RUY JOSÉ
EBER FERREIRA
INKS

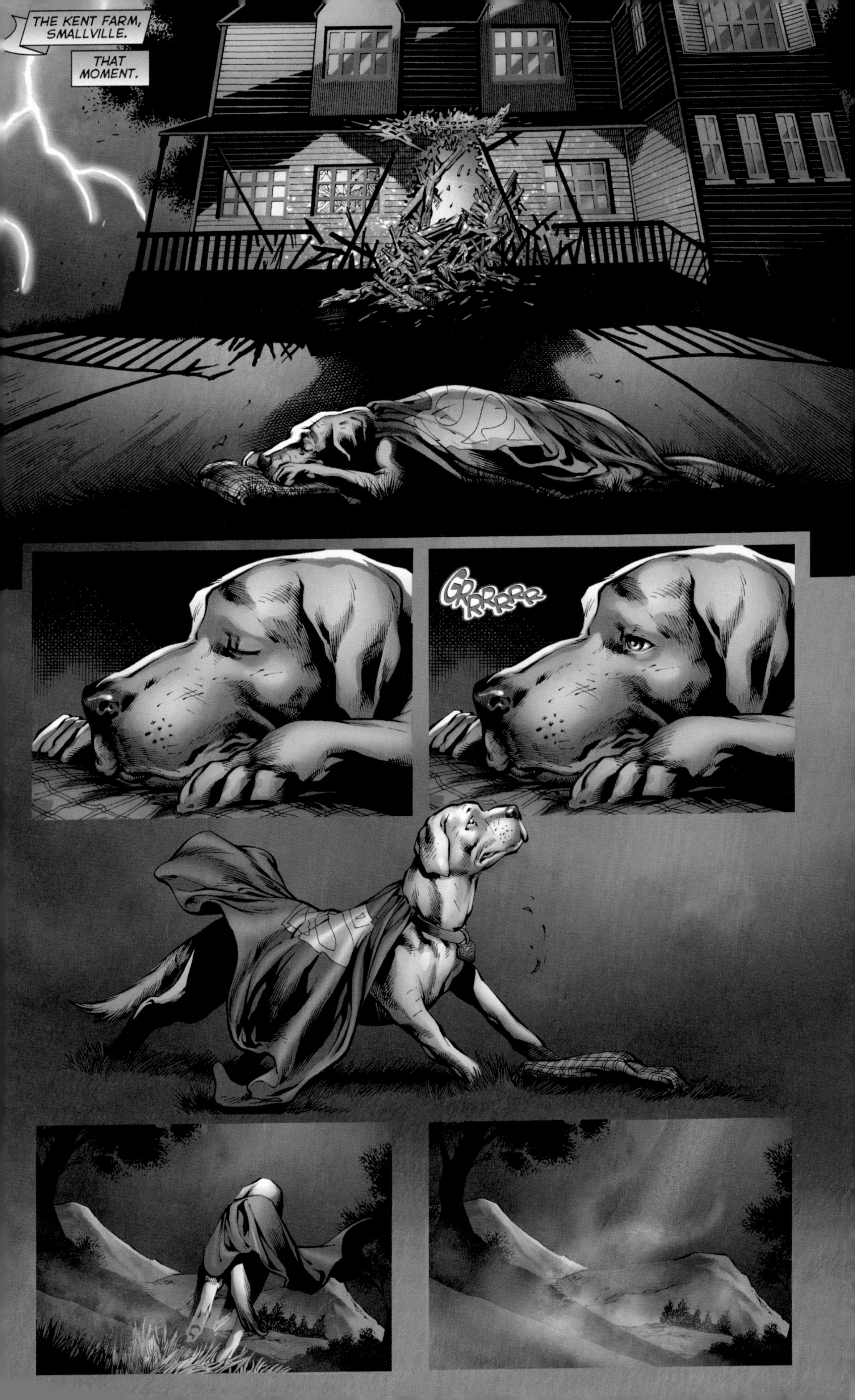
THE KENT FARM, SMALLVILLE.
THAT MOMENT.
GRRRRRR

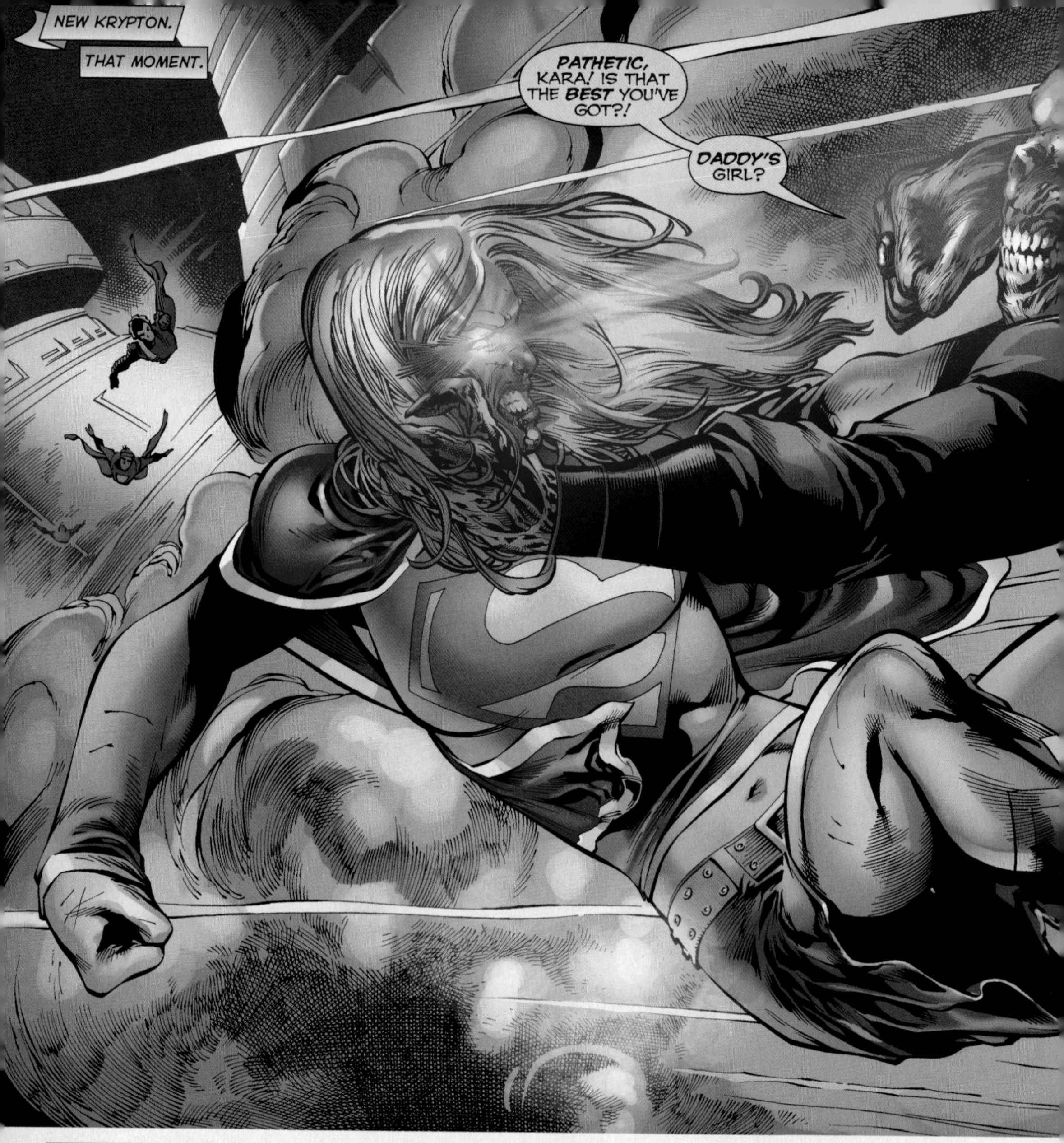
NEW KRYPTON.
THAT MOMENT.
PATHETIC, KARA! IS THAT THE BEST YOU'VE GOT?!
DADDY'S GIRL?

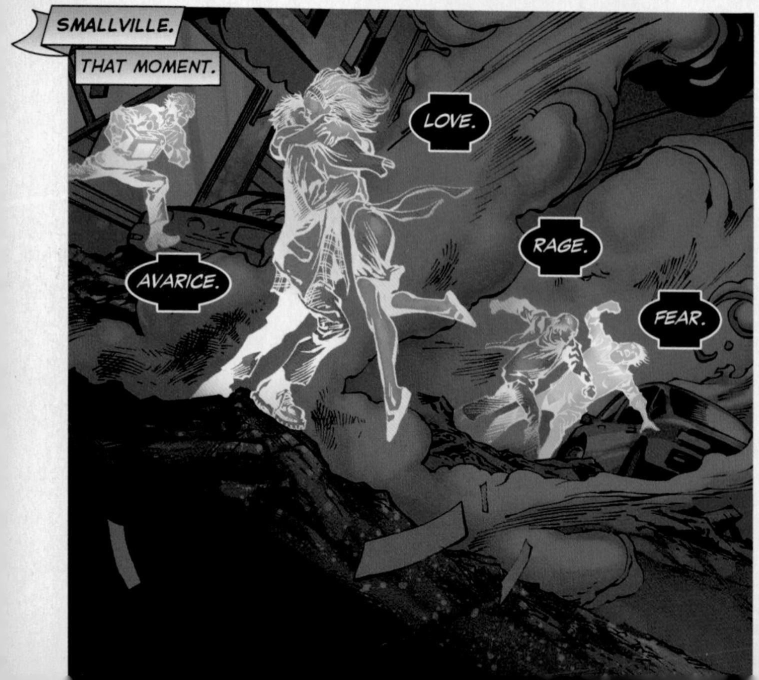
SMALLVILLE.
THAT MOMENT.
LOVE.
RAGE.
AVARICE.
FEAR.

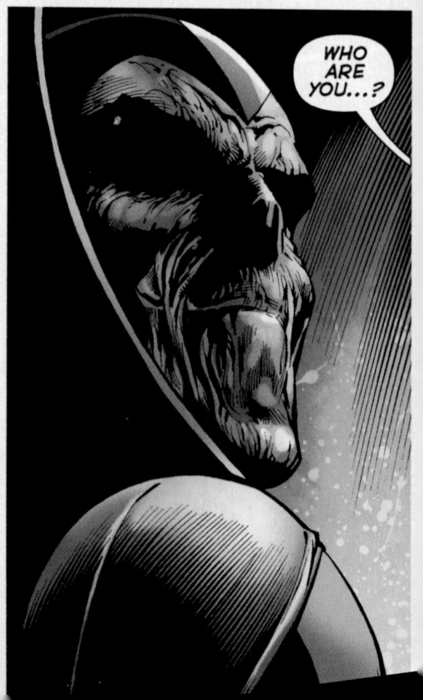
WHO ARE YOU...?

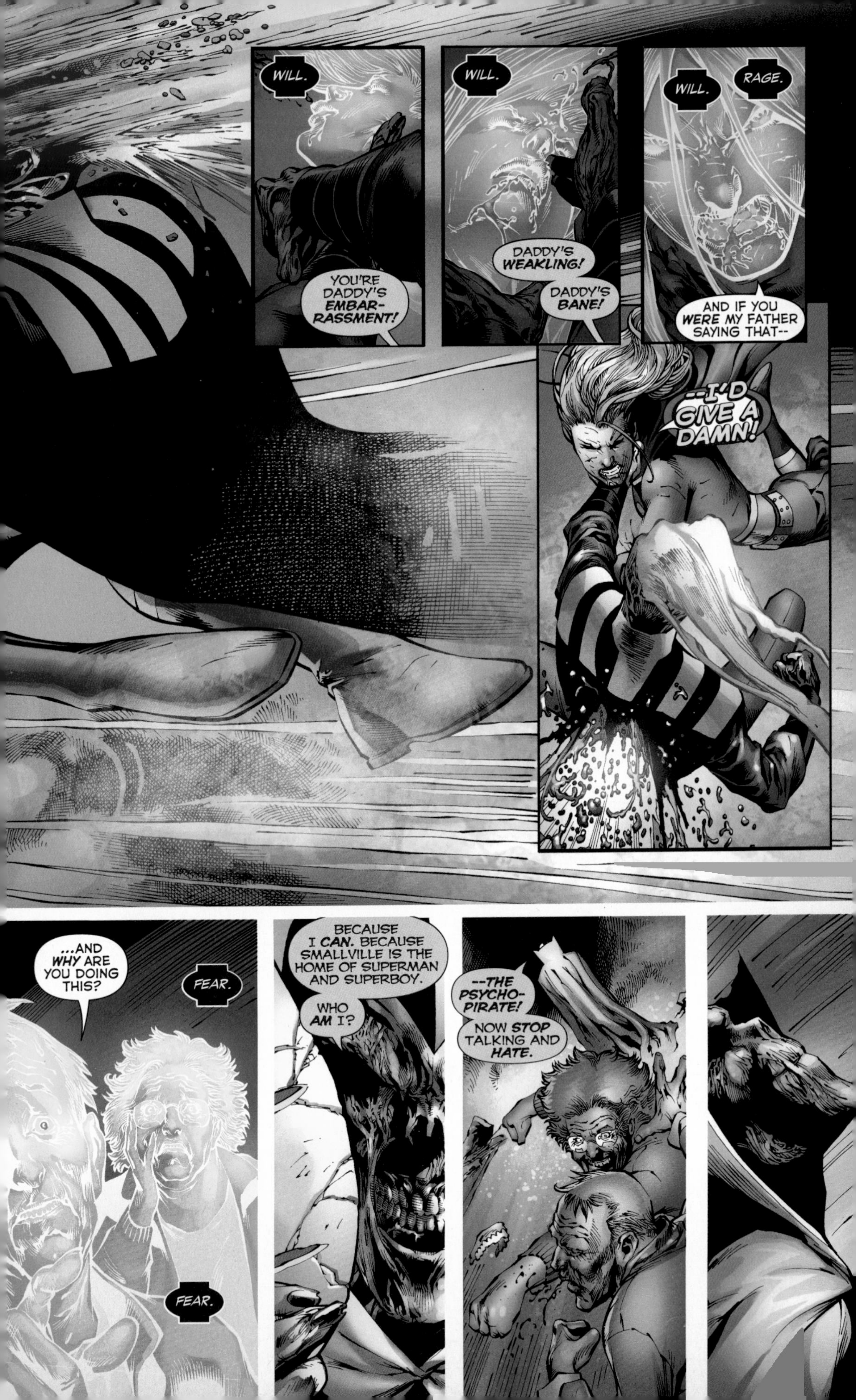
WILL.
YOU'RE DADDY'S EMBAR-RASSMENT!
WILL.
DADDY'S WEAKLING!
DADDY'S BANE!
WILL.
RAGE.
AND IF YOU WERE MY FATHER SAYING THAT--
--I'D GIVE A DAMN!
...AND WHY ARE YOU DOING THIS?
FEAR.
FEAR.
BECAUSE I CAN. BECAUSE SMALLVILLE IS THE HOME OF SUPERMAN AND SUPERBOY.
WHO AM I?
--THE PSYCHO-PIRATE!
NOW STOP TALKING AND HATE.

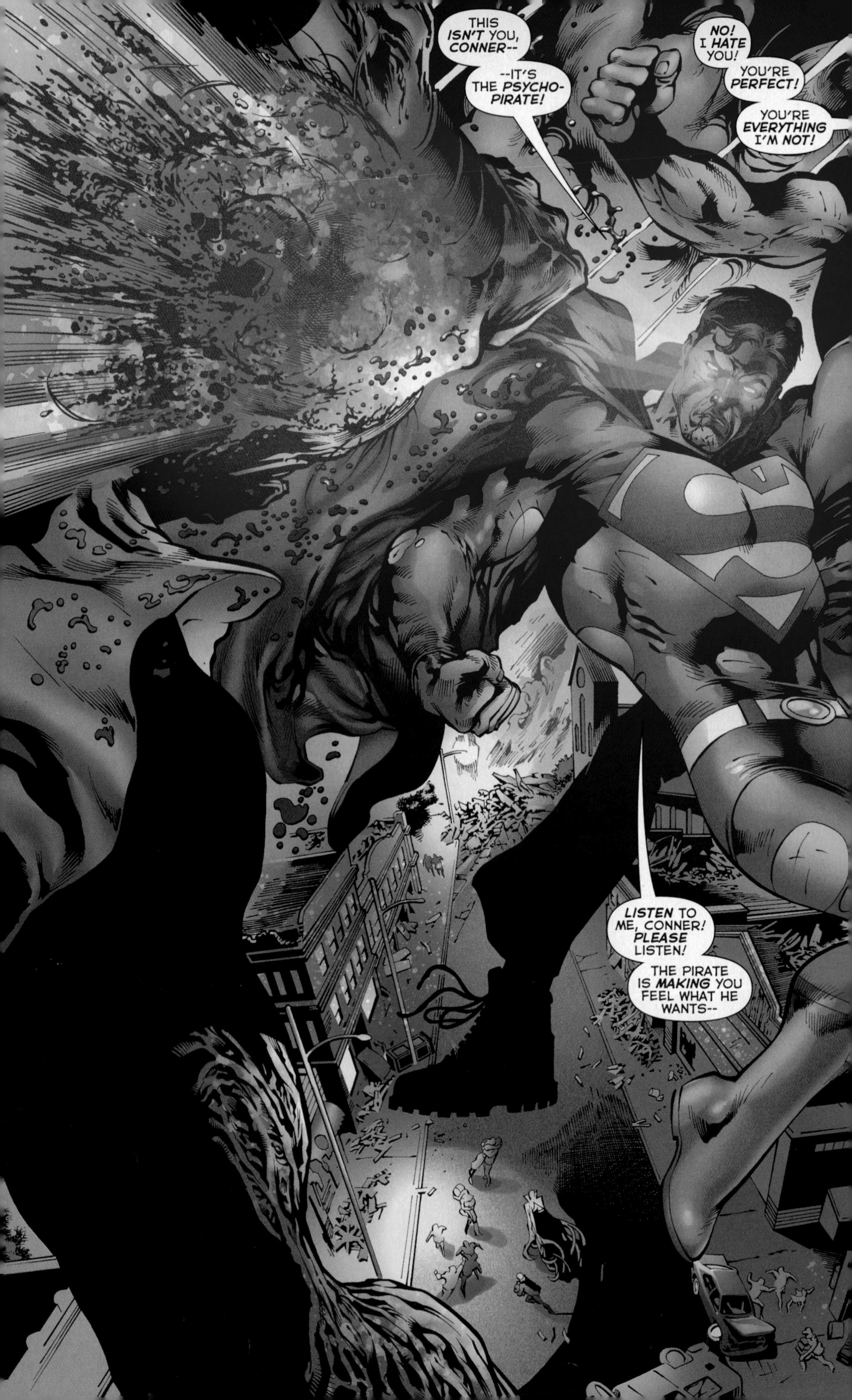
THIS ISN'T YOU, CONNER--
--IT'S THE PSYCHO-PIRATE!
NO! I HATE YOU!
YOU'RE PERFECT!
YOU'RE EVERYTHING I'M NOT!
LISTEN TO ME, CONNER! PLEASE LISTEN!
THE PIRATE IS MAKING YOU FEEL WHAT HE WANTS--

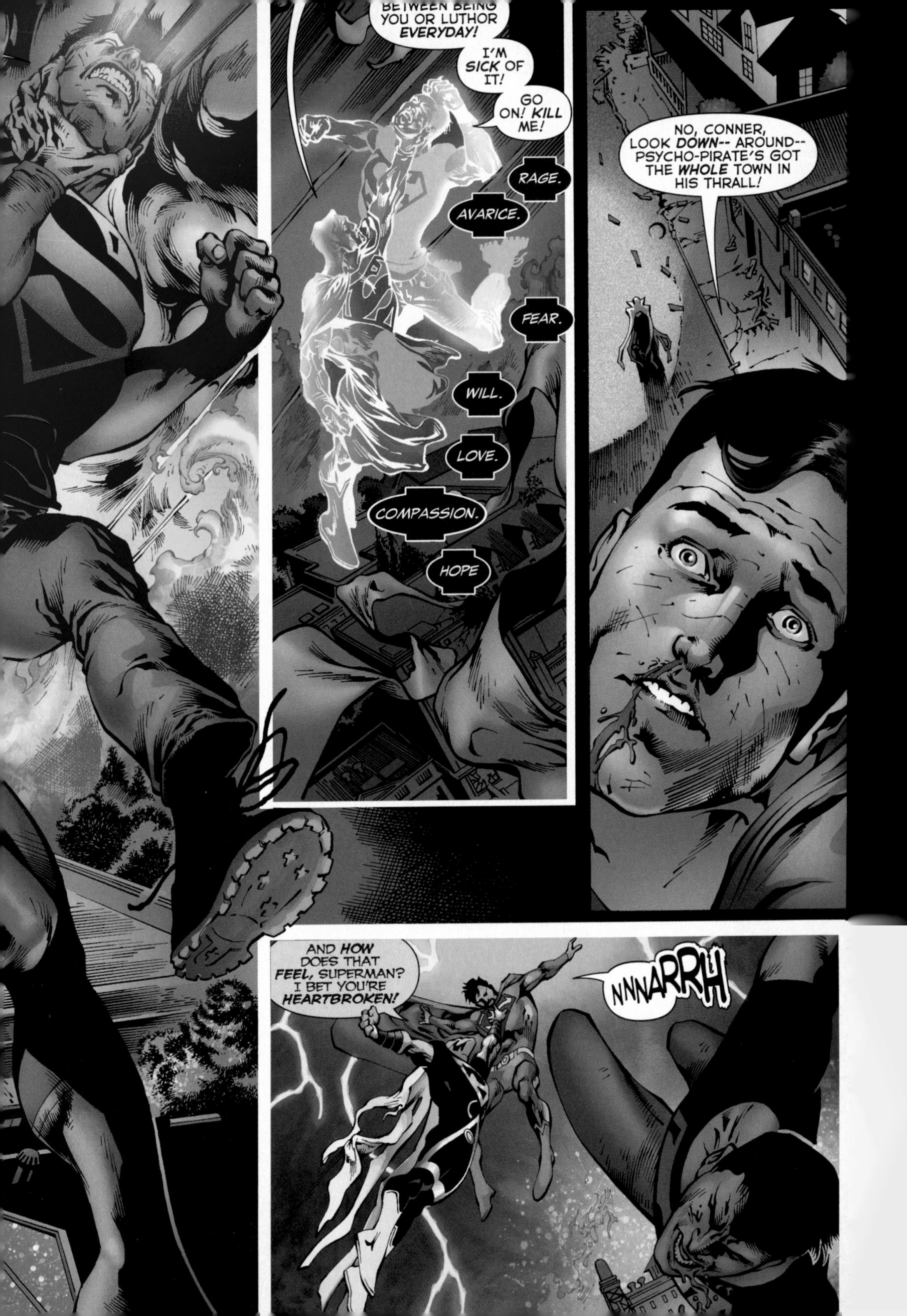

BETWEEN BEING YOU OR LUTHOR EVERYDAY!
I'M SICK OF IT!
GO ON! KILL ME!
RAGE.
AVARICE.
FEAR.
WILL.
LOVE.
COMPASSION.
HOPE
NO, CONNER, LOOK DOWN-- AROUND-- PSYCHO-PIRATE'S GOT THE WHOLE TOWN IN HIS THRALL!
AND HOW DOES THAT FEEL, SUPERMAN? I BET YOU'RE HEARTBROKEN!
NNNARRH

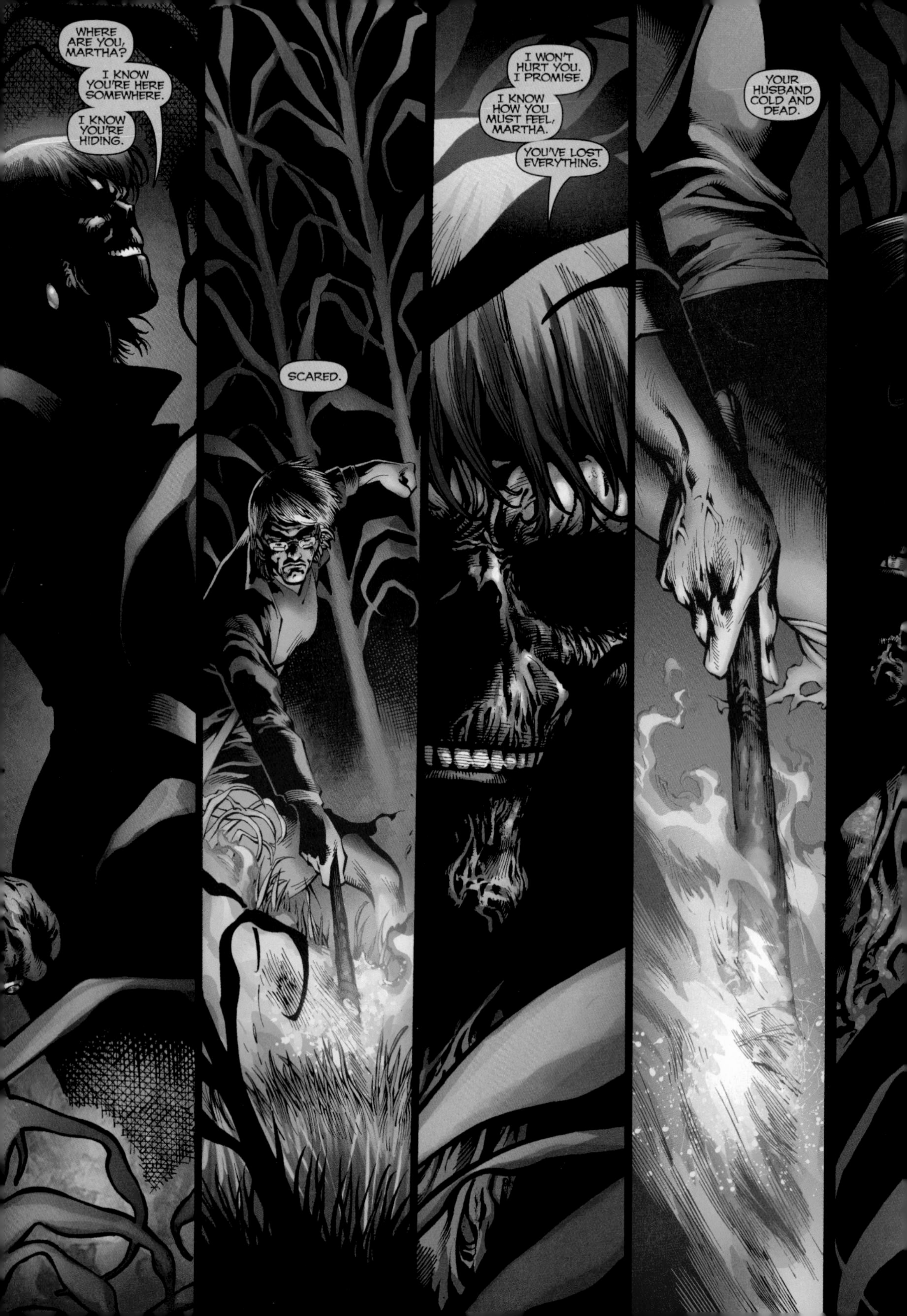
WHERE ARE YOU, MARTHA?
I KNOW YOU'RE HERE SOMEWHERE.
I KNOW YOU'RE HIDING.
SCARED.
I WON'T HURT YOU. I PROMISE.
I KNOW HOW YOU MUST FEEL, MARTHA.
YOU'VE LOST EVERYTHING.
YOUR HUSBAND COLD AND DEAD.

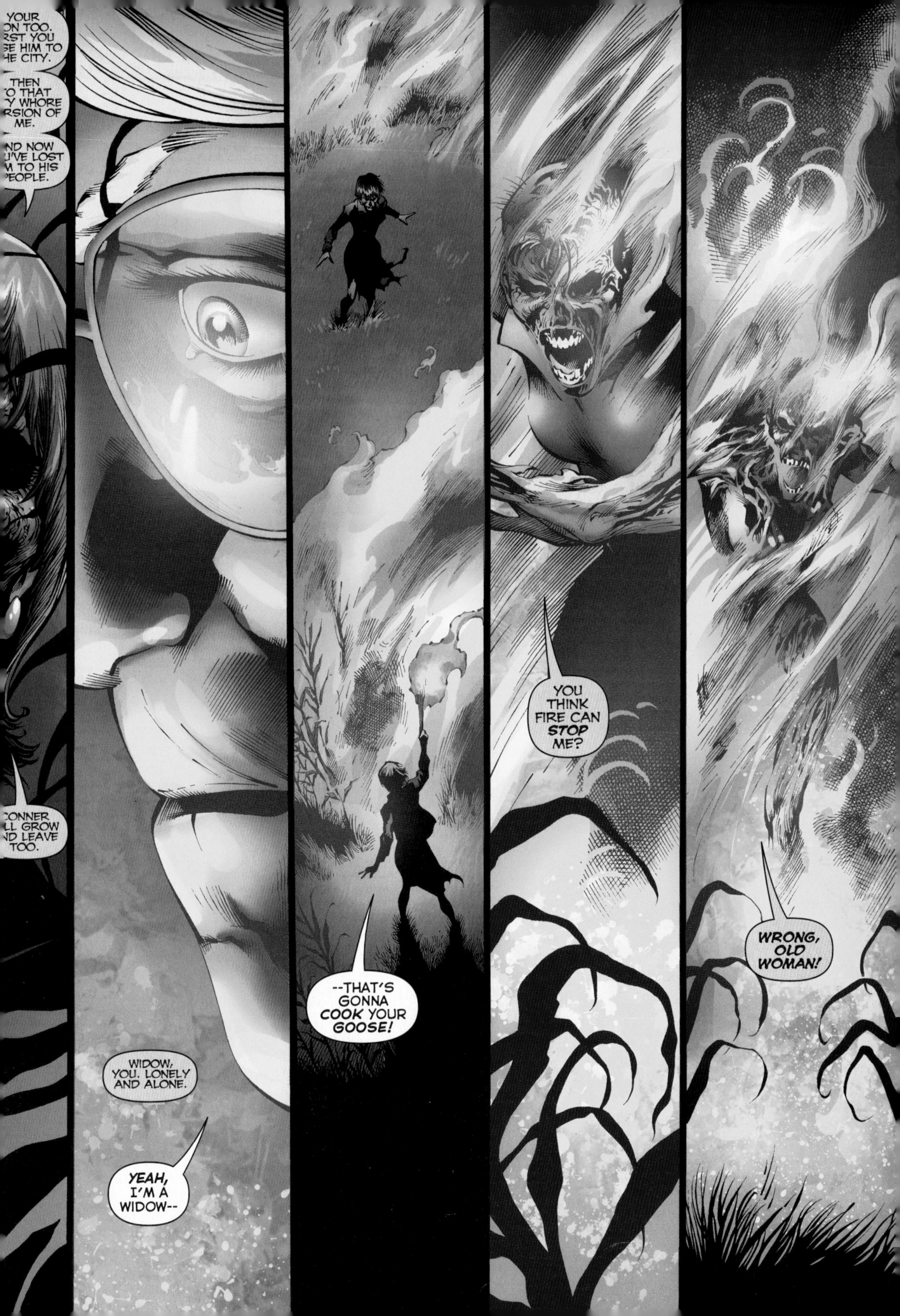

YOUR
ON TOO.
RST YOU
SE HIM TO
HE CITY.
THEN
O THAT
Y WHORE
RSION OF
ME.
ND NOW
U'VE LOST
M TO HIS
PEOPLE.
CONNER
LL GROW
ND LEAVE
TOO.
WIDOW, YOU. LONELY AND ALONE.
YEAH, I'M A WIDOW--
--THAT'S GONNA COOK YOUR GOOSE!
YOU THINK FIRE CAN STOP ME?
WRONG, OLD WOMAN!

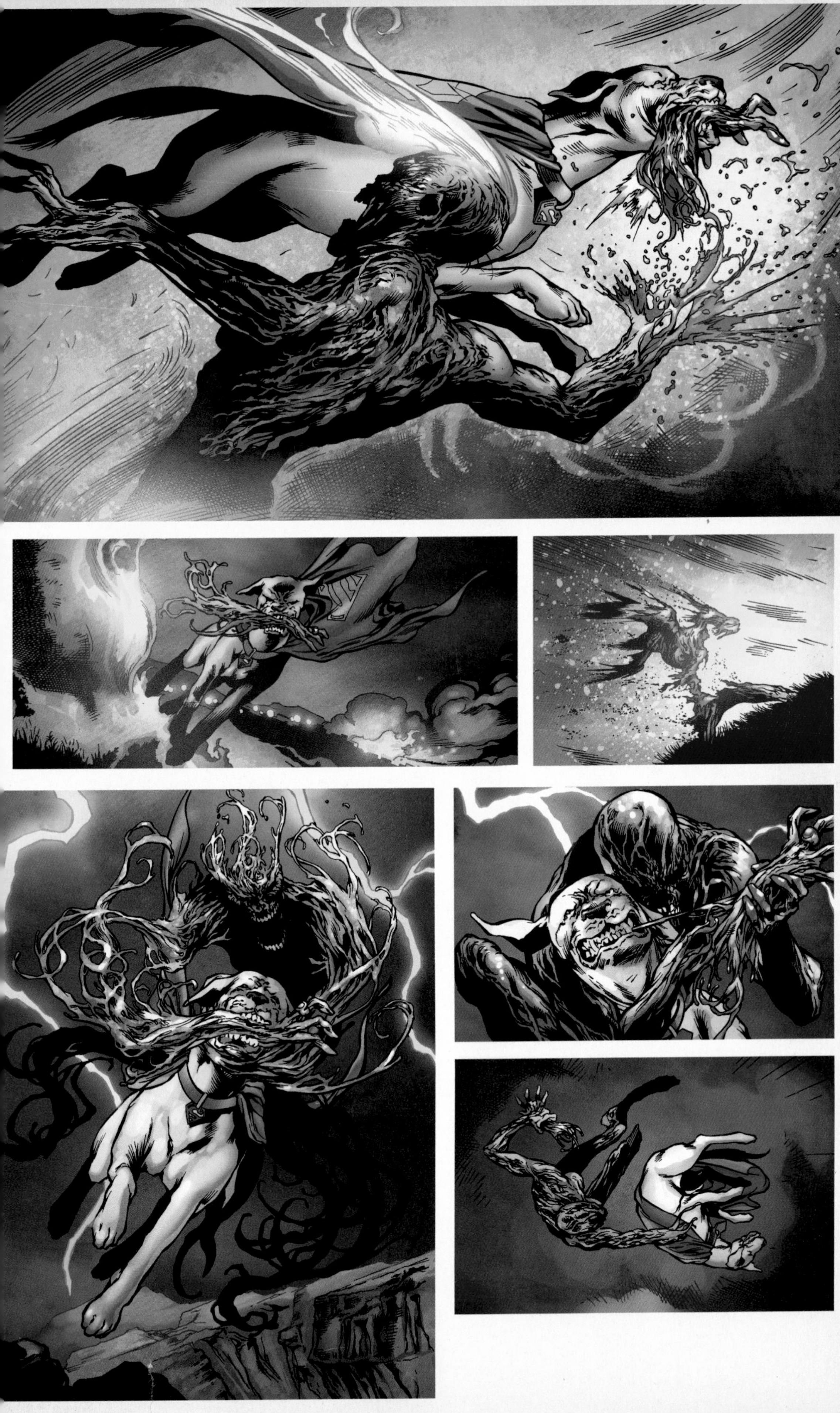

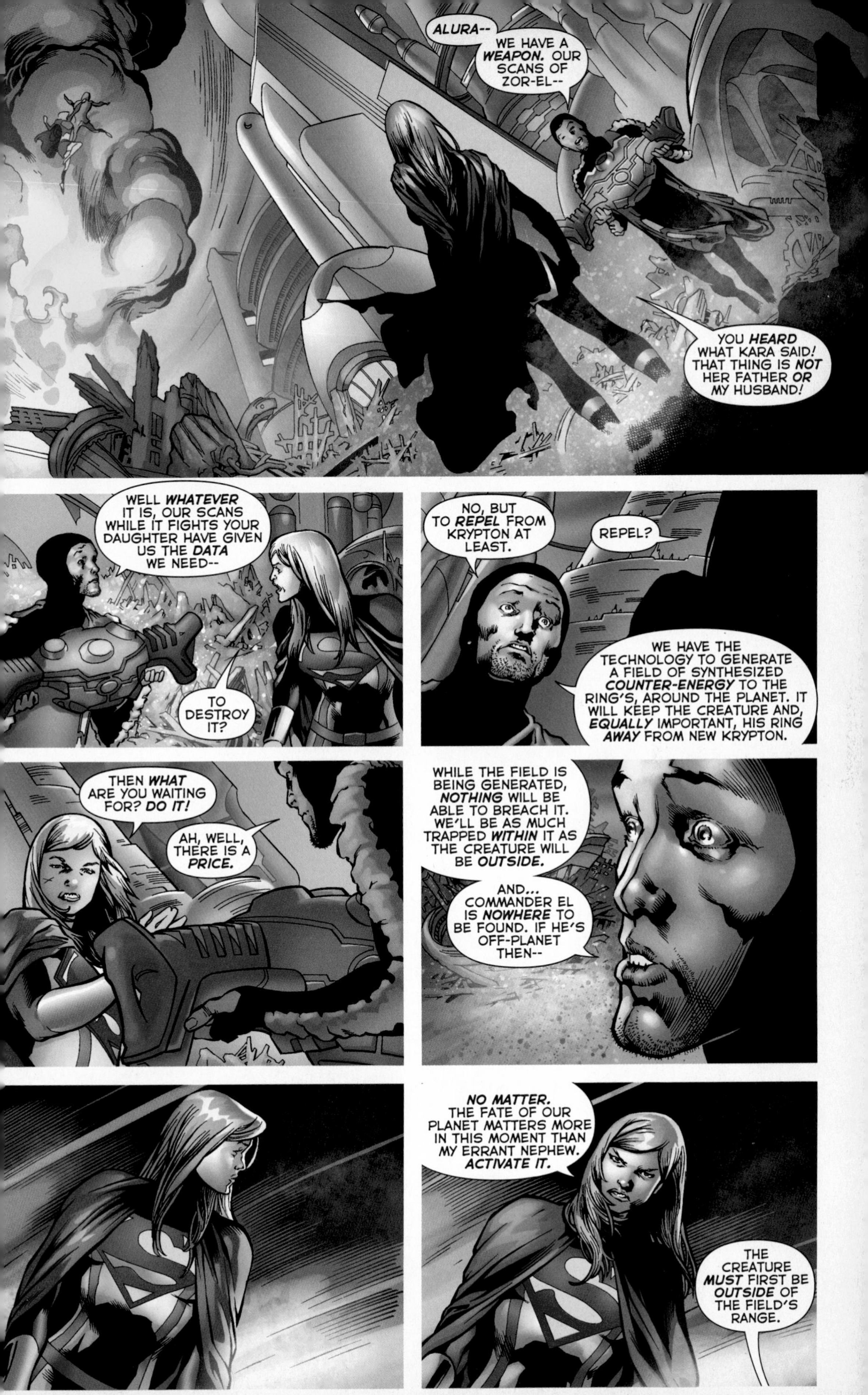

ALURA--
WE HAVE A *WEAPON.* OUR SCANS OF ZOR-EL--
YOU *HEARD* WHAT KARA SAID! THAT THING IS *NOT* HER FATHER *OR* MY HUSBAND!
WELL *WHATEVER* IT IS, OUR SCANS WHILE IT FIGHTS YOUR DAUGHTER HAVE GIVEN US THE *DATA* WE NEED--
TO DESTROY IT?
NO, BUT TO *REPEL* FROM KRYPTON AT LEAST.
REPEL?
WE HAVE THE TECHNOLOGY TO GENERATE A FIELD OF SYNTHESIZED *COUNTER-ENERGY* TO THE RING'S, AROUND THE PLANET. IT WILL KEEP THE CREATURE AND, *EQUALLY* IMPORTANT, HIS RING *AWAY* FROM NEW KRYPTON.
THEN *WHAT* ARE YOU WAITING FOR? *DO IT!*
AH, WELL, THERE IS A *PRICE.*
WHILE THE FIELD IS BEING GENERATED, *NOTHING* WILL BE ABLE TO BREACH IT. WE'LL BE AS MUCH TRAPPED *WITHIN* IT AS THE CREATURE WILL BE *OUTSIDE.*
AND... COMMANDER EL IS *NOWHERE* TO BE FOUND. IF HE'S OFF-PLANET THEN--
NO MATTER. THE FATE OF OUR PLANET MATTERS MORE IN THIS MOMENT THAN MY ERRANT NEPHEW. *ACTIVATE IT.*
THE CREATURE *MUST* FIRST BE *OUTSIDE* OF THE FIELD'S RANGE.

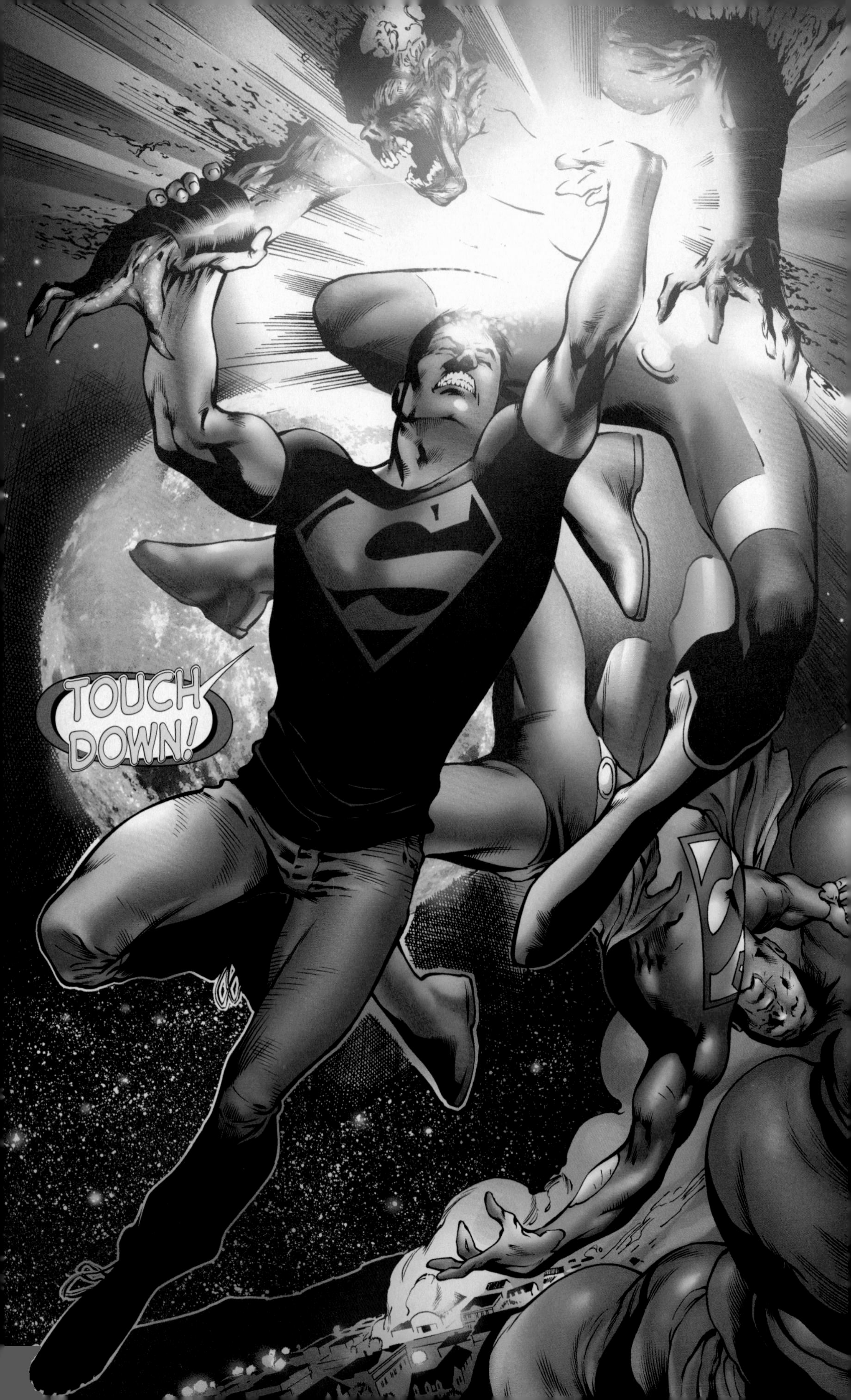
TOUCH DOWN!

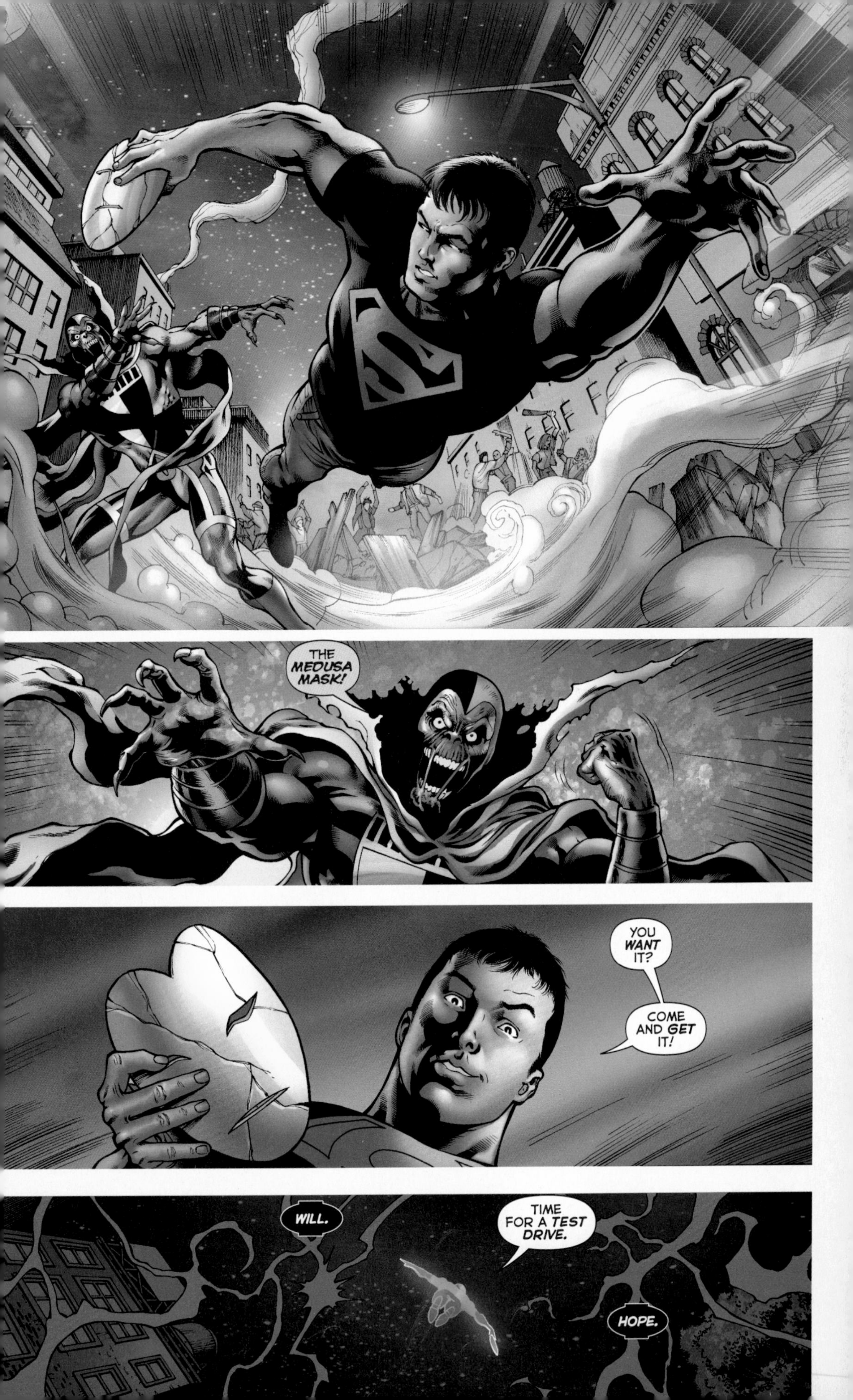
THE MEDUSA MASK!
YOU WANT IT?
COME AND GET IT!
WILL.
TIME FOR A TEST DRIVE.
HOPE.

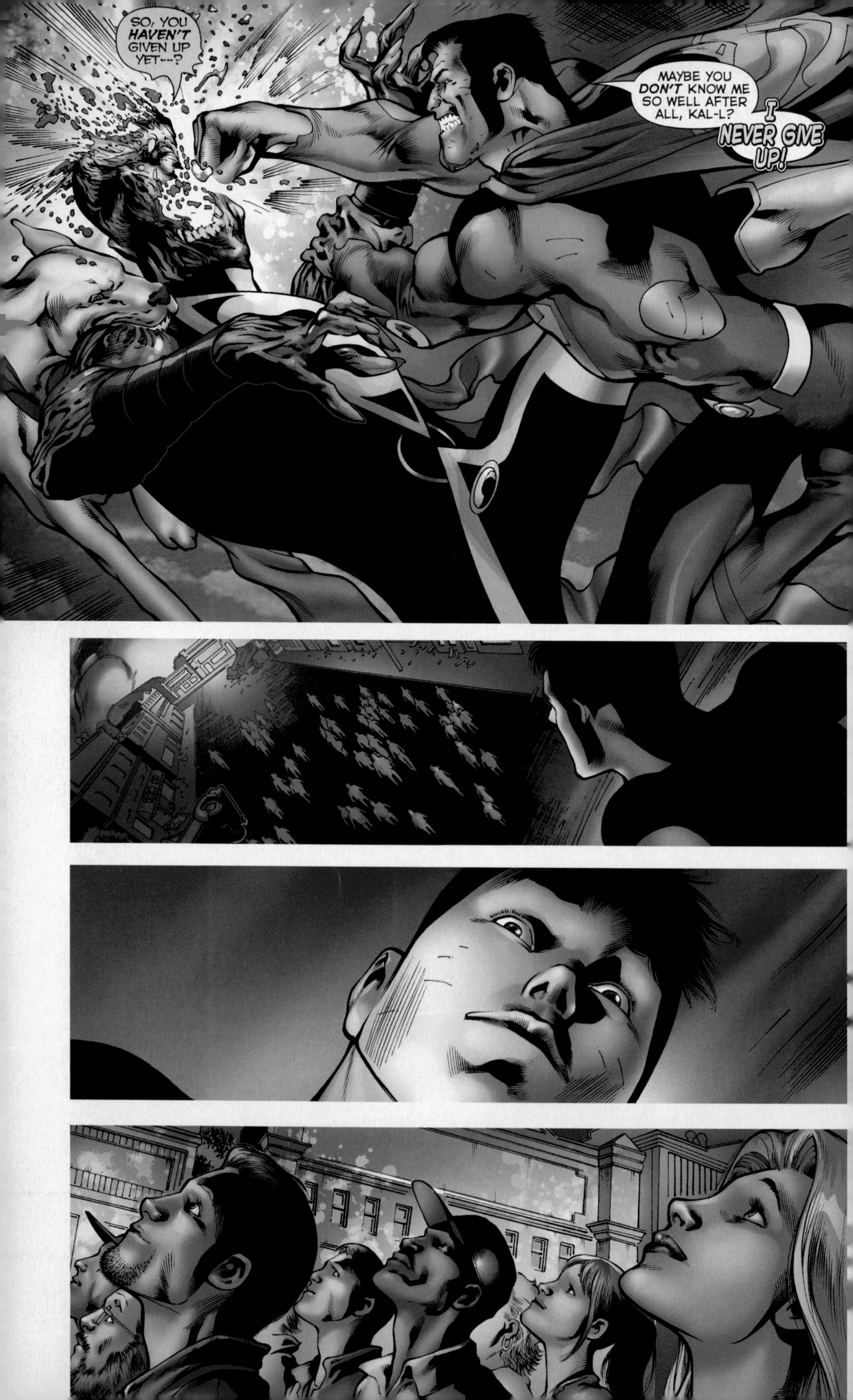
SO, YOU HAVEN'T GIVEN UP YET--?
MAYBE YOU DON'T KNOW ME SO WELL AFTER ALL, KAL-L?
I NEVER GIVE UP!

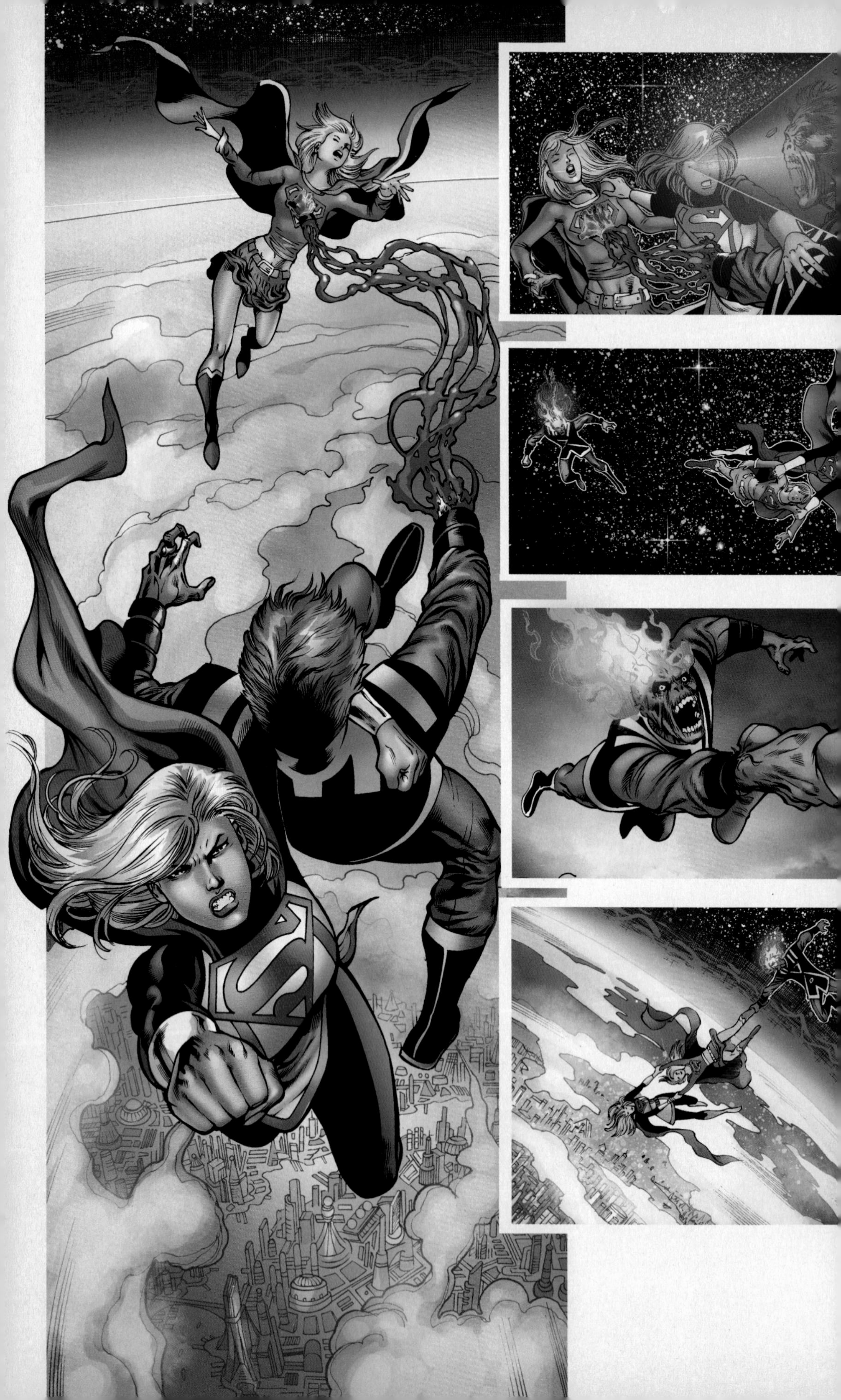

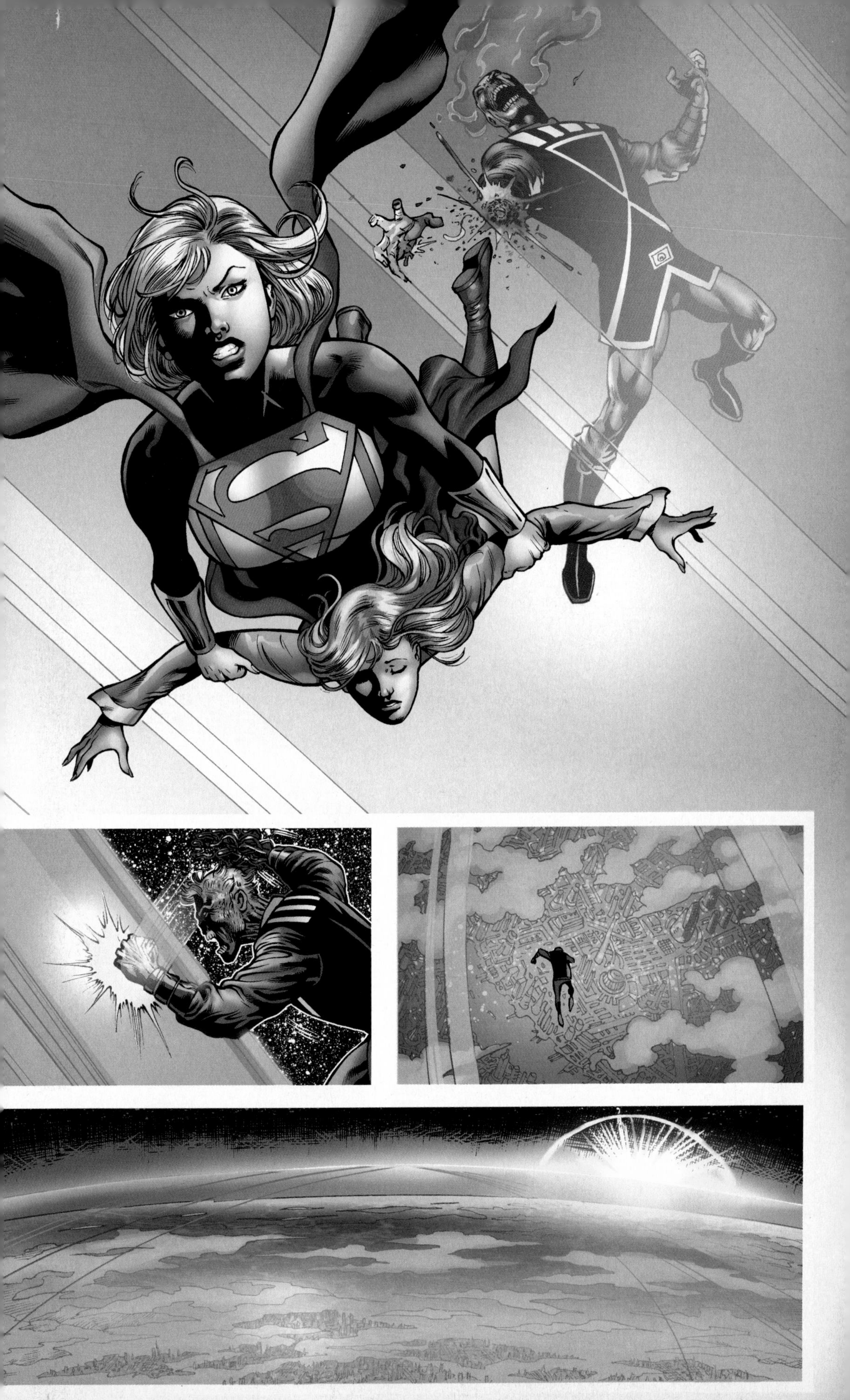

SMALLVILLE.

KAL-L...

...FEEL

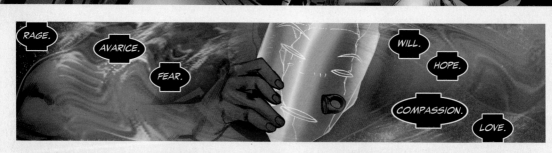

RAGE.

AVARICE.

FEAR.

WILL.

HOPE.

COMPASSION.

LOVE.

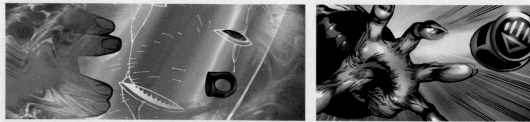

END.

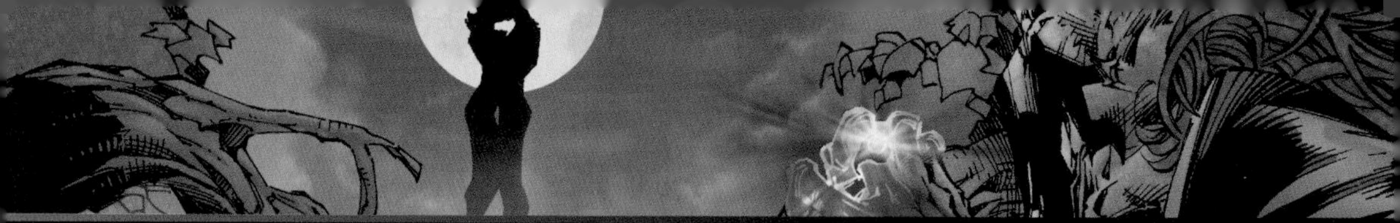

WHEN DEATH COMES KNOCKING

J.T. KRUL
WRITER

ED BENES
PENCILS

**ROB HUNTER
JON SIBAL
JP MAYER**
INKS

DEATHSTROKE

THE H.I.V.E. NEVER SHOULD HAVE HIRED YOU TO GO AFTER THE TITANS, *SON.* THAT'S WHAT GOT YOU KILLED.

GRANT WILSON

"WHEN IT COMES TO GRIEF, EVERYONE DEALS WITH IT IN THEIR OWN WAY.

THEY'RE STILL PAYING FOR THAT MISTAKE.

"WHEN LOVED ONES ARE *TAKEN* FROM US, SOME CAN NEVER SEE BEYOND THOSE RESPONSIBLE. SOME ARE FOREVER DRIVEN BY A DESIRE FOR *PAYBACK.*

RED STAR

"OTHERS GO INWARD, FACING THE GRIEF HEAD-ON, LIKE A FREIGHT TRAIN.

"GOOD AND BAD, THEY CLING TO THE MEMORIES BECAUSE IT'S ALL THEY HAVE.

VODKA

NA ZDOROVYE.

RAVAGER

"AND FOR THOSE INCAPABLE OF COPING, THEY DO THEIR BEST TO IGNORE THE GRIEF ALTOGETHER...

WE'RE DONE.

YOU GOT THREE MINUTES TO GET OUT OF HERE BEFORE I CUT IT OFF.

"...IN ANY WAY POSSIBLE."

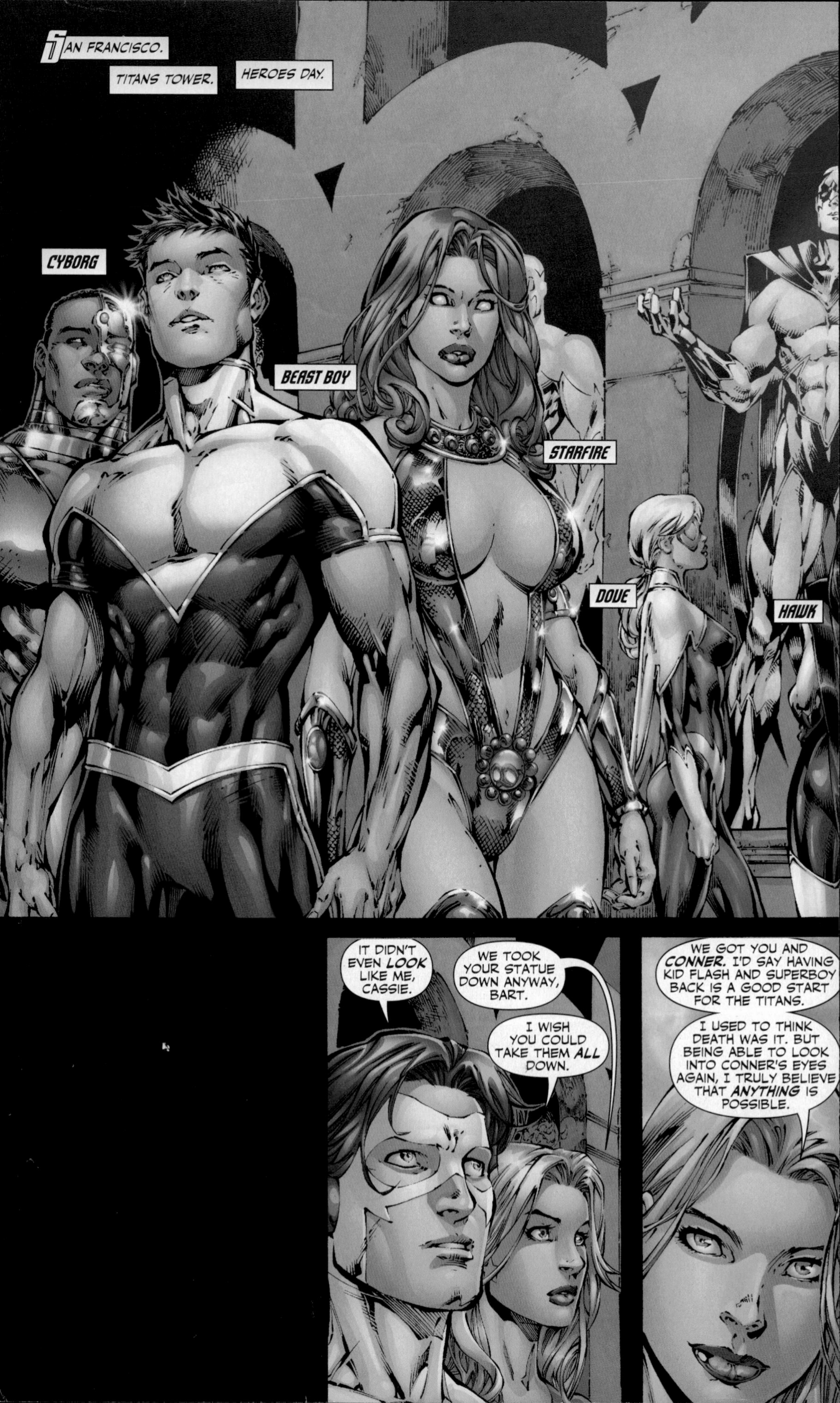
SAN FRANCISCO.
TITANS TOWER.
HEROES DAY.
CYBORG
BEAST BOY
STARFIRE
DOVE
HAWK
IT DIDN'T EVEN LOOK LIKE ME, CASSIE.
WE TOOK YOUR STATUE DOWN ANYWAY, BART.
I WISH YOU COULD TAKE THEM ALL DOWN.
WE GOT YOU AND CONNER. I'D SAY HAVING KID FLASH AND SUPERBOY BACK IS A GOOD START FOR THE TITANS.
I USED TO THINK DEATH WAS IT. BUT BEING ABLE TO LOOK INTO CONNER'S EYES AGAIN, I TRULY BELIEVE THAT ANYTHING IS POSSIBLE.

GEO-FORCE

BUT WE FACE THE GRIEF TODAY JUST LIKE WE WOULD ANY VILLAIN.

DONNA TROY

WONDER GIRL

KID FLASH

YEAH. *TOGETHER.*

ROBERT HAD JUST GOTTEN HIS SECOND TOOTH.

SOME OF US HAVE *CHEATED* DEATH. ME, MORE TIMES THAN I CARE TO REMEMBER. BUT FOR MOST, CASSIE... DEATH IS THE END.

IF DEATH CAN REALLY BE A TWO-WAY STREET, I WISH IT WOULD WORK FOR MORE THAN PEOPLE LIKE US.

TERRY AND MY SON, ROBERT, DIDN'T DIE FIGHTING BROTHER BLOOD OR TRIGON. IT WAS JUST A RANDOM CAR ACCIDENT.

REALLY CAPTURED HIS *SMUG* SMILE.

WHEN I FIRST BECAME *DOVE*, I THOUGHT THE SAME THING. BUT THAT WASN'T WHO HANK WAS. IT WAS JUST HIS *ARMOR*.

NOBODY SAW THAT BUT *ME*.

HANK WASN'T SMUG, HOLLY. EVERYBODY SAYS THAT, BUT THEY DIDN'T KNOW HIM. NOT REALLY.

I HEARD ENOUGH STORIES ABOUT THE *GREAT* HANK HALL TO KNOW WHAT HE WAS.

POMPOUS, EGOTISTICAL... *SEXIST*. SOUNDED LIKE A TOTAL *TOOL*.

ALL I KNOW IS, THE LORD OF CHAOS *TRADED UP* WHEN HE APPOINTED ME THE NEW *AVATAR OF WAR*.

YOU CAN ROMANTICIZE HANK LIKE HE WAS A MARTYR IF YOU WANT. BUT REMEMBER...IN THE END, HE DIED A *BAD GUY.*

HOLLY, TEARING HANK DOWN WON'T MAKE YOU A BETTER *HAWK.* IT'S NOT A *COMPETITION.*

WHATEVER. SAVE THE BIG-SISTER ADVICE FOR ONE OF YOUR *CHARITY* CASES.

"*DON HALL OF EARTH.*"

DOVE

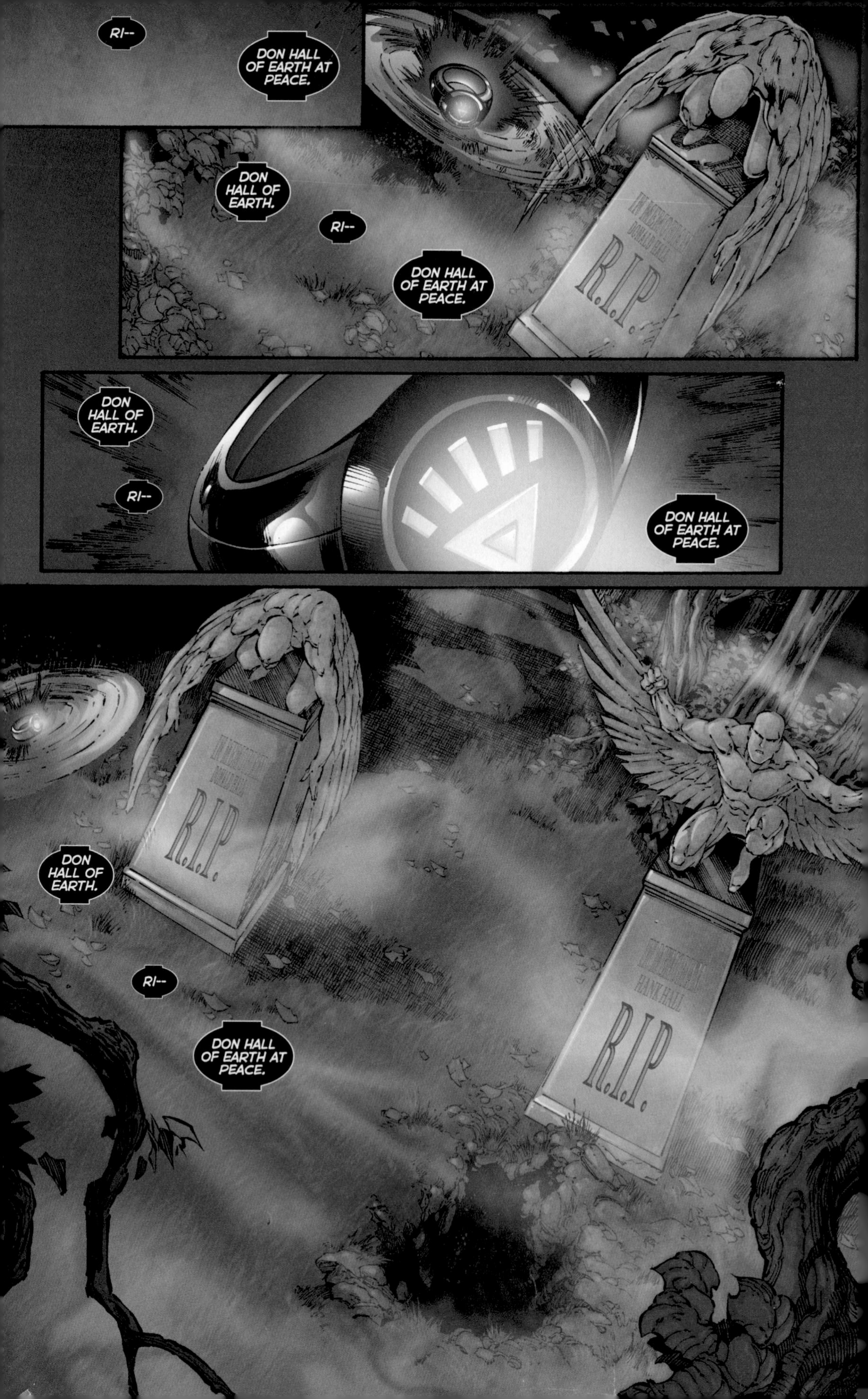
RI--
DON HALL OF EARTH AT PEACE.
DON HALL OF EARTH.
RI--
DON HALL OF EARTH AT PEACE.
R.I.P.
DON HALL OF EARTH.
RI--
DON HALL OF EARTH AT PEACE.
R.I.P.
DON HALL OF EARTH.
RI--
DON HALL OF EARTH AT PEACE.
HANK HALL
R.I.P.

OKAY, PSYCHO-STALKER! YOU GOT OUR ATTENTION. COME OUT, COME OUT WHEREVER YOU ARE.

DO YOU HAVE TO SHOUT?

RAGE.

WHAT? THE LIBRARY'S CLOSED. I DON'T THINK THE RULE ABOUT SILENCE APPLIES.

WHOEVER IS OUT THERE, YOU DON'T NEED TO PROVOKE HIM.

THEY STARTED IT. I'M JUST GOING TO FINISH IT.

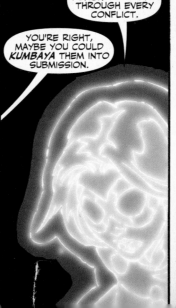

YOU CAN'T PUNCH YOUR WAY THROUGH EVERY CONFLICT.

YOU'RE RIGHT, MAYBE YOU COULD KUMBAYA THEM INTO SUBMISSION.

WELL, WELL, WELL. GUESS IT'S LADIES' NIGHT.

HANK?!?

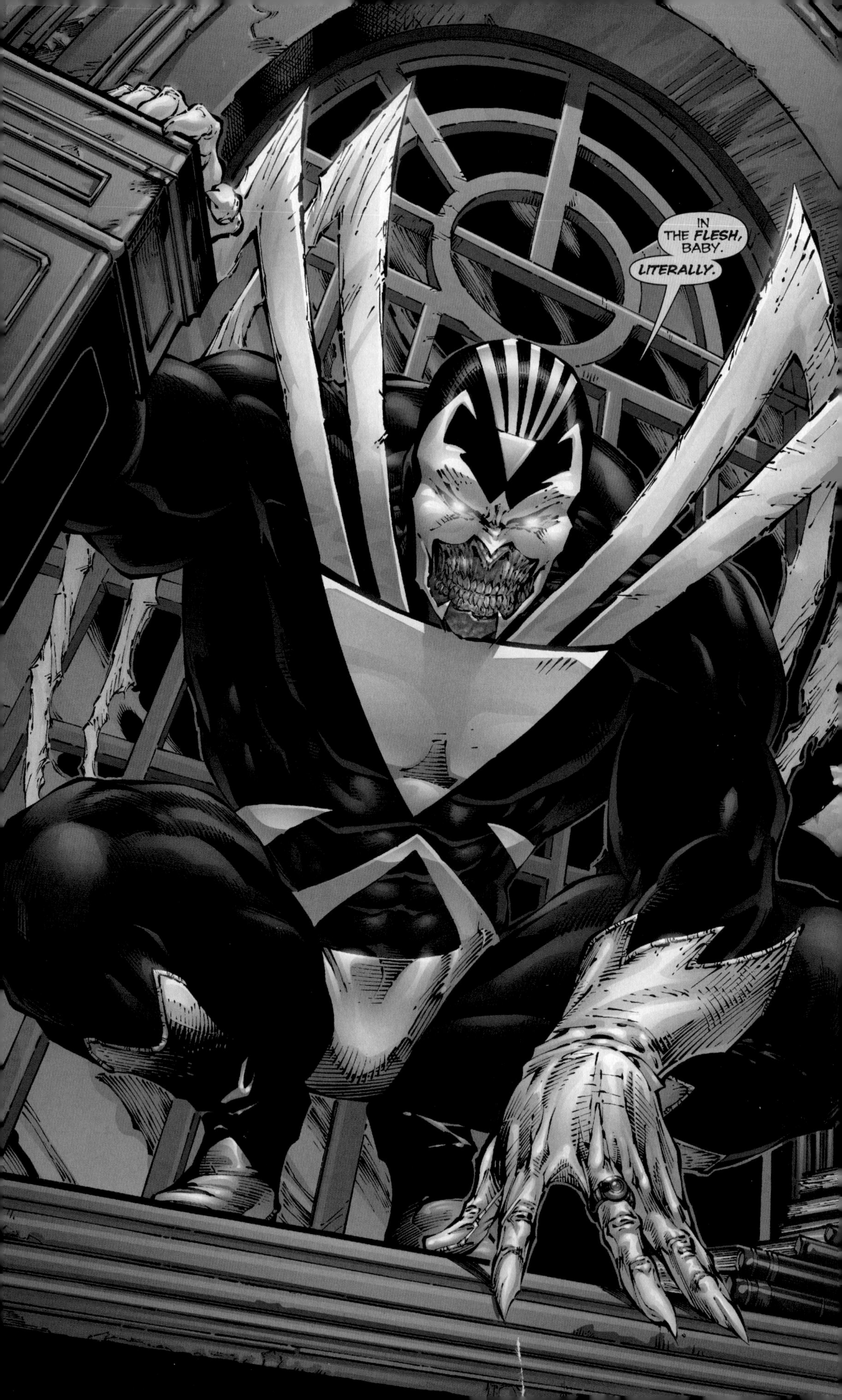
IN THE FLESH, BABY.
LITERALLY.

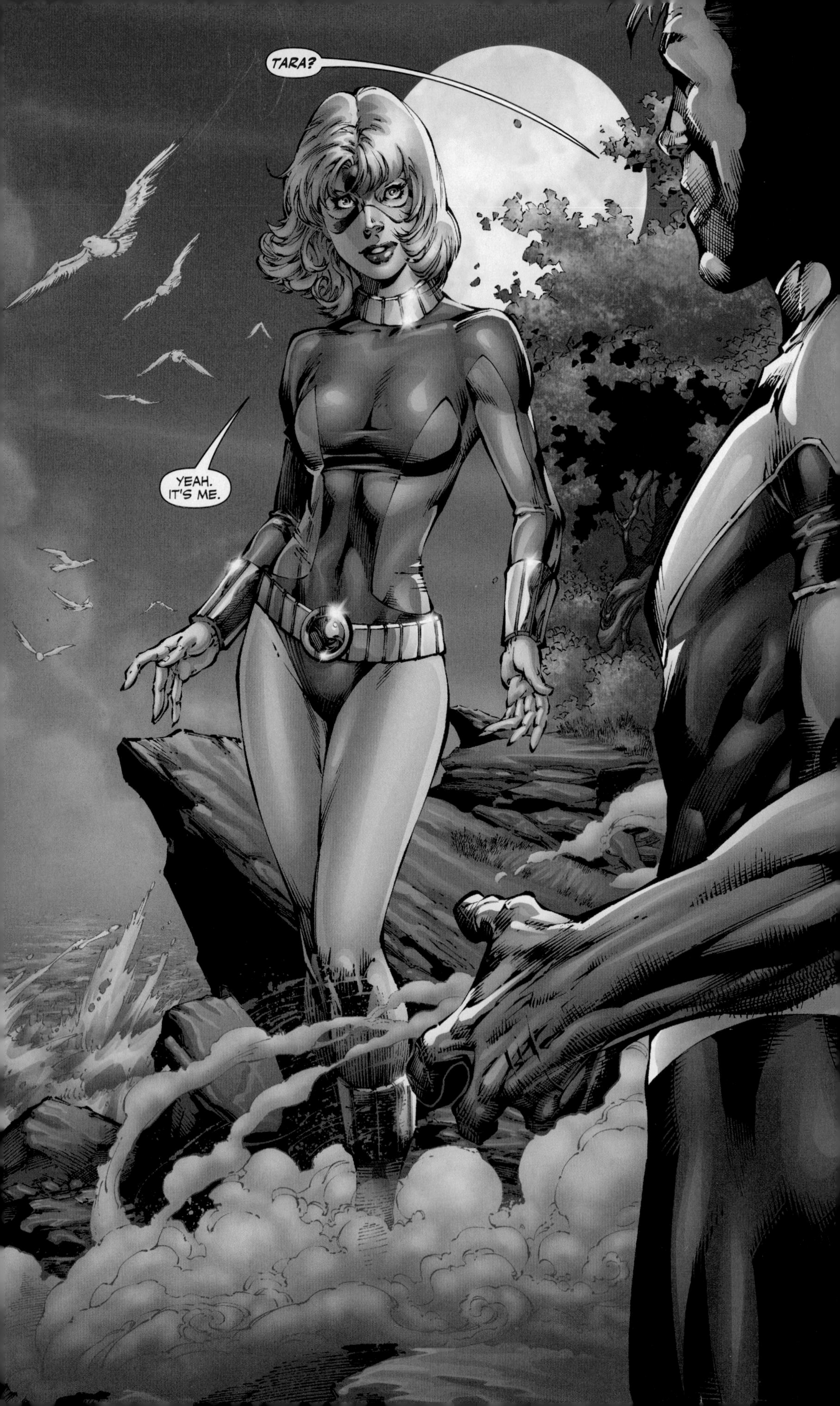
TARA?
YEAH. IT'S ME.

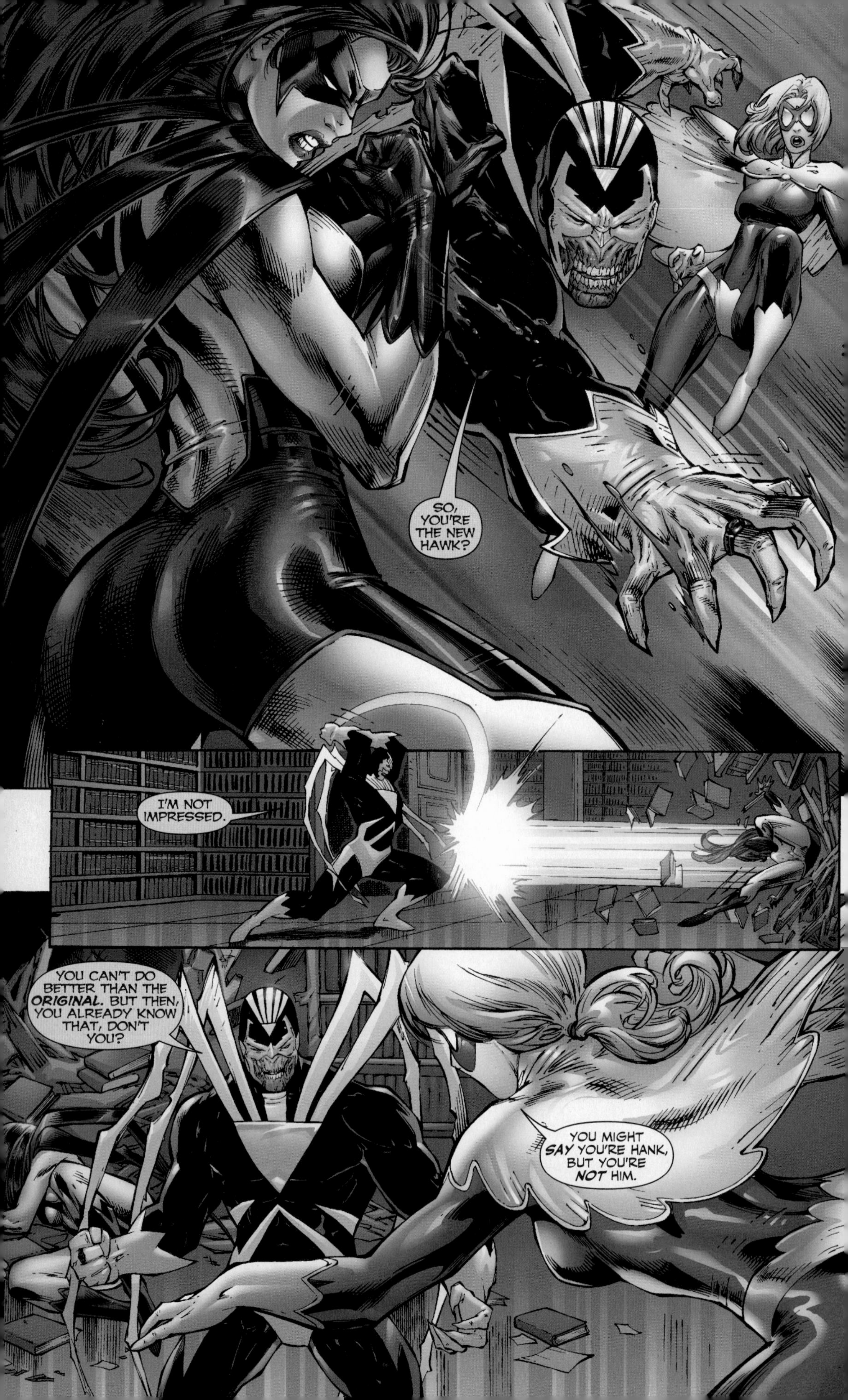
SO, YOU'RE THE NEW HAWK?
I'M NOT IMPRESSED.
YOU CAN'T DO BETTER THAN THE **ORIGINAL.** BUT THEN, YOU ALREADY KNOW THAT, DON'T YOU?
YOU MIGHT ***SAY*** YOU'RE HANK, BUT YOU'RE ***NOT*** HIM.

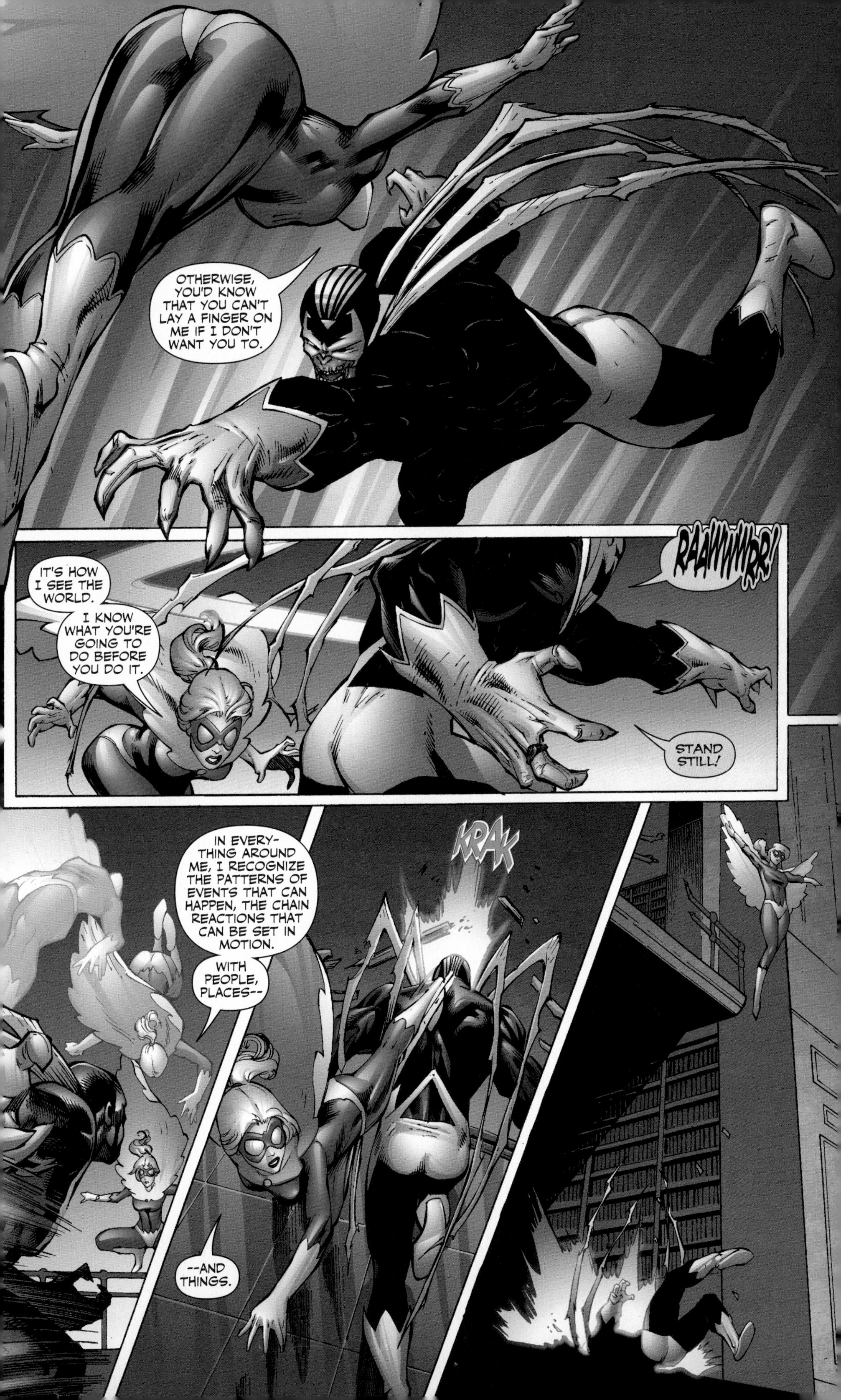
OTHERWISE, YOU'D KNOW THAT YOU CAN'T LAY A FINGER ON ME IF I DON'T WANT YOU TO.
RAAWWWRR!
IT'S HOW I SEE THE WORLD.
I KNOW WHAT YOU'RE GOING TO DO BEFORE YOU DO IT.
STAND STILL!
IN EVERY-THING AROUND ME, I RECOGNIZE THE PATTERNS OF EVENTS THAT CAN HAPPEN, THE CHAIN REACTIONS THAT CAN BE SET IN MOTION.
WITH PEOPLE, PLACES--
KRAK
--AND THINGS.

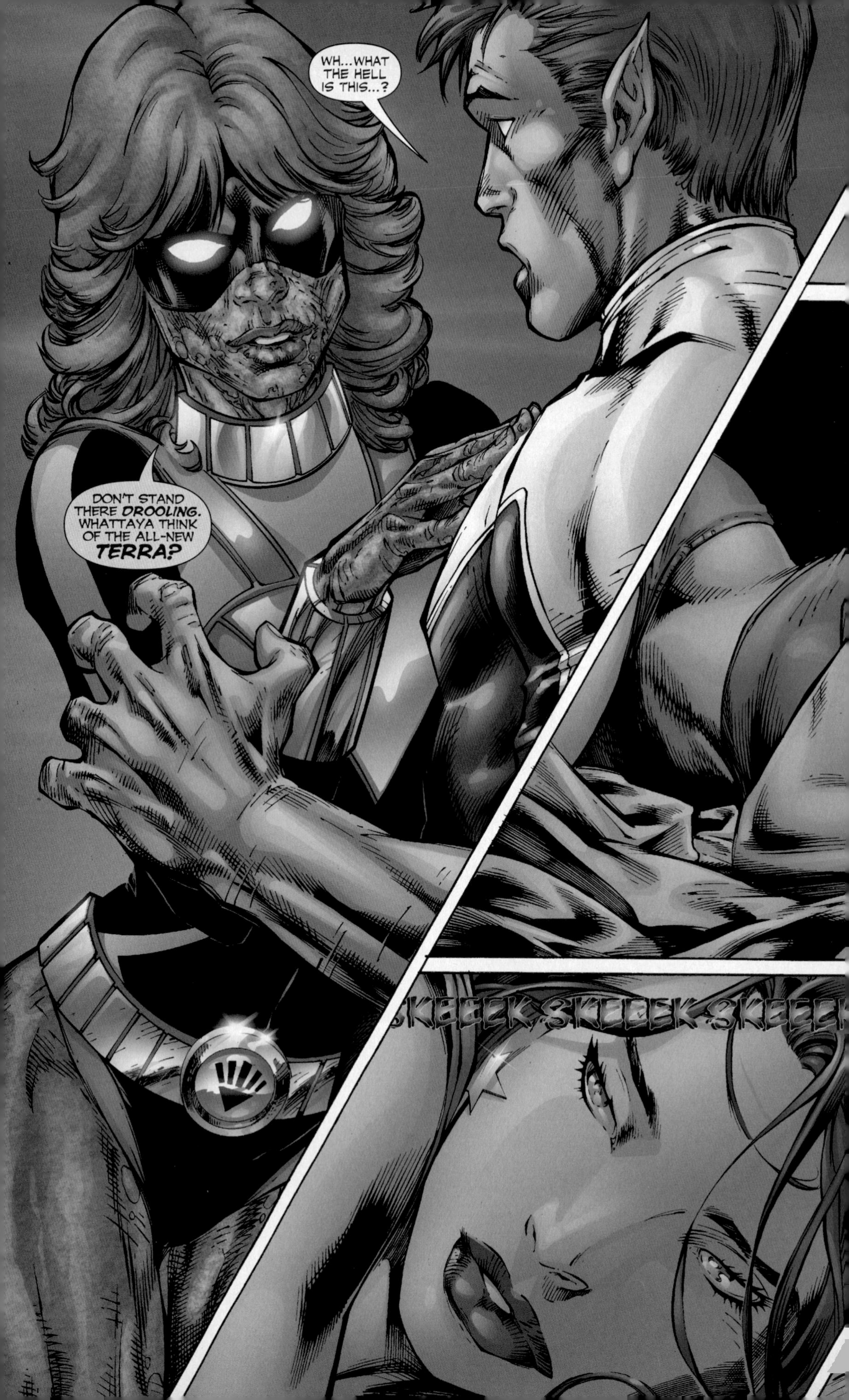
WH...WHAT THE HELL IS THIS...?
DON'T STAND THERE DROOLING. WHATTAYA THINK OF THE ALL-NEW TERRA?
SKEEEK SKEEEK SKEEEK

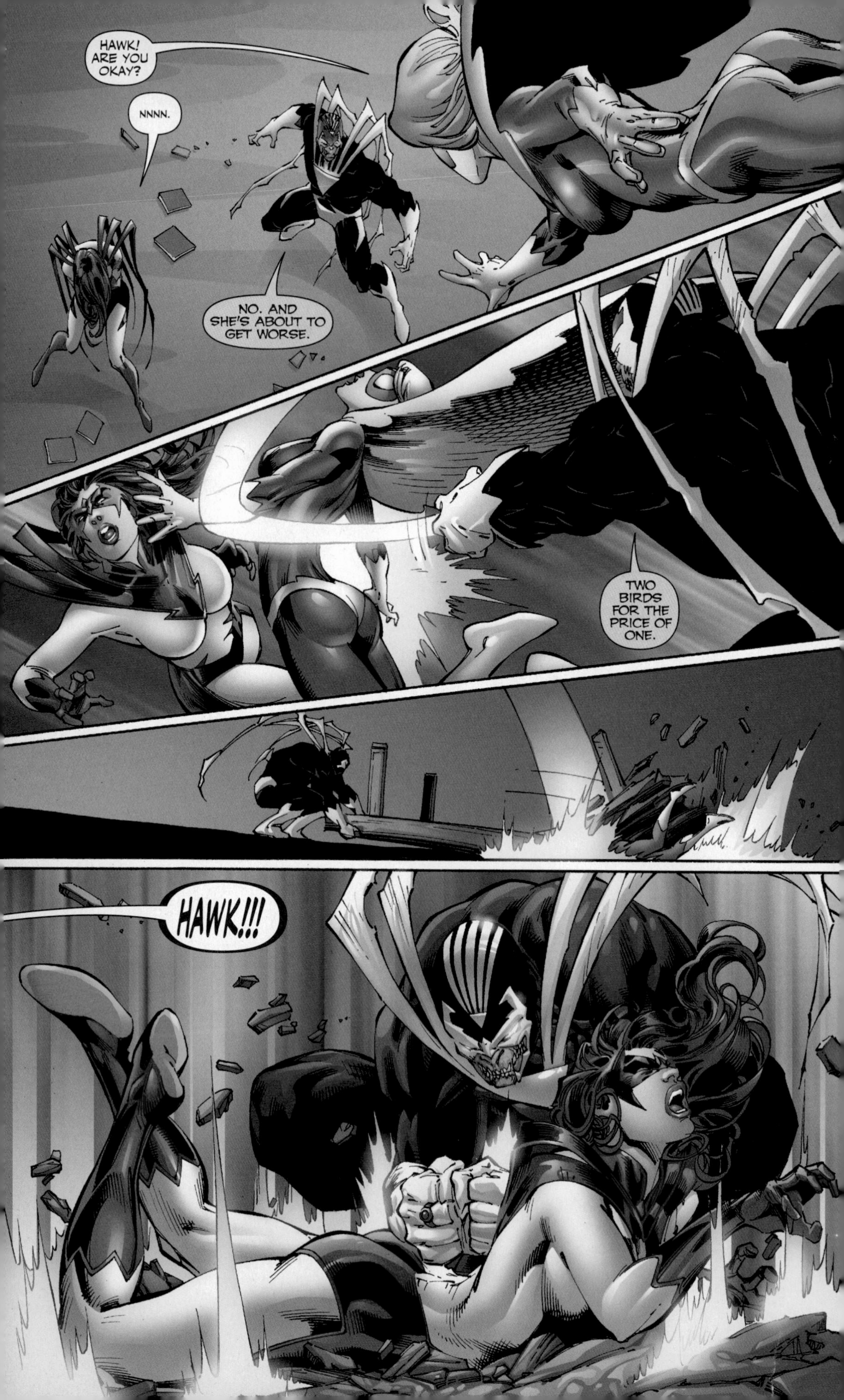
HAWK! ARE YOU OKAY?
NNNN.
NO. AND SHE'S ABOUT TO GET WORSE.
TWO BIRDS FOR THE PRICE OF ONE.
HAWK!!!

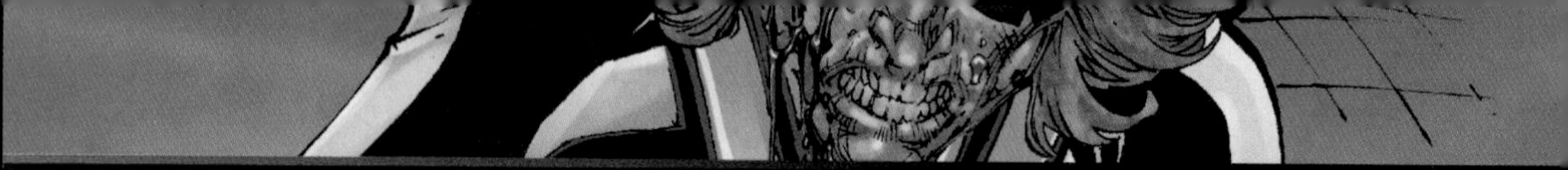

BITE THE HAND THAT FEEDS

J.T. KRUL
WRITER

ED BENES
PENCILS

SCOTT WILLIAMS
ED BENES
INKS

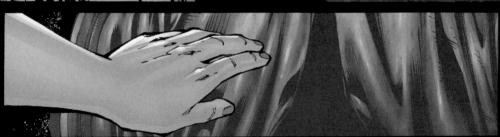

I TRIED TO PUT HIM DOWN FOR HIS NAP, HONEY--

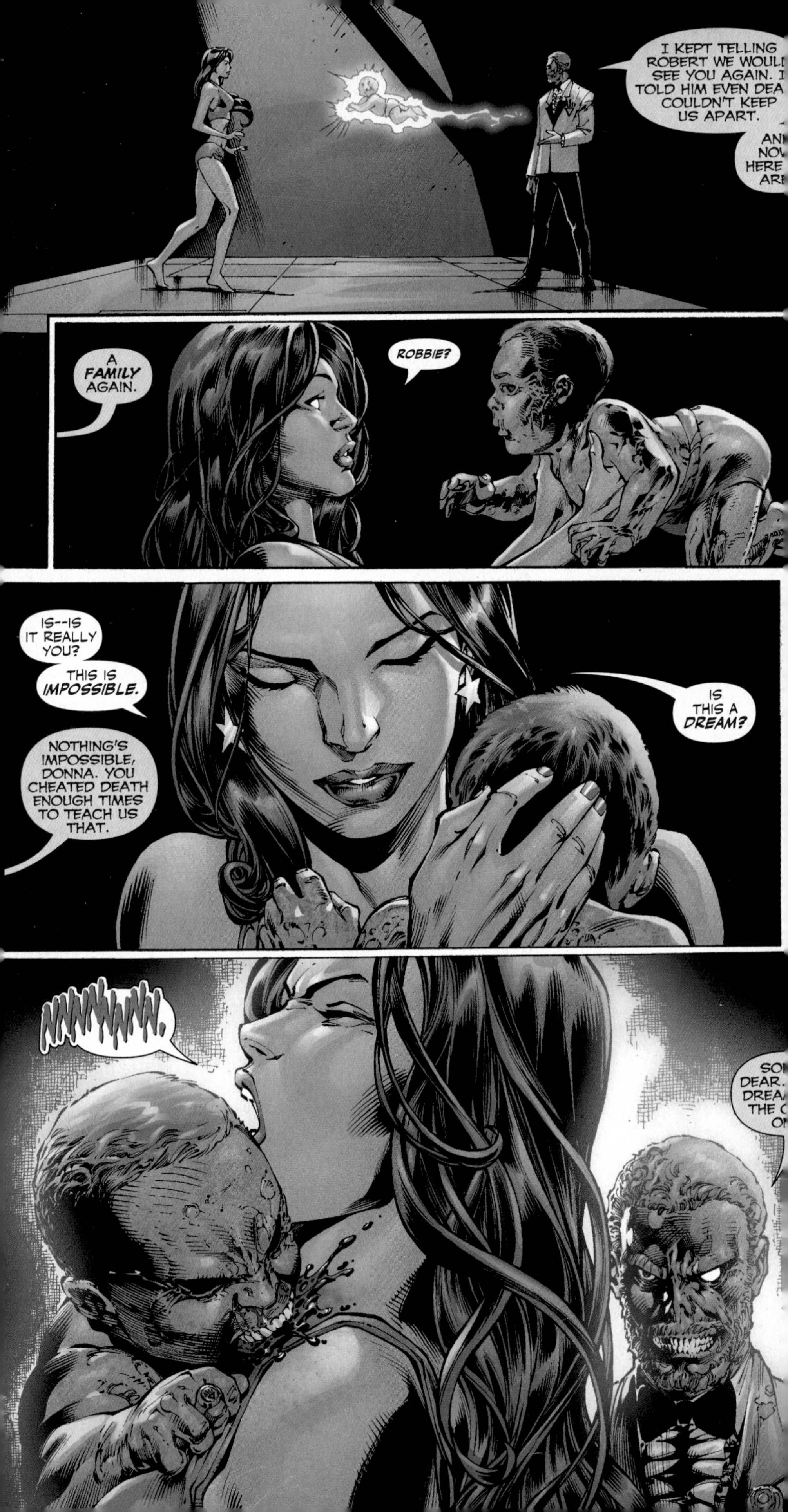
I KEPT TELLING ROBERT WE WOUL
SEE YOU AGAIN. I TOLD HIM EVEN DEA
COULDN'T KEEP US APART.
A FAMILY AGAIN.
ROBBIE?
IS--IS IT REALLY YOU?
THIS IS IMPOSSIBLE.
IS THIS A DREAM?
NOTHING'S IMPOSSIBLE, DONNA. YOU CHEATED DEATH ENOUGH TIMES TO TEACH US THAT.
NNNNNNN.

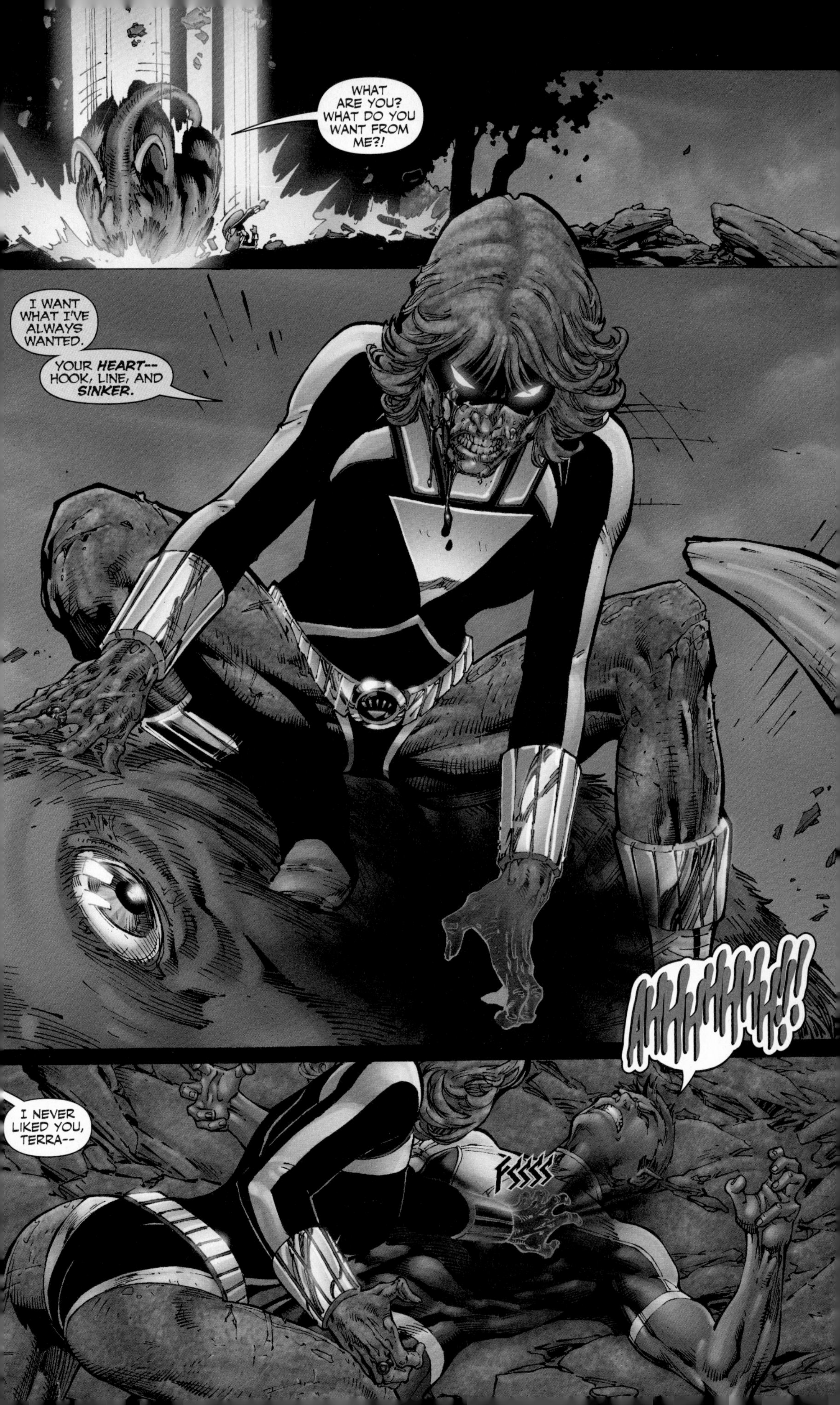

WHAT ARE YOU? WHAT DO YOU WANT FROM ME?!
I WANT WHAT I'VE ALWAYS WANTED.
YOUR **HEART**-- HOOK, LINE, AND **SINKER**.
AHHHHHHH!!
I NEVER LIKED YOU, TERRA--
FSSSS

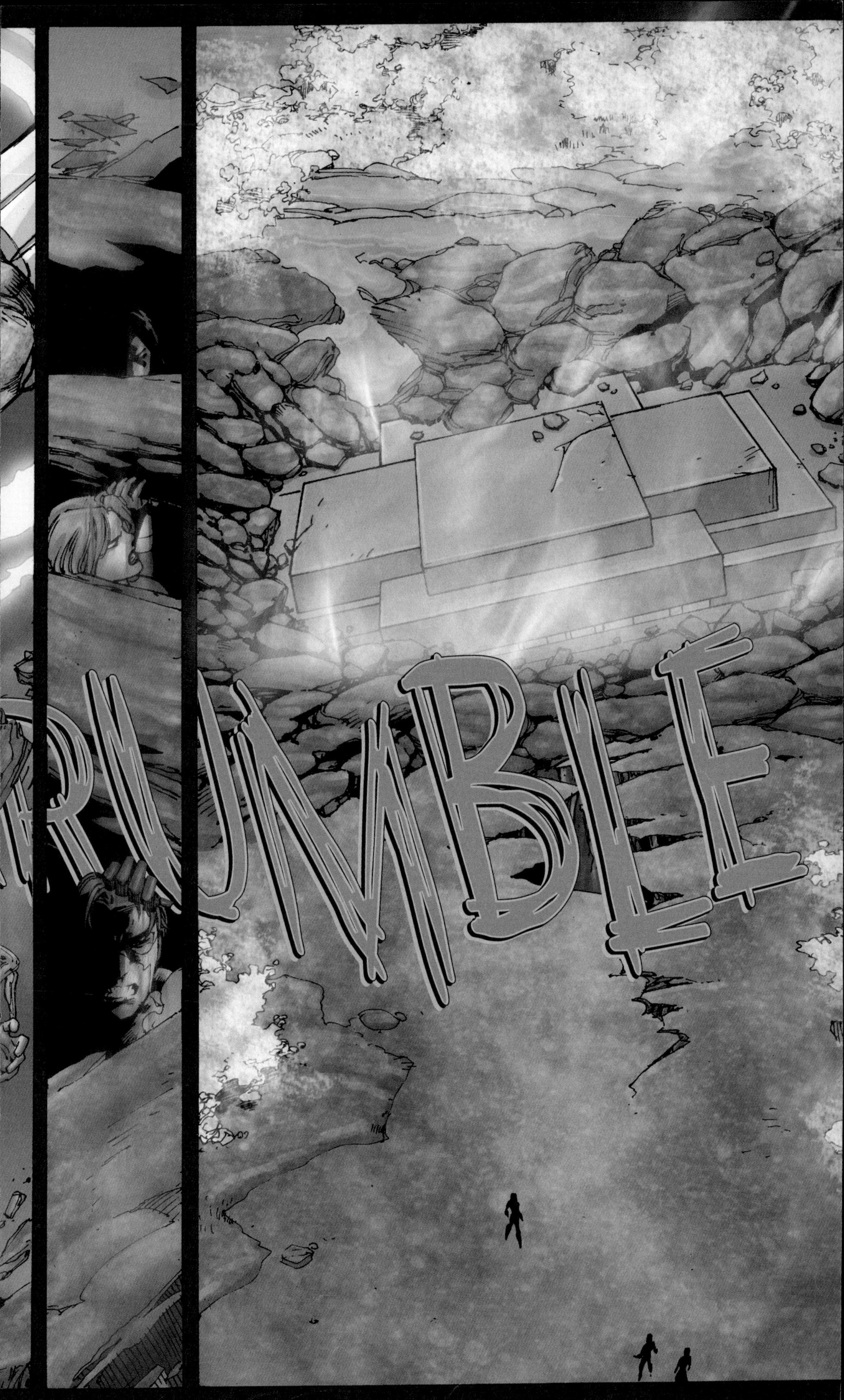
RUMBLE

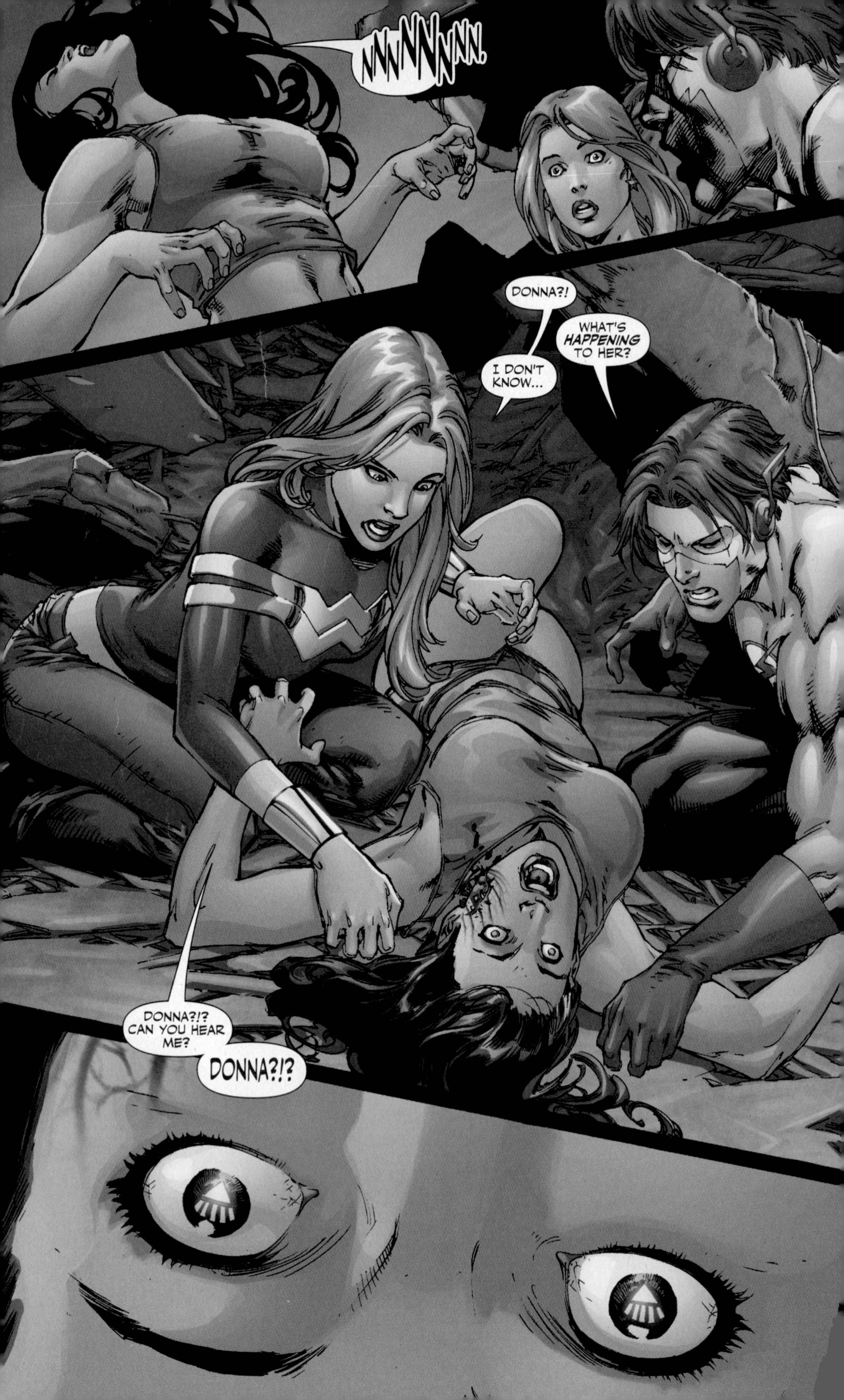
NNNNNNNN.
DONNA?!
I DON'T KNOW...
WHAT'S *HAPPENING* TO HER?
DONNA?!? CAN YOU HEAR ME?
DONNA?!?

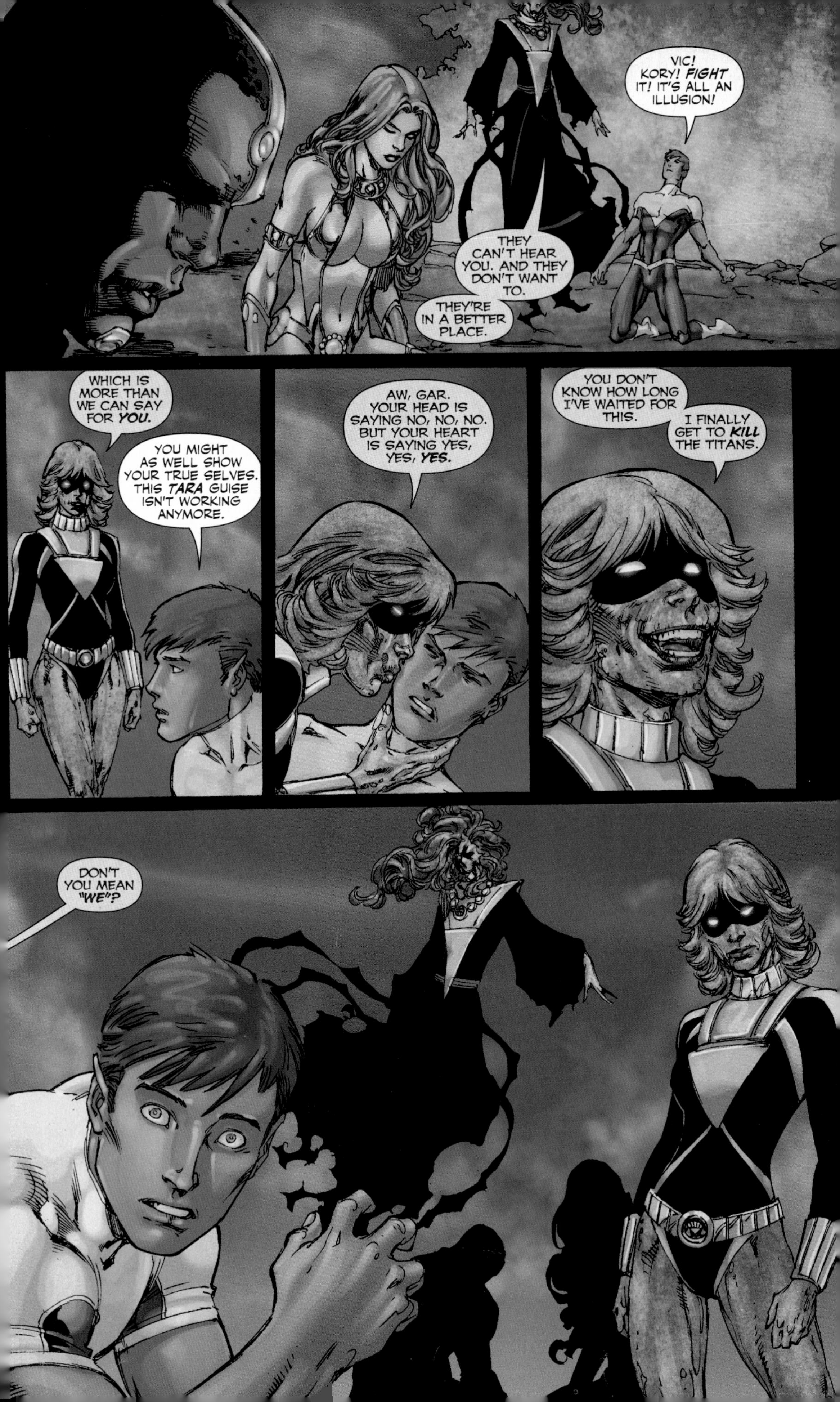

VIC! KORY! *FIGHT* IT! IT'S ALL AN ILLUSION!
THEY CAN'T HEAR YOU. AND THEY DON'T WANT TO.
THEY'RE IN A BETTER PLACE.
WHICH IS MORE THAN WE CAN SAY FOR *YOU.*
YOU MIGHT AS WELL SHOW YOUR TRUE SELVES. THIS *TARA* GUISE ISN'T WORKING ANYMORE.
AW, GAR. YOUR HEAD IS SAYING NO, NO, NO. BUT YOUR HEART IS SAYING YES, YES, *YES.*
YOU DON'T KNOW HOW LONG I'VE WAITED FOR THIS.
I FINALLY GET TO *KILL* THE TITANS.
DON'T YOU MEAN *"WE"*?

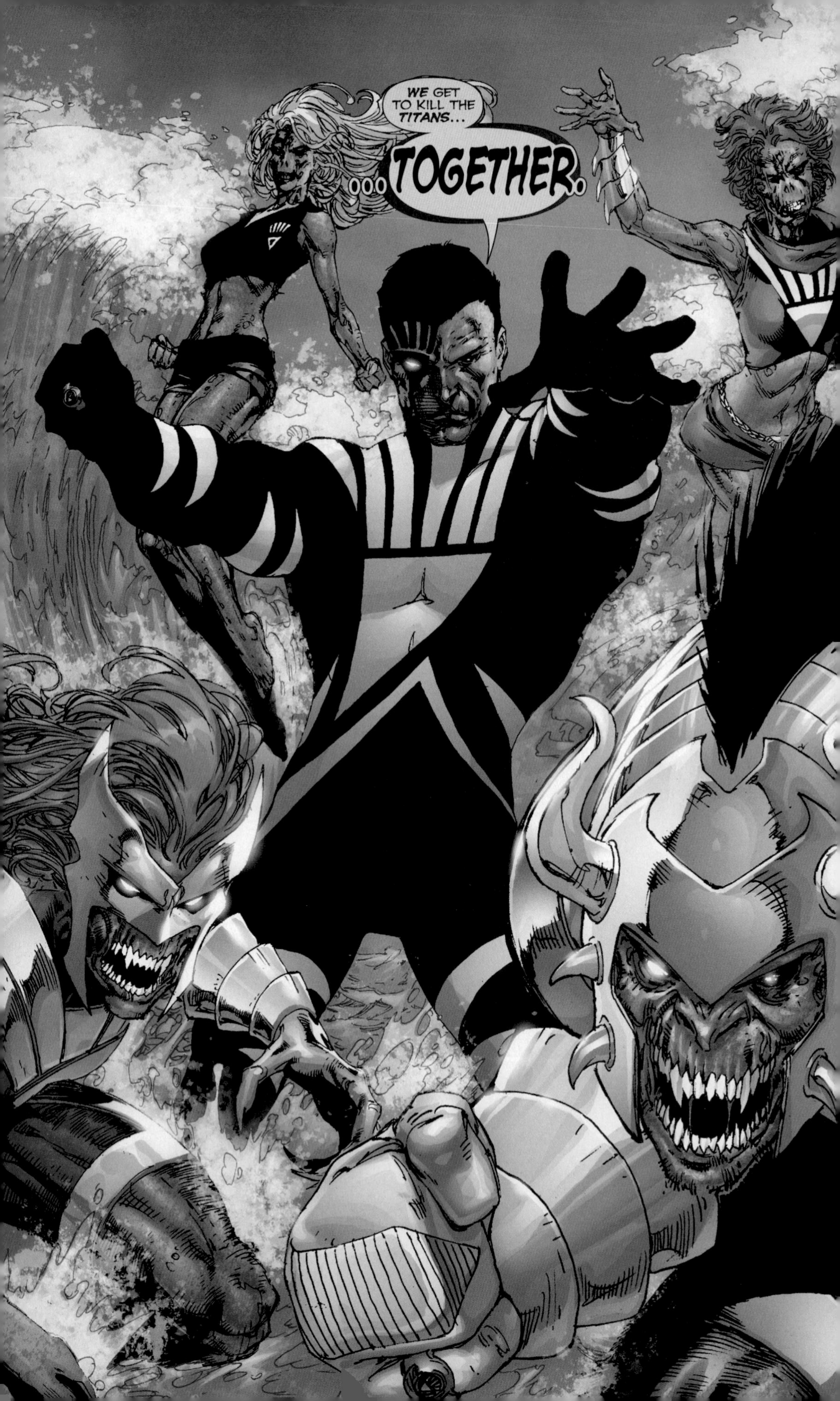
WE GET TO KILL THE TITANS...
...TOGETHER.

WHEN DOVES CRY

J.T. KRUL
WRITER

ED BENES
ARTIST

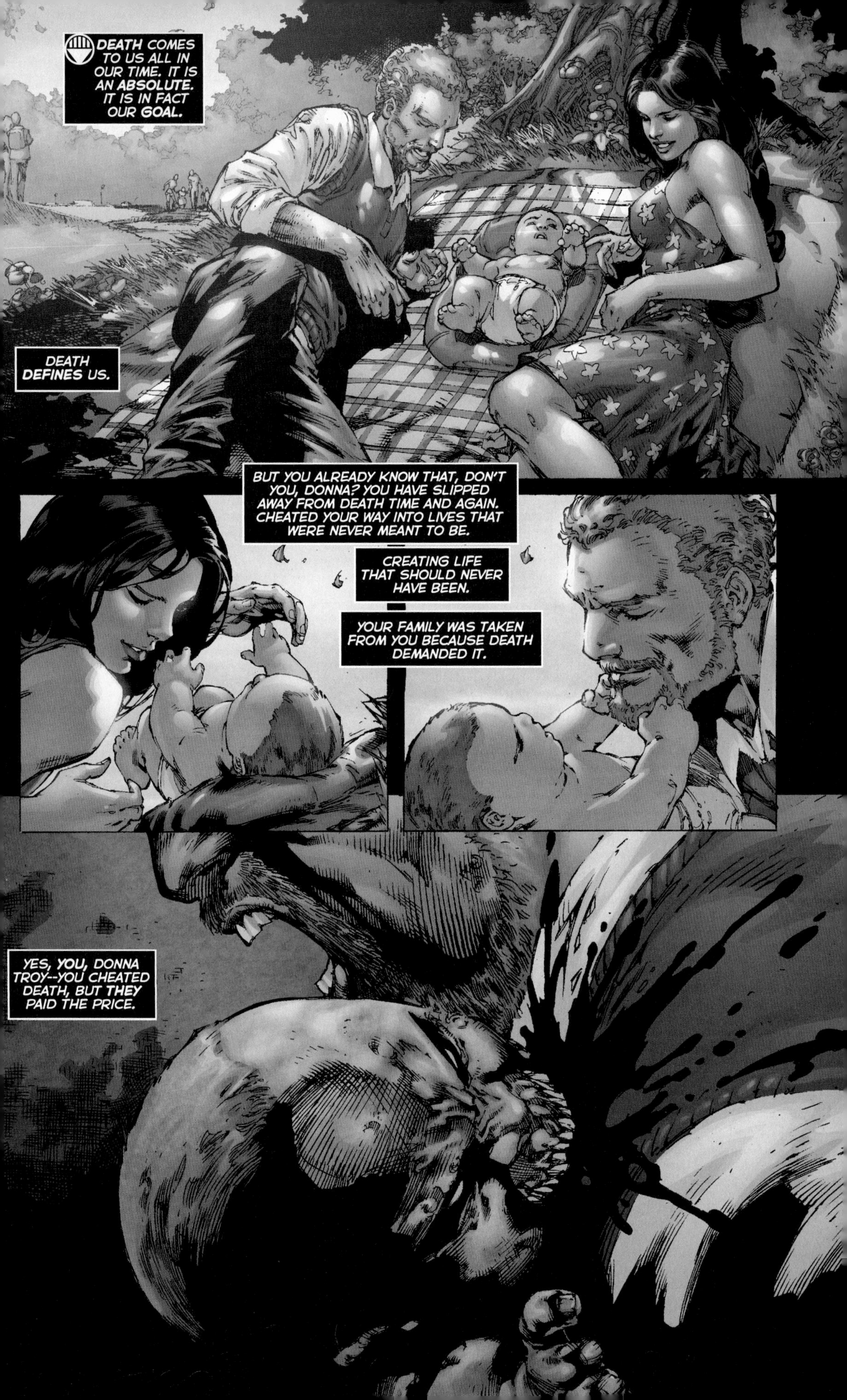
DEATH COMES TO US ALL IN OUR TIME. IT IS AN ABSOLUTE. IT IS IN FACT OUR GOAL.
DEATH DEFINES US.
BUT YOU ALREADY KNOW THAT, DON'T YOU, DONNA? YOU HAVE SLIPPED AWAY FROM DEATH TIME AND AGAIN. CHEATED YOUR WAY INTO LIVES THAT WERE NEVER MEANT TO BE.
CREATING LIFE THAT SHOULD NEVER HAVE BEEN.
YOUR FAMILY WAS TAKEN FROM YOU BECAUSE DEATH DEMANDED IT.
YES, YOU, DONNA TROY--YOU CHEATED DEATH, BUT THEY PAID THE PRICE.

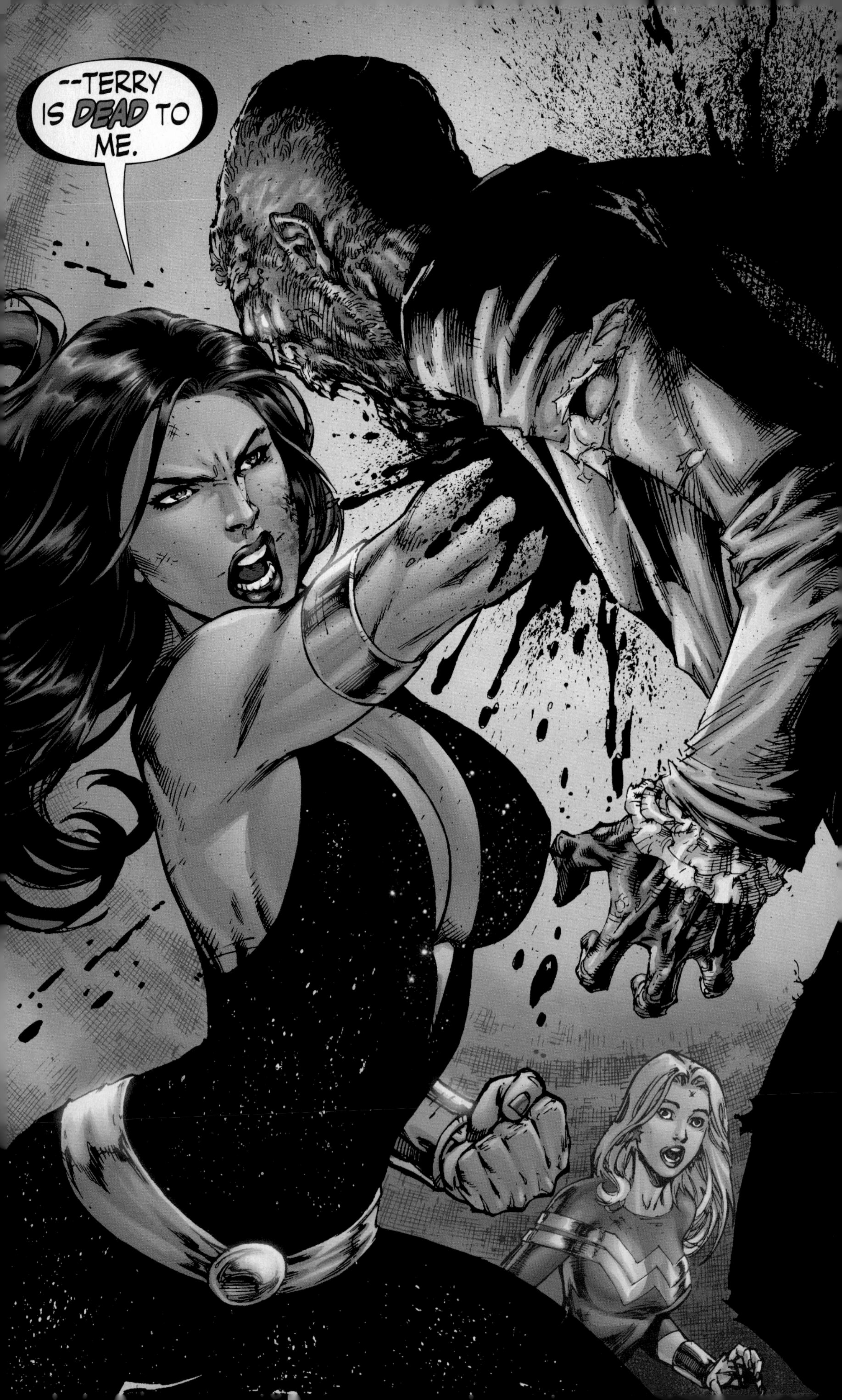
--TERRY IS DEAD TO ME.

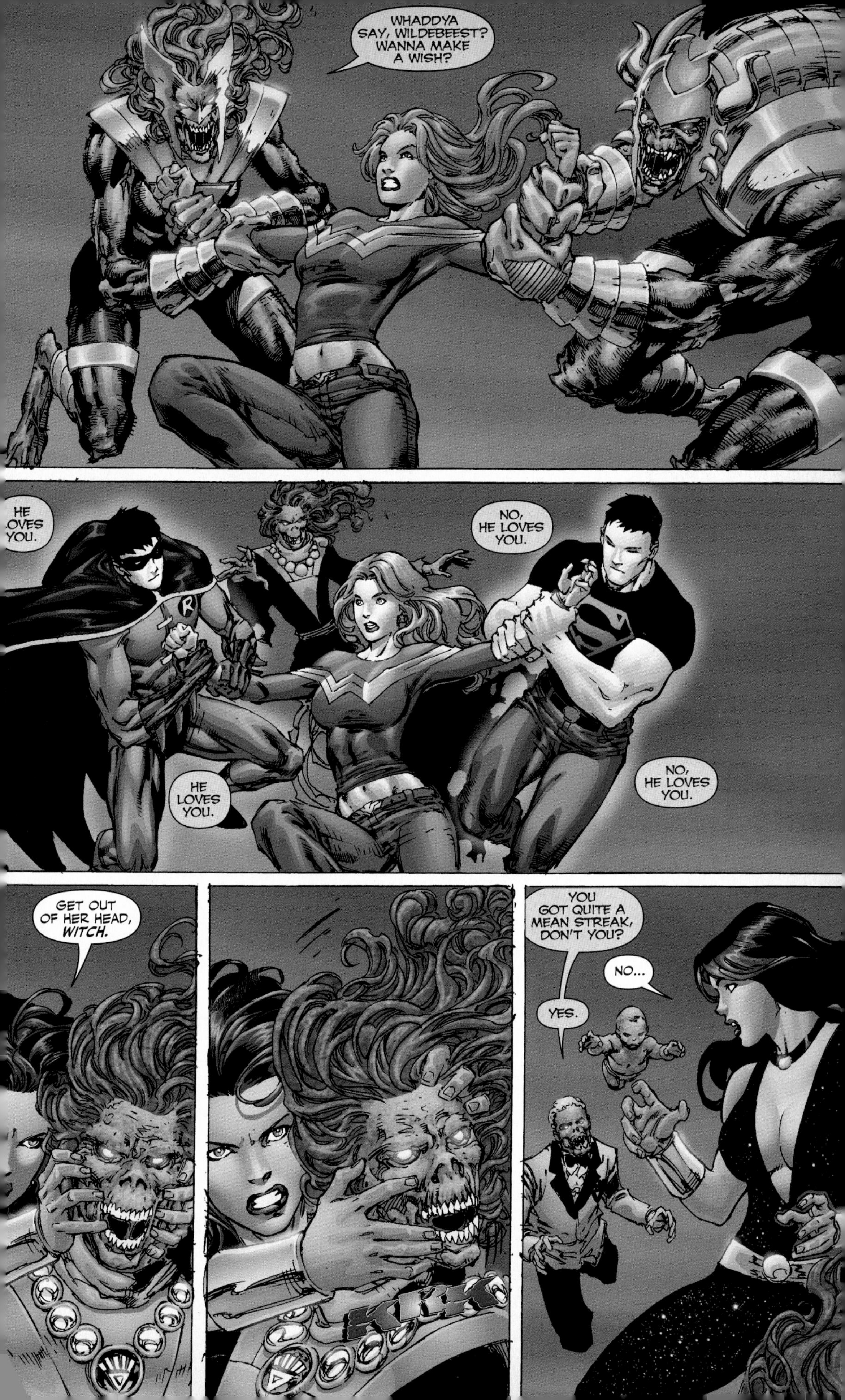
WHADDYA SAY, WILDEBEEST? WANNA MAKE A WISH?
HE LOVES YOU.
NO, HE LOVES YOU.
HE LOVES YOU.
NO, HE LOVES YOU.
GET OUT OF HER HEAD, *WITCH.*
KKK
YOU GOT QUITE A MEAN STREAK, DON'T YOU?
NO...
YES.

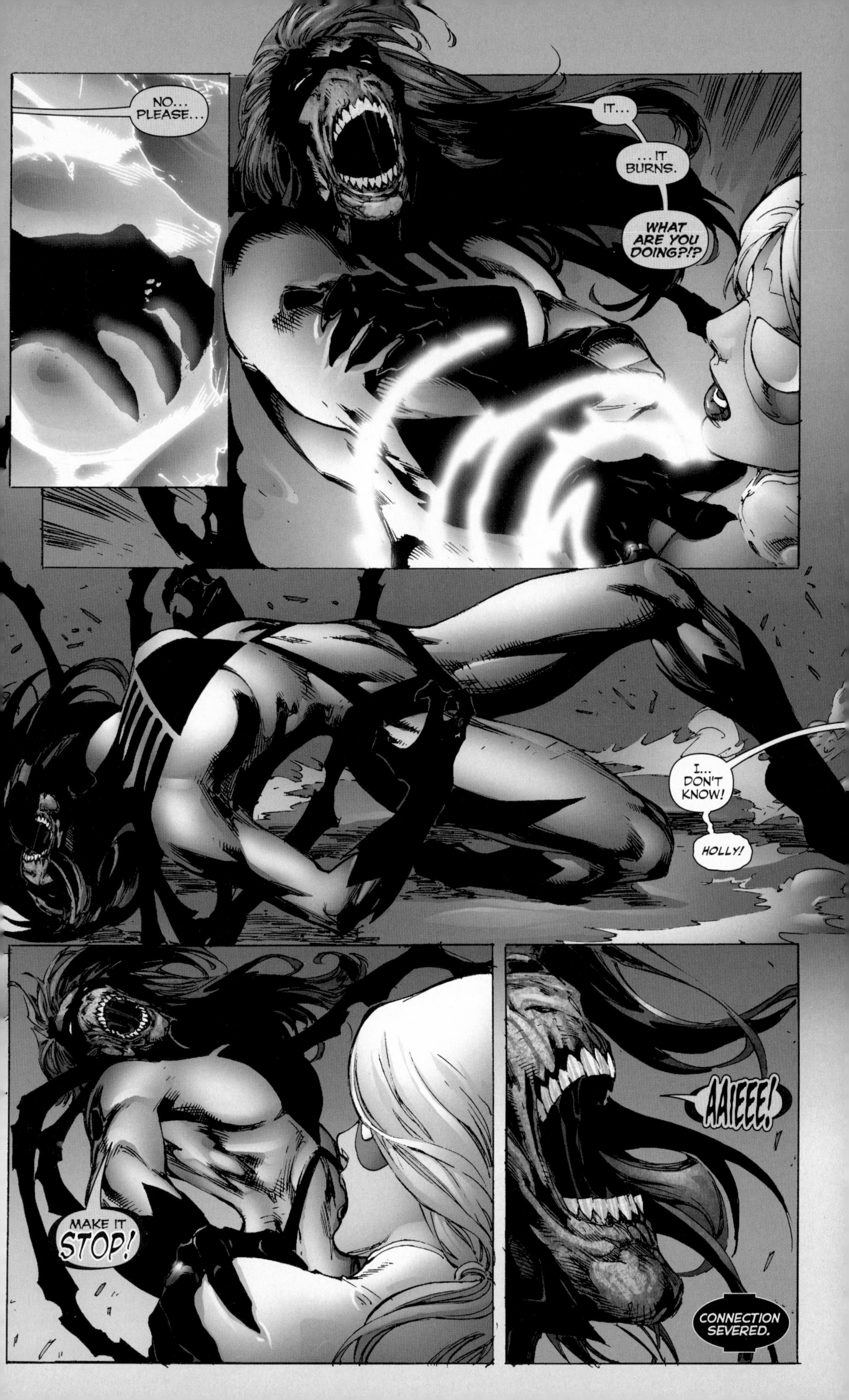
NO... PLEASE...
IT...
...IT BURNS.
WHAT ARE YOU DOING?!?
I... DON'T KNOW!
HOLLY!
MAKE IT STOP!
AAIEEE!
CONNECTION SEVERED.

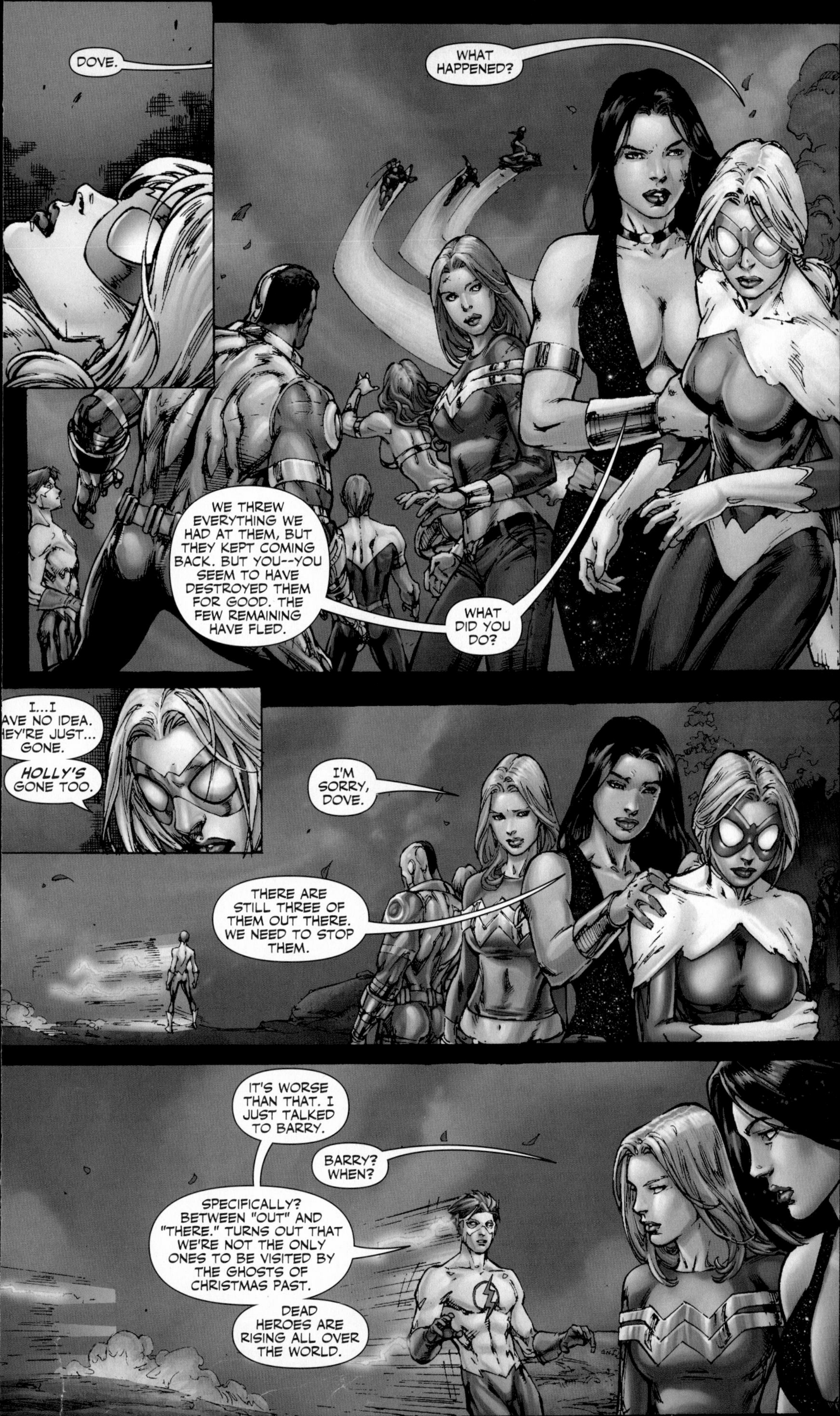
DOVE.
WHAT HAPPENED?
WE THREW EVERYTHING WE HAD AT THEM, BUT THEY KEPT COMING BACK. BUT YOU--YOU SEEM TO HAVE DESTROYED THEM FOR GOOD. THE FEW REMAINING HAVE FLED.
WHAT DID YOU DO?
I...I AVE NO IDEA. HEY'RE JUST... GONE.
HOLLY'S GONE TOO.
I'M SORRY, DOVE.
THERE ARE STILL THREE OF THEM OUT THERE. WE NEED TO STOP THEM.
IT'S WORSE THAN THAT. I JUST TALKED TO BARRY.
BARRY? WHEN?
SPECIFICALLY? BETWEEN "OUT" AND "THERE." TURNS OUT THAT WE'RE NOT THE ONLY ONES TO BE VISITED BY THE GHOSTS OF CHRISTMAS PAST.
DEAD HEROES ARE RISING ALL OVER THE WORLD.

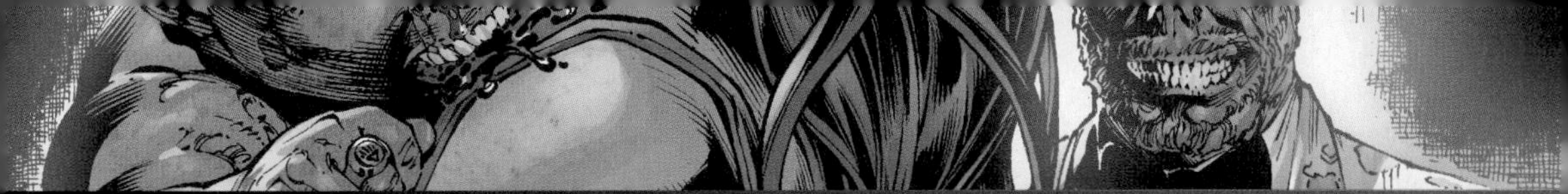

BLACKEST NIGHT
BLACK LANTERN CORPS
VOLUME ONE
VARIANT COVER GALLERY

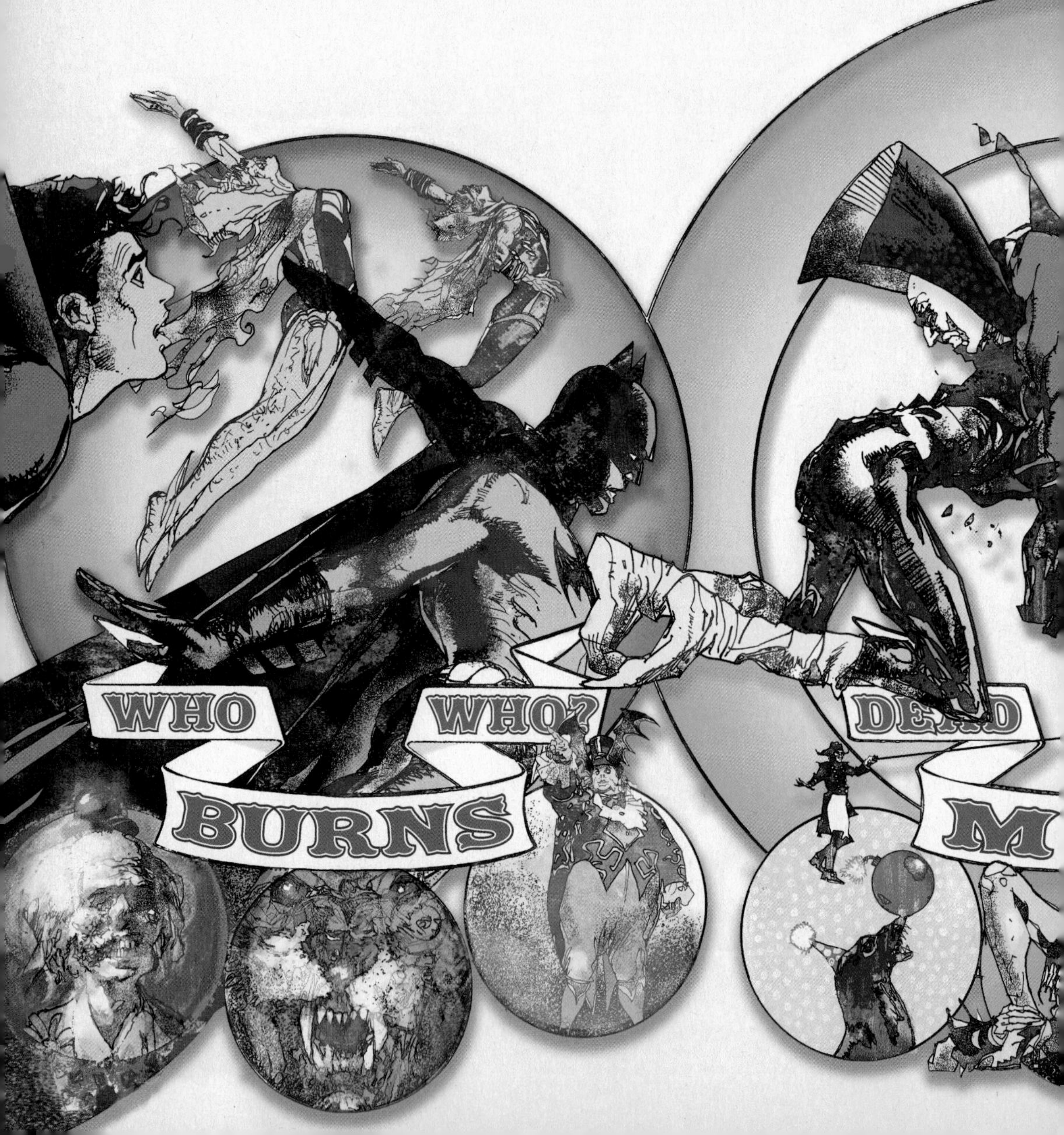
WHO
WHO?
DEAD
BURNS
M

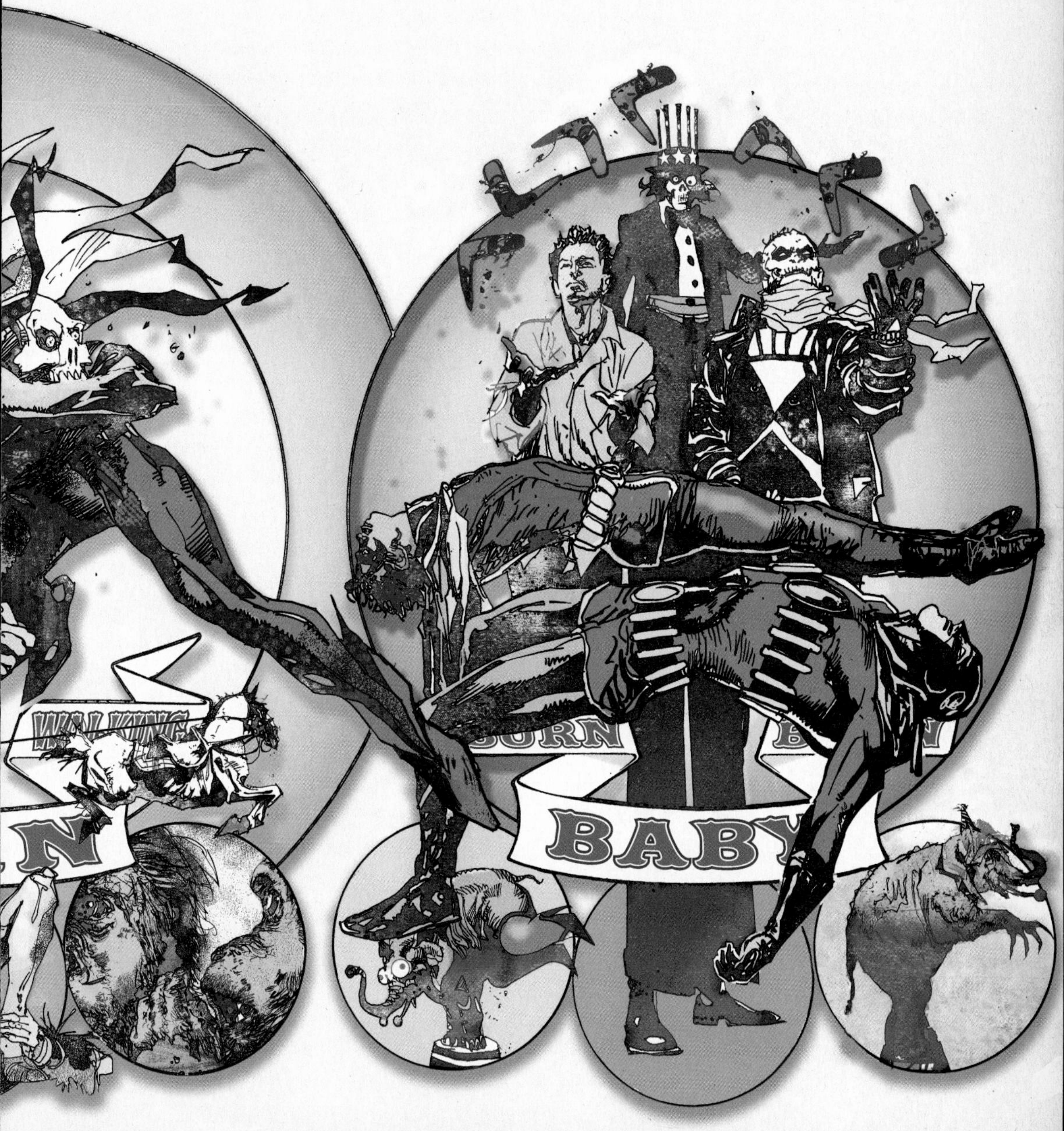
BURN

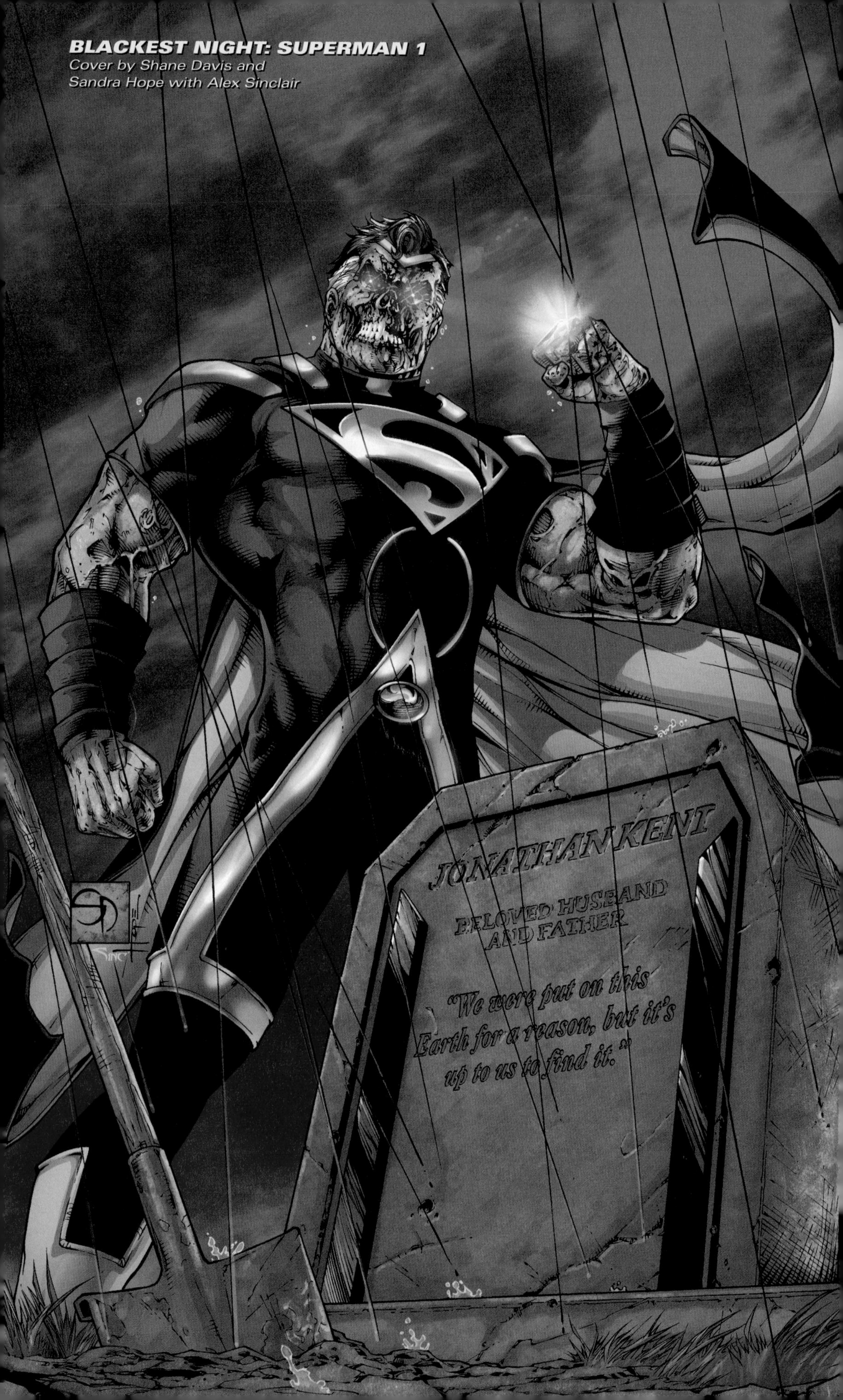
JONATHAN KENT
BELOVED HUSBAND AND FATHER
"We were put on this Earth for a reason, but it's up to us to find it."

BLACKEST NIGHT: SUPERMAN 1

Cover by Shane Davis and Sandra Hope with Alex Sinclair

BLACKEST NIGHT: SUPERMAN 2
Cover by Shane Davis and
Sandra Hope with Alex Sinclair

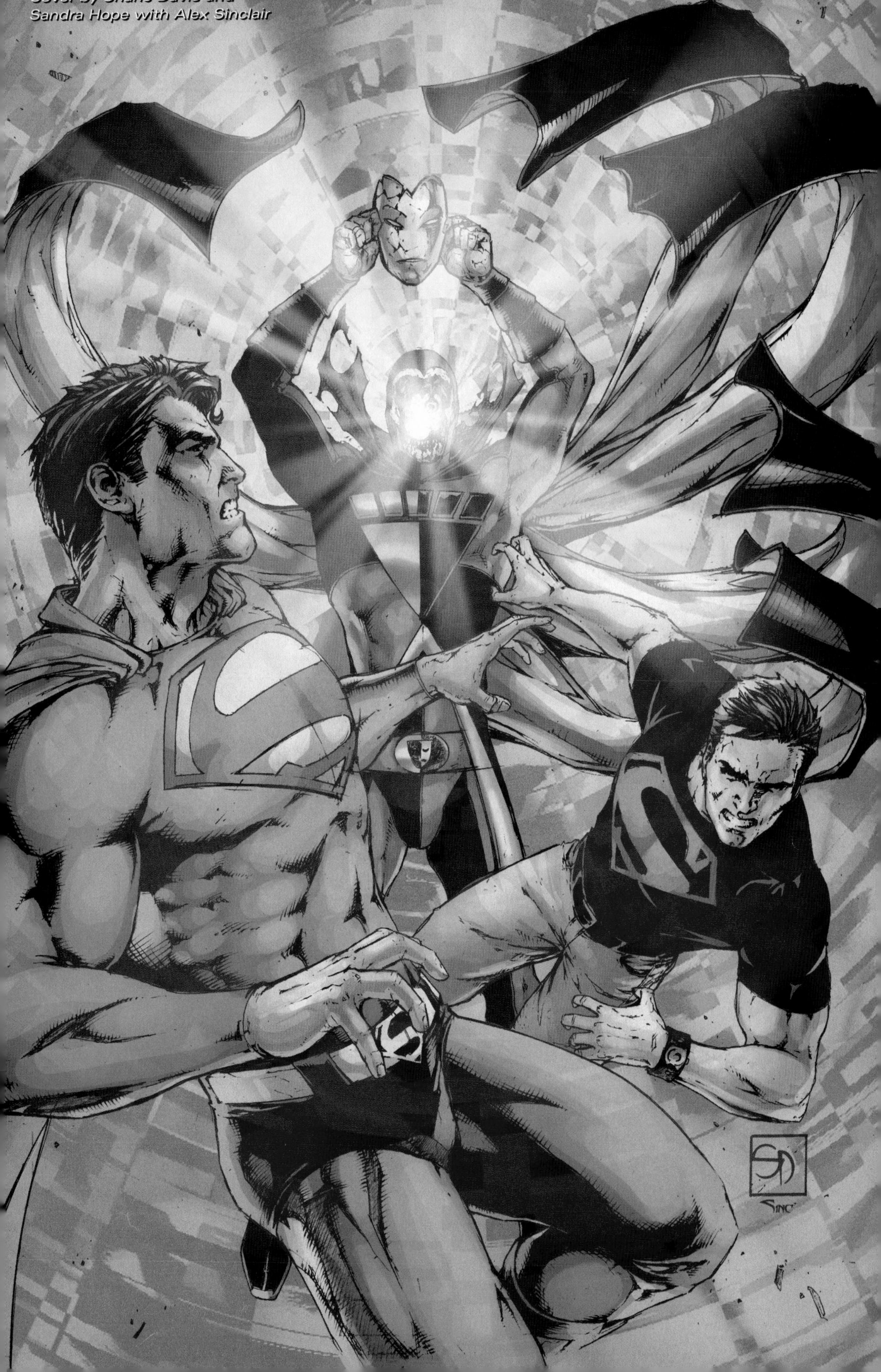

BLACKEST NIGHT: SUPERMAN 3
Cover by Shane Davis and
Sandra Hope with Alex Sinclair

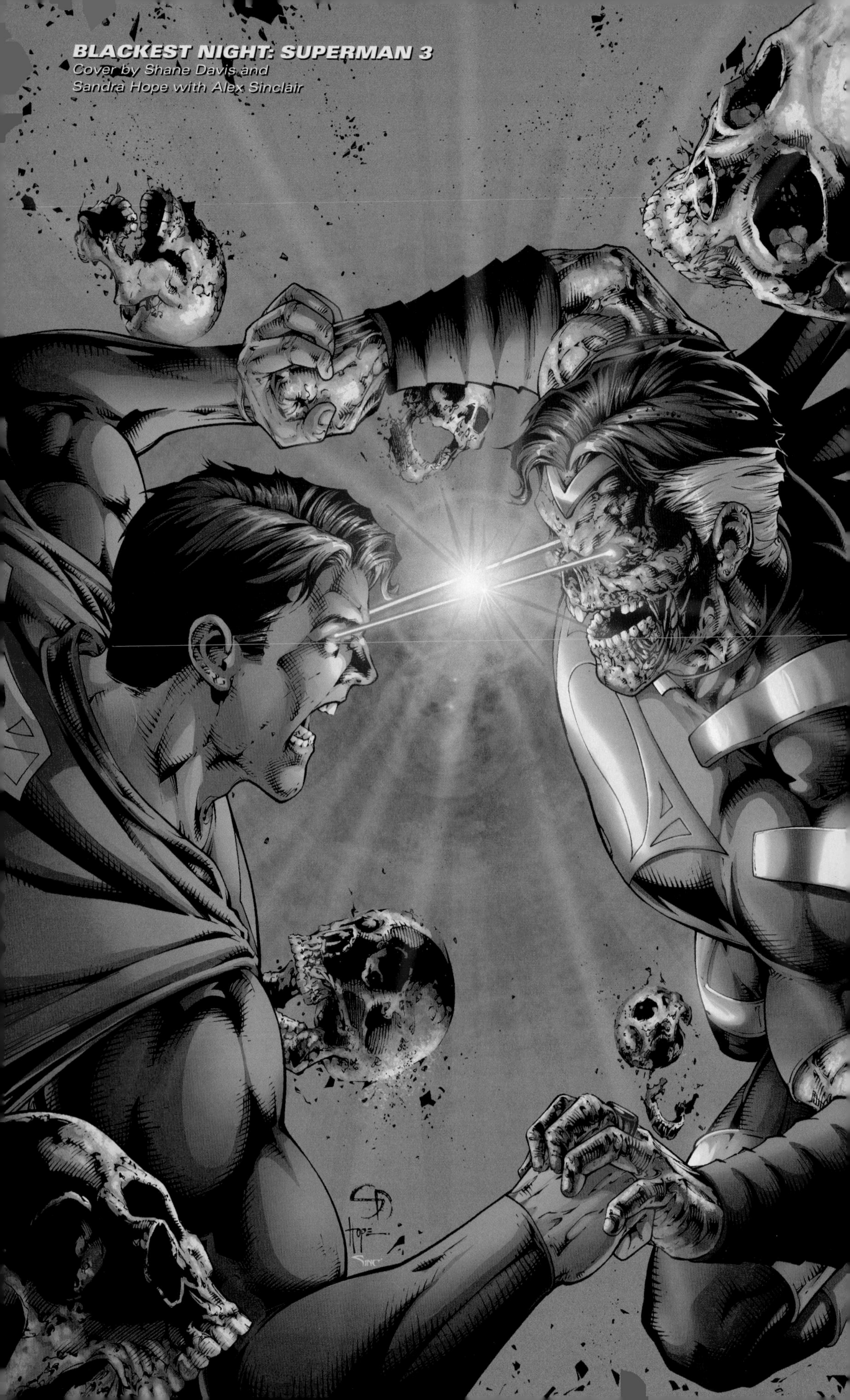

BLACKEST NIGHT: TITANS 1

Cover by Brian Haberlin

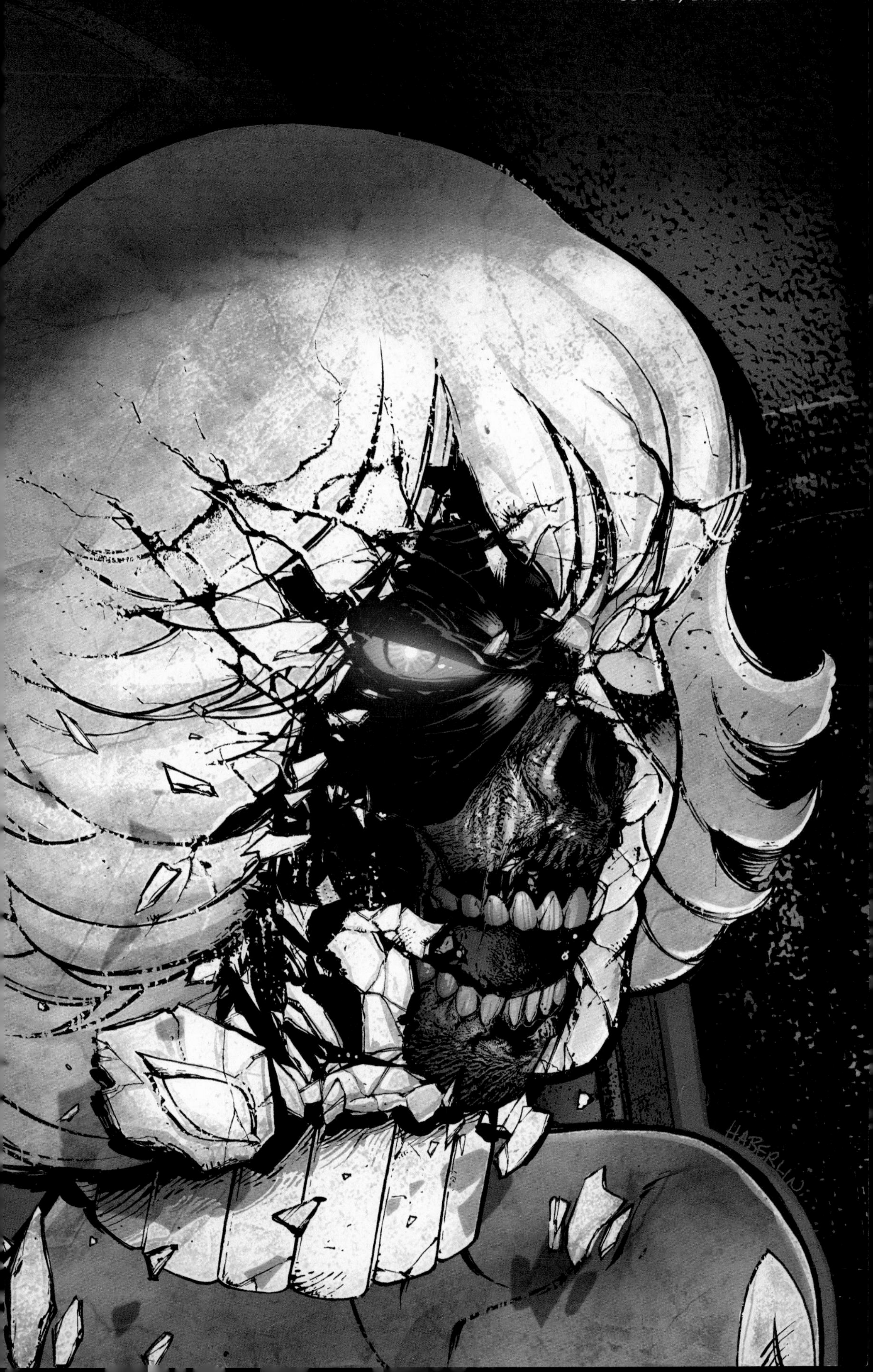
HABERLIN

BLACKEST NIGHT: TITANS 2
Cover by Brian Haberlin

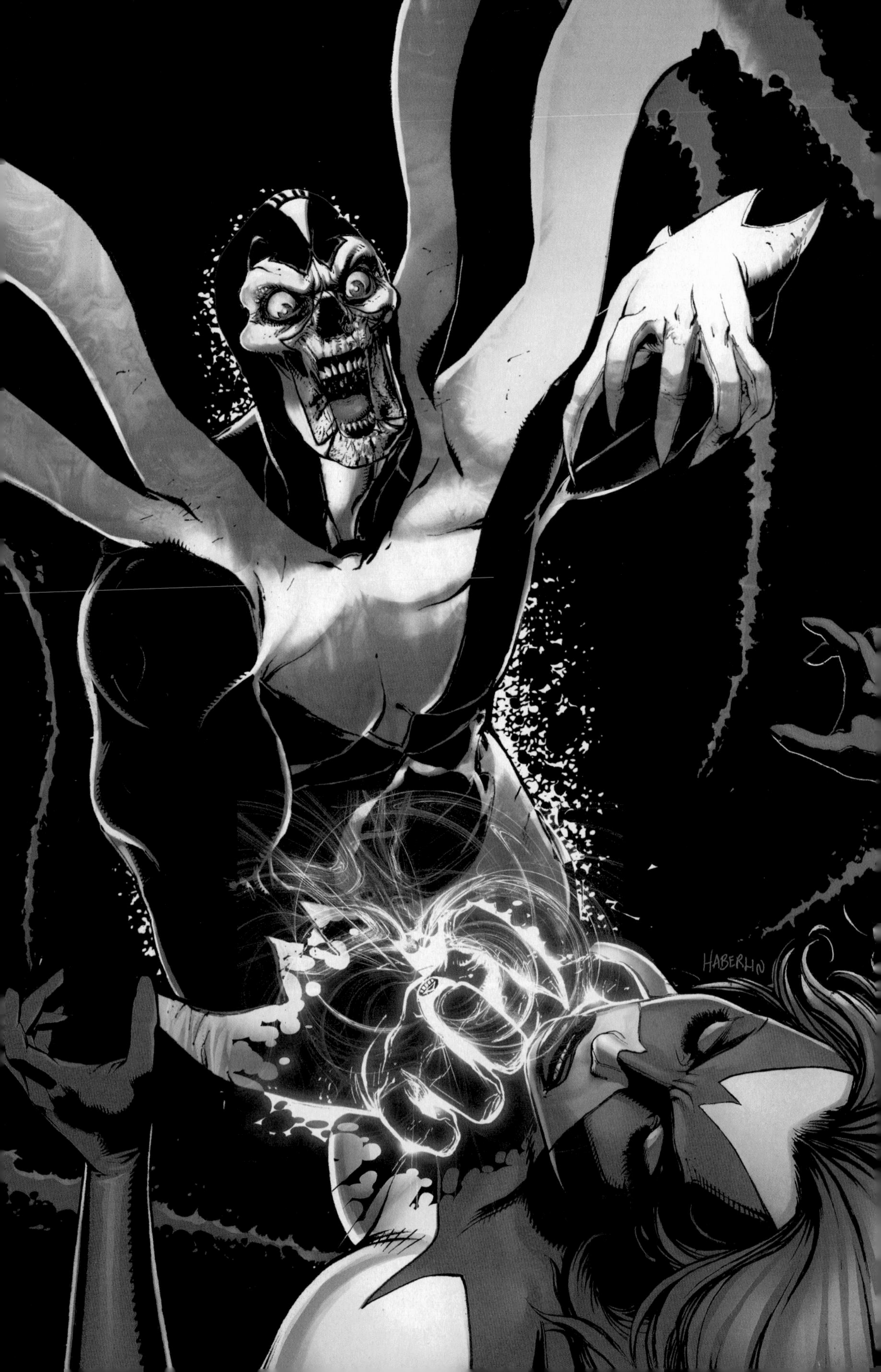
HABERLIN

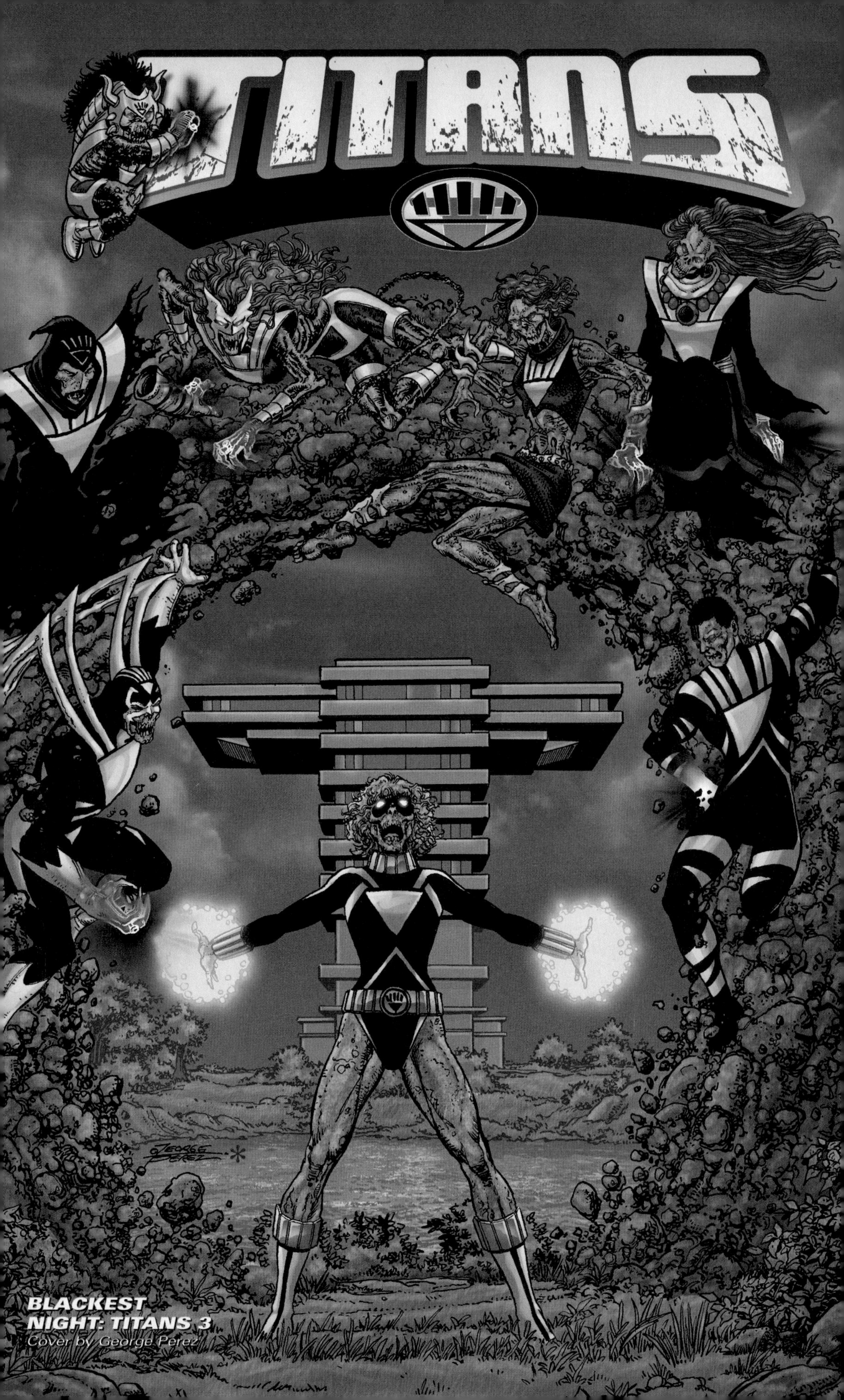
TITANS

BLACKEST NIGHT: TITANS 3
Cover by George Perez

BLACK LANTERN BATMAN VILLAINS

Designs by Joe Prado

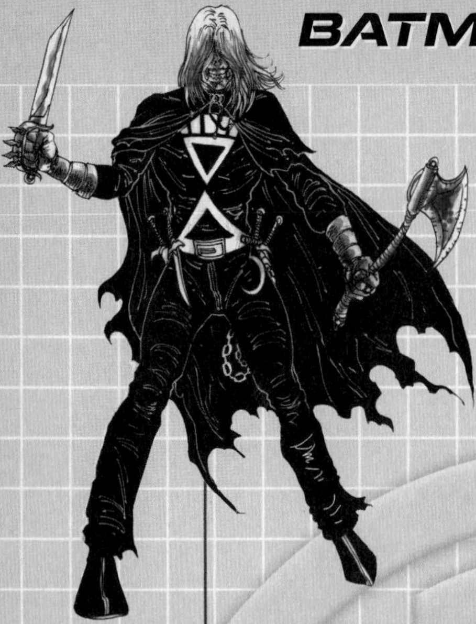

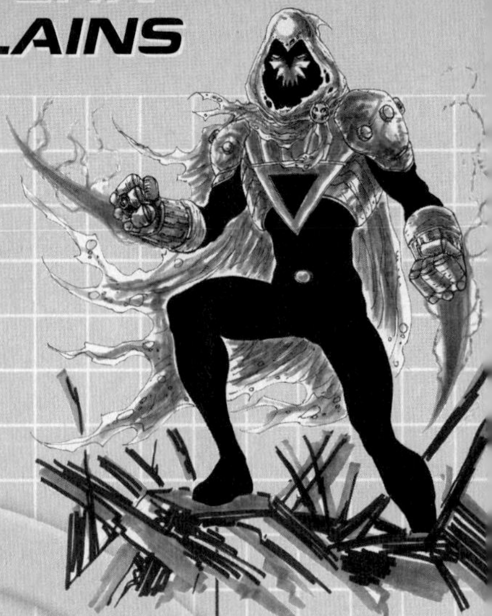

BLACK LANTERN ABATTOIR

ALTER EGO: ARNOLD ETCHISON

A CRAZED SERIAL KILLER, ABATTOIR FELL TO HIS DOOM WHEN JEAN PAUL VALLEY, WHO WAS THEN ACTING AS BATMAN, REFUSED TO ASSIST HIM. AS A BLACK LANTERN HE NOW SEEKS BATMAN, NOT KNOWING THAT DICK GRAYSON IS THE CURRENT ONE.

BLACK LANTERN AZRAEL

ALTER EGO: JEAN PAUL VALLEY JR.

HIGHLY INTELLIGENT COMPUTER EXPERT JEAN PAUL DISHED OUT HIS OWN BRAND OF JUSTICE AS THE VIGILANTE AZRAEL, BUT AFTER FACING HIS OWN ULTIMATE JUSTICE IN THE FORM OF TWO BULLETS, BLACK LANTERN AZRAEL CONTINUES DEALING OUT DEATH TO THE RESIDENTS OF GOTHAM CITY.

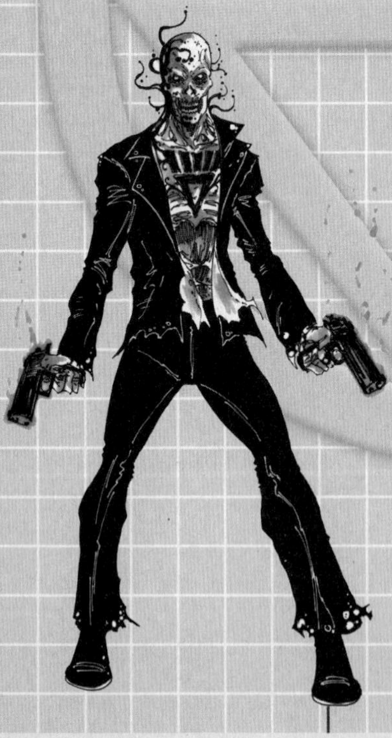

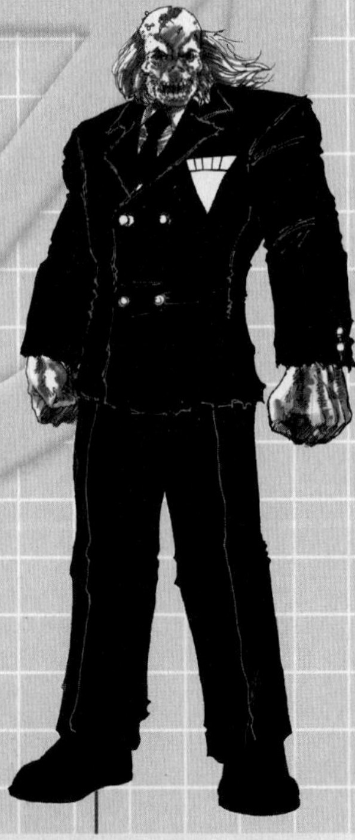

BLACK LANTERN BLACK MASK

ALTER EGO: ROMAN SIONIS

A GENIUS CRIME LORD WHOSE MASK WAS BURNED INTO HIS FACE. HE WAS LATER MURDERED BY CATWOMAN AS RETRIBUTION FOR HIS MANY VICIOUS CRIMES.

BLACK LANTERN BLOCKBUSTER

ALTER EGO: MARK DESMOND

SUPER STRENGTH AND STAMINA COULD NOT PROTECT BLOCKBUSTER FROM A GUNSHOT TO THE HEAD FROM TARANTULA.

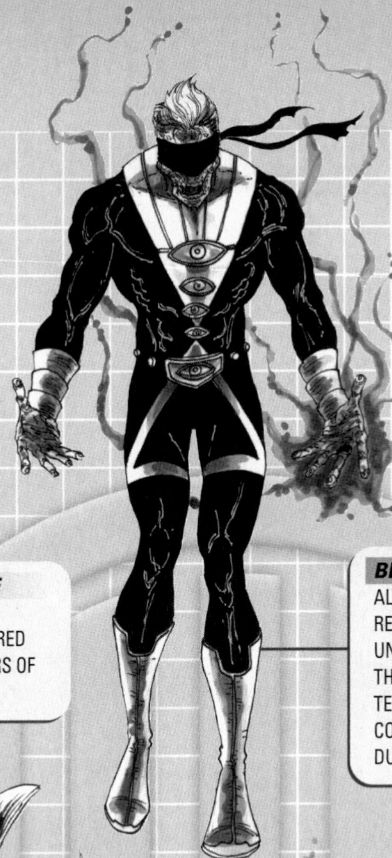

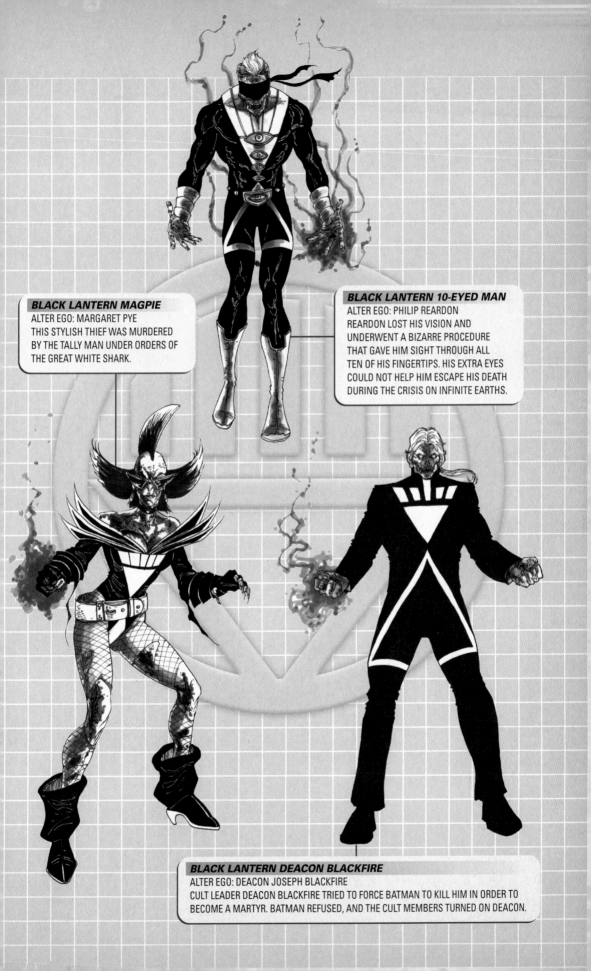

BLACK LANTERN MAGPIE

ALTER EGO: MARGARET PYE

THIS STYLISH THIEF WAS MURDERED BY THE TALLY MAN UNDER ORDERS OF THE GREAT WHITE SHARK.

BLACK LANTERN 10-EYED MAN

ALTER EGO: PHILIP REARDON

REARDON LOST HIS VISION AND UNDERWENT A BIZARRE PROCEDURE THAT GAVE HIM SIGHT THROUGH ALL TEN OF HIS FINGERTIPS. HIS EXTRA EYES COULD NOT HELP HIM ESCAPE HIS DEATH DURING THE CRISIS ON INFINITE EARTHS.

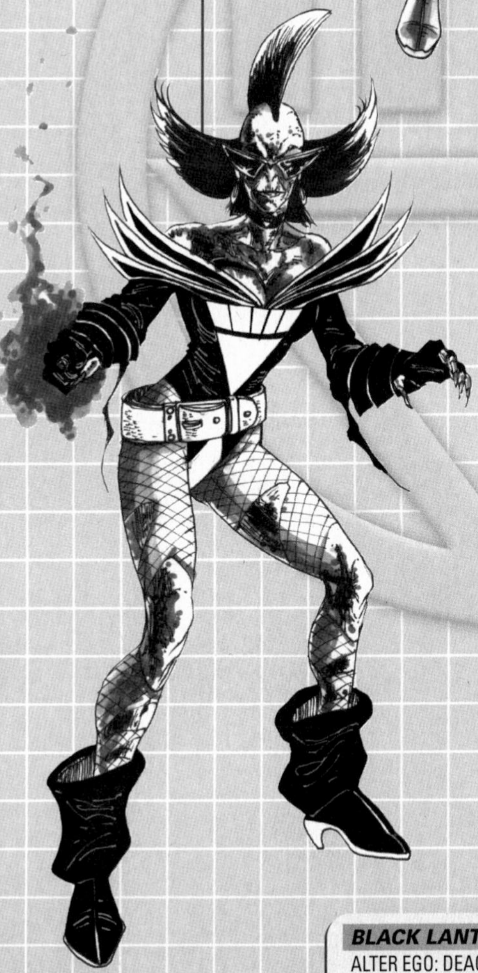

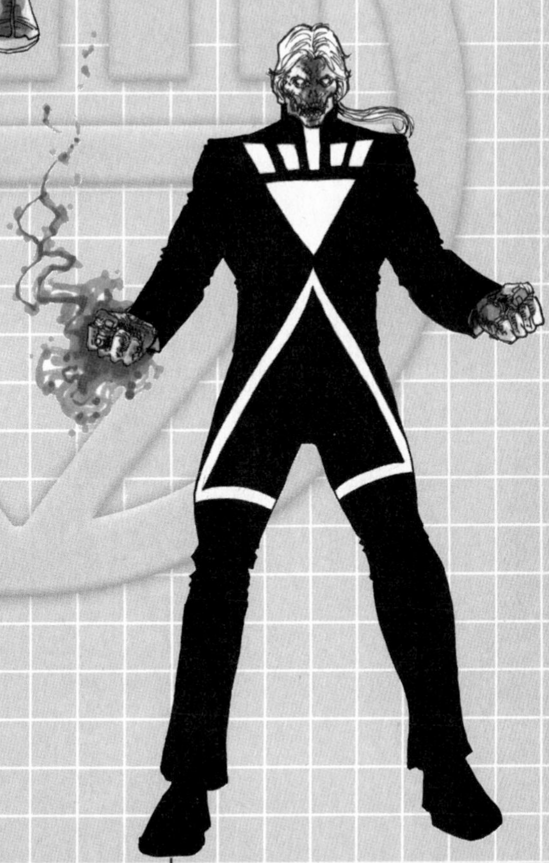

BLACK LANTERN DEACON BLACKFIRE

ALTER EGO: DEACON JOSEPH BLACKFIRE

CULT LEADER DEACON BLACKFIRE TRIED TO FORCE BATMAN TO KILL HIM IN ORDER TO BECOME A MARTYR. BATMAN REFUSED, AND THE CULT MEMBERS TURNED ON DEACON.

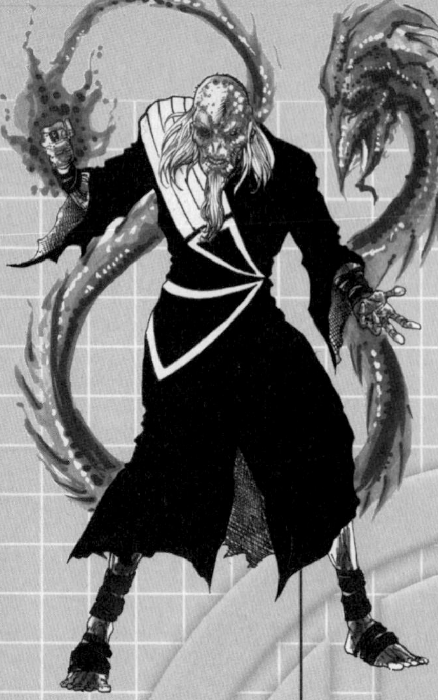

BLACK LANTERN SENSEI

ALTER EGO: UNKNOWN

A MASTER MARTIAL ARTIST WHO WAS ONCE IN CHARGE OF THE LEAGUE OF ASSASSINS, THE SENSEI MET HIS END WHEN HIS CORRUPT SOUL WAS JUDGED UNWORTHY.

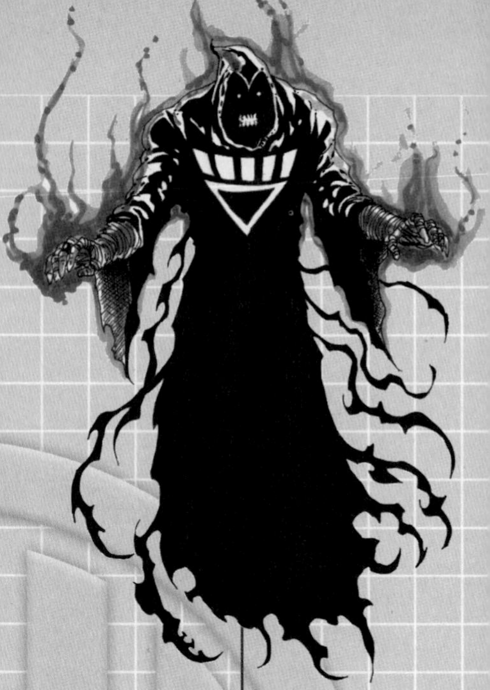

BLACK LANTERN SPOOK

ALTER EGO: VAL KALIBAN

SPOOK, WHO POSSESSED IMPRESSIVE HYPNOTIC SKILLS, WAS DECAPITATED BY DAMIAN WAYNE, THE SON OF BATMAN.

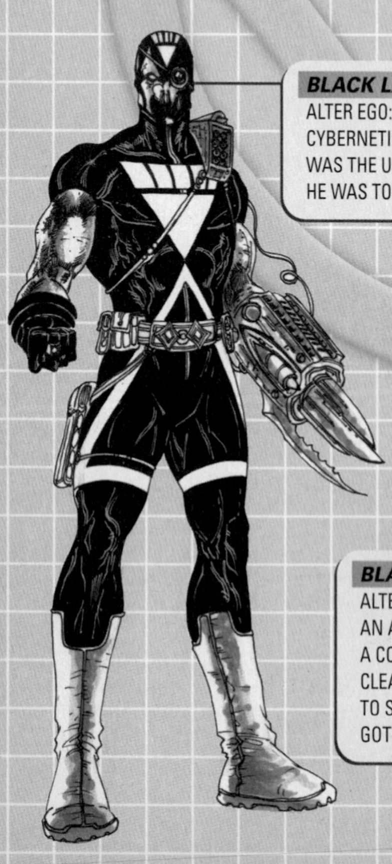

BLACK LANTERN KGBEAST

ALTER EGO: ANATOLI KNYAZEV

CYBERNETICALLY ENHANCED, KGBEAST WAS THE ULTIMATE ASSASSIN UNTIL HE WAS TOSSED FROM A ROOF.

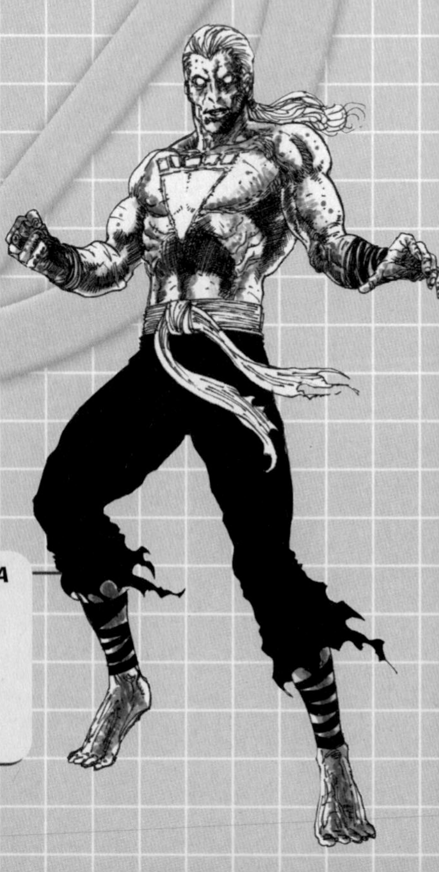

BLACK LANTERN KING COBRA

ALTER EGO: UNKNOWN

AN AVERAGE CRIME LORD WITH A COBRA COSTUME, KING COBRA CLEARLY WASN'T STRONG ENOUGH TO SURVIVE ON THE STREETS OF GOTHAM CITY.

BLACK LANTERN TRIGGER TWINS
ALTER EGO: WALT AND WAYNE TRIGGER
THE TRIGGER BROTHERS WERE EXPERT
MARKSMEN UNTIL THEY BECAME THE BULL'S-EYE.

BLACK LANTERN VENTRILOQUIST
ALTER EGO: ARNOLD WESKER
A PSYCHOTIC CRIMINAL WHO BELIEVES
HIS BOSS IS A DUMMY NAMED SCARFACE,
ARNOLD WAS SHOT AND KILLED, LEADING TO
THE INTRODUCTION OF A NEW VENTRILOQUIST.

BLACK LANTERN TONY ZUCCO
ALTER EGO: BOSS ZUCCO
TONY ZUCCO IS THE MAN WHO HAD
THE FLYING GRAYSONS' TRAPEZE
ROPES CUT, LEADING TO THE BIRTH OF
DICK GRAYSON AS ROBIN. HE WAS
MURDERED BY A RIVAL CRIME BOSS.

BLACK LANTERN TITANS

Designs by Joe Prado

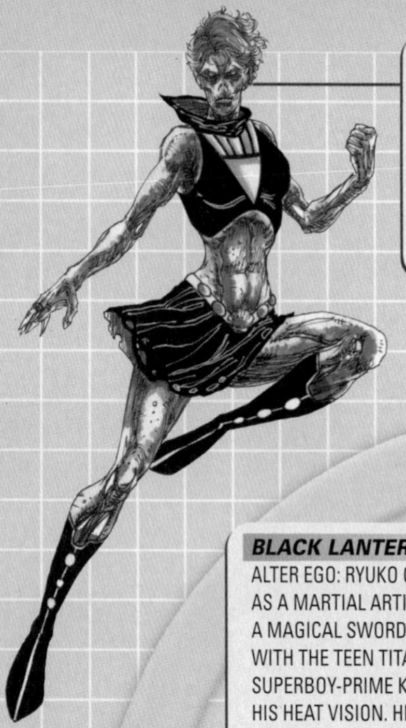

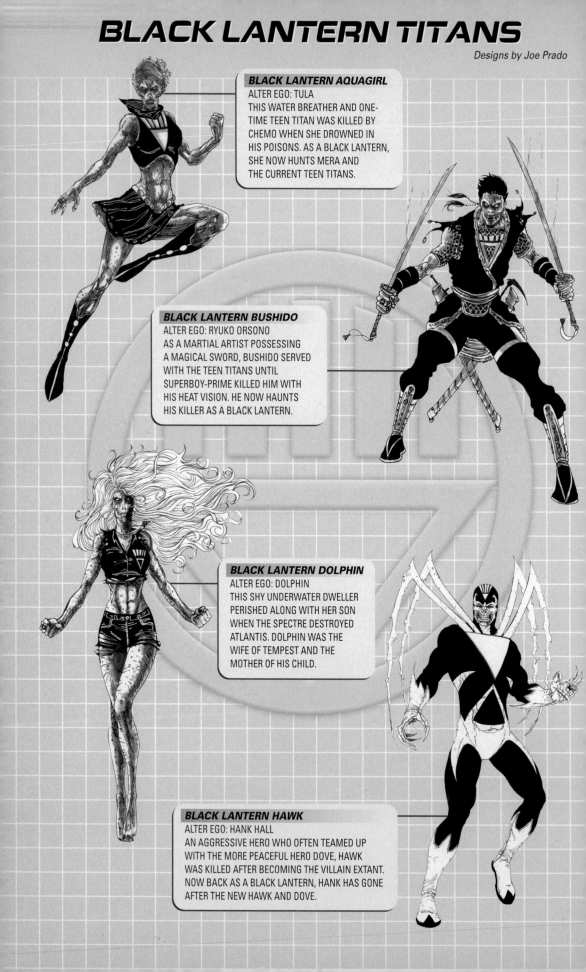

BLACK LANTERN AQUAGIRL

ALTER EGO: TULA

THIS WATER BREATHER AND ONE-TIME TEEN TITAN WAS KILLED BY CHEMO WHEN SHE DROWNED IN HIS POISONS. AS A BLACK LANTERN, SHE NOW HUNTS MERA AND THE CURRENT TEEN TITANS.

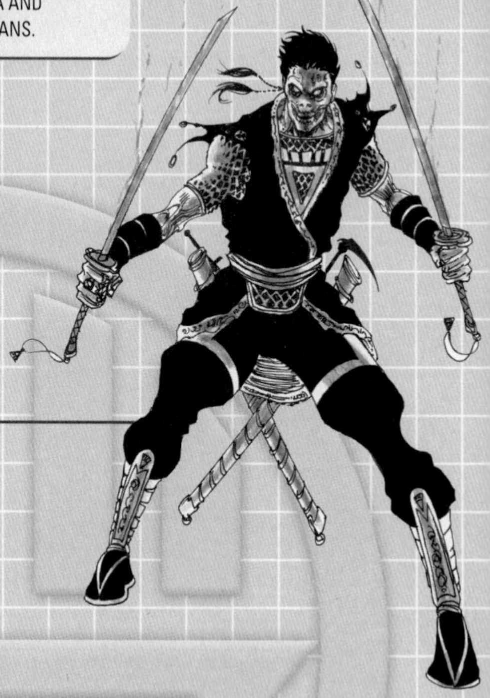

BLACK LANTERN BUSHIDO

ALTER EGO: RYUKO ORSONO

AS A MARTIAL ARTIST POSSESSING A MAGICAL SWORD, BUSHIDO SERVED WITH THE TEEN TITANS UNTIL SUPERBOY-PRIME KILLED HIM WITH HIS HEAT VISION. HE NOW HAUNTS HIS KILLER AS A BLACK LANTERN.

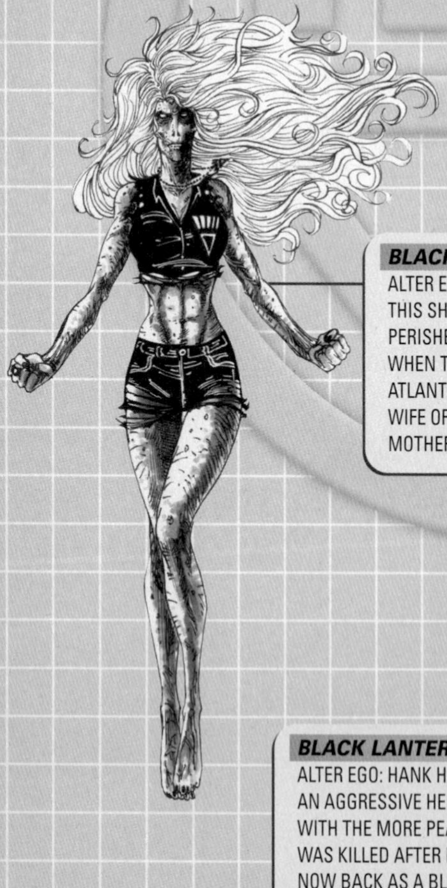

BLACK LANTERN DOLPHIN

ALTER EGO: DOLPHIN

THIS SHY UNDERWATER DWELLER PERISHED ALONG WITH HER SON WHEN THE SPECTRE DESTROYED ATLANTIS. DOLPHIN WAS THE WIFE OF TEMPEST AND THE MOTHER OF HIS CHILD.

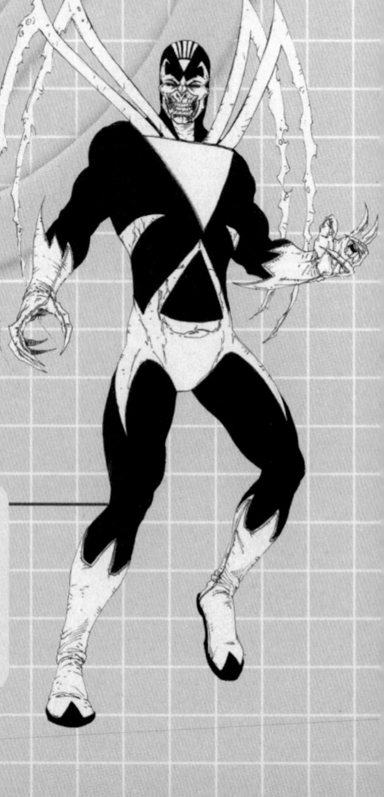

BLACK LANTERN HAWK

ALTER EGO: HANK HALL

AN AGGRESSIVE HERO WHO OFTEN TEAMED UP WITH THE MORE PEACEFUL HERO DOVE, HAWK WAS KILLED AFTER BECOMING THE VILLAIN EXTANT. NOW BACK AS A BLACK LANTERN, HANK HAS GONE AFTER THE NEW HAWK AND DOVE.

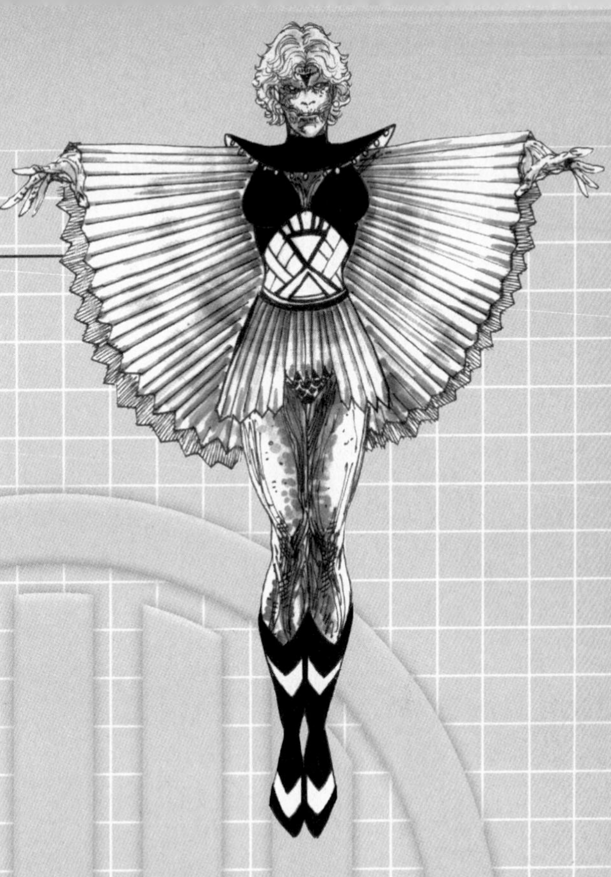

BLACK LANTERN KOLE

ALTER EGO: KOLE WEATHERS

KOLE CAN CREATE CRYSTALS FROM THIN AIR AND FLY. SINCE DYING AT THE HANDS OF THE ANTI-MONITOR, SHE'S BEEN REVIVED AS A BLACK LANTERN, HUNTING FOR THE HEARTS OF THE TITANS.

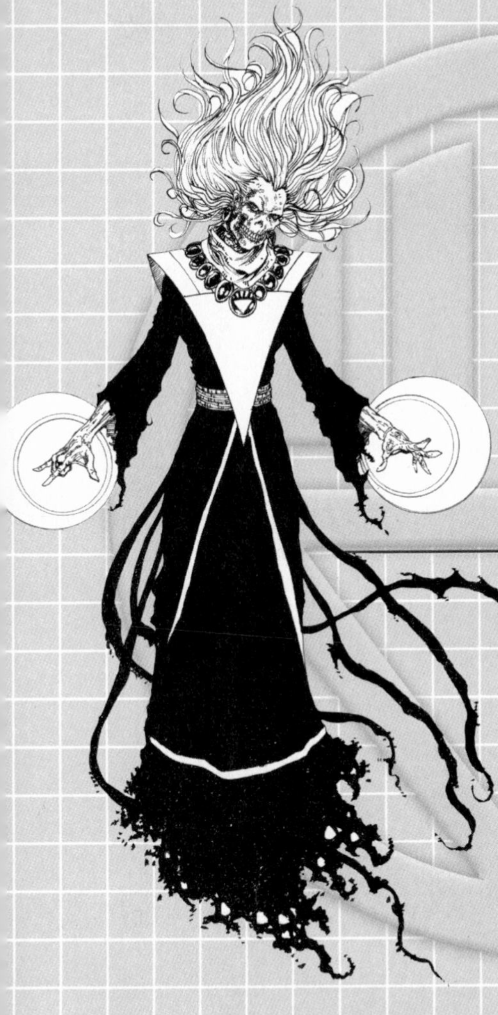

BLACK LANTERN OMEN

ALTER EGO: LILITH CLAY

THIS PRECOG AND TELEPATH COULD NOT PREDICT HER OWN DOWNFALL, AS HER NECK WAS SNAPPED BY AN EVIL SUPERMAN ANDROID.

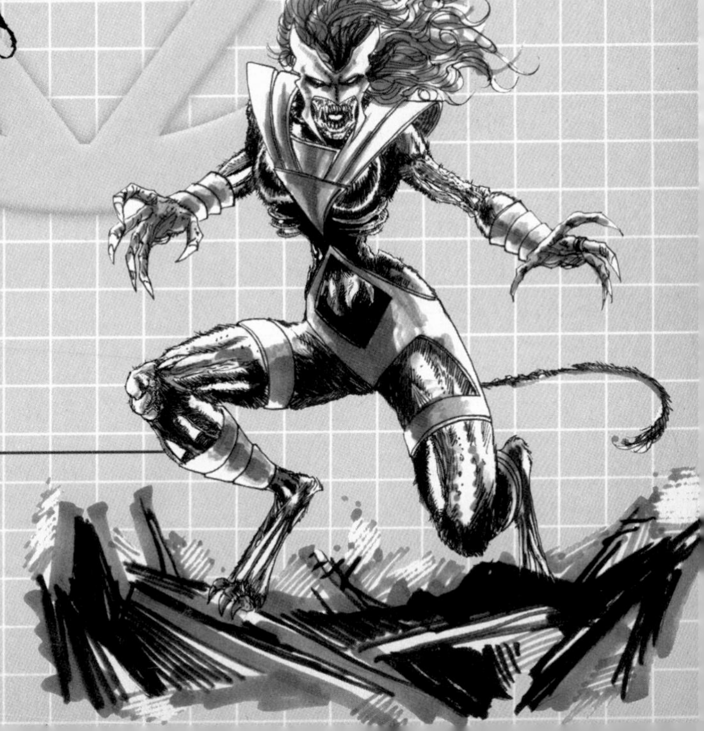

BLACK LANTERN PANTHA

ALTER EGO: ROSABELLE MENDEZ

FORMER TITAN PANTHA HAD HER HEAD PUNCHED CLEAN OFF BY AN ENRAGED SUPERBOY-PRIME. HER CAT'S-EYE VISION GREATLY ENHANCES HER BLACK LANTERN ABILITIES.

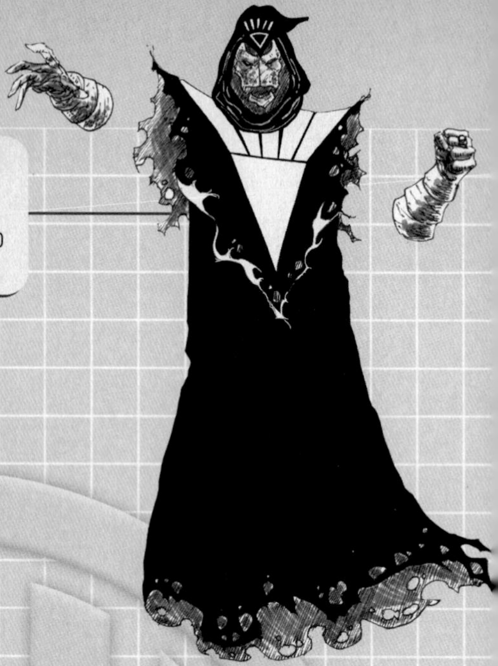

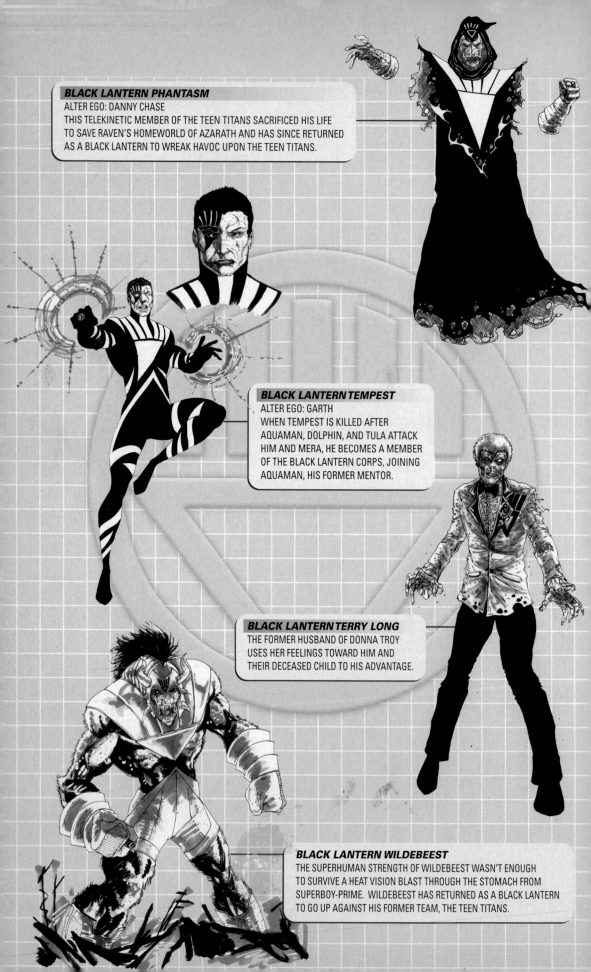

BLACK LANTERN PHANTASM

ALTER EGO: DANNY CHASE

THIS TELEKINETIC MEMBER OF THE TEEN TITANS SACRIFICED HIS LIFE TO SAVE RAVEN'S HOMEWORLD OF AZARATH AND HAS SINCE RETURNED AS A BLACK LANTERN TO WREAK HAVOC UPON THE TEEN TITANS.

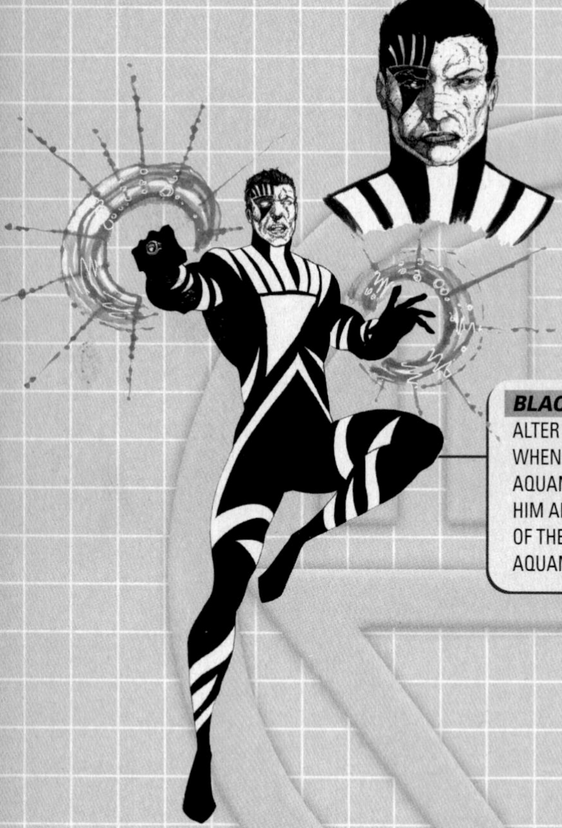

BLACK LANTERN TEMPEST

ALTER EGO: GARTH

WHEN TEMPEST IS KILLED AFTER AQUAMAN, DOLPHIN, AND TULA ATTACK HIM AND MERA, HE BECOMES A MEMBER OF THE BLACK LANTERN CORPS, JOINING AQUAMAN, HIS FORMER MENTOR.

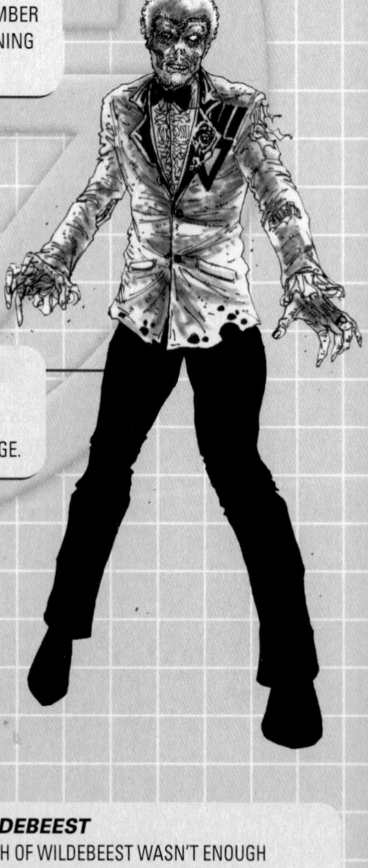

BLACK LANTERN TERRY LONG

THE FORMER HUSBAND OF DONNA TROY USES HER FEELINGS TOWARD HIM AND THEIR DECEASED CHILD TO HIS ADVANTAGE.

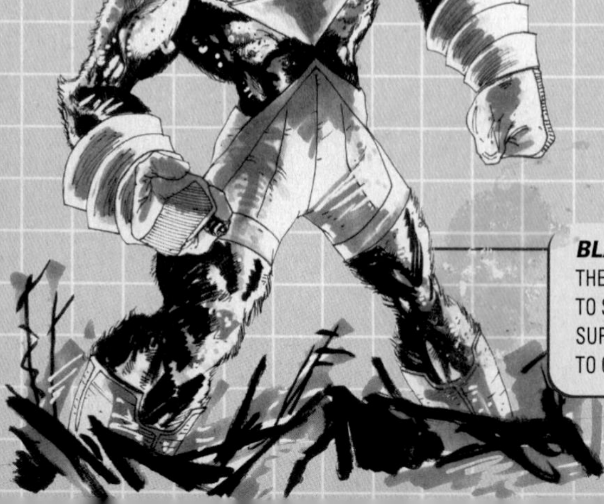

BLACK LANTERN WILDEBEEST

THE SUPERHUMAN STRENGTH OF WILDEBEEST WASN'T ENOUGH TO SURVIVE A HEAT VISION BLAST THROUGH THE STOMACH FROM SUPERBOY-PRIME. WILDEBEEST HAS RETURNED AS A BLACK LANTERN TO GO UP AGAINST HIS FORMER TEAM, THE TEEN TITANS.

BLACK LANTERN TITANS VILLAINS

Designs by Joe Prado

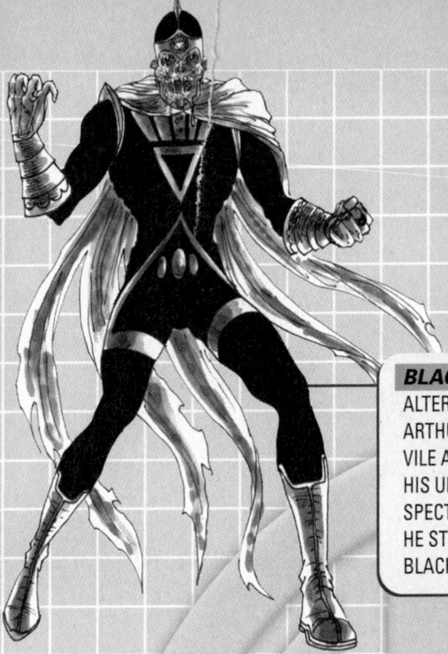

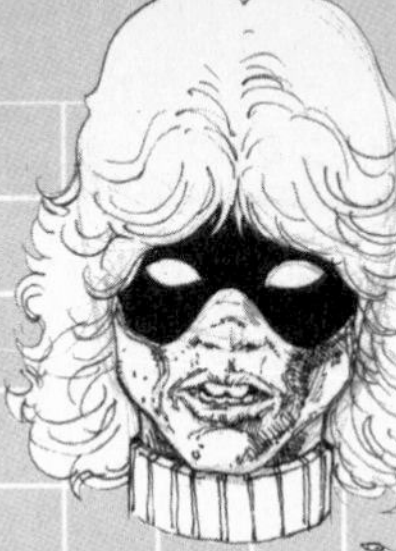

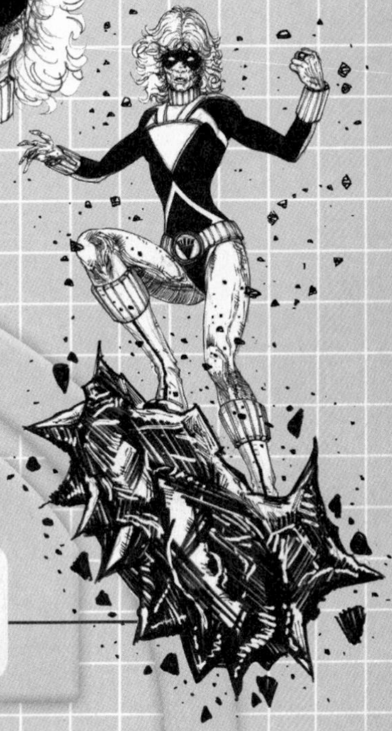

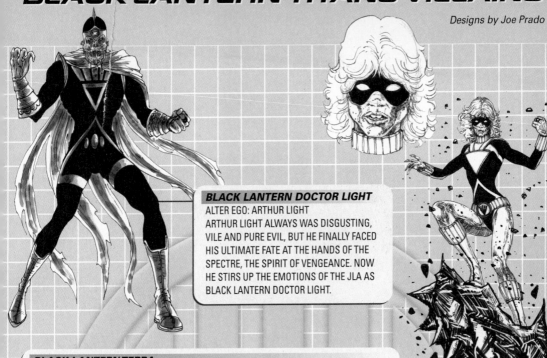

BLACK LANTERN DOCTOR LIGHT

ALTER EGO: ARTHUR LIGHT

ARTHUR LIGHT ALWAYS WAS DISGUSTING, VILE AND PURE EVIL, BUT HE FINALLY FACED HIS ULTIMATE FATE AT THE HANDS OF THE SPECTRE, THE SPIRIT OF VENGEANCE. NOW HE STIRS UP THE EMOTIONS OF THE JLA AS BLACK LANTERN DOCTOR LIGHT.

BLACK LANTERN TERRA

ALTER EGO: TARA MARKOV

TERRA ALWAYS PLAYED BOTH SIDES. AS A BLACK LANTERN SHE POSES A TERRIBLE THREAT WITH HER EARTH-CONTROLLING POWERS BUT EVEN MORE AS AN EXCELLENT LIAR.

BLACK LANTERN MADAME ROUGE

ALTER EGO: LAURA DE MILLE

WITH A SPLIT PERSONALITY, MADAME ROUGE IS OFTEN TORN BETWEEN GOOD AND EVIL. WITH HER ELASTIC POWERS, ROUGE HAS PROVEN TO BE A DEADLY THREAT GOING UP AGAINST THE DOOM PATROL AND TEEN TITANS UNTIL ULTIMATELY BEING KILLED BY BEAST BOY. NOW THAT SHE IS A BLACK LANTERN SHE'LL DOUBTLESS CONTINUE TO BE A FORMIDABLE ADVERSARY.

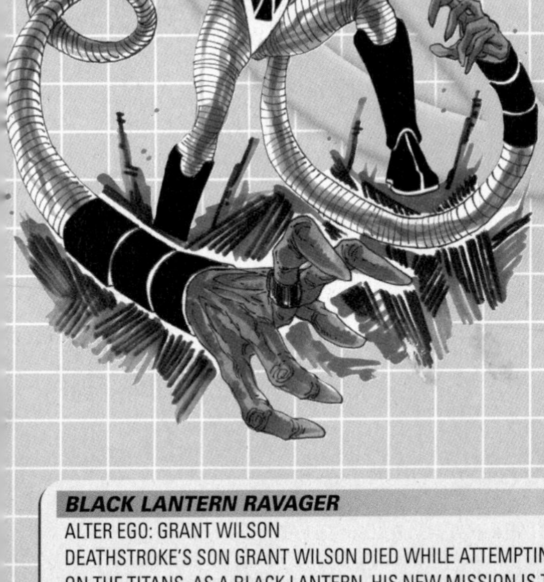

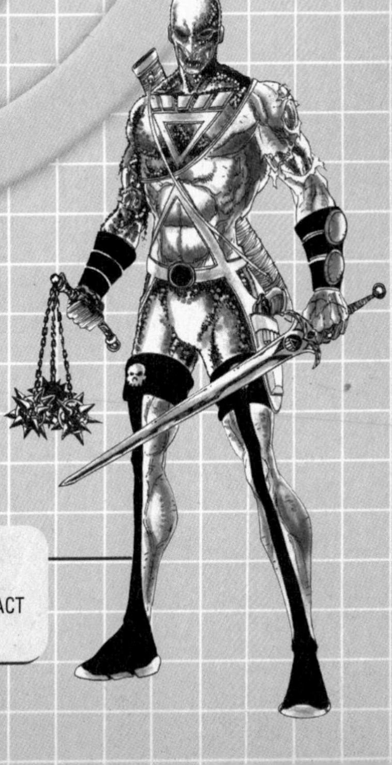

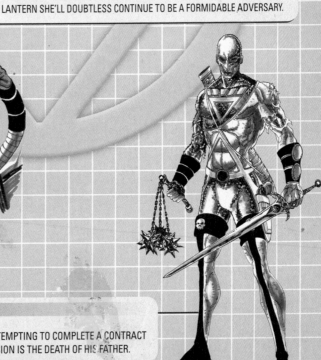

BLACK LANTERN RAVAGER

ALTER EGO: GRANT WILSON

DEATHSTROKE'S SON GRANT WILSON DIED WHILE ATTEMPTING TO COMPLETE A CONTRACT ON THE TITANS. AS A BLACK LANTERN, HIS NEW MISSION IS THE DEATH OF HIS FATHER.

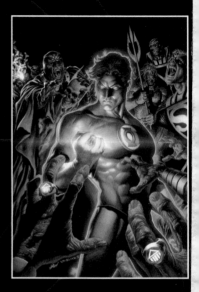

COMICS BLACKEST
Tomasi, Peter J.
Blackest Night. Volume one,
Black Lantern Corps